Hannes Wessels

◆

MEN OF WAR

The Fighting Few Who Took On The World

EX MONTIBUS MEDIA
26 Caledon Street,
Darling 7345.
:
Text © Hannes Wessels
Images © Richard Stannard.

Cataloguing-in-publication data is available from the
South African National Library.

All rights reserved.
No part of this book may be reproduced or transmitted in any form or by any means, electronic or mechanical including photocopying, recording or by any information storage and retrieval system, without permission from the publisher in writing.

Every reasonable effort has been made to trace copyright holders and to obtain their permission for the use of copyright material. The author and publisher apologize for any errors or omissions in this work and would be grateful if notified of any corrections that should be incorporated in future reprints or editions of this book.

Cover design: Kristen Barrett.
Editing: Steve Lunderstedt
Proof reader: Jerry Buirski

First edition, first impression 2020

For a complete list of **EX MONTIBUS MEDIA** titles, please contact:
Email: admin@exmontibusmedia.co.za
Telephone (27) 73 777 2745
www.exmontibusmedia.co.za

Contents

Dedication...iv
Author's Note...v
Acknowledgements..vii
Chapter One: Taking On The World..........................1
Chapter Two: Into The Bush................................19
Chapter Three: Into the Army..............................28
Chapter Four: Operation Big Bang..........................44
Chapter Five: Making of an enemy..........................60
Chapter Six: Leaving Rhodesia.............................83
Chapter Seven: The War Escalates.........................123
Chapter Eight: Pseudo Operations.........................149
Chapter Nine: Back to the SAS............................175
Chapter Ten: Assassinations..............................193
Chapter Eleven: Beginning of the end.....................218
Chapter Twelve: The end of Rhodesia......................263
Chapter Thirteen: Southbound.............................280
Chapter Fourteen: From the Seychelles to the Single Cells..........304
Chapter Fifteen: Back to war.............................338
Addendum on Viscounts....................................360
Sources Consulted..365
Books..366
About the author...367

Dedication

To all the good young men from Umtali Boys High who died too young in three wars. For so small a school the sacrifice was enormous.

Roll of Honour

1914-1918

W. E. Bennett
C. E. Green
R. G. Hart
V. Karrant
C. Kelleher
J. Norris
E. St. C. Tulloch
E. Taylor

1939-1945

Raymond Amm
Frederick Austin
Maurice Beckley
Peter Berry
Cecil Blyth
Harold Bromwich
Cecil Browne
George Bulloch
John Boyd-Clark
Arthur Cockerell
Peter Duff
Felix Edwards
Derek Erasmus
Arthur Everett
Jack Green
John Harrold
Christopher Holland
Frank Holman
Ashley Jackson
Hugh James
Charles Lees
Douglas Leggo
Ralph Lenton
Lex Love
Wilfred Love
Neville Mansell
Paul Markides
Dennis McBeath
Ronnie Methuen
Arthur Moore
Christoffel Nezar
Gordon Parkin
Douglas Rail
George Reid
Patrick Reid
Thomas Roberts
William Rose
Neville Scholtz
Desmond Searle-Crossley
Peter Sutton
Kathleen Tulloch
Peter Uren
Louis van der Linde
Nicholas van der Merwe
Jacobus van Lelyveld
William Venter
John Watson
Clifford Whitehead
Robert Williams

1968-1979

26. 3.1968	Reginald Binks	R.L.I.	1964-1967
26. 3.1971	Harry Young	Air Force	1959-1964
24. 3.1973	Bruce Davison	4R.R.	1962-1965
22. 8.1974	Gary Lloyd	3 Ind.R.R.	1969-1973
19. 7.1975	Eben Potgieter	R.L.I.	1972
8. 8.1976	Maurice Clipston	4R.R.	1942-1945
14.10.1976	Roderick Hayworth	4R.R.	1951-1954
15.10.1976	Albert Newman	4R.R.	1959-1961
9.11.1976	Nicholas Gregory	1R.R.	1964-1968
12.12.1976	Gregory West	3 Ind.R.R.	1970-1975
20.12.1976	Aubrey Murphy	6 Ind.R.R.	1974-1975
20. 3.1977	Jeffrey Barnard	Depot R.R.	1966-1971
6. 4.1977	Ronald Barton	4R.R.	1959-1963
12. 5.1977	Philip Nicholas	B.S.A.P.	1971-1976
26. 6.1977	Alan Hill	2 Ind R.R.	1970-1975
7. 9.1977	Godfrey Webber	1R.A.R.	1967-1971
20.12.1977	Mark Langerman	4R.R.	1967-1970
12. 1.1978	Antony Camacho	R.L.I.	1972-1974
23. 1.1978	Johannes Vorster	4R.R.	1968-1971
4. 6.1978	Tony Carroll	3 Ind.R.R.	1971-1976
27. 6.1978	Bruce Thompson, S.C.R. 2 Ind.R.A.R.		1964-1969
2. 9.1978	Peter Fairbanks	5 Ind.R.A.R.	1972-1977
18.12.1978	David Mirams	Intaf	1952-1957
18.12.1978	John Barry	S.A.S.	1971-1976
2. 1.1979	Douglas Havnar	10 R.R.	1966
2. 1.1979	Kerry Fynn	Air Force	1956-1960
4. 1.1979	Erwin Lombard	B.S.A.P.	1972-1977
5. 1.1979	Leonard Moriarty	1st Engineers	1969-1971
11. 1.1979	Clive Cripps	S.A.S.	1969-1971
17. 4.1979	Michael Moore	R.L.I.	1973-1977
18. 4.1979	Nicolaas van Niekerk, B.C.R. R.L.I.		1972-1974
24. 4.1979	William Perkins	4 R.R.	1971-1973
11. 5.1979	Steven Needham	B.S.A.P.	1970-1975
18. 8.1979	Donald Baker	B.S.A.P. Reserve	1934-1938
12. 9.1979	Simon Edridge	B.S.A.P. Reserve	1966-1968
2.10.1979	Kevin Tennent	Grey's Scouts	1975
9.11.1979	Kingsley Harris	B.S.A.P. Reserve	1954-1960
28.11.1979	John Mann	B.S.A.P. Reserve	1960-1965

Being someone interested in history and particularly the history of Southern Africa, I have often felt the best way to record periods of time is through the eyes of people who were there and then try my best to explain how they saw events unfold. I have tried to do that in this publication.

Although we did not know each other well and I was junior to him, Richard Stannard and I go back a long way to our days at Umtali Boy's High School. I was not present on the fateful afternoon when he pushed his luck too far and was 'asked to leave' but I do remember hearing all the chatter on the events of the day. We have remained in touch ever since and after the books I did on the SAS with Darrell Watt and Andre Scheepers were generally well received, we decided to do this one together.

Books about war are inevitably replete with sad stories of death and suffering against a background of people in high places playing recklessly with the lives of others which is never easy to record. In the course of writing this book I was blessed to work with someone as forthright and honest as Richard, but also to enjoy the levity that comes with being witness to his boundless optimism and marvellous sense of humour. He exemplifies the Rhodesian way of laughing in the face of sometimes impossible adversity. Thanks to him, this account is, I believe, enhanced and lightened by the recollections of a spirited man who has never taken himself or his predicaments, too seriously. And very often, with great soldiers, egos take centre stage and recollections become distorted to fit a version of events that suit the individual's needs; this certainly does not apply to Richard who has at all times shown himself perfectly relaxed with the facts, no matter how they portray him and he was ever-ready to accept the blame for mistakes.

Some of the events covered in this book have been written before by me and by other authors; but as is the nature of war, every battle and every situation is a complex combination of events and personalities which bears telling from different perspectives which is what I have tried to do. As is invariably the case with history, I cannot claim that all the facts presented are absolutely correct but I have tried my best to be accurate and, as much as possible, I have tried to let the actual soldiers tell the stories in their own words.

I have received criticism in the past for only presenting one side of the story and through the eyes of mainly white soldiers. Maybe I should plead guilty. But writing about a war in which one was involved, in a dispassionate and objective tone is not an easy task when one holds strong views on some of the fundamentals, however I have attempted in this book to silence some of my critics.

As Richard served with the Selous Scouts and operated with some of the great black soldiers of the time, including former enemy fighters, I have enjoyed including some of the exploits of these truly remarkable men. They give us all a fascinating lesson in the incredible results that can be achieved against the odds in the course of multi-racial endeavour underpinned, not by skin colour, but by ability, bravery and commitment to one another and a common cause. It is somewhat ironic, some may even find this proposition laughable, but I truly believe the most powerful and persistent lesson to be learned from the story of the Selous Scouts is that racial barriers are not insurmountable and the benefits of tearing them down are extraordinary.

Buttressing my effort to balance and broaden the narrative, I have also been able to weave into this account the story of one of the enemy from the time he boldly elected to leave school to join 'the struggle', his travels and travails through training in Tanzania and the Soviet Union, then on to the battlefields back in his homeland. I hope these recollections are as poignant and powerful for the reader as they were for me as the writer.

The Rhodesia/Zimbabwe story is one of triumph and tragedy and the denouement is a sad one. Few young countries packed as much action into so short a timeline with lead players as colourful and controversial. This book taps into that rich reservoir of remarkable people and extraordinary events.

Acknowledgements

There is no chance of writing a book like this without being able to tap into the kindness and goodwill of the men who served in these difficult times, who share a common desire to have our history recorded as accurately and fairly as possible.

To this end I am indebted to my editor Steve Lunderstedt who is a far better historian than I, who cast his eagle-eye over these pages and helped me enormously. Tom Thomas and the Selous Scout Association for allowing me the use of their photographs and some of the written material from the book 'The Men Speak'. In this regard my sincere thanks also to Jonathan Pittaway who compiled and published the book. Adam van der Riet for his help with photographs. To Andrew Field and the BSAP Regimental Association for allowing me the use of some of their photographs. Special thanks to Chas Lotter, the 'Bard of Rhodesia', for allowing me to use his poignant and such pertinent, poetry. Professor Richard Wood for allowing me the use one of his excellent maps. Pete Winhall for use of his collection of old Rhodesian newspapers.

As with my previous books on the war, I am indebted to Darrell Watt who has been supportive and generous with his time and knowledge. Special thanks to Tim Callow, Andrew 'Stan' Standish-White, Ken Bird, Keith Samler, Allan Hider and John 'Jungle' Jordan for their written contributions which have broadened the narrative and added so much to the story. And Barry Jolliffe, Frans Botha and Rob Riddell for their input regarding some of the events related herein.

MEN OF WAR

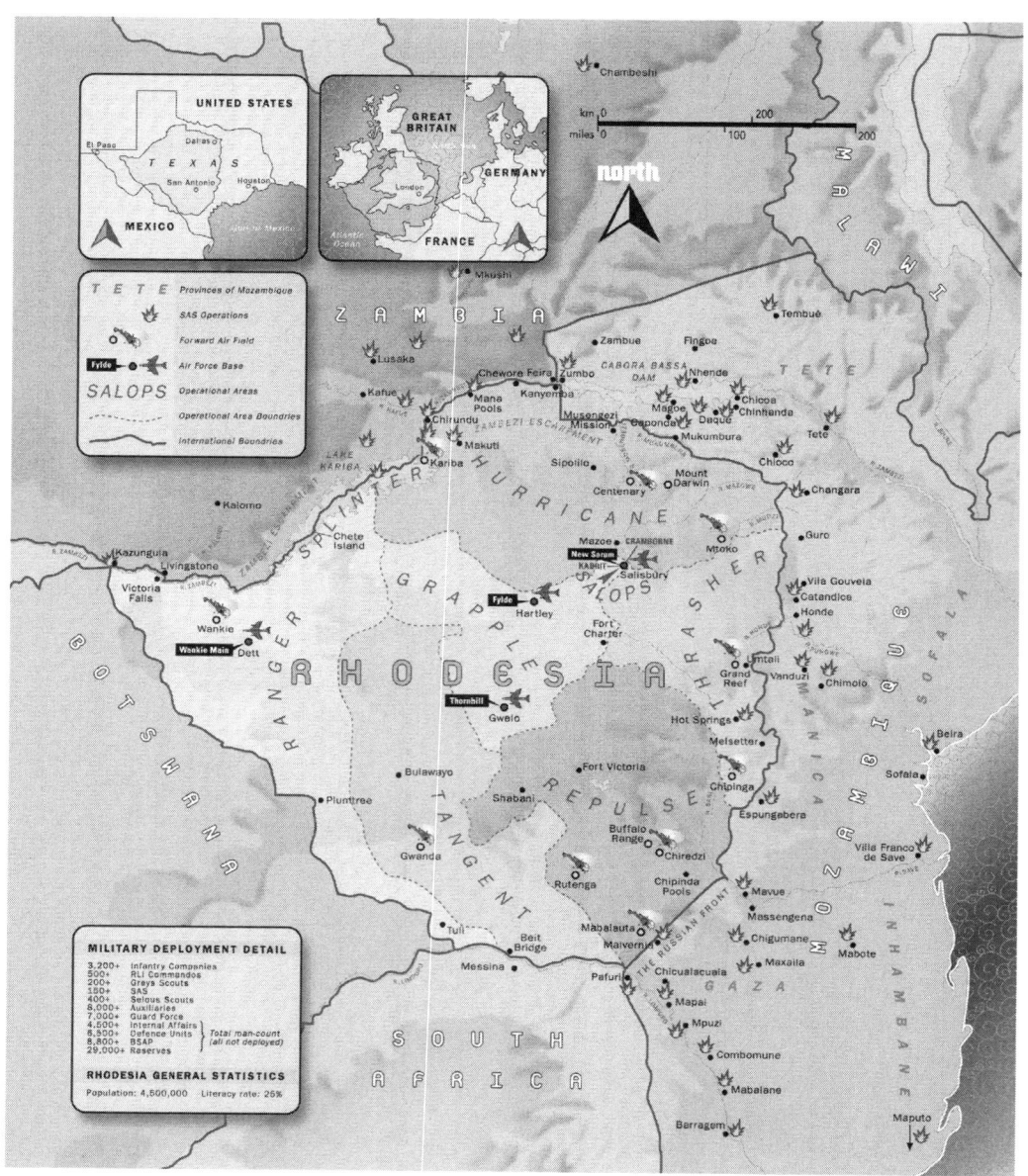

Rhodesia Operational Areas and Hot-Spots.

Chapter One

We have forgot who fired the house,
whose easy mischief spilt first blood,
under one raging roof we lie
the fault no longer understood. (Laurie Lee.)

♦

Taking On The World

First Farmer Falls

On the night of Saturday 4th July 1964, factory foreman, Pieter Oberholzer, accompanied by his wife Johanna and three-year-old daughter was driving home at night from Umtali to their home near the highland village of Melsetter where they lived in the shadow of the majestic Chimanimani Mountains when he spotted rocks strewn across the road. Forced to halt, he exited the car and went to remove them when he was assaulted and stabbed by members of a gang hiding on the side of the road.

"As he stopped, he got out and they threw stones at him," Johanna recalls. "I can remember seeing four Africans around the car. They came up and I saw one raise a knife above his head and stabbed down at my husband. It was so quick and all in such a rush that I did not see how many times he was stabbed. It was quite a long knife. Stones were coming from all around. I could not see very well. They broke the windscreen with stones. I got a stone on my jaw."

Despite having been knifed seventeen times in the chest and stomach, he staggered back to his vehicle and with the attackers trying to set the car alight he crashed through the boulders as another vehicle approached which put the killers to flight. By this time Pieter was dead. Johanna and child were rescued and rushed away and the gang returned later to slit his throat, smash his face with rocks and pin a note on his chest with a dagger. The note let it be known that the 'Crocodile Gang' had struck, and they would strike again.

He was the first European victim of politically motivated racial violence since 1896 when 244 white settlers were murdered in the tribal rebellions against European occupation. In a sense, The Oberholzer murder marked the beginning of a war that would last for 16 years. One of the members of the gang, although not present at the murder, was Zimbabwe President Emmerson Mnangagwa.[1]

Later in that year Mnangagwa would plant an explosive device in a locomotive. Investigations revealed his identity, location and address and he was put on trial. Initially sentenced to death, lawyers argued he was below the minimum age to suffer the death penalty and the sentence was commuted to one of life imprisonment.

Politics leading to UDI

Just three months before the murder, on the 13th April, the course of Rhodesian history changed when Ian Smith replaced Winston Field and became Prime Minister of the then Southern Rhodesia, charged with securing independence, restoring order to the restive townships and steadying jittery white morale.

With Robert Mugabe already serving a 21-month sentence following a conviction in March 1964 under the country's security laws, Smith quickly jailed Joshua Nkomo, whom he had identified as a primary source of the unrest. While Mugabe languished in Salisbury Prison, Nkomo was dispatched to Gonakudzingwa, a detention camp in the remote southeast of the country. "It was a horrible place," reported Nkomo later. "The lions were just outside so we were always frightened of being eaten."

With excitement running high, many expected Smith to declare independence unilaterally from Britain immediately and fearing this eventuality, British troops were placed on alert in Aden. Instead he addressed the nation in measured terms: "No one in the British government, including Harold Wilson the Prime Minister, disputes the fact that Rhodesia is better governed and better prepared for independence than any other in Africa, but they insist on a transfer to black majority rule. This we fear will lead to the destruction of our country and all we have worked so hard to build." To

---

[1] Mnangagwa had grown up in Mumbwa in then Northern Rhodesia where, as a petty criminal, he was brought before the courts on more than one occasion. Facing a lengthier sentence he joined ZANU, left the country and went to China for military training.

CHAPTER ONE

gauge the country's mood, he embarked on a countrywide tour and found the majority happy to let him lead and they would simply follow.

Smith and his ministers worked hard to find a formula for a constitutional agreement but to no avail. On 3rd November, Harold Wilson told the Commons that the gap between the two sides was unbridgeable and even if the majority of Rhodesians supported the settlement, he reserved the right to determine what would finally apply. He also told Smith that any agreement would have to be acceptable to the Commonwealth and the country's African majority. This was the final straw for Smith, who declared a State of Emergency two days later.

Ron and the RLI

Away from the political arena Smith was trying to get a feel for the mood of the military with many senior officers unhappy with the prospect of a break from the Crown. One who saw it very differently was Ron Reid-Daly, then RSM (Regimental Sergeant Major) of the RLI (Rhodesian Light Infantry).

"I like to think I played a small role in helping Ian Smith steel himself for making the big decision to declare UDI. Prior to this there was quite a lot of dissension in the army and indeed in the civil service, about the ramifications of this. Some of the senior ranks, most notably the army commander, General 'Jock' Anderson, were very much opposed to the move and this left Ian Smith wondering if he would have the support of the military.

"Just before he made the call in 1965, he came to the RLI barracks and I invited him to the Sergeants' Mess for a drink. One turned into many and the RLI NCOs let it be known in no uncertain terms that they were up for the fight and would back the PM to the hilt if he chose that route. Later I walked Ian Smith to his car and he was very quiet for a while then he stopped and said: 'Thanks Ron, I'm now happy that if it comes to a fight the men will be behind me and that has given me great peace of mind!' It was only a few months later UDI was declared and as promised the RLI was right behind him. 'Jock' Anderson refused to support Ian Smith and he took early retirement, not wanting to be part of a process that he saw as unconstitutional. Many years later Ian Smith reminded me of that night and said it was a decisive moment in him making up his mind to make the declaration that would change the course of our history."

UDI Declared

On the evening of 10th November, Rhodesia High Commissioner in London, Brigadier Andrew Skeen delivered a confusing and irrelevant verbal message to Smith. Smith and his cabinet later decided that on the morrow, 11th November, the declaration would be made. Much deliberation went into the wording of the document. It was eventually left to Messrs. Rudland, Ross, Williams and van der Byl, together with a calligrapher, to fashion the declaration. PK van der Byl insisted on including the words: "To us has been given the privilege of being the first Western nation in two centuries to have the determination and fortitude to say — so far and no further." His paean to his adopted country would soon arouse strong emotions.

At around 9am, Harold Wilson phoned Salisbury. He pleaded with Smith to act with restraint and resist those "with the bit between their teeth". Smith listened but was tired, distant and uncooperative.

An hour later, Smith, together with his ministers and deputies gathered in the Phoenix Room of the Milton Buildings in Salisbury, to sign the unilateral declaration of independence. The last time any such event had occurred was on 4th July 1776, in Philadelphia when the Americans seized their independence from Britain.

The prominent Rhodesia historian Dr Richard Wood says that the declaration had been planned for the day before. However, the government, hoping for a last-minute concession from Britain, held back the formal announcement for 24 hours. The resulting coincidence between Armistice Day and UDI enabled the Rhodesian government to ambiguously claim that their act of rebellion was aimed, not so much at the Crown, but at Harold Wilson's Labour government. Armistice Day was 11 November 1918 when the guns fell silent in World War I (1914-1918). Commemorated ever since as a Remembrance or Memorial Day for those who died in wars.

Smith used his regular lunchtime newscast to break the news to the country's 225,000 whites and several million blacks. In words echoing the American 1776 declaration he set out the case for independence, stressing the patience of Rhodesians in the face of British Labour Party treachery.

From a constitutional point of view the Rhodesian government and all

CHAPTER ONE

who served that government were in a state of rebellion against the Crown and this had treasonous implications for all civil servants of British ancestry who were under immediate pressure from Westminster to resign their posts or fear the consequences.

One such individual was British South Africa Police (BSAP) Inspector Peter Stannard, then the Member in Charge at Marlborough Police Station in Salisbury. "I remember there was panic at home," related son Richard. "I was 12 years old and it was all a bit vague to me but then dad came home and said to mom and us kids that we would have to leave the country. This came as a huge shock. He explained that the government was now in rebellion against the Crown and he had to be loyal to the Queen and that meant resigning from the police. Little did I realise it then, but we Rhodesians were about to go to war against the world and I was going to be very involved in that war."

Britain prepares for war

In neighbouring Zambia, reaction was swift. Fearing attack from the 'rebels' to the south, President Kenneth Kaunda requested immediate military assistance. Harold Wilson was quick to oblige and in a letter to the United States of America President Lyndon Johnson he laid out his response.

MEN OF WAR

"We decided to meet the second request by sending a squadron of Javelins[2] to Ndola. The operation, which has been planned on a contingency basis for some time, will start today and should be completed by Tuesday or Wednesday of this week. The Javelins will go into Ndola, the radar environment to Lusaka and men of the RAF regiment will go to both airfields and possibly to Livingstone as well to guard against sabotage etc. We shall thus be in occupation of all the main airfields in Zambia. We have made it a condition of acceding to this request that Zambia will invite no other foreign forces into the country without our agreement." Additional British plans for the invasion of Rhodesia were extensive.

What Harold Wilson didn't tell the USA president was that there was serious dissension within the RAF about being deployed and to possibly engage in battle old friends and colleagues in the Rhodesian Air Force. In one case, Barry Taylor was a serving officer in the Royal Rhodesian Air Force[3] and his father was across the river in the RAF. Despite the fact that they were being prepared to attack Rhodesia, Salisbury (ATC) air-traffic-control kindly vectored the aircraft in to their landing-strips in Ndola and Lusaka. Soon after arriving in Zambia, two members of the RAF contingent defected to Rhodesia, much to the embarrassment of the British Foreign Office.

Two Javelins were placed on immediate standby in Lusaka, while the rest of the squadron was tasked with flying routine patrols on the Zambezi river. With Salisbury ATC monitoring them, Rhodesian Hunters and Canberras were frequently dispatched to the river to make their presence known. These encounters invariably ended up with the opposing pilots waving warmly at one another.

Late December an infantry company was sent to what was then Bechuanaland[4] to be in position on the country's western flank and to provide protection for the BBC facility tasked with broadcasting anti-Rhodesian propaganda in a bid to incite a black revolt within the country. Additionally, the army's Strategic Reserve including the 16th Parachute Brigade, Aiportable Infantry and 1 Para were readied for deployment.

---

[2] Gloster Javelin - a twin-engined T-tailed delta-wing subsonic night and all-weather interceptor aircraft that served with the RAF from February 1956 until 1968

[3] The 'Royal' was dropped in March 1970 when Rhodesia became a Republic

[4] Bechuanaland became independent Botswana on 30th September 1966

CHAPTER ONE

The Royal Navy was to provide two aircraft carriers which were to be sent into the Mozambique Channel carrying strike aircraft and interceptors. Two ships carrying Royal Marine Commandos were readied to sail to Tanzania from where they would move south into Zambia and closer to the Rhodesian border. Light armour was to be airlifted into Zambia.

Prior to a ground invasion, RAF long-range bombers flying out of Kenya were to bomb the country's main airfields including the air force bases at Thornhill outside Gwelo and New Sarum near Salisbury. The main airports were then to be seized and secured by men of 22nd SAS. They would be followed by the Paras and then the infantry which would be used to secure all road and rail routes and all the main centres of government including the country's broadcasting studios. A team trained by the BBC would immediately begin broadcasting in English and the vernacular. Kariba Dam and the power generating station was to be seized following a combined assault including Paras and light-armour. Additional troops and equipment were readied at bases in Malta and Libya. Once the military was in full control and the Rhodesian Security Forces disarmed and neutralised a governor was to be installed backed by a contingent of British policemen.

On the 19th December the United Nations (UN) Security Council voted unanimously for harsh and comprehensive sanctions against Rhodesia while excitable Organisation of African Unity (OAU) members threatened to sever diplomatic relations with London if the rebellion were not crushed immediately. Petrol rationing was introduced within Rhodesia and Rhodesian assets in the UK were seized.

In a moment of considerable irony given the fact that war clouds loomed large, Ron Reid-Daly was awarded an MBE on the 31st May 1966. "I think they must have regretted it afterwards," said Ron, "but I had done my bit for the Empire and would have liked to do more but they seem to have lost interest before we did!"

The Tiger Talks

In one of the first engagements of the war, sometime in March 1966, 47 armed ZANLA[5] men crossed the Zambezi into Rhodesia and split into two groups. The one set about blowing up power lines near the farming town of

---
[5] Zimbabwe African National Army. Armed wing of ZANU. Came to be based in Mozambique and led by Robert Mugabe.

Sinoia. They were quickly engaged by police details and seven members of this group were killed. While men from the Rhodesia Light Infantry (RLI) were deployed in the area in the aftermath, this was the early stages of the war and the army played second fiddle to what was seen as essentially a police operation. The other group made their way to the Hartley farming area, where on the 17th May 1966 they attacked the Viljoen homestead, killing farmer Johannes and his wife Johanna (Babs). The two children, aged three, and nine-months, survived.

On the 1st December 1966, Smith led a Rhodesian delegation for talks with Wilson's team aboard HMS *Tiger* on the Mediterranean Sea. Consigned to the 'B' cabins in the battlecruiser's bowels, Jack Howman, then Minister of Defence, recalled the indignities of second-class-citizenry.

"The British attitude to us was one of Victorian paternalism and condescension. At times insufferably arrogant. Perhaps," he went on, "this is understandable for in the British view, had we not had the impertinence, the audacity, to defy, indeed to challenge the power and the authority of Her Majesty's government and were we not the first of our kind for 200 years to do so?"

Surprisingly few disagreements surfaced except for the mechanics of the return to 'legality'. Wary of possible British perfidy and despite Wilson's bullying, Smith advised that he would need cabinet approval before signing. Wilson became in turns apoplectic and menacing, finally threatening force if Smith did not sign.

On the last day of the talks Howman related the events. "We came into the Admiral's day-cabin to find Mr. Wilson in an absolute fury. I have never before seen a man indicating such vicious malevolence as this man did at that moment. 'You will sign these documents! I will not have Britain humiliated! You will sign before you leave this ship!' he shouted."

"I believe something happened to Mr. Wilson that evening, that he received a call either from his own government or from another source; that he was put on the spot, and I am convinced that he was petrified that we should leave the ship without submitting ourselves to his jurisdiction. ... his attitude was one of a fearful, panicked man who in seeking to ride a tiger was trying to pull us on too."

On the 5th December 1966, after an exhaustive cabinet meeting, Smith announced fundamental acceptance of the Tiger principles but refused to

CHAPTER ONE

abandon the country's constitution. Particularly repugnant to the Rhodesian leadership was the demand that they surrender control of the country's security forces to the command of a British governor. The next day Britain requested widened mandatory sanctions at the United Nations.[6]

On the 1st August 1967 a major armed incursion took place at Batoka Gorge east of the Victoria Falls when 79 ZAPU[7] and South African ANC[8] men crossed into Rhodesia from Zambia. This was the second attempt at crossing; the first ending in chaos when there was a near mutiny among the men. Chris Hani (later assassinated) and Joe Modise, who would later become South African Minister of Defence under President Nelson Mandela in 1994 were part of the group.

They made for the Deka river inside the Wankie game reserve then split into two groups tasked with establishing bases in Tjolotjo Tribal Trust Land and the Nkai farming area from where they were to attack white-owned farms in the surrounding areas. The operation was blown when one of their members was captured by a Rhodesian African Rifles (RAR) patrol acting on police information and *Operation Nickel* was initiated. One Special Branch policeman serving at the time insists Modise was actually passing information to a Rhodesian 'handler'.

Following up on the information gleaned from the captured insurgent the RAR immediately went into action before being joined by Two Commando of the RLI. Out of the 79 that had infiltrated, 29 were killed and 17 captured. A further 29, most of them members of the South African ANC, were arrested in Botswana.

"This was a turning point in the war," remembers Reid-Daly. "It forced us to take a long hard look at ourselves and review our tactics. For the foreseeable future the Zambia border remained the focus of our attentions."

---

[6] Smith was justified in doubting British sincerity. After the 1980 settlement at Lancaster House, the transition to majority rule was expedited with unseemly haste once control had been ceded to a British governor. Undertakings were ignored and voters were massively intimidated by Mugabe's forces, resulting in a highly questionable election result.
[7] Zimbabwe African Peoples Union. A rival resistance organisation led by Joshua Nkomo and dominated by the Matabele tribe.
[8] African National Congress.

MEN OF WAR

Battlefield Zambezi

Early 1968, Darrell Watt was patrolling the Zambezi escarpment. "We were in some very wild and rugged country looking for enemy sign when we stumbled upon an old man living completely alone far from any other humans. We had an interpreter with us, and I asked him to explain this man's circumstances. We gathered that he had been thrown out of his family and told to live on his own which he had been doing for years. His only neighbours were the lions, leopards, elephant, rhino and the other game that was abundant in the hills. We asked him where his family were, and he said they were many miles away living in the Chewore Mountains.

"He was smoking something out of a pipe and was holding hot coals with his fingers to keep it burning. I watched him take a long hard pull on the pipe and then he had a coughing convulsion and I thought he was going to die. His dress was very primitive, just animal skins and nothing on his feet. He was living off the land, setting snares for small game and birds and eating berries and 'bush-spinach'. We gave the old man what we could, and he was very grateful but I was curious and wanted to find his family so we set off in the direction he indicated looking for human tracks. The further we went into those mountains the thicker the bush became, the steeper the slopes and there seemed to be rhino behind every bush. As always, they were very aggressive and we were constantly having to duck, dive and jump up trees to avoid being knocked over but the only way we could continue was on the well-worn elephant paths which was where all the animal traffic was. Every now and then I would climb a large anthill to look for sign of movement. We were up one of the gullies when we noticed a herd of elephant descending just across the ravine and going in closer, we found foot-prints. I had a feeling then we were being watched but continued the climb to the top of the escarpment, rested on a rock knoll and the view of the valley below was breathtakingly beautiful. Through our binoculars we watched herds of antelope and buffalo below. I was hoping to see smoke or hear human noise, but it was deadly quiet when we lay up for the night. All we heard in the darkness was rhino snorting and elephant trumpeting and snapping branches.

"First light we were up and I was excited when we cut tracks of about ten people, including some children, walking barefoot away from us. My hunch was right, these wild people knew we were there and were keeping their

CHAPTER ONE

distance. They had never seen Europeans before and were understandably nervous. The local guide suggested we put food on some flat rocks in the open and then move back a distance where they could see us and know we were going to do them no harm. We did this and then sat back and waited. Eventually, they emerged slowly and nervously from out the thickets like wild animals wearing animal skins and some were carrying axes. They moved carefully towards the food and inspected it closely before picking it up and holding it. Then they suddenly seemed to know it was sugar, salt and sweets along with what else we could spare and they snatched it all up and ran back into the bush and out of our sight. It was an amazing experience; I thought this is how the cavemen lived and they were still living in an ancient world, well removed from where we found ourselves. We had to get back to fighting a war and I envied them a little. We never saw them again and I often wonder what happened to those wild people.

"It was only a few months later that the next big incursion was intercepted middle of March 1968 when a game ranger cut heavy tracks on a huge path near the security road going to the Angwa River. The 'Figure 8' boot prints he noticed, were unusual and the alarm was raised."

One of the young policemen in the Lomagundi area at the time the report came in was Ken Bird. "My first Police posting after the gruelling Morris Depot training and lengthy Hendon system driving course, was to Karoi. I was still nursing tarmac burns from falling off my heavy government-issue British motorcycle, when I presented my travel warrant at the Salisbury railway station, on a wet, cold and windy morning in January 1967.

"The clerk directed me to a short freight train with a single guards-wagon at the rear. It was rather austere with green upholstery and slept two. Apart from the guard, I was the only passenger. The whistle blew, the steam engine took up the strain and, with excitement mounting, we began puffing our way to my unknown future, seventy-five miles northwards. It was going to take a while, though, because we never seemed to go any faster than walking pace. Arriving at Sinoia Station after dark I was collected in a police Land Rover and taken northwards to my new post.

"My first briefing, the morning following the train ride, was by the Member in Charge and I was shocked to learn that the police area was considered at high risk for terrorist infiltration from Zambia. As someone who enrolled to be a policeman I had never even considered anti-terrorism as part of the environment that we would have to cover. My dreams of patrolling the virgin wilds in Rider Haggard mode began to deflate. It wasn't long, as a totally untrained anti-terrorist operator, I found myself foot-slogging, with a heavy pack and unfamiliar FN FAL rifle, following up lone terrorist tracks from locals reporting strangers in the tribal area. Our follow-up group was a complement of four, all equally untrained, with more chances of losing our collective virginities, than getting to grips with slippery terrorists.

"I had been there for 12 months, when, on the 14th March 1968, at about 4pm I was called into a briefing by 'Furb' Thomas, the Member in Charge. Five of us were to respond to a report of a terrorist incursion into Rhodesia, somewhere in the Zambezi Valley. Our orders were to leave at 3am the following morning and drive far into the valley to rendezvous with a National Parks ranger who would indicate alien boot-spoor in his area of jurisdiction which was the Chewore Wilderness Area. With the expertise of our specialist tracker, Sergeant Mavire, we were to confirm or disregard the boot prints as being terrorists or simply illegal persons.

"We were uplifted by chopper and flew into the designated area and with the help of Mavire we had little trouble confirming they were indeed terrorist tracks indented into the basalt soils of the valley by Russian-issue boots with a number '8' figure incorporated into the bar pattern of the sole. Time was probably past midday. The chopper lifted off, we were alone in the silence left behind, our orders were to standby for a RAR (Rhodesian African Rifles) section, under command of a sergeant major. We had just kick-started *Operation Cauldron*!

"The RAR section of eight men deployed to us late that afternoon. No time was wasted, and we took up the tracks immediately. We followed till sunset then set up an ambush on a small river. The banks were green and grassy, almost having a manicured park look and the water was clear, cold and tasted delicious. We slept well, without incident, and continued on tracks early the following morning.

"The terrain became more rugged as we traced rocky ridges but all the time we were following in the same direction as the water was flowing. The summer rains had come and gone, the flow of water was ebbing, disappearing and reappearing, filtered to crystal clarity through the granular sands.

"The terrorists, from the chopper activity, must have been aware that

CHAPTER ONE

their presence had been noted, but the tracks we were on were now two days old. Crossing to a thick riverine embankment, hidden from aerial surveillance, was a cleared sleeping and cooking area about the size of half a football pitch. In the gloomy tree canopy enclosure, something had caught the eye of the RAR Sergeant-Major and he recovered a Cuban military cap, from behind a bush. His one word, 'Zapu', came from his previous experiences on *Operation Nickel* in the west of the country. A careful 360° circular sweep registered a tally of about 60 to 80 terrorists and on transmitting this information, we were ordered to pull back immediately and go into ambush mode.

"We were all too aware we had almost no training for this sort of task apart from humping through the mountainous Mavuradonha Mountains for ten days on completion of recruit training and firing the new FN rifles, so we were a little out of our depth. It seems that this fact had not been overlooked by Police General Headquarters. Accordingly, our small unit followed instructions – to hunker down and ambush while the army specialists organised themselves.

Ken Bird continued:

"The following morning, we were told to stand-by in our position and shortly after sunrise the RAR were relieved by 14 Troop, 3 Commando, Rhodesian Light Infantry, under Lt Bert Sachse. His senior NCO was Basil Rushworth. Others in the Troop were 'Pop' Henwood, 'Spike' Stone, Rob Korb, CJ Swanepoel and Eric Ridge. With them was an SAS 'call-sign,'[9] commanded by Sergeant Joe Conway, with Darrell Watt, T.C Woods and 'Stretch' Franklin.

"But first there was a sweep of the abandoned camp. Hidden, again in the tree foliage, were about a dozen Russian made carbines, SKS and AKs. We also found the remains of a rhino they had poached and an attempt to fabricate a handgun holster out of zebra hide. A trooper commented that morale appeared high amongst the 'gooks'[10].

"We then joined the RLI and tracked down the river-bed, seeing spoor winding in and out while some of the enemy seemed to head into the increasingly high ground now closing in on the river like parallel walls. I felt

---

[9] Section of four or eight men with a designated radio identity.
[10] Slang for guerrillas, originally used in Vietnam.

fear then and even now, looking back, it was a highly dangerous situation we were in. We were moving with some stealth, but the warning bark of a big male baboon boomed out at us and focused my mind on the fact that we were moving observed. I thought it probably meant that there were no gooks between the baboon troop and us.

"Taking a smoke-break at around lunch time elicited some humour always found within groups of fighting-men, along with some wishful thinking. Being a Saturday afternoon, everyone was in agreement that our time would be better spent pissing it up at La Boheme night club in Salisbury.

"Late that afternoon we moved onto a hill next to the riverbed. Away from the likely action, we were allowed to listen to the 'Forces Requests' with Sally Donaldson on our short-wave radios. It was little embarrassing for some of the soldiers with messages from girl-friends like 'Keep your pecker down,' and 'Crave you 'til I peg'. Popular song of the time was Manfred Mann with 'The Mighty Quinn'. It was all just so casual and the banter among the troops was jocular but there was little doubt about their aggression. This was clear in their entire demeanour, the professional way they carried their weapons and their trained eyes.

"The sun set and a huge moon took over. For anyone less scared than me, they may have considered themselves camping in paradise. The night air was pleasantly cool, there were whispered sounds of the rivulets running over rock, soft sighs as the warm sands gave up their heat and for the first time in my life I heard the nocturnal cacophony of night-jars, owls and the bewitching laugh of an hyena. The pungent scent of carrion carried on the night air. For me, I decided I'd definitely prefer to be drinking and flirting at 'La Boheme'. The only other sound of the night was one of ours; Dennis Castell-Castell, oldest trooper in the BSAP,[11] snoring like a chainsaw and being woken every ten minutes by the guard. Dennis always gave the same irascible reply of, 'get some fucking ear plugs'.

"We took up the tracks again, early the following morning. The streams of water, heated by the previous day's sun, had cooled overnight and we filled our water bottles. As the sun climbed higher, the water warmed enough for lovely bathing, during smoke-breaks, in the isolated rock and sand catchments.

---

[11] British South Africa Police.

CHAPTER ONE

"Then we were taken to the command-base, known as Dean's camp, where they were building a bridge on the Angwa. That night Dennis Castell-Castell, from his rucksack, produced a bottle of his clear moonshine drink, which he flattened all on his own. The drink, known colloquially as 'Nipa', had the required affect. Dennis regaled everyone with his rude songs. Under threat of detention, he was silenced, and the Zambezi valley was surrendered, once more, to the sounds of wildlife."

Meanwhile, Watt and the SAS were moving fast in pursuit of their quarry. "The first full day we did about 30 kms," he recalls. "It was hot, our packs were heavy, but we wanted to nail these guys. We walked till it was dark then slept on the tracks. Joe Conway shat me out for not standing when on guard. I said I stayed low because I didn't want to be silhouetted in the moonlight and shot.

"The group we were after was about 30-strong and was a mix of Zapu and ANC. Their heavy boots made tracking easy and at one point I jumped in a chopper and was able to track them from the air which speeded up our pursuit considerably. It got very tense through thick bush, down gorges and up narrow ravines where we were very exposed to fire from above. When we got in the area of Dean's Camp, we waded waist-deep through the Angwa River. Once across, I told Joe we very close to them and being only four we were going to struggle to deal with them. This is when Bert Sachse arrived with his RLI Troop and two National Parks game-scouts as trackers. The game-scouts were not happy; this was not what they had signed up for and they were so scared they were shaking with fear. I had to show them a FN bullet and tell them that our bullets are stronger, but I could see we needed to get them out of harm's way as much as possible and told them to go to the back and I would take the lead on spoor. I also told Joe to tell Bert and his men to follow a distance behind and track us to reduce the sound of us advancing. I could see the bruised grass and writhing ants having been recently trampled on and knew the shooting was about to start. By this time, we were nearing the escarpment and I found where they had just laid an ambush up a river-line and then had hurriedly abandoned the position. I spied a small hill and told Joe to wait while I climbed it and glassed the area. Up I went and just as I thought, there they were. What immediately caught my eye was how light-skinned some of them were, unlike our Africans. They were wearing green jackets.

"Quickly and quietly we got the RLI into extended line on the higher ground and we were perfectly positioned on the ridge line. Bert gave the order to fire and I reckon 25 of them were dead in seconds. I got in close at about 30 metres and blasted away with a shotgun. What a fabulous weapon at close-quarters. I ended up swearing at them in Shona and Joe told me to shut up as I was making too much noise! I give them credit for putting up a very good fight, but we had the advantage of being on higher ground. At that point they called themselves 'FROLIZI'.[12] All the equipment was Chinese, and we helped ourselves to the jackets. That was that, we nailed all of them; Bert got a BCR,[13] I got fuck all!"

"We watched the action from a hill looking down into the valley," remembers Ken Bird. "Suddenly, we heard very intense gunfire followed by grenades exploding. It was the SAS and RLI blokes making contact. We watched as a military fixed-wing began aerial firing in the near distance. The firing seemed to last for a long time and from the military presence we were able to monitor the radio chatter of the troops in close contact with the gooks. The same soldiers that we had bid goodbye to the day before.

"Choppers flew in for the wounded soldiers; a shattered femur and a leg twisted at an odd angle, another trooper with a forearm wound that directed the offending round into his rifle butt. We then linked up with the RLI and set up a stopper-group in the riverbed, against a rocky midstream island. Within two hours it was all over, and we went into the contact zone.

"In my short tenure in the BSAP I had obviously seen some dead bodies, but no stretch of the imagination could give insight into the devastation that the FN 7.62mm does to a human, especially a tumbling ricochet. There were dead gooks lying all over a rocky area. Some had limbs attached only by several sinuous chords; one had an empty cavity within his cranium, covered only by his long, uncut woolly hair flap. Another seemed to have been split in two with a well-aimed rifle grenade penetrating and exploding his lower body. One of the RLI blokes was dead. Someone said the dead gooks were Cubans, they had yellow skin. They were, in fact, the typical cross breed of the South African Eastern Cape tribe[14]; they were the armed wing of the South African ANC.

---

[12] Front for the Liberation of Zimbabwe
[13] Bronze Cross of Rhodesia
[14] The Eastern Cape tribe are the Xhosa

CHAPTER ONE

"Back at base someone produced a five-ton Bedford. We loaded the dead gooks and drove to Karoi police station. We had plundered the recovered packs, or what was left after the soldiers had taken their first choice. I had found a set of 'Figure 8' boots and we all sported the tinny badges that the gooks carried. Presumably they would have handed these out on a victory parade.

"We were met by 'Furb'; his sarcasm was toxic as always. A tubby, eye-bulging CID Inspector, reeking of his lunch time binge, loudly announced that we would all be charged for wearing the enemy badges. The bodies were removed to the mortuary and I knew I could never face routine police work again. Something had been triggered in my psyche, a recognition that hunting terrorists was the greatest adrenaline rush one would ever experience. My life would never be the same again!"

During the same operation, a store-owner near the town of Mangula reported a suspicious presence and a police reaction resulted in the capture of a further six terrorists who revealed that the number of infiltrators was larger than Rhodesian intelligence had anticipated.

Another contact followed involving the RLI and RAR who met heavy resistance, culminating in an airstrike. This had little effect, but follow-up operations continued during which enemy detachments were intermittently engaged and a war of attrition ensued. With the enemy in disarray, orders were radioed from Lusaka for the infiltrators to evacuate but tracking teams effectively interdicted their withdrawal.

When a captured insurgent agreed to take the RLI to his base-camp, Training Officer Lt Ron Reid-Daly was given command of the assault, using troops still in training. The group they were tracking included ANC fighters heading to South Africa and they had entered the Doma farming area on their way south. When the guide's information proved erroneous and the camp's location had to be re-evaluated requiring an approach through open country, Reid-Daly had to quickly alter his plan, reducing the numbers in his assault-group to release men for the flanks. He then attacked and on hearing rifles being cocked, opened fire. When a terrorist appeared around an anthill he was shot dead but the rest of the enemy fled into thick bush with the RLI in determined pursuit. Though Reid-Daly had organised his men into a sweep-line, a hidden terrorist, using an RPD[15], fired killing Troopers

---

[15] Soviet designed 7.62 Light Machine Gun.

Reggie Binks and Christopher Wessels.

Activities had to be terminated when night fell but the next day two wounded enemy were tracked and captured. By this time, 28 insurgents had been killed and 15 captured. One wounded terrorist was found half-eaten by crocodiles and another partly consumed by lions.

"This operation had proved a great success," recalls Ron. "By the end of it, 123 men had infiltrated and 69 had been killed and 50 captured. We had six men killed. The death of Reggie Binks was particularly sad because he was so young, and this forced a re-think on how early we would deploy young soldiers in the future."

Chapter Two

The war has crept in
On the places I knew
In my wandering, bachelor days,
Devoured them

♦

Into The Bush

Legal Beadle

While the soldiers were fighting it out in the Zambezi Valley, a pivotal legal battle was unfolding and negotiations with the British government resumed when another round of talks took place on the warship HMS *Fearless* on 9th October 1968. Harold Wilson changed his tack and was markedly more hospitable this time, even upgrading Smith to the Admiral's cabin. Accompanying Smith were Jack Howman and Des Lardner-Burke. Although progress was made, nothing was signed when the talks broke up four days later. Sticking points for Smith was Wilson's insistence that the Smith government renounce the current constitution and transfer power back to the Crown while a new constitution was drafted and put to a referendum. The political stalemate continued.

A Royal Marine on board HMS *Fearless* at the time of the talks was Jock McKelvie. He had spoken to Ian Smith on the ship and had been so impressed that he had resigned from the Marines and joined the Rhodesia Light Infantry. He would win the Silver Cross of Rhodesia during the war.

At the same time, drama was unfolding in the Rhodesian courts where three black Africans, convicted of brutal murder were insisting upon a right of appeal to the Privy Council in London on the grounds that Rhodesia remained a Crown Colony which gave them legal access to the British, rather than the Rhodesian courts. The appeal was dismissed, and Her Majesty the Queen promptly intervened that night by written decree, summarily commuting their death sentences to life imprisonment. The politicians remained silent while the matter was taken on appeal to the

Rhodesian Appellate Division. Presiding was Sir Hugh Beadle, a Salisbury-born Rhodes Scholar. He attained the rank of Captain in WWII before becoming Chief Justice in 1961 and ironically, a Privy Councillor in 1964 when he was knighted. Beadle however was undaunted, he declared the Royal Order invalid and upheld the sentence which was carried out the next day, triggering a furious response from the British and international media.

Peter Stannard, having delayed a decision to resign from the police, at the time a Chief Superintendent based in Rusape in Manicaland Province, 80 kms from Umtali, watched this legal battle unfold with great interest. In a sense the court was putting a legal stamp of approval on the political decision to 'rebel' against the Crown and he and his colleagues were faced with a choice again; resign now from the service and remain loyal to the Queen or become a fully-fledged 'Rhodesian Rebel' and remain in the BSAP.

He weighed his options in the context of the times. Despite the political turmoil, fuel rationing, sanctions and isolated incidents of civil unrest, life was good for the 'coppers' and for most Rhodesians. The Police Club was a lively meeting place where cheap beer was quaffed in large quantities and the police fielded competitive cricket and rugby teams which played on most weekends. Across the border in Mozambique, the Portuguese appeared firmly ensconced and access was easy for the Umtali people who nipped frequently across to Vila Manica and Machipanda to fill up with fuel and enjoy the food, fine wine and warm Mediterranean hospitality. A local blend of Rhodesian jingoism seemed to sweep the country. Against this backdrop, Peter decided he and the family would tough it out and stay with the 'rebels'.

Expulsion

But rebellion ran in the Stannard blood because at school his son Richard was of the same mind, albeit, in a different context. The long-serving, and highly-regarded headmaster of Umtali Boys High School, Ken 'Coney' Fleming, was at his wits end with the boy. Despite repeated warnings, soliciting the help of his parents, and multiple canings, he could not get the unruly boy to conform.

"I was a nightmare at school anyway but then tragedy struck and made my mood worse. I was enjoying the weekends on the farm in Odzi with my Uncle Paul Mather-Pike, who had served with Peter Walls in the Rhodesian

CHAPTER TWO

SAS in Malaya. It was a Sunday morning when he called me to the tractor shed and I never forget walking in to see him looking grim.

'Rich, it's time, for you to become a man,' he said. I stared blankly back at him.

'Your brother Mark died last night after a bicycle accident. Pack up son, we leave for Salisbury in an hour.'

I was dazed and bewildered. I found out later, he had been hit by another cyclist and concussed. On admission to hospital, they did not think it was serious, but he had a subdural haematoma and died in the night. My mom and dad never recovered from the loss.

"Back at school I really struggled with his death and felt a sense of guilt because I had been distant from him and now he was gone. Not long after this, I bunked out of the boarding-house and went through the bush and over the border into Mozambique where I got myself seriously plastered. When I returned that night, I was out of control and threatened prefects and masters with various forms of violence. When Coney heard about this, he had had enough of me.

"The Housemaster came and told me I had been expelled and to pack my kit. My dad arrived in his uniform, red with rage and I thought he was going to kill me!

'You are a complete embarrassment,' he screamed, 'we've all tried with you and failed! Only one thing for you – I'm sending you to the army! Sixteen years old - they will take you as a 'boy-soldier'! I don't know what else we can do!'

"Unbeknown to my father and me, at that very time, the military authorities were having another look at the regulations concerning 'boy-soldiers'. This was in the wake of the death in action of Reggie Binks who had just been killed aged 16.[16]

"My dad had been a captain in the 9th Gurkha Regiment before he came to Rhodesia, along with his brother Dan, and joined the police, so soldiering ran thick in his veins. He knew I might make a decent soldier and decided the sooner the better to keep me out of trouble but I was not in that much of a rush and prevailed upon him and my poor mom, Melody, to give me a chance to at least get an 'O Level' certificate. When they calmed down they

---

[16] Reggie Binks was 16 years and four months old when he was killed in action.

agreed, and I was sent to Marist Brothers College in Que Que.

"Here, a new and ugly challenge awaited because some of the priests were paedophiles. A couple of the boys told me about this one particular master who would come into the dormitory at night, slide his hand under the blankets and fondle the boys. I said 'no problem, my dad's a cop; I'm going to report this guy and he'll deal with it.' That's what I did, and dad was quickly on to it and the offending priest was chucked out the school. This didn't make me too popular with some of the staff, but I managed to keep my head down and pass.

"While the army was certainly an option, my dad spoke to me and said I should, 'Go forth and carve a career for myself in Internal Affairs.' It all sounded a little mundane but then, when I found out more about it, I gathered I would probably be sent into the bush and that pleased me. I had visions of bundu-bashing, crossing crocodile-infested rivers and fighting off lions in an effort to civilise the natives and it sounded better and better.

"At this time Ian Smith had pretty much given up on finding a settlement with the British Labour government and Rhodesia declared itself a republic under a new flag; the 'Green and White' replaced the old and the colours that we would soon serve under with such pride and devotion became part of our lives.

Internal Affairs

"Few of Rhodesia's critics ever understood the reason why there was a division of land in the country between Africans and Europeans, but the original intention was an honourable one. After the occupation, the country was actually run by Cecil Rhodes's British South Africa Company which set aside almost half of the land for the sole occupation of the natives. This was done to protect them against land speculators and the divisions were drawn up along ethnic lines so as to preserve tribal identities. The idea from the beginning was to interfere as little as possible with the traditional leaderships in the administration of what would become known as Tribal Trust Lands and European ownership of property in these areas was forbidden. The Department of Internal Affairs (Intaf) was then formed to assist chiefs and headmen in the general upliftment of the tribal populace through the provision of health and educational services, the dissemination of advice on agriculture and husbandry and trained personnel were deployed

CHAPTER TWO

to integrate African Customary Law into the system of Roman Dutch Law introduced by the settlers. Leading figures in this process were the District Commissioners who were highly educated men, well versed in local lore, language and culture, dedicated to helping the Africans. This is where I found myself in 1971 when I was posted to Murewa in the north-east of the country as a cadet-officer.

"My boss, the District Commissioner (DC), was Wally Walters. A tall, highly intelligent man with a commanding presence he was committed to his job and dedicated much of his life to helping the Africans improve their quality of life. Following in the colonial tradition, only very highly qualified men of impeccable integrity were entrusted with this sort of authority He kept saying to me, 'You need to deliver character, Richard!' Below him there were two District Officers (DO's), Johnson and Charlie Nicolle, whose father had headed the Department of African Affairs. Charlie was a dapper dresser, always turned out in a well cut, three-piece pin-striped suit. I looked a little shabby next to him in my simple safari-suit, stockings and 'veldskoens'('vellies').

"What came as a rude and sudden surprise to me was the amount of studying we were expected to do after a full day's work. The pressure was immediately applied to learn the local language, the history of the area, the customs of the tribe, the customary law, how the administration of justice was enforced and how settlement of civil disputes was conducted. There were four sub-Tribal Trust Lands in the area we administered and my initial responsibility was to supervise the payment of the government grants to chiefs, headmen and their staff. The days were often tiring, travelling long distances over rough roads in my Land Rover.

"As a cadet I was also responsible for supervising the dipping of the African cattle. It never ceased to amaze me how far in the air the beast would leap when I stabbed it with the electronic cattle-prodder. While I found it quite amusing then, little did I know, I would soon be on the receiving end of the same device and I wouldn't be laughing. This dipping programme proved highly effective at the time.

"My home was a little one-roomed house opposite the DC's office and the courts. I had Henry the old cook, he was well into his 70s and sported an impressive moustache. He had retired from government service but said he came back to work to escape his nagging wife. He cooked wonderful meals on the old wood-stove and he was stimulating company. Blackwell was the gardener looking after me. He provided my hot water by firing up a 44-gallon drum in the evening. We had no electricity and Henry would light the paraffin lamps before supper. Then, with the lamp on my desk I would get to my books. Often the mosquitos were bad in the evenings to add my annoyance at having to study.

"Jock was the local postmaster and on weekends he and I used to load up my old 1947 Chevvy and drive through the Pungwe TTL to go fishing on the Mazoe River where we caught Bottlenose and Catfish. On the way back I would load up the car with firewood for my boiler and stove.

Father John Bradburne

"It all became more interesting when I was given the additional responsibility of paying the lepers from the leper colony at Mutemwa. The colony was run by John Bradburne, an English monk, musician and mystic who had come out to Rhodesia in the early 60s.

"He had been an officer in the 2nd Battalion, 9th Gurkha Regiment – my father's regiment - in Malaya when the Japanese attacked allied forces under General Wavell. Facing tanks with no armour and no anti-tank weapons his battalion was pushed south. When Singapore fell, a calamitous defeat which Churchill described as 'the worst disaster and largest capitulation in British history,' Bradburne and fellow officer Captain James Hart decided to escape - separate from the main body of men. Surviving off what the jungle provided they made steady progress until Bradburne succumbed to cerebral malaria.

"Eventually, he and Hart made it to the coast, commandeered a Sampan and made for Sumatra but their first attempt nearly ended in disaster when they were caught in a storm but made it back to the mainland. On the second crossing they made it to Sumatra and then on to Dehra Dun in India to re-join the 9th Gurkhas where my grandfather James Stannard was serving as the RSM. Thereafter he joined Orde Wingate's Chindits and continued the fight against the Japanese. Ever the eccentric, Bradburne fascinated the Gurkhas with his routine of climbing a tree in the jungle and playing the flute for them. During this time, he met Lt. John Dove who he befriended and it was Dove who became a Catholic priest after the war and went to Silveira Mission in the then Southern Rhodesia. Working at the mission

CHAPTER TWO

were Robert Mugabe's two sisters and the staff there were to become very involved in subversive activities against the Rhodesian government. After contacting Dove, 'seeking a cave in Africa where I can pray', Bradburne came to Silveira in 1963 and made a home for himself in the chicken coop where he would be exposed to as little human company as possible. He was then introduced to the Mutemwa Leprosy Settlement near Mtoko in the north-east of the country in 1969 and decided immediately this was where he wanted to stay.

"When I met him, he was living alone in a mud hut but spent a lot of time in a cave. He told me how, when he almost died of malaria in Malaya, he had prayed and Jesus Christ had revealed himself to him when he looked into the sky and from that moment on, he felt he had a role to fulfil in life that was divinely ordained and he expected to die a martyr.

"He was absolutely devoted to his lepers and they to him. They called him, 'Baba John' (Father John). Every day he would wash the worst cases himself and carry them on his back when they were unable to walk. He was fiercely protective of his patients who, in the main, had been banished from the villages and from their families, making them lonely outcasts. On Sundays he would say mass for them, deliver the blessed sacraments and play the organ to accompany the hymn singing.

"I grew used to them but at first I was shocked. They were hideous to look at with their weeping lesions, festering sores, skin nodules, facial disfigurement and fingerless hands. In Shona lore they were believed to have upset ancestral spirits and nobody wanted them near. John was constantly in conflict with the local villagers and headmen because he would not allow their cattle to encroach on the area set aside for the lepers. He had planted fruit-trees for his patients and the locals would steal the fruit which drove him into a fury. Although a priest, he had also been a soldier and he had a temper on him.

"One day after we had finished paying them, I remember listening in on a discussion about John, and the Africans in conversation firmly believed he was indeed a man in touch with God. They talked about how he was always in the presence of birds but more importantly for them, he was often seen with Bateleur Eagles circling above him and these raptors were considered by the African spirit-mediums to be connected to their ancestral spirits. They said bees built their hives near him and believed this was also a sign of some mysterious relationship he had with the natural world.

"He took his job a lot more seriously than I did. The lepers would have to queue up weekly on the spotlessly polished verandas outside my office to receive the cash support provided by the Rhodesian government. I would pay each one, one at a time and they had to sign for it, those who could not write had to make a thumb-print. Some came in with no thumbs so I said I could not pay them. This caused consternation and screams of disapproval until I relented and handed over the cash. Father Bradburne was not at all amused. Another problem for the lepers was Jock the postmaster's dog. The lepers smelled terrible and when they came to the offices for their money the dog would smell them and cause havoc sending the lepers scurrying for cover. Such was the commotion on one occasion, Wally Walters heard the noise and came hurrying to investigate. At this point there were lepers scrambling all over the polished verandas trying to get away from the dog and the DC was furious. Jock and I got a serious ear-bashing and the postmaster was told to get his dog locked up.

"While most of the country was quiet at that time, reports were filtering in of anti-government political activity and we were warned to be on the lookout for hostile elements associated with ZANU[17]. They were thought to be establishing a presence in neighbouring Mozambique through an alliance with Frelimo which was successfully increasing its footprint in the colony as the Portuguese appeared to be tiring of war. BSAP Special Branch officers, Peter Stanton and Winston Hart had their informers in the area and they were picking up disturbing signals. The information was passed up the chain of command but it seems not everyone in the security hierarchy was paying attention.

"Meanwhile John, through his total commitment to the poor and the sick in the area was making himself a target because he was visibly undermining the message being put out to the people that the whites were there only to rape and plunder. The same applied to us in Internal Affairs. The Zanu political commissars and operatives could see how effective we were in administration and poverty alleviation and they set their sights on our destruction.

"An early enemy tactic was to intimidate the locals into refusing to dose their cattle at the dips. Unfortunately, they succeeded in destroying them

---

[17] Zimbabwe African National Union.

CHAPTER TWO

and the spray-races and some of the dip-attendants were murdered. As a result, hundreds of thousands of cattle, roughly half of the African herd, would needlessly die. The next target was the chiefs and headmen who were targeted as 'collaborators' or 'sell-outs' and warned to stop engaging with us on pain of a serious beating or death. In the course of the war that would follow hundreds of these good people would be tortured, maimed and murdered.

"By the end of my first year in internal affairs I was also given the responsibility of registering births and deaths. This was tedious admin and I began to lose interest in my job. On the one weekend I jumped into my old Chevvy and headed for Salisbury at full speed looking for some action. I went straight to *Le Coq D'Or* nightclub in the middle of town, had a few beers and picked a fight with the biggest bloke in the bar. Well, this was a huge mistake; he fucked me up badly and I ended up flying head-first down the stairs into the hands of the police before being taken to hospital. A bottle in my face caused cuts needing stitches and some of my teeth were knocked out. My father was furious when he heard. I arrived back at work, battered and bruised, and Wally Walters sat me down. 'Richard,' he said, 'this sort of conduct is not acceptable for a Cadet Officer in Internal Affairs. I don't think this is where you belong, and I think you will do a lot better in the army.' He was right; and without much further ado, I prepared myself for a career change.

Chapter Three

I am nineteen
Padre.
Why then do I feel so old and worn?

♦

Into the Army

Llewellin Barracks

"Like thousands of young Rhodesians before me I walked nervously through the gates of Llewellin Barracks in January 1972. Named after a former Governor General of Rhodesia, Lord Llewellin, it was a bleak place built mostly out of corrugated iron. It had been hastily constructed in 1939 as one of the new bases for training young pilots from all over the world, to fly for the Royal Air Force in WW II. In 1956, it was taken over by the army and became a Territorial Force Training Centre, then later Depot Rhodesia Regiment.

"At the time I reported for my service there had been riots around the country in protest against an agreement reached between Ian Smith and the new British PM, Sir Alec Douglas Home which would have broken the political impasse but it was subsequently rejected.

"Mom and dad dropped me off at the boom on a sunny Monday morning and bade me farewell. Little did I know but I was just steps away from being part of an army that would test me to the limit over most of the next years.

"I grabbed my suitcase, turned for one last wave and walked gingerly towards the gates. The boom lifted and I noticed the Military Police, the 'Redcaps' eyeing me out. I barely had time to attempt a friendly smile when they went berserk and the screaming began. 'Run you little cunt – and don't stop till you see the rest of the 'Fresh Poes!' I charged off with my suitcase until I saw where all the rest of the similarly confused conscripts were gathering and it was mayhem. One of men hurling endless abuse and who stood out was Sergeant-Major Jock Hutton, a WWII veteran who had jumped into occupied France prior to the Normandy landings.

CHAPTER THREE

"The rest of the day was chaotic as hundreds of us ran around being yelled at and abused by the instructors. We rushed from one point to the other collecting the kit we would be issued with to see us through the training. Two of most clothing items, from socks to underpants to caps and combat-jackets, mess-tins, knives and forks, badges, berets. At the end of it we were buried in all our new possessions. Just to make us look even more stupid we were ordered to wear our 'Cunt-Caps' (combat-caps), combat-jackets, shorts, socks and takkies. Then haircuts – a bloke by the name of Skinner took just about everything off in 10 seconds. Blokes who arrived with nicely groomed locks looking quite smooth suddenly looked like complete idiots.

"We were then split into platoons, began running around the old airfield so the instructors could see who was fitter and stronger and then the medical exams where we were prodded and inspected ending with the downgrading of anyone with physical defects that made them unfit for full infantry training.

"Once the initial thinning-out was over the actual training began with runs in the early morning, two hours on the drill-square, weapon-training and the assault course. The shouting and abuse seldom stopped, and any mistakes were immediately punished by some form of physical exercise. The gum-poles were a big part of the physical training; three men to a pole and round and round the airstrip. There were casualties with some collapsing from exhaustion. Then at the end of the day it was back to our beds in our barrack rooms to clean and polish boots and brass for the morning inspections. Daily inspections were done by the corporals and they were tough but the weekly inspection done by the Company Sergeant Major (CSM) was very difficult and would often end with beds being upended and kit strewn around the barrack-room floor. We would then have to get to work cleaning up the mess. When the white gloves were worn by the inspecting officer we knew we were in for a hard time. Surfaces would be hand-brushed and any dust or dirt that appeared on a glove would trigger some sort of punishment. Sometimes the individual was singled out but more often than not it was the entire platoon.

"Operating quietly in the background was a small group of black batmen who would shine boots and clean kit for a fee but if caught you were in big trouble. They also ran a lucrative trade smuggling in contraband booze and other banned commodities.

"The biggest fear for the recruits was being caught doing something seriously wrong, being charged and sent to Brady Barracks, outside Bulawayo, where the Detention Barracks (DB) were. A pretty brutal place run by CSM Pretorius, a former heavyweight boxer, notorious for hammering his inmates; he was probably the most feared man in the Rhodesian Army.

"Weapon training was intense, and we were all very familiar with our weapons before we eventually went to the range to fire them. Any action on the range that was considered unsafe drew a very angry response from the instructors and anything serious like an AD (accidental discharge) carried the possibility of a spell in DB.

"Sunday church came as a huge relief. All quiet and civilised, nobody shouting at us and if you were not in need of spiritual renewal you could get some badly needed sleep which is what most ended up doing. After four weeks of training we were allowed in the Troopies' Canteen if we had passed our weekly inspection, and after ten weeks the first phase of our training was complete, and we were allowed a weekend home.

"On return to barracks we were offered the chance to apply for postings to other army units such as the medical corps, engineers and signals and some were selected for a leadership training course from which they would select corporals and sergeants. For those of us who stuck with the infantry course we trained in conventional warfare but the emphasis was on counter-insurgency and we did several exercises outside Bulawayo getting used to the challenges we would face and the tactics we would use, out in the field of operations.

Two Independent Company

"On completion of our training we were given a few days off then back to Llewellin and we were trucked to Kariba town as part of Two Independent Company Rhodesia Regiment which was based there, tasked with patrolling the lake-shore and the Zambezi River as far down as the bridge at the border-town of Chirundu.

"This was like being on one long walking safari. Before deploying we were given a lecture by Pete Clements and Rex Pretorius, two of the original Selous Scouts, on basic bushcraft and how to handle wild animals in the bush without having to kill anything. Both of these guys were real 'bushmen' who could live off the land indefinitely.

CHAPTER THREE

"We spent most of our time patrolling the river-line looking for tracks of 'terrs'[18] but this was a quiet phase of the war and there was not a lot of human activity. There was however, plenty of animal activity and the area was full of black rhino who did not like us, so we spent a lot of time on the run from these beasts. Very often they would charge from short range and a section of weary soldiers would bombshell and be sent racing off in different directions looking for a tree to climb at great speed. On pain of death did anyone shoot in self-defence; National Parks Rangers were quick to investigate any shootings of game by the army and the presumption of innocence was always in favour of the animals so we ran for our lives rather than risk jail.

"My friend Rory Beary, who had previously been hurt by a charging rhino while serving with 'Two Commando' of the RLI, was later convicted

FIVE BULLETS IN SLEEPING RHINO

Herald Reporter

BULLET HOLES in a rhinoceros carcass indicated the animal was either lying down or sleeping when it was shot, a game ranger told Karoi Magistrate's Court yesterday.

Mr. Oliver Coltman of the Department of National Parks and Wild Life Management, said there were no signs that the rhino had been charging when it was shot.

He was giving evidence against Corporal Rory Eugene Beary, of the Second Commando, 1st RLI, who had pleaded not guilty to shooting the rhino on November 7.

Similar charges against three other troopers were withdrawn.

Beary was found guilty of unlawfully hunting and shooting a black rhino at Chewore Game Reserve, in the Zambezi Valley.

The hearing was adjourned for sentence on August 17.

The magistrate, Mr. E. D. Vosloo, said Beary's evidence was untruthful in part. He thought it probable the rhino was asleep or lying down when it was shot.

Beary claimed the rhino was charging the Army patrol when it was shot.

Mr. Coltman told the Court: "In the past 18 months I have collected the carcasses of 44 dead rhinoceros in the reserve. This is an absolutely unnatural number to have died in this period of time."

He said the rhino shot by the patrol was about 4½ years old and weighed 3 000 lb.

He had gone to the scene of the shooting with members of his staff after a report that an army patrol had shot a charging rhino.

BULLET HOLES

"We searched the area thoroughly and found the carcass in a river bed," he said. "There were no tracks of a charging rhino at all in the area. We searched it very carefully."

Mr. Coltman said five bullet holes had been found in the rhino. Two were in the chest and three in the groin.

"It would have been virtually impossible to hit a rhino in those positions if it were charging at you," he said.

"To hit the rhino in the chest like that it would have had to be lying down or sleeping."

The rhino's skull, which was produced as evidence, had no bullet holes.

Corporal Beary told the court his patrol had come upon the rhino suddenly. They were within eight yards of it when they first saw it and had stopped at once.

"After a couple of minutes I began to back away," he said.

It was then the rhino had charged.

"I considered my entire patrol was in great danger and I shot first at its feet but that had no effect. I then shot at the head and it stumbled and veered off to our right," said Corporal Beary.

When the rhino reached the river bed, other members of the patrol had fired at it.

He could not understand why there were no bullet holes in the skull.

Mr. R. Codron, of the Directorate of Legal Services, Ministry of Defence, for the accused, said Beary had been in scrapes with rhino before and had once been injured while running away from one.

---

[18] Slang for terrorists.

of poaching, fined and given a suspended jail sentence for killing one. In court he told the magistrate he only fired in self-defence at close range when they stumbled on the animal in a ravine but Oliver Coltman, who was the Ranger in the area, went to the scene to investigate. In his evidence he explained to the court that the animal's tracks before death did not indicate a charge and the placement of the bullets that hit the animal in the side suggested Rory was lying and the magistrate agreed. This sent a strong signal to all of us to run rather than shoot.

"In another incident a group of elephant stampeded onto an RLI patrol and one of the troopies fell trying to escape. A cow-elephant grabbed him, tossed him and was attempting to kneel on him and crush him to death when another trooper, Peter Pitman charged into the rescue and started beating the animal in the ribs with his rifle. This had no effect and he then used his rifle butt to beat its ear and that must have hurt because she backed off and both soldiers survived.

"Lions were also a problem, particularly at night. Only a month before I went to Kariba, RLI Lieutenant Al Tourle who had been awarded the Bronze Cross for gallantry, was killed by one. While giving a briefing to the men a lion came out the dark and pounced from behind, grabbed him by the neck and dragged him off into the bush. One of the troops reached for his rifle, fired over the lion's head and the cat ran away but Tourle's neck was broken. By morning, even with medical attention, he was dead.

"While the patrolling was hard going, we saw no action against the enemy. Back in Kariba we had a good time in the pubs and on the lake, but they kept us fit with runs down the hill from the barracks and back up again to the top. It was known as the 'ski-run' and on a hot day, it was gruelling exercise.

"We went to the range regularly to hone our shooting skills and on one of these exercises I first clapped eyes on Darrell Watt. He was with Andy Chait and they were firing AK-47s. I was immediately struck by the size of his powerful legs watching them use their weapons and it was easy to see that these two guys were real professionals and we were just amateurs. I think it was then that I first thought about joining the SAS and becoming a real soldier.

"As it turned out, towards the end of the year, we were redeployed to the northeast of the country where the SAS were operating. The Portuguese

CHAPTER THREE

ARMY HERO KILLED BY LION

Herald Reporter

A RHODESIAN ARMY OFFICER, Lieutenant Albert Knight Tourle, died after being mauled by a lion while he was on duty in the Zambezi Valley, the Ministry of Defence announced yesterday. No further details of the attack were released.

Lieutenant Tourle was awarded the Bronze Cross of Rhodesia last October for his gallantry and "outstanding qualities in leadership" during security forces engagements against terrorists.

On one occasion his initiative led to the elmination of nine terrorists, six of whom he accounted for himself.

Lieutenant Tourle was also an accomplished shottist. He won the Queen's Medal in 1966 and was several times runner-up in this event. In 1968 he shot for the Rhodesian Bisley team in Bloemfontein.

It is understood that a second Rhodesian Army officer, Lieutenant Frederick Watts, was also mauled by the lion. Lieutenant Watts is believed to be recovering at the district hospital in Kariba but his condition is not serious.

LIEUT. A. K. TOURLE

were still in control and our BSAP Special Branch had gathered information about new infiltration routes opening up from camps in Zambia, running through Mozambique and into Rhodesia. The 'Porks', as we referred to the Portuguese, were not always happy to have our troops operating there but the SAS had been given permission and we went in after them to see if we could find any enemy movement. We found a lot of burned-out kraals but not much else.

"Back in Rhodesia our base was on an airstrip near the border town of Mukumbura and on the other side of the strip was the SAS camp. Dick Paxton was there with a 'Provost' fixed wing which was being used for airstrikes in support of the Portuguese. Not knowing what I was going to do after my service ended at the end of the year, I wandered over to introduce myself and to see if there were any openings for me.

The first chap I engaged was Noel Robey. I immediately noticed a lion, badly tattooed on his chest and when I looked him in the eyes, I realised I was not very welcome.

'What the fuck do you want here?" he said.

'I just thought I might have a look at joining the SAS,' I replied politely.

'Fuck off you little cunt,' he said, 'no room for runts here!'

'Is there an officer I can speak to,' I asked.

'No, just fuck off back to your camp!'

I stood my ground and when he realised I wasn't leaving he softened and grunted something about Major Harvey, pointed in his direction and walked off in a huff.

"I made my way gingerly into the camp, asked where the major was and found him in his tent. I explained who I was and that I was interested in joining up and he was helpful. He asked me how old I was and when I told him I was 19, he said, 'You better hurry and get on selection before you get too old!' I left my name and he said they would get in touch to let me know when the next selection was being run.

To the SAS

"Early 1973 I received word that I was to report for duty at Cranborne Barracks in Salisbury. Although I had already completed one recruits' course, I had to start from scratch and go through the whole recruit training programme once again.

CHAPTER THREE

"With that behind me, I went on a selection course which began at Cranborne. Nick Breytenbach was with me and Danny Smith, who was one of the early heroes, was one of the training sergeants. The 'pre-rev' which was 24 hours of hell really started to get the better of me and Francie who had come from the Australian SAS was a big help. He kept reminding me that this was just a phase, to hang in, bite the bullet and I'd get through it. We were in and out of the RLI swimming pool most of the night, carrying big steel balls and we had to hump a truck chassis around on our shoulders with instructors within swearing at us from the cab. The morning runs were long, we were carrying heavy packs and we were not allowed water, so thirst became a big factor. Quite a few of the chaps threw in the towel at this stage. Those that kept going through the 'pre-rev' were loaded into trucks and we set off on the long, cold drive to the Inyanga mountains on the eastern border.

"There we started the daily speed-marches up and down the mountains, having to find our way by careful map-reading through some very rugged country, to specific points within a specific time. The last day was the hardest, we had to climb Mt. Inyangani, the highest mountain in Rhodesia and we had to complete the task within a set time limit. I just made it.

"Out of roughly a hundred who had started the course, eight of us passed including Nick Breytenbach and Nigel Willis. I really got on well with both of them. Then we were loaded back on the trucks and hit the road back to Salisbury. Our first stop was the 'Winged Stagger' where we had to down a yard of ale in seconds or you had to try again. Although we had passed selection, we still had our parachute course to do and then we would have to go operational before being eligible to receive our colours."

First SAS Operation

"My first external operation," remembers Stannard, "was with Koos Loots and Fletcher Jameson and we parachuted into Mozambique to join the SAS based at Makombe on the Zambezi river where Rob Warraker was running the show. I was very happy to see Darrell Watt and Andy Chait were there along with Dave Scales, who was running the signals. They were already veterans in a sense and we 'fresh-poes' were quite intimidated by them.

"At this stage, the Portuguese seemed to have lost the will to fight and they had very much confined themselves to their bases while doing very little in the way of aggressive tactical deployments. With Frelimo growing in confidence, they had invited their Zanla allies to take advantage of the situation and use this part of Mozambique as a reasonably safe route into Rhodesia.

"The lack of aggression being shown by the 'Porks' had encouraged Frelimo to go on the attack and they frequently showered the Portuguese bases with rockets and mortars. Most of the troops we spoke to were just biding their time and trying to stay alive long enough to go back to Portugal. During the rains the going was particularly hard and on my one parachute jump I landed in mud, was buried up to my chest and thought I was going to die there. Fortunately, the other guys found me and pulled me out. But the bush in places was thick and stinging-nettles were a problem. It was almost impossible to anti-track and the enemy had their *mujibas*[19] out reporting on our movements.

"We went out in four-man, hunter-killer groups with orders to find and engage the enemy. It was not long before I saw my first kill when we spotted a lone 'gook' with an AK and a youngster who was unarmed. Andy Chait dropped the armed guy and we let the little guy go. I walked up to have a look. Brought up a Catholic, I did some soul-searching. This guy's death had been so sudden; one minute he was walking in front of us and then he was no more. My first experience of the 'quick and the dead'.

"Then we started to run into bigger groups of Frelimo and they were up for the fight. We were often outnumbered and outgunned and they started to give us a very hard time. They must have been very angry that we Rhodesians had arrived to complicate their plans when they felt they had the 'Porks' pretty much beaten.

"On one deployment with Jop Oosthuizen in command and Hennie Pretorius, we had four contacts in one day with big, well-organized groups and we were boxed in. Jop was injured and taken out, leaving Hennie to take command. Hennie managed to extricate us, but it was very close and we did think they were going to surround us and take us all out. Having been under that sort of pressure and on the run in a sense, it was not good for morale. Then the South Africans arrived commanded by Jan Breytenbach.

---

[19] Youthful enemy collaborators.

CHAPTER THREE

He had just been in Biafra and had seen quite a lot of action.[20] He was not at all impressed with us. When he heard what had happened, and that we had made no kills, I remember his fierce blue eyes boring into me as he gave us hell for not being more aggressive.

"We were a little peeved on receiving this dressing-down. He was an officer but not in our army and the South Africans were there to watch and learn, not command. Our orders were to hunt and kill Zanla groups, not engage Frelimo and we were heavily outnumbered against them. We felt this was all a little over the top at the time.

"February 14th always sticks in mind. Brian Robinson was at the base and when he was around we were all a little nervous because he took no crap. He knew it was Nige Willis's birthday and Nigel was about to be deployed. Just before they moved out he approached Nigel and said, 'Happy birthday Willis, now for fuck's sake don't get shot on your birthday!' As it turned out, late that afternoon his call-sign walked into a well-planned Frelimo ambush, Nigel took a burst of RPD fire in the chest and was killed instantly."

Two months later, on 25th April 1974, the Portuguese government of Marcello José das Neves Alves Caetano fell in a coup led by General António Sebastião Ribeiro de Spínola, and the wheels were soon in motion to ditch the Portuguese African Empire and transfer power to the nationalist movements in the colonies.

"It all happened so quickly," recalls Stannard. "We felt we were getting on top of the situation and stemming the flow of Zanla into the country when we were told the 'Porks' were handing over and going home. It was a real blow. In a hostile world we had effectively lost our last ally apart from South Africa and the South Africans were showing themselves to be friends only when it suited them. We were ordered to stop our operations and prepare to return to Rhodesia.

"Back in Rhodesia it was a bit of an anti-climax but the SAS decided that we needed more guys that could speak the Shona language to make us less dependent on interpreters, particularly for interrogation purposes. For some odd reason, because I was never much of an academic, I was one of five, along with my great pal Nick Breytenbach, selected to do the three-

---

[20] The South Africans were sent there to help the French-backed Biafrans who were fighting to secede in Nigeria. The Nigerian regime was backed by the British.

month language course to be conducted by Phillipa Berlyn, a renowned linguist and academic at the University of Rhodesia. Her husband was Dick Christie, a former WW II fighter pilot, law professor and an Air Force reservist who flew Dakotas operationally, sometimes taking the SAS deep into Mozambique and Zambia.

"Well, poor Phillipa; I don't think she had any idea of how hard it was going to be to teach us anything. All of us had joined the SAS looking for action and here we were sitting behind desks in a classroom, wearing collar and tie, trying to learn a difficult language that we weren't terribly interested in being able to speak. She did her best and all credit to her but then I think she tumbled to the fact that she was wasting her time; none of us were very good linguists and we were never going to be fluent. We suggested that we have some of our lessons in the 'Winged Stagger' because classroom was too boring. She had a wonderful sense of humour and although a little reluctant at first, she agreed and off we went to the pub to learn Shona. With the barman assisting her as a tutor in this pretty hopeless effort she started to really enjoy herself and these visits to the pub became increasingly frequent, to the point where I think she was enjoying the boozing as much as we were. At the end of three months we had little to show for it other than big bar-bills but she had become a great friend to all of us.

"Having completed the course, and back in the bush, we had a contact and the gooks were mortaring the shit out of us. Rob Warraker was in command when we entered a village where we suspected the gooks had been hiding out. They had a *mujiba* who looked like the guy to get information from, so I, with my new linguistic skills, was immediately summoned to do the interrogation in fluent Shona. Well, the moment I opened my mouth, I think everyone knew, I had not learned a damn thing. Rob was furious.

"Brian Robinson was also not impressed with my performance and I think I was irritating him so he came up with a new task for me. Solid intelligence from central Mozambique had become sketchy and he wanted to send somebody with a military background, under cover into the area to see what was actually going on. Having a still valid British passport, I was selected as one of the spies but there was a problem trying to figure out what my cover should be, when it was suggested that Phillipa accompany me, with her posing as a journalist and me as her assistant.

"So off I went with her, across the border and we travelled as far as

CHAPTER THREE

Vila Pery (soon to become Chimoio) with me looking for signs of military movement and other matters of strategic value. In Chimoio we were actually very warmly received by the Frelimo officers and men who were in very high spirits in the knowledge that the country was soon to be theirs and the long fight many of them had been anticipating was not to be. It was quite a weird feeling for me being so close to these guys. Little did they know I had only recently been trying to kill them and I would soon be trying to do so once again. Already, the white Portuguese were very unsettled and starting to leave. All the slogans and graffiti were about the communist revolution that was underway and how a 'workers' paradise' was about to become a reality. As it turned out, for the whites, their worst fears were soon realised and they lost everything soon after Samora Machel came to power.

PK van der Byl.

In August 1974, Ian Smith, to the surprise of many, appointed PK van der Byl as Minister of Defence, replacing Jack Howman.

"His appointment as Minister of Defence, was an immediate tonic for us," recalls Ron Reid-Daly. "Morale improved immeasurably throughout the armed services when news of this development filtered through. I loved the guy. He was eccentric, outrageous at times but what a fantastic sense of humour he had. Whatever he did, he did with gusto and enthusiasm.

"Soon after his appointment I remember he phoned Peter Walls and asked him to have a uniform made up for him. It must be said that PK and General Walls never really hit it off. He wanted it made to his own specifications with an English-style high-collar and buttons in all the right places. Having found out that the RLI were wearing shorts rather than longs he asked for something along the same lines but smarter. He then arrived for a visit in a helicopter in a camouflage, cavalry-type shirt and these beautifully tailored shorts out of which came these long thin legs. He was carrying a heavy calibre hunting rifle; a .450 double I think. It all looked bloody funny but I tell you he could walk and he could shoot.

"He then spoke to the local army commander and said, 'right what patrols are going out because I'm going with and I need to kill something as soon as possible.' There was a lot of 'but ... but ... but' from the army commander but PK cut him short; '... don't but me .... I'm the Minister of Defence and I'm telling you to send me out into the field,' he said."

"I was posted to number 7 Helicopter Squadron in 1974 by which time the civil war in Rhodesia was well on its way," recalls Peter Simmonds. "On this occasion I had just completed a four-week trip on operations in Mt. Darwin situated in the northeast of the country and was looking forward to 10 days rest at home away from the war. On my first day back at New Sarum Air Force Base I wasn't pleased when my boss, Squadron Leader Eddie Wilkinson, told me that an Air Task had come in and there was no-one left on the Squadron to do it but myself. There had been a recent cabinet reshuffle in government and Mr. P.K. van der Byl had just become our new Minister of Defence.

"P.K., as he was affectionately called, had decided that the best way to get to know the military and to show how serious he was in his new portfolio, was that he should tour the front line. My Air Task was to fly him around the northeast operational area.

"We only had 'fire-forces'[21] from Mt. Darwin eastwards and south down to Pungwe in the Mrewa district. I was tasked to spend one night each in Mt. Darwin, Marymount Mission and Pungwe with P.K. while he got to know the various Army commanders and their men in each place.

"Eddie Wilkinson briefed me to take an Alouette II for the job, to fly low in the operational area so as not to be shot at, but not so low as to frighten the Minister. I was then to drop him back at the Squadron where the Commanding Officer of New Sarum would be waiting to greet him before he drove home on the Friday so he was home for the weekend. I hadn't met P.K. before but had seen him on television and was therefore aware of his colourful eccentric character but I can't say I was ready for him when I did meet him for this trip. On Tuesday 2nd my Flight Engineer, Steve Stead and I, prepared the Alouette II with enough fuel to fly us safely to Mt. Darwin. Steve and I each had a tiny bag with clothes and toiletries for three nights in the bush and a stretcher packed under the back seat of the aircraft. The two of us took up very little space in the aircraft.

"P.K. duly arrived on the Squadron with 'Wilkie' in attendance. His car drove up to the helicopter and introductions and handshakes took place. I noticed that the new minister had somehow managed to find a full set of smart camouflage clothing for the trip. His attire was conspicuous in that he wore no rank on his shoulder at all, but his green and khaki longs were

---

[21] Quick reaction airborne shock-troops with attack aircraft in support.

CHAPTER THREE

different because he held them up with a brightly coloured red and yellow stable-belt. He had kept the belt from his earlier days as an officer with the 7th Hussars during the Second World War in Italy. He must have dug deep in the attic for this belt. Then his bedroll was hauled out of the car boot and I wondered if we would ever get it into the tiny Alouette II. It was bigger than a 44-gallon drum and it was obvious he intended being comfortable. Then two large bags came out of the car. One must have had clothes in it and the other, much heavier, clinked suspiciously but somehow we managed to squeeze it all into the cabin. He was also hanging on to what looked very much like an elephant gun. He was well known for elephant hunting and was determined to take it. No-one suggested he change it; he wanted to put 'his gun' to good use on this trip.

"The chopper was frightfully heavy but we managed to take off and flew away north over Borrowdale. We then passed over the granite hills and valleys of Domboshawa and on to Bindura, before descending to 50 ft. above ground level for the rest of the trip to Mt. Darwin.

"Right from the start P.K. was chatty and excited but he let me know within 10 minutes of leaving New Sarum that he was to be dropped in the Botanical Gardens near his house, off Second Street Extension when we returned on the following Friday. Wilkie had been explicit that he must be brought back to New Sarum where he would meet the Station Commander, but P.K. was insistent that he would be dropped near his house and wouldn't accept the instructions I had been given. I thought it was odd that he should be worrying about the end of his trip before it had begun but as he said with a little ceremony in his very English accent, 'It's all been organised, Peter! I've arranged for people to meet me there, so it cannot be changed, we must land in the Botanical Gardens!'

"Ten minutes from Mt. Darwin, I warned Operations on the radio that we would be arriving soon and discovered that a 'contact' was in progress west of Mount Darwin. 'The King', Colonel Dave Parker, was running operations in Mt. Darwin and suggested we change frequency so that the Minister could hear the 'punch-up' taking place over the radio.

"P K was delighted when we changed to 'Channel Two' and immediately badgered me to join the contact. He wanted to be put down on his own in the contact area with his elephant gun; 'On high ground please, Peter, as I like to attack downhill. I'd like to bag one of these chaps and this is an ideal

MEN OF WAR

opportunity, don't you think?' All this was said seriously in the strangest of accents and Steve Stead was gagging in the back of the aircraft.

"There was no chance I could do what he asked of course, but I felt I owed it to him at least to ask 'The King' if we could fly at height over the contact area for a look at it from a distance.

"Colonel Dave Parker was adamant in his next instructions.

'Get the Minister to Mt. Darwin, now, Simmo! He is not to be allowed anywhere near the contact, I will get him as close as he needs to be on the map in my ops-room when he lands!' P.K. heard the transmission and looked disappointed. All the while Steve kept a straight face, seemingly oblivious to the goings on of pilots, officers and ministers around him.

"After we landed, P.K. saw out the rest of the contact in the ops-room and spent the afternoon pouring over maps, tactics, and strategies and getting to know the men involved in the war. He enthusiastically chatted to soldiers and managed to attract even the roughest 'troopies' attention with them saying they wanted to 'kyk this new oke' (see the new guy). That evening he endeared himself in the Officers' Mess with his quaint stories and three bottles from the clinking bag. The Minister knew a thing or two about winning us over and we were well lubricated by his Scotch whisky, fine wine and beguiling character.

"The following day he wanted to visit Karanda Mission on the way to Marymount Mission. 'The King' had told him that we had taken some seriously wounded soldiers there recently and that the renowned American surgeon at the Mission had kindly patched them up before sending them on to Salisbury General Hospital. He had probably saved the soldiers' lives and since we were never really sure whose side any of these missionaries were on, it was considered a good idea to encourage them by sending the Minister to thank them personally for their action.

"We were not expected and landed unannounced at the airfield where the Karanda Mission pilot was attending to his Cessna. When our blades stopped turning he wandered over and I persuaded P.K. to leave his elephant gun in the aircraft. The pilot didn't know who P.K. was so I told him this was the Minister of Defence for Rhodesia and explained why we were there. He was most impressed with all this and insisted on calling P.K. 'Your Highness' for the rest of the visit. Steve Stead and I made no effort to correct him and it seemed P.K. had no intention of putting the pilot right either. He

CHAPTER THREE

obviously preferred to maintain his 'no rank on the shoulders' stance and his new 'Your Highness' title. It seemed to me that it actually suited him. The pilot showed us to the surgeon who was appropriately thanked with a little pomp before we moved on in a cloud of dust to Marymount Mission.

"Halfway there we flew over a couple of African women carrying huge suitcases on their heads as they walked along a lonely path in the middle of nowhere. P.K. immediately wanted to check them out '…in case they are carrying weapons of war'. This was a Minister like no other we had seen before. He was determined to be directly involved. He was a contact waiting to happen. No other senior politicians had been this far into the bush before and frankly, even the good ladies from the Border Patrol Welfare Fund had ventured deeper into the Operational Zone than any of the Ministers I could remember. I felt there would be no harm in letting him have a look in the suitcases and who knows, they may have contained something they shouldn't. I looked for a suitable area and landed. I asked the long-suffering Steve Stead to accompany P.K. with his own weapon for the suitcase inspection. Steve's face gave nothing away as he galloped away with his FN after the Minister who was by now bounding through the bush with his enormous gun held menacingly at the ready. By the time I got airborne and overhead the offending suitcases were open on the ground and the African ladies were standing nearby with their hands up in the air. P.K. was 'hoiking' colourful clothes out of the suitcases with the barrel of his gun. There was clearly nothing sinister hidden away in the suitcases and P.K.'s disappointment was obvious, even from the air. We left the ladies to continue their haulage and moved on to Marymount Mission."

Chapter Four

No man outlives the grief of war
Though he outlives its wreck;
Upon the memory a scar
Through all his years will ache. (William Soutar)

♦

Operation Big Bang
August – October 1974

"My first big attack was *Operation Big Bang* in October 1974," remembers Stannard.

"We received orders to go into Zambia. Special Branch had passed on information about a ZIPRA[22] camp somewhere in the vicinity of the Mazanga River. Chris Schulenburg, 'Mac' MacIntosh and Joe Bressler did the initial recce after crossing the Zambezi about 50 kms downstream from the Victoria Falls. The recce-team picked up movement and signs of an enemy presence but could not pin-point the camp and returned to Rhodesia. A few weeks later 'Schulie' went back in with Mick Graham and Bob MacKenzie.

"At some stage Schulie picked up vehicle movement and saw these guys digging a bloody great hole and could see they were burying stuff; he quickly deduced it was probably an arms cache and this was where they were camped. He and his recce-team then returned to Rhodesia to report his findings then went back in with the three section commanders to identify the camp and establish how the assault would take place. About forty of us were then briefed at our HQ in Salisbury and mobilized to do the attack. We were flown down to a bush strip near the DC's camp at Sidinda Island and there we readied ourselves. Dudley Coventry was in overall command and Garth Barrett was to lead the actual attack. Schulie then came back and did the final briefing. Unbeknown to us, I think Zipra were watching our every move as we were going through the motions."

"In the afternoon before the deployment some cattle came through

---
[22] Zimbabwe Peoples Liberation Army. Armed wing of ZAPU based in Zambia.

CHAPTER FOUR

the edge of the camp, along with two *mujibas* who had been sent to check us out, but we were not sufficiently alarmed," remembers John Riddick. "The Zodiacs to be used in the crossing were stashed at the mouth of a dry river-bed about one kilometre upstream, around the side of a kopje. Mac McCrimmon and one other were left to guard them."

"Forty-three of us crossed, at 9pm with Garth Barrett taking the lead and we marched in single file into the night," remembers Stannard. "I think it was, at that time, the biggest external operation of the war. To their credit the enemy was not panicking. Little did we know at the time, but as we moved into Zambia they were moving in the opposite direction into Rhodesia and just as we were about to attack them, they were about to do the same to us."

Back at the base Riddick remembers: "We were not left with a lot of men; two guys with the boats about one kilometre away and no radio contact with them as it was on the blind side of the hill. Three signallers; Farmer, Alexander and Tennis. I was the 'rookie' medic with 'Dup' du Preez and Scottie McCormack in charge. Willie Erasmus was tasked to run the Zodiacs on retrieval and there was Dudley Coventry and Phil Cripps."

"I had put my bed in the shadow of a big tree trunk," remembers Willie. "but the moon was inconsiderate enough to move exposing me to moonlight. I woke up with a bang. I was suddenly flat on my belly about two metres from my bed. I would not have thought that muscle spasm could jerk you that far. My left arm was numb, and I had a dull ache in my belly. I was being covered in dirt as the bullets hit the ground just in front of my face. What initially saved my life is that the first shot threw me into shadow and they could not see me. I looked up and was amazed at how close these two terrs were to me; only about 10 feet. They each emptied a magazine, changed mags, fired a few more shots then took off. During all this I was hit twice more; left shoulder and between the buttocks. I was lucky I was only hit four times."

"The gooks took Dudley Coventry completely by surprise," recalls James Framer, "and opened up on him at point-blank range hitting him in the calf and thigh, and scalping him, knocking him out cold. Phil was on the south-side of the camp on guard, and ran to his 'bivvy space' where he caught a round in the upper arm, passing close to the nerve and giving him wrist droop for about a year!

"As our tent was blacked out the terrs could not see it however Cpl Tennis, in the Signals Tent, exited at a great rate of knots leaving the tent flap wide open and showing light on us guys sleeping on the ground. I could hear Phil Cripps and Willie Erasmus groaning and Major Coventry calling out. I ran into the tent to switch off the light and in doing so lost my night vision making it difficult to find the correct microphone to call for air support. I made my contact with the signaller at the Wankie Air Base who answered immediately and quickly summoned the pilots and gunner to assist us. I stayed only a couple of minutes inside the tent and ran back outside and jumped in our rubbish hole and faced into the incoming fire. One of the guys was firing back and I started firing as well however I heard Phil Cripps groaning and crawled out to him under the moonlight to help. Then I called to Cpl Riddick (the medic) to help. He was busy attending to Willie, using a flashlight to find a vein in his arm so he could insert a drip. I told Phil to stop groaning as it was giving our position away and I calmed him down by telling him I had just come out of South Vietnam and knew what I was doing. I also told him that if the gooks appeared I would blow them away. Gunfire was still going on.

"I had the A63 radio with me and I heard the chopper pilot asking me to hold down the presell switch so that he could pinpoint our position using his homing device. After a minute or so the pilot had got a fix and not long after I heard the fighter aircraft swoop down over our camp and he told the chopper pilot that he would give him top cover just in case they tried to shoot him down.

"Cpl Riddick by then had done all he could for the casualties. I'm certain his quick and courageous reaction saved Willie's life. The chopper landed and we all helped in loading the wounded. Looking at Willie I did not fancy his chances. Then they were airborne and on their way to Wankie Hospital."

"We were high up in the escarpment on the North Bank, well into Zambia and heard the firing," recalls Dave Hodgson. "As we looked back we could see green tracer way down below us and knew our base-camp was under attack. It bothered us as we did not know if they had been 'taken out' or not and if so, we would struggle to get back across the Zambezi and back to safety."

"Having heard of the attack, things were happening fast back in Salisbury," remembers Riddick. "Ken Philipson was organising every able-

CHAPTER FOUR

bodied soldier in the squadron, including the National Service guys, and they boarded a Dakota for the flight to come in and assist us. Nothing was said to Barrett or Schulie about the attack as they might have aborted the operation.

"That afternoon the Bedford RL was sent down the airstrip to collect more fuel, and about 800 metres down the road, 'Torty' King on the back was told to look out for landmines. Just as the warning was issued the front wheel hit a mine in the road. That night, bright moonlight and wide eyed, 'Dup', Scottie, and I had no sleep again."

Meanwhile, Barrett and his men, having walked through the night, took up positions before dawn and sought shade in the stifling heat to wait out the day. After nightfall they were on the move again and walked until the early hours of the following morning. Satisfied they were in the right place, Schulenburg and Barrett positioned the men tactically with stop-groups strategically placed to cut off those fleeing the assault group which would charge in from the north.

As the sun rose and all became clear, Schulenburg shot the lone sentry and that was the trigger for a roar of fire and pandemonium as the assault-group charged in for the kill. Some defenders fought for their lives while others fled in a blind panic.

"I was with John Rossier in one of the stop-groups," remembers Stannard. "The attack went in, we had fleeting glimpses of gooks running like hell and we engaged them with accurate fire. Then a sweep-line went in to clear the camp followed by the demolitions group under Rob Warraker. They had to go down a huge hole to get the job done while we went and laid landmines."

"I joined the demolitions team under Rob," recalls Dave Hodgson. "We had been in the stop-group directly in line with the assault-group so we had a few kills as most of the terrs ran in our direction. When the shooting was over and all went quiet the search of the area commenced and as suspected, the bunker in the centre of the base provided entry through a trap-door to a massive arms cache below which was on a scale unlike anything ever seen before thus far. After selecting what could be carried back to Rhodesia the rest was readied for destruction.

"'Bags' Styles and I set the charges," remembers Hodgson. "And we made a very 'big bang' indeed. It was heard over 50 kms away and such was the size of the blast, we were worried the Zambian Air Force would arrive from Livingstone where they had a squadron of fighter-jets. Thankfully nothing showed up and we made it back safely. But, in hindsight I think we were too cocky. We were the finest anti-terrorist unit in the world during the 1970s and we should have known better than to leave our base-camp exposed. It should have been better protected."

"We were definitely too big for our boots," recalled Darrell Watt. "Zipra were getting very good at identifying vulnerable targets that were not expecting to be attacked and going for them. They were without doubt very brave buggers and needed good hidings to put them back in their place."

"After Vorster's Détente things went quiet for us and most of the army as the South Africans kept pressure on us not to be too aggressive in the hope that there would be a political settlement," says Stannard. "We all knew it was not going to happen and all this did was give the enemy a chance to lick their wounds and prepare for the next offensive. Morale in the SAS during this time was very low as the South Africans stopped or slowed the supply of fuel and supplies into Rhodesia to put pressure on Ian Smith. P.K van der Byl, the Minister of Defence came to see us in the bush to tell us what was going on and he tried to cheer us up. He arrived, immaculately dressed carrying an AK. I think he was as frustrated as we were; he wanted to go into attack mode in a big way.

"At this time there were other problems in the SAS. Brian Robinson was a very competent OC but he was not terribly popular with a lot of the men. Ron Reid-Daly, on the other hand, was charismatic and very popular and with the formation of the Selous Scouts a lot of our guys elected to ask for postings to the Scouts. In no time at all we were down to about 40 fighting men and if the drain had continued I don't think the SAS would have survived. A big factor in the unit remaining viable was the introduction of National Servicemen to boost our numbers. At the time this was not well received by the regular soldiers who resented their admission and set out to give these guys a hard time. Thankfully, they toughed it out and out of their ranks came some of our best soldiers."

"I was one of the early NS guys to make it into the Squadron," remembers Frans Botha. "I was intake 136 and completed my recruit's course with the RLI in May 1974, before we were given an opportunity to try the SAS selection. Eight of us passed, including Barry Deacon and Barry Jolliffe

CHAPTER FOUR

and we were very excited about our prospects but in the barracks, we soon realised we were not very welcome. The Regulars[23] definitely resented us being there. They were all on 3-5-year contracts and maybe they felt we had come into an elite unit through the back door but we were all left wondering if we should not have just stayed in the RLI. On our first visit to the Troopies pub, 'The Winged Stagger', we were just approaching the entrance when some of the older soldiers inside saw us coming and slammed the doors shut in our faces. It was another rude reminder that we were not wanted there.

"Not being welcome there, on the weekend, Barry Deacon and I went to the Le Coq d'Or nightclub in Salisbury to have a few beers and a bit of fun. It was a favourite meeting place for army guys and the RLI boys were a permanent presence there. As a result, it was pretty rough at times, but it was a very popular watering-hole for the troops.

"Barry and I were sitting at the Round Bar, minding our own business, when I took my leave to go to the gents for a piss. While I was away, something was said about us being 'fresh poes' because I came out to find Barry in a furious fight, then saw John Rossier, one of the older SAS soldiers and a corporal, going down with blood all over the place and Barry still beating the hell out of him. As I approached him, Bruce Fraser, also a corporal in the SAS, came towards me with that look in his eyes and I knew a fight was on. We went at each other and eventually tumbled down the stairs, out the front entrance and into the streets where we ended up laying into one another among the dustbins. Eventually I got the better of him and he was man down asking me to stop. At the end of it, we had to take stock of the fact that two new soldiers, with no rank and no colours, had just decked two corporals and humiliated them in a public place. We took a taxi back to Cranborne and went to bed wondering what would come of this but fearing for the worst.

"Next morning early the summons came early. We were ordered to the office of Major Knight-Willis where we would be dealt with; both expecting time in DB before being thrown out the SAS. We were marched in and brought to attention, then allowed to stand at ease before being given a chance to explain what happened. We told him that we had not gone looking for a fight but that there was hostility being directed at us new blokes and

---

[23] 'Regulars', in the Rhodesian Army were career soldiers and 'Territorial Force' (TF) troops were reservists. NS were National Servicemen.

it was clear they did not want us in the Regiment. This had triggered the aggression and we were pretty sure Rossier and Fraser had decided to fuck us up and get us chucked out. The major listened very quietly to everything we said and then much to our delight and surprise he spoke.

'Alright boys, that's all fine by me. Try not to repeat this behaviour but you can go now.'

"We both breathed a huge sigh of relief and then made it to the dining hall for breakfast. Sitting there with black eyes and badly bruised faces were Rossier and Fraser.

They looked away when we walked in but I think that fight was the ice-breaker that changed the way the Regulars looked upon us NS chaps. We had shown them we could hold our own with the best of them in a fist-fight and we were not going to be pushed around. From then on everything changed and the NS guys went on to make a major contribution in making the Rhodesian SAS what it became."

Ceasefire. Ken Bird - Mashumbi Pools

On the 11th December 1974, a reluctant and wary Ian Smith agreed to an immediate cease-fire and allowed the release of political detainees. One of those released under pressure from South Africa, was Robert Mugabe who would soon slip away into Mozambique with the help of Jesuit priests who were friendly with the then Assistant Commissioner of Police, Peter Allum. Not long after Mugabe's departure, Emmerson Mnangagwa was also released.

The *quid pro quo*, guaranteed by South African President BJ Vorster, was that Zambia and Mozambique would bring to an end the armed incursions. This did not happen and the Rhodesian defenders lost ground as their restraint was ignored and incursions continued.

Sensing a major strategic shift, Ian Smith sought an alliance with South Africa and Portuguese hardliners to defend everything south of the Zambezi river rather than see Frelimo take control but the winds of change were blowing hard; Vorster was nervous and Samora Machel's dream of a Marxist dictatorship in Mozambique was prematurely at hand. Having established a transitional government, Machel made it clear he would be totally committed to the 'liberation' of Rhodesia, thus making 3,000 kms of frontier extremely vulnerable.

CHAPTER FOUR

"Mnangagwa's release and deportation to Zambia raised some eyebrows," recalls Ken Bird. "He was not a political detainee but a convicted saboteur. Tony Bradshaw, then a high-flying Chief Superintendent in BSAP Special Branch, handled the whole exercise. Word was that Mnangagwa was recruited as an informer in exchange for his release. So he was effectively being sent back to Zambia to spy for us. But then out of the blue and to everyone's surprise Bradshaw resigned his commission abruptly and went back to the UK. I now think he was working for MI6 all along and they decided he would be better placed to run his agents from there and for the Brits, rather than for us so he was called back by his real bosses. His two big pals were Mike Edden and Dan Stannard. Most of us now believe Edden was passing information to the Brits and I'm certain Stannard was passing on to Mugabe's people.

"At this time, I was based at Mashumbi Pools in the Zambezi Valley at the confluence of the Hunyani, Dande and Ambi rivers. From there I was running informers, some of whom were moving into Mozambique and back, trying to get information on enemy infiltration routes and timings. Although the army had been pulled back into a defensive pattern because of the cease-fire, we were pretty sure this was going to be a brief respite and we worked hard to keep the intelligence flowing. But it was not all war; we remained, essentially policemen and our duty was to serve the people in the area as best we could. The uniformed branch under me were also encouraged to continue exercising their role in investigating crimes and making arrests, in the true zero-tolerance approach practiced by the BSAP, a strong virtue practiced throughout our proud history.

"Primitive tribal people lived along the tributaries flowing into the great Zambezi. Their levels of flow ranged from pools sustained by granular sub-surface water to raging torrents, capable of tossing huge trees in which no human could survive. After the summer rains the levels dropped rapidly and the deep waters slowed sufficiently for humans to cross. Traditionally, the tribal chiefs were protected by their own messengers and aides and one of their duties was to cross the deep river waters ahead of the senior dignitaries in order to clear the way.

"Things never happen in singularities and I received a report from a tribal runner about an elderly woman who had been bitten by a venomous snake so I took the DC's boat and cruised the river all the way up to Chikafa,

MEN OF WAR

on the Mozambique border, mindful of the fact that this could be a false story to lure me into an ambush. We parked the boat then marched inland to a village where I was introduced to the victim who looked very healthy indeed and this annoyed me; I'd taken quite a risk thinking this was a life or death situation and this was clearly not the case. I remonstrated with the excited elders who explained they had tied the bark of a tree around her thigh and lo and behold, the swelling went down and the pain disappeared. Nothing more I could do so I threw a couple of aspirin into her cupped mouth, washed them down from my water bottle and bade them farewell.

"The sun was sinking and a late afternoon thunder-storm was blowing slowly in from the north but also approaching was beer-time in my magnificent 'pole and dagga' pub back at the camp where I used to sit, sometimes alone, and imagine I was surrounded by beautiful women lusting for my attentions. I pull-started the motor and with the comforting hum of the engine I sailed safely home.

"On nearing the little jetty, I noticed a worried look on the face of one of my African constables.

'Sah,' he shouted excitedly, 'the chief's messenger has been bitten by crocodile!'

This was not what I wanted to hear when getting ready for a beer at sundowner time and I suspected it was not too serious but could not be sure; duty, once again, called and the thunderstorm that threatened was breaking. Wind whistled through the mopani leaves, ominous dark clouds billowed across the sky, rolling thunder boomed across the valley and bolts of bright lightning lit across the horizon. We set off as fat droplets of rain came down on us and the afternoon calm was rudely replaced by storm and a sense of panic.

"We had not gone far when we came upon the exhausted rescue party carrying the casualty from the Ambi where the croc attack had transpired and the sight was a gruesome one. The young man, blessed with a magnificent build, had been bitten multiple times but one wound indicated his whole torso must have been in the monster's mouth because it enveloped his entire chest and back with deep, jagged wounds. His sternum had been crushed exposing bits of creamy cartilage and white tips of shattered ribs which I knew posed a potentially huge problem internally. His hand was ripped right through both sides leaving him with bloody pieces of flapping flesh

CHAPTER FOUR

for fingers. On his upper thigh was another bite that looked dangerously close to his femoral artery. He had lost a lot of blood, his presentation was way beyond my rudimentary medical capabilities and I quickly summoned an army medic who set up an intravenous drip and requested an immediate 'casevac'.[24]

"We then moved him to the airstrip and an incoming Police Reserve Air Wing (PRAW) aircraft was circling above the low cloud, trying desperately, but to no avail, to locate a break in the ceiling for a rapid landing and take-off. We waited anxiously while the afternoon faded into dusk, the sun sank lower and the sounds of the little fixed-wing faded away to whence he came from. I was left with a heavy heart and a young man who I knew well, might now die.

"The army-medic was superb; he carefully cleaned all the wounds with Betadine, kept the intravenous fluids flowing all night, pumped his patient full of antibiotics, suppressed the intense pain with morphine, wrapped him in a warm sleeping bag and soothed him with the reassurance that all was going to be fine in the morning.

"With the first crack of dawn we heard the angel of mercy in the sky; a farmer who flew in the reserves, and he swooped to the rescue. We quickly laid our man on the floor of the little plane and the pilot, all smiles waved us farewell then powered down the bush-strip and out of our sight *en route* to hospital in Salisbury. I was relieved, I felt we had done our best but I had a strong sense of foreboding; I was pretty sure septicaemia would have set in and with deep bites like those inflicted on him by filthy crocodile teeth, I didn't hold out much hope.

"On my return to camp I immediately hauled in one of the Tsetse Department hunters to consign the crocodile to history. He waited patiently for some days before the reptile showed himself in his sights and he dispatched it with a single shot to the head with a heavy calibre rifle. Two days later the croc, a massive white brute, surfaced belly up and as his decomposing gases built up, probably farted himself all the way to the Mozambique border.

"The late rains continued and it was on a clear, moonlight evening that I heard a distant explosion, far away to the north. We had a full commando from the RLI camped across the river. From their commander I found out

---

[24] Casualty-evacuation.

that another group of soldiers were moving at night and had detonated a landmine on the Mozambique border. A soldier had lost his leg.

"One of our choppers flew out thanks to a bright moon that gave him a horizon and returned safely to our jungle airstrip with the dying warrior and their medic. We had set up a temporary illuminating path using small gas cookers and an air force fixed-wing landed to take the casualty back to Salisbury. A Land Rover with dimmed lights marked the extreme end of the strip. The light aircraft needed all the length and power to get airborne, but his wheel clipped the top of the vehicle. He managed to climb for a while but then went into a death-dive. We found them in the morning and they were all dead. Killed were Air Lt Brian Murdoch, No. 4 Sqn, RhAF, Cpl Thomas Michael Parker, 8th Bn, RR, and L/Cpl Roger John Povey, 2nd Bn, RR. The latter two were the landmine casualties being casevacced.

"It was a sad time, but my spirits lifted and I almost fell off my chair when, sitting under a tree, I saw this familiar figure stride jauntily into my camp wearing a huge smile. It was the 'crocodile-man'; he had walked some distance to thank me for helping him and to tell me he was fit as a fiddle. But he also wanted to regale me with the story of his great adventure on leaving the valley following his accident. It was as if he had just journeyed to outer space; this was a very primitive man who had lived his entire life in the wilds, who had just been in an aeroplane to a sophisticated hospital in the capital city. Coming from where he did, this was a chance venture into a world he barely knew existed and with his wide-eyed innocence, he described every piece of the journey to me in detail. The city and all the people and traffic had blown him away and he seemed to assume I had never been there either. He told me the most terrifying part of his adventure was dealing with the white matron at the hospital who shat[25] on him for not following a daily walk and exercise routine.

"At the time we were living pretty rough so when someone, somewhere 'borrowed' an old 'Gypsey' caravan from some unknown government department benefactor, I did not ask too many questions. How the hell they got it down the rough escarpment, only they knew but it was a welcome opportunity to improve my standard of daily living in my new home on wheels (albeit punctured and thus flat) which made me the proud 'owner' of the only mobile holiday-home in the entire Zambezi Valley. The thin

---

[25] Slang for being chastised.

CHAPTER FOUR

aluminium skin was not going to stop any bullets but the lure of luxury was enough to forsake the relative safety of the trenches. At night our bravery was bolstered by lots of beer and bullshit and we knew we were easy pickings for a determined enemy but for some strange reason we were not attacked. Even on nights when I was the only white man in the entire area, the gooks never tried their luck! The mission statement of our pub was to 'defend it to the last beer'! Inside, was hand-painted sign, in a Gothic font stating:

"Through these portals piss the finest fighting men in the world".

"On return from one uneventful patrol, I received a visit from old Chief Chitsunga whose people lived along the Angwa river. He was deeply disturbed when he reported that a series of huts had been forcefully entered at night by two white youths and they had indecently assaulted young teenage girls in the village. Now as far as I was aware, the only two white youths on the Angwa lived in the 'Protected Village' compound near Dean's Camp which fell under the authority of Jim Herd, the District Commissioner (DC).

"I was pissed off so we set off immediately; Chief Chitsunga, a BSAP Patrol Officer and an African constable in full uniform, right down to the spit and polished boots and leggings. The two men went to the villages, spoke to the complainants, recorded statements, identified the two accused who were the men I suspected and we went to arrest them. They were read their rights, cuffed and shackled in front of a large, approving audience, loaded up and readied for the bumpy drive to the main district police station over the escarpment at Sipolilo. On our way we met up with Jim Herd and explained what had happened and who the suspects were. He was livid and requested permission to tie them to a tree right there and then and flog the bastards as an interim exercise before the courts involved themselves. He was even angrier when I denied his request.

"On arrival, they were detained in the quaint little Sipolilo cell block that housed the odd poacher or chicken thief, and then, with our job done, we went back to our base and forgot all about them. But that was until the Rhodesian military got wind of what happened and because they were National Servicemen, the army authorities decreed that they had jurisdiction despite the fact that they were serving in Internal Affairs. The civil authorities would have to stand aside and the suspects would be arraigned at a military courts-martial convened under a judge advocate. It was clear the military preferred their Detention Barracks which were hellish, to civilian

MEN OF WAR

remand centres and they wanted these blokes to feel the pain.

"For the courts martial, there was a convoy of eight military vehicles in all that drove in, ranging from heavy troop carriers to Land Rovers, carrying all the legal people, support staff, and armed protection. Proceedings started the next day and the trial was held in one of Jim Herd's offices. The military had not wasted any time in applying their drills. Both prisoners were shorn of hair, dressed in old camouflage shirts and trousers and lace-less boots, and this was before they were even sentenced. The fear in them was atmospheric; the tales of what horrors awaited them at the hands of the Pretorius brothers at the infamous Brady Barracks DB were designed to create terror.

"On entering the witness box, I immediately received a severe reprimand from the bench for my sock-free dress, with rugby shorts and a torn green tee shirt. I explained that this was the best attire I could muster from my Spartan wardrobe but the court was unamused. My evidence was brief, but I did speak up on behalf of the one young prisoner, who I felt had been led astray and appeared contrite.

"At the end of day one, it was hot as hell and everyone retired to the mud hut that served as the BSAP 'wet' canteen. Rustic and cool, unpainted earth walls made from red clay, the pub served delicious cold beer but the music was limited because the only record we had was a tinny rendition by the 'Bee Gees' which screeched forth from the lid of an old record player. A lone lamp swung from a rafter to provide a little light.

"It was a busy night for the barman. There were defence officers from the air force, prosecuting officers from the army, a stenographer, cooks, guards and other admin people, all piling in for a beer. Due to an ancient order, the prisoners, because they were considered soldiers, could not be detained in the police cells and had to have an armed guard with them at all times. This meant that the armed guard, who wanted to join the fun, had to bring them to the pub where he chained them to an old hitching post outside so he could keep an eye on them while he got plastered.

"Everyone was having a grand time when I was joined at the bar which had a heavy wooden top, by the DC, Jim Herd, and the Judge-Advocate presiding, a Lt. Colonel, who had an Uzi sub machine gun slung across his back, which he placed on the bar counter.

"The night wore on, the Bee Gees screeched on in the background

CHAPTER FOUR

while we were in a heated discussion about how many elephant we were going to have to shoot the following week as part of a population reduction exercise. Then the DC had had enough of the Bee Gees so he picked up the judge's Uzi from the bar and shot out the speaker, then he shot the light out, plunging us into blackness with the Bee Gees now sounding like a group of Donald Ducks. This was followed by panic and pandemonium as people fled into the night abandoning the bewildered prisoners to a fate unknown. The judge, Jim and I carried on drinking.

"The following day the trial was concluded after the complainants had given their evidence and the judge retired to consider verdict and sentence. The tribespeople were taken back to their villages in high spirits.

"I popped in to say goodbye to Jim Herd and via the hand-cranked telephone exchange he received a call from one of the Deputy Commissioners of the BSAP. The previous night's bar shooting had been reported. Jim put his phone onto a speaker system for me to listen in. My name came up as the main perpetrator; 'Young Bird is a maverick' said the voice. But, credit to Jim, he claimed full responsibility and the conversation ended, with both laughingly agreeing that the less said, the better. So it died a natural death.

"As I left, I saw the forlorn prisoners, shackled and cuffed in the back of a troop carrier. They were on their way to begin their lengthy sentences in the dreaded Detention Barracks. Their penance would not end with the completion of their detention punishments for, upon release, they would be escorted, under close security to Llewellin Barracks to begin, afresh, infantry and drill training. With luck they might have time served taken into account. Someone commented that they would return to semi freedom as very fit young men.

"Events such as this were incidental to the war, but there was rarely a dull moment and I felt that our obvious commitment to the rule of law which transcended race, brought us closer to earning the trust of the locals whose support we would need in the tough years ahead. The BSAP had historic ties with the people who lived on the rivers and in the Regiment's detached, disciplined way, blended with fearless zero-tolerance, they had laid the firm foundations for a highly constructive relationship with the rural Africans. I often felt I was just a passing performer in a beautifully presented stage play. We came, we went - we were duty bound to hold up the honour of the force and we were extremely proud of what we stood for.

"From Sipolilo, I drove the long way home, back down the 'Alpha Trail' to Mashumbi and on arrival I was thrilled to see that the boys were back; the SAS had swung in, business was about to get back to normal. It was time; the cooling autumn breeze meant the rains had gone, the bush was thinning and its dense green cover would soon lose its leaves. In short, the breeze carried on it a fresh promise of blood and these special soldiers had picked up the scent. Vorster's stupid 'Détente' exercise was effectively dead.

"I will never know now but I often think back to those heady days and like to believe the fairness and indeed compassion, I and my colleagues showed the tribes-people of the valley in those troubled times, did pay dividends in our ongoing struggle to defeat a ruthless enemy. The more we worked with the people and for them, the more I was hearing from my informants, and eventually I had enough information to start making some deductions which helped me focus more accurately on where the enemy was coming from, where they were crossing into Rhodesia and how their support network in the country sustained them. Eventually, after collating the intelligence available to me I was able to point, fairly convincingly, to a staging base at a place known to the locals as Chintopa along the Angwa River where it flows into Mozambique. I passed my reports up the chain of command and my spirits lifted when in early March, the SAS arrived out of the blue, and based up on the Mashumbi airfield under the command of Captain Bob MacKenzie with the softly spoken, Lt. Martin Pearse as his second in command.

"While I had little direct contact with them and was not told of their plans, a 12-man patrol under Martin's command soon slipped away, breached the minefield and slunk into Mozambique under the cover of darkness. Near Chintopa, he selected his ambush position, set up a bank of Claymores and began the long wait. Five long days later, with the men keeping movement and noise to an absolute minimum under hot, humid conditions, an unsuspecting group of terrorists marched slap into the trap and in my view, probably one the classic ambushes of the modern war era ensued. The brilliant positioning of the Claymores ensured a shrapnel-hell blasted the terrorists before the machineguns tore into them and the bullets ripped them to pieces.

"Unfortunately, in sweeping the area in the aftermath 'Rocky' Walton was hit in the leg and his femoral artery was severed leaving him in a

CHAPTER FOUR

critical condition. The medic was quick to apply a tourniquet to stop the bleeding and gave him Morphine for the pain but casevac that night to Salisbury proved impossible and time was a matter of life and death. He was evacuated at first light, made it to Andrew Fleming hospital but died soon after his arrival. The route on which the ambush took place was the same one we had been watching thanks to the flow of local intelligence.

Martin Pearse's citation for his Military Forces' Commendation reads as follows:

"Whilst employed on operations Captain Pearse was in command of a 12-man patrol carrying out the task of a long-term ambush. The bush was extremely thick and finding a suitable position proved a difficult task. After he had been lying in ambush for five days, 24 terrorists walked into the position. Pearse sprang the ambush which resulted in 13 immediate kills. Further intelligence gained indicated that 15 terrorists had been killed in this ambush and also that a number had been wounded. Pearse's skill in sighting the ambush and the determination to wait and kill resulted in a highly successful contact."

Chapter Five

True merriment comes from those
Who have looked into their own open graves
And walked away again
To find life again.
Whereon the world is richer

♦

Making of an enemy

Guerrilla Training

In the enemy camp, as the war escalated and the demand for trained fighters grew, one of the main training camps filling this need was Morogoro in southern Tanzania and there, a tough, well-educated 18-year-old caught the instructors' eyes. His name was Robson, born in 1956 in Bikita in south-eastern Rhodesia. One of eight children, the son of a mine-cook, he excelled at junior school and in doing so impressed Father Francis from Silveira Mission. Father Francis was the same man who helped John Bradburne begin his Rhodesian journey and he secured Robson a scholarship to St George's College in Salisbury, which was then one of the top private schools in the country. There he performed well academically and on the sports fields. However, unbeknown to his school-pals, away from sport and studies, Robson had joined the African National Council Youth Wing and was becoming increasingly politicised.

In what should have been his penultimate year, prior to completing his final exams, he joined his white friends for a meal at a Wimpy Bar in downtown Salisbury. Also present was a group of boisterous bikers, who noted with visible displeasure the presence of a lone black man in an establishment that was mainly patronised by whites. When the young Robson's food arrived one of the bikers insisted it was in fact his order and moved to take it off the table. An altercation ensued and this then turned into a fight resulting in the arrival of the police who arrested those involved

CHAPTER FIVE

in the affray and took them to the police station for questioning.

Robson, knowing he had been the victim of an unprovoked, racially motivated attack, felt that the police investigators were too hard on him and too soft on the people who had assaulted him. He came away from the incident embittered and soon found his way to Chishawasha Mission outside Salisbury where he knew militant political activists were working on plans to overthrow the white minority government. There he engaged a recruiting agent who explained to him the risks involved in leaving the country for military training but exhorted him to do the honourable thing and prepare to fight and die for what was right and in the interests of the black majority.

He agreed and accepted the challenge immediately. Along with a small group, Robson made his way to Bulawayo where they linked up with other volunteers and then on to the border town of Plumtree. There they were met by a guide who warned them of the dangers ahead, avoiding the Rhodesian security forces and the consequences of being caught. Some lost their nerve and opted out. Those remaining, roughly a hundred, then proceeded on foot to the frontier defined by the Ramakwevana river and crossed illegally into Botswana.

"When we crossed the border we then decided that with such a big group, if anything happened it was going to be a disaster, so we split in half. When we left the country, we did not know that there were two parties leading the fight against the Rhodesian government. No one knew that there was Zapu and Zanu. The first group arrived at Francistown Police Station and the group was received by a Zanu representative. When our group arrived a Zapu representative, the late Comrade Nathan Dube met us and so although I was a Shona, I was signed up by a party mainly supported by the Matabele people.

"While at Francistown Police Station all our particulars were taken. We were given new names and I was given the name of Nhamo Tafirenyika. After all the documentation, we were taken to the local prison for safekeeping because the Botswana government only gave recruits transit rights; they did not want us staying long in the country. We stayed at the prison for two nights. The following day we were taken to the airport where we boarded Zambia Airways and flew to Lusaka. There, we were met by Zipra people who took us to Lilanda Township. At Lilanda we stayed for four days and then moved to Mwembezi Transit Camp under the command of Comrade Todd. That is where our training started. We stayed in this camp for more than two weeks, waiting for OAU transport to take us to Tanzania for training.

"The OAU vehicles finally arrived and took us to Morogoro Camp in southern Tanzania for full military training. We went via Mbeya and at Mbeya we collected other comrades who were also there for training. We arrived at Morogoro and were met by the Commandant, then Colonel Dube, Colonel Moyo and several Ghanaian instructors led by Captain Dako.

"We commenced our course in July 1974. It was at this point we Shonas started asking why we were being trained by Ndebele-speakers and asked where were the Shonas. We were uncomfortable being separated from the recruits with whom we shared a tribal allegiance and sought permission to continue our training at the Zanla training base in Iringa but this was denied. A group of us then decided to go to Morogoro town and report to the Tanzanian soldiers who we would ask to hand us over to Zanla. We left at night and made it to the Tanzania army camp where we introduced ourselves and asked permission to switch to the Zanla base to continue our training, however this request was refused and we were returned under arrest to our camp, before being imprisoned in Mangerere Prison in Morogoro town.

"While in prison I started growing hair between my legs (*zvindakwenya*). I asked for some sort of medication from the prison warders and a bottle of something was provided which I applied but then developed terrible blisters. The wounds were so bad I had to be taken to the local hospital where I stayed for almost a month. The wounds were so raw and painful I could not move. I remember during this period I had 72 injections. Eventually I was withdrawn to camp where I had to finish my treatment and my wounds healed finally.

"I then worked hard and emerged one of the top recruits. The training was very tough, but we were well supplied with food from the Soviet Union and some of our instructors were Zimbabweans who had been trained in Soviet military academies, so they were very good and thorough. We ran like hell and did lots of assault courses. Later, we did them under live fire so if you lifted your head up you were killed. They said, 'train hard – fight easy', they kept telling us the enemy was dangerous, so we better work hard and listen to what they told us. We spent a lot of time on the shooting ranges firing heavy and light weapons. I was young and did not drink, most of the

CHAPTER FIVE

other chaps were the same and discipline was strict but we were motivated. We were trained on Soviet radios and other military equipment. Indiscipline was not tolerated; normally, fierce beatings followed.

"In December 1974 our company, which was the first to be deployed was formed. Our Platoon Commander was comrade Erick Ndondo, Company Commander was Carlos Mudzingwa and Chief of Operations was comrade Gordon Munyanyi. At the end of the course we were tired but excited and very keen to get into action against the enemy back home. I was made an officer and told I and my men would soon be transported by road to Zambia from where we would prepare to infiltrate into Rhodesia

"We were split into three sections and then we drove south into Zambia where we were met by Gordon Munyanyi. He took us to a camp near Kariba Dam in the Chipepo area. The camp was in the Gota Gota mountains on the Zambian side. Gordon warned us that what awaited us was no joke; that the enemy was dangerous and very alert so we were told to be very careful of lighting fires at night and to be aware that the Rhodesians were capable of picking up tracks from the air so we were told to do the best we could to hide our prints. We slept there for a night and observed the Rhodesian side during the day. Our mission was two-fold; recce the area and establish a permanent presence in the area.

"We crossed the lake at where it was widest because the Rhodesians were ambushing the narrow crossing points. We left Zambia at last light, loaded up all our food, ammunition, weapons and equipment into an inflatable with an outboard motor and set off on the 30 km long trip across the water. We decided to paddle all the way because we were afraid the noise of the engine would attract enemy attention. We arrived on the Rhodesian side in the early morning hours. As soon as we made land we concealed our equipment and stayed at the crossing point for the rest of the day. Then we moved into the Mapongola Hills to find bases. Three days after establishing our base in the mountains we went back to the lake to collect our spare weapons and food to move them to the hills close to the operational area.

"To establish a presence in the area we had to convert the Tonga people to our cause, but it turned out to be a more difficult task than we anticipated. We were the first insurgents in the area and the people had heard nothing about us or what we were fighting for. Even Comrade Shumba who was Tonga-speaking had difficulties in trying to convince the people that we were fighting to liberate them and that they should support us. Meantime, we sent out patrols and did our best to gather information. All the time, we had radio contact with our commanders back in Zambia.

"In about March 1975, we were visited by our company commander Comrade Carlos Mudzingwa. He brought the message about ongoing talks with the Rhodesian government and we were told to hold the fighting for a while because there was the possibility of a political agreement. We told him that the enemy was placing us under increasing pressure and the food situation presented a big problem because the local people were not supportive enough of us. They wanted to be left alone and have no part in the war. Because they would not feed us we decided to start shooting wild game for the pot despite the fact that Gordon had warned us not to do this. We were about 30 kms inland near the escarpment when one of our men shot an impala. This was a big mistake and although we did not know it at the time, the shot was heard by the enemy.

"Our situation deteriorated and nine of us then volunteered to return to our cache near the lakeshore to collect more supplies including tins of Russian beef. We noticed that there was more enemy activity on the lake which concerned us but we had no idea that a Selous Scout call-sign was watching us from their observation point on top of a mountain. Then a spotter plane appeared overhead. We were tired but found a place to hide and rest as we thought we would only approach the cache under cover of darkness. But they had worked out where we were hiding and they tracked us down and opened fire. We immediately returned fire but then helicopters arrived and the fight intensified. We were caught on flat ground, so I said to the other guys let's run for the hills and find places to hide. While climbing the hill we heard the soldiers on the radio talking to the pilots and their section commanders on the ground, so we found thick cover and went into hiding. One of our men was wounded and left behind and Section Commander Mlope Sibindi was never seen again. I took over command of the surviving six. I told the men to sit tight and not fire. We were very relieved when the sun set and in the dark that night, I saw a light which may have been a soldier's cigarette and that gave me an idea of which way we should move out of the area and away from danger. Following game-trails, we walked with animals also moving away from the lake so it would be difficult to track us. We then walked hard for two days back into the Mapongola Hills.

CHAPTER FIVE

"We were relatively safe there but hungry because food continued to be a problem and we were told to move our area of operations closer to the town of Gokwe. There, we were careful to remain in good cover during the day and move only at night. We were pleased when some of the villagers took pity on us and started to bring us *sadza*[26] and water on a regular basis. Some fishermen also came by and gave us some of their catch. But by this time we had decided to try and make it back to Zambia.

"From the mountains where we were hiding to Kariba Dam, the Rhodesians had sealed the whole area, making it very difficult for us to go north and across the lake. We had to take a circuitous route around them and walked for 10 days through wild country before we reached people who would help us. We were always careful to sleep a safe distance from their homes because we did not know if the locals were on our side or not but eventually we managed to cross safely back into Zambia.

"When back in Zambia, I was very pleased to hear I had been selected for officer training at the Soviet Military Academy in Leningrad. I was one of 38 picked to go from Dar es Salaam. It was a long five-month course and very intensive with very professional instructors. One of them, Major Victor Chernenko, became a lifelong friend. Also there, were troops from Angola who we came to know well and liked. It was mainly military training but there was political instruction too. The Russians also warned us that the Rhodesians were tough and were not going to be beaten easily so we had to prepare for a lot more fighting."

Officers Course January 1975

"In January 1975 I was posted by Major Brian Robinson to the School of Infantry to commence officer training," remembers Richard Stannard. "We first had to pass through the Officers Selection Board. During this process we were given various aptitude tests and exercises in solving imaginary problems. This involved the writing of essays on a variety of topics, most of which I did not know an awful lot about.

"When the brainstorming was done there was a vigorous physical component. We had to tackle the assault course carrying a heavy drum over and under all the obstacles. To assist us in this task, a few short planks and a rope was provided. It was a test of our ability to think fast when physically

---

[26] Maize-meal porridge.

tired, a combination of mental agility and physical strength. On average, only about 10% of candidates applying for the course passed. Pure brute strength or a university degree did not cut it – they were looking for attitude and character they could mould into confident young officers who could be trusted to lead men into battle. At the end of it there were 28 of us who had passed the initial selection and we were permitted to commence the 13-month course.

"We all arrived at the School of Infantry on the same bus. Once through the gate we all knew that we were in for a tough time. I was happy to have my friend and fellow SAS corporal, 'Mac' Macintosh along with me. As a trained soldier, it was my second basic recruit course but I could see this was going to be very different. The Commandant at the School then was Lt. Colonel George Lloyd, known as 'Classy' because he had a very aristocratic accent and demeanour.

"Once we had been through all the stores and issued our prescribed kit and equipment, the roadshow started with Colour Sergeant Reed, a wiry guy with crooked teeth, screaming obscenities.

Colour Sergeant Lou Hallamore was our 'drill-pig'.

'You mangy bunch of fucking recruits – fall in on the parade square!' From that moment on, we would not walk again for a very long time; for the entire first phase we would be on the double.

"That first evening, we were introduced to our Shona batmen whose job it was to wash and iron all our uniforms and starch our khaki drill pants until they were pieces of cardboard. These wonderful blokes had a great sense of humour and quickly sized us up and gave us nicknames in the vernacular. One of the cadets walked quickly on his toes and was named 'Nguruve' which translates into pig in Shona. Sadly, these guys read him right because this guy didn't do too well with his personal hygiene and always looked like he had walked through a bush backwards. His failings brought forth many communal punishments and this became increasingly irritating. Eventually, after two weeks we couldn't take it anymore and three of us dragged Nguruve into the showers. There we used 'Vim' a scouring agent and a rough floor-brush and proceeded to scrub him raw. He squealed like a pig, had to be committed to the camp clinic and we never saw him again. It was all part of the process; he had become a liability and we could not carry him forever, so we rid ourselves of him. He cried like a banshee.

CHAPTER FIVE

"It was the African batmen who nick-named me 'Kafupi' which translates to 'short-arse', and it stuck instantly because it amused everyone enormously, particularly the drill instructors who didn't like me messing up their sessions.

'For fuck's sake Stannard how can you take a 20-inch pace when you're only 18 inches tall – get off my fucking parade square!' And with that I would march off and stand at ease under the shade of a tall tree which overlooked the square while the rest of the squad did endless about turns and slow marching steps in the boiling sun.

"By week four, blokes were burned to a crisp, necks had gone from red to dark brown and our ears were a scaly mess of sun-dried skin mixed with pink blotches of raw cartilage. Bored, during Classical War lectures I used to amuse myself by picking pieces of skin off my ears and flicking them across at Cadet 'Jug' Thornton who invariably sat in front of me and to my left. This pissed him off but pleased the ants that I would study closely as they rushed in to devour the tiny flakes of dry skin on the floor.

"There was always a bucket of water at the front of the lecture room. Cadets that were too tired to follow the intricacies of Classical War were regularly invited to immerse their heads in a bucket of cold water to reignite their interest.

"Our days were long and demanding. We would be out our beds at 4.30am to start shining boots and buckles, waxing floors, cleaning toilets and getting ourselves ready for our daily morning inspection. If anyone in the barrack room failed, we were then to move our lockers, footlockers, beds and equipment all the way to the parade square and stand inspection there. The standards were ridiculously high; the fibres on our blankets were scrutinised to ensure that they were all carefully brushed to run the same way. I quickly learned it was better to sleep rough on the floor next to my bed and save myself some toil. We would all take turns 'boning' our black stick boots with an iron and a hot spoon using precious 'Kiwi' polish. This magical 'shiner' was sometimes hard to get owing to sanctions. It may sound trivial now but then we were ready to give anything for the polish because it was the only one that mixed with spit and cotton wool to make the toecaps shine like mirrors – so smooth even flies skidded off them!

"On one particularly memorable occasion someone committed some minor offence and Major Burford, one of our senior instructors, had a fit. He ordered us to dig a hole six foot by six foot in the kopje behind the barracks which was all shale and rock. We had to complete the task by first light and be ready for the RSM inspection in the morning. Digging with picks and shovels proved pointless; we were barely able to scrape the surface. In despair we snuck off and hired a jackhammer from a depot in Gwelo and spent all night taking it in shifts drilling in the side of kopje. The staccato sounds resonated throughout the entire School of Infantry and we imagined them all in their beds laughing their heads off. We were nearly done when an order came from the Officer's Mess to stop immediately; they couldn't sleep it was about 2am in the morning and no longer funny. Somehow, we managed to sort ourselves out, finish the job, make the inspection and pass.

"There were times when I hated the lectures more than the physical pain. Major Mick McKenna from the RAR would drone on about Sun Tzu (circa 500), 'The Principles of War', selection and maintenance of the aim, maintenance of morale, offensive action, surprise, security, concentration of force, economy of effort, flexibility, cooperation and administration. I kept thinking what the fuck has this got to do with the war we have to fight. I know some of the basic principles were applicable but in the main, much of this course was a waste of time and I and many of the other guys became increasingly restless. Meanwhile, my mates in the field were dying. The news of 'Rocky' Walton's death came as a very sad shock; he was very well liked and respected.

"Finally, we finished the Classical War theory with a live exercise, commanding troops advancing on an enemy position. We had national servicemen as our soldiers, and we all got to work digging trenches and filling sandbags. To construct a berm, we laid dummy minefields and put up rolls of good old barbed wire in front of our dug-in positions. At all times the instructors watched us closely. Each cadet had a spell as a platoon commander tasked with positioning his machine-guns and mortars, setting arcs of fire and delivering orders. Targets were logged and relayed to the mortar-men. It was a tough five days in and out of trenches with rigid routines to follow and I was pleased to remind myself I was unlikely to find myself fighting this sort of war.

"Once this exercise was over we were taken on an 'escape and evasion' exercise in the Selukwe Hills not far from where Ian Smith had his farm. There, we had to move long distances from one place to another without

CHAPTER FIVE

being captured by 'enemy' troops deployed in the area to track us down. Accurate map-reading and night orientation were key. We were given virtually no food and a lot of weight to make the going as hard as possible. We ended up doing most of the marches at night and successfully avoided being captured. When we were famished Major Burford appeared on the scene looking very friendly and asked us if we would like some food.

"The offer was very welcome but it was not immediately clear where the food was coming from until a Land Rover appeared on the road coming towards us in a cloud of dust, slowed alongside where we were resting and discharged three squealing piglets out the back before roaring off into the distance. The poor piglets wasted no time in racing off into the bush while we all looked on askance. A bark from Major Burford broke the brief silence.

'Well what the fuck you waiting for? Fuck off after them.'

We all tore off like lunatics into the rocky hills and in a frantic effort to run them down but they found refuge in an antbear hole so we had to dig down and grab the poor blighters before dragging them to the surface. Nobody enjoyed the slaughter, but we had little option; we ran sticks through them and roasted them on an open fire. The meat was delicious and the crispy skin tasted just like the pork scratchings that I would order in the pub when downing a cold Castle beer; (never a Lion for me, always Castle)… and lots of it.

"Once our bellies were full I think we relaxed too much because we were tricked into entering a dark cave to look for something and when we emerged into the sunlight there stood the frightening black faces of a company of fully armed RAR soldiers who wasted no time in manhandling us into handcuffs behind our backs and pulling hoods over our heads. It came as a nasty surprise, but we should have been expecting something because we knew there was an interrogation phase to come and as they had not managed to 'capture' us they had decided on deception as a means to an end.

"It was cold and our combat clothing was removed leaving us with pants, no socks, and no shoes. We were slung into a stinking mud-hole where we lay for a while, utterly helpless when we had hessian sacks pulled over us and then a torrent of cold water was hosed onto us with such force I started to panic because I couldn't breath and I thought I was going to suffocate, drown and die; we were being 'water-boarded' in modern day parlance and it's a terrifying experience. Gasping desperately for air, the wet sack sealed my mouth and nose off from the air I craved. The water stopped momentarily but then someone stood over me and slowly pored another bucket over my head. I could hear individual cadets moaning nearby and then the sounds of heavy boots as soldiers arrived to drag individuals out of the mud one at a time to go to the interrogation tent.

"What we did not know at the time was three members of our Military Intelligence were waiting to try out some new techniques on us. All the other guys were taken and I ended up alone in the mud-hole waiting for the pain to come. Eventually, at about midnight, I was dragged into the tent, hooded and shivering with cold. I was forced to my knees and a bright light was shone in my face, temporarily blinding me. Exhausted, angry and vengeful I was slumped in a chair in a room full of people I could not see. Just as I managed to breathe normally again someone came behind me and another bucket of freezing cold water poured down on my head. Immediately, I again felt I was going to drown and die. It was almost too much, I was suddenly overcome by a white-hot fury, my temples pounded, my mind screamed and I felt my eyes were popping out of my head the rage was so all consuming. I was desperate to identify the people responsible and take revenge – God alone knows what would have happened had I been unleashed but the water stopped, and I was able to breathe again.

"Then the usual crap about the SAS started. No matter where I went in the Rhodesian Army, there was always someone wanting to have a dig at us. I think they left the best to last because I was an SAS soldier, who had seen some action and I had a reputation for a short temper. Unlike some of the officers who were running this course, who had never heard a shot fired in anger. They were going to take their time with me.

'So, you think you SAS are tough guys?' said one of them.

'Fuck off,' I said.

With that I was jabbed hard in the stomach with a cattle prodder that sent a powerful bolt of hot pain exploding through me that threw me off the chair, on to my back where I landed hard and lay trying to gather my senses. Still hooded, I then took a hard punch in the solar plexus which took my breath away.

'Give us the information,' said a threatening voice. I lay there telling myself to listen to that voice carefully and remember it for later so I might

CHAPTER FIVE

find the guy and kill him. His breathing sounded laboured and I thought to myself he is probably a fat, useless, rear echelon sergeant who smokes and eats too much. I was shaking with anger when this moron ripped my pants down and started mocking my genitalia.

'Call that a prick,' he screamed to the accompaniment of roars of laughter from the gallery. I was shaking with anger when I received another prod and another shock from the cattle prodder, this time in the ribs and I convulsed with pain while listening to the howling behind me. All I could think of was killing one of them.

"Forty years later, I still have a pathological hatred for those people concerned. I understand the need for such an exercise, but they went way over the top with me that night and I do believe I was singled out for special attention. As far as the techniques are concerned, I thought they were crude and unsophisticated.

"They are lucky I was unable to seek divine retribution. Little do they know but I did find out who was involved and I did plan revenge. I found out where they lived, what their movements were and the best place for me to confront them. Luckily for them, I discussed my plans with close friends and they dissuaded me. They are very lucky but fuck you Major Burford for allowing it to go on for so long into the early hours of the morning before you called them off. I'm happy to say they damn nearly killed me, but they never came close to breaking me. Quite a few of the cadets did not come through this phase and were promptly kicked off the course.

"Eventually, we, the remaining officer cadets moved up into senior rank accommodation where we each had our individual rooms and our own Mess and dining room where our food was served on immaculate white tablecloths with silver cutlery. We had the bar to ourselves as long as we conducted ourselves as gentlemen. Some horseplay was tolerated in the Mess but there was a fine line drawn between what was acceptable and what was not. Unfortunately, I had a habit of not always seeing the line and that was my downfall.

"However, the cursed Shine Parades were over, and the instructors started to relax a little, but we still had tough physical training every morning on the rugby field and then the assault course had to be tackled with us carrying logs and in full battledress.

"Well over the worst of it with three months to go before being commissioned as Second Lieutenants in the Rhodesian Army, I was confident I was home and dry. There was some excitement over the preparations being made for our passing-out parade which was to be a rather grand affair with dignitaries in attendance, generals, our friends, families and the RAR band playing. We would be marched on to the square as cadets and off it as officers.

"With all this to look forward to and feeling very pleased about my future, I jumped into my VW Beetle and headed to Salisbury for a party where I knew I would see some of my old SAS chums. I knew some had been on exciting operations and I was looking forward to hearing their reports.

"Unfortunately, there was some sad news to be had. By this time, in June 1975, Mozambique had become an independent republic under a Marxist government led by Samora Machel. This was a troubling development because it opened up our entire eastern border to infiltration.

"The week before my trip to Salisbury, a four-man group, including Gary Stack, Mike Smith, Kelvin Storie and Ginger Thompson, were on a reconnaissance patrol in Mozambique, south of the Zambezi, when ambushed by a large group of Frelimo who must have been watching them. Kelvin was killed instantly, and Ginger was wounded but they were completely outnumbered and overrun. Ginger managed to hide, while Mike and Gary hastily withdrew, but with a river behind them, they then found some high ground from which to fight back. By this time the Frelimo were moving into cover near where Kelvin lay. Their commander, a big fat guy, then came out into the open and started kicking his body around and this was too much for Gary and Mike who then drilled him. This then drew the rest of the Frelimo platoon back into the open and Gary and Mike put down sustained, accurate fire, which killed more of them and put them to flight. Fortunately this rear-guard action saved Ginger and they also managed to recover the radio and codes that Frelimo were about to grab from Kelvin.

"After the piss-up in Salisbury, my plan was to return to the School of Infantry in the early hours of the morning, so it was a long way to go for a party and back, but I knew the Guard Commander and knew he would cover for me if I was late. Unfortunately, I was late and he was not on duty, so I was booked AWOL (Absent Without Leave) and on my return placed under close arrest. I sat rather glumly in the cells chatting to the Regimental Policemen awaiting news of my fate. Word was it was touch and go; they

CHAPTER FIVE

were pondering whether or not to chuck me off the course.

"After an agonising wait, I was told I was to be charged formally, brought before the Commanding Officer (CO) and confined to barracks until further notice. At this stage we had completed most of our counter insurgency training and were completing courses at Brady Barracks in Bulawayo on Signals and Military Engineering. All the other cadets were free to do as they wished over the weekends while I was forbidden to leave the camp confines.

"Although I had blotted my copy book, all I had to do going forward was behave and do as I was told which sounds easy, but I was restless and a little angry when we came to the official Officer Cadets Dining In Night. This was a serious, formal occasion where we cadets were expected to be on our very best behaviour. Senior officers were decked out in their smart, scarlet Mess dress with butterfly collars, the wives and girlfriends in long dresses and us in our Greens with white epaulettes and belt.

"Stupidly, Mac Macintosh and I decided to get to our Mess early and have a few 'warming' beers before the main event. What started as a few, quickly became many as we laughed and swapped stories and in all too short a time, we were both seriously drunk. By the time the senior officers and wives in their ballroom gowns arrived outside to have their welcoming cocktails Mac and I were flying! Well not flying exactly but we were dancing together on the bar, drinking beer out of an ice bucket and singing at the top of our voices. The arriving guests were greeted by the sight of the two of us leaping about the bar attired only in stick-boots, berets and underpants. It was hard to imagine any other place or situation where this sort of behaviour would be more unacceptable.

'What the hell are you two playing at?' shouted an officer and I looked long enough to see my girlfriend, beautifully dressed in her ballgown, with tears streaming down her face.

'You're an inconsiderate bastard Stannard,' she rightly said, and with that she fled into the darkness never to be seen again.

"Once again, I sat myself down on the gold floor of a cell in a military jail and pondered my plight. The Red Caps came and took my belt and bootlaces in case I tried to commit suicide.

'Nice underwear Cadet,' said the Guard Commander snidely; glanced at me with contempt, then the door clanged shut as he disappeared. A brain full of booze gave up on me and soon I was snoring.

"Next day came with a bang. Heavy boots at the cell-door, the rattling of keys and guards barking orders. I was dressed in my combat fatigues and being a prisoner, marched at the double from the cells up the driveway to the office of the Officer Commanding the School of Infantry.

Once outside his office, the RSM took over and his voice boomed in my ears as he instructed me to look six inches above the head of the CO and no lower. Again at the double I was marched into his office and brought to attention. There was a brief silence then Colonel Lloyd spoke clearly and concisely.

'Your conduct is unbecoming that of an officer in the Rhodesian Army. You lack the finesse we require. Stannard, I want you to think about this on your way back to your regiment. You are officially Returned To your Unit (RTU).'

'March him out RSM,' he commanded, and I was quickly on my way.

"With that, I was done. I handed my kit back to the QM stores and went to pay my batman. They had all heard the news of my demise and were laughing loudly. They shook my hand warmly and assured me I would be back soon. No way, I thought to myself, I'm done with this bullshit. I then went to bid my comrades' farewell. They laughed and reminded me the next time they saw me I'd have to salute and call them Sir. I jumped in my Beetle and they were all there to wave me goodbye. Passing the barrier, I gave the guards a mock salute and they gave me a finger. My officers course was well and truly over and I didn't have a lot to show for it.

"In a hurry, I headed back to Cranborne Barracks, looking forward to seeing my old pals. I drove straight to the Winged Stagger Corporals' Mess where I was pleased to find Billy Grant, James Hayden and Ian Suttill. I was expecting a lot of verbal abuse and I was not disappointed. But they were pleased to have me back and that cheered me. Just when I was settling in for a long drinking session the Adjutant appeared to tell me to report to the CO Major Brian Robinson immediately. Bloody hell, that was quick I thought. My fun was over.

Robinson wasted no time with pleasantries. I had barely come to attention when he started.

'What the hell was all that crap about, Corporal Stannard? We expected

CHAPTER FIVE

better from you. Think of the taxpayer - how much it has cost to put you through that year.' I must admit, the last person I was thinking about was the Rhodesian taxpayer but he had a point. Then he got angrier.

'Get out of my sight,' he said menacingly, 'I'm putting you right back on operations and you're off to Mozambique on the first flight out of here.'

"And sure enough, within a short space of time I was back in Mozambique in the bush, dodging bullets, eating sardines, dog biscuits, drinking sweet tea, stinking like a hyena, swatting tsetse flies and struggling with prickly heat. I had not taken my boots off in a week and didn't dare. I was sure the smell would alert every Zanla terrorist in the country. I thought somewhat wistfully about my Officer Cadet mates dining on fine china with smart waiters in attendance and chuckled. Here I was, in the middle of 'Injun Country' staring at three black faces staring back at me wondering what our chances were of making it home alive. But then I cheered myself – for fuck's sake I was home where I belonged, and I was with my mates. What more could a man want?"

Shadreck the Poacher

While the war escalated along Rhodesia's eastern border the National Parks Game Rangers remained vigilant and aggressive in trying to protect the wildlife in their sanctuaries, but because of the deterioration in the security situation with landmines and ambushes an ever present threat, they faced mounting challenges. The game-rich Gona re Zhou[27] area in the southeast of Rhodesia, south of the Sabi River, which bordered on Mozambique provided rich pickings for ivory and meat poachers who crossed the border with the support of Frelimo forces deployed in the area to assist Zanla. The kingpin was a formidable Shangaan hunter called Shadreck who was the most wanted ivory poacher in the country. From the late 1960s when his elephant poaching activities first became known, every warden and ranger in the region was after him. A brilliant bushman, fearless and an excellent marksman he used a variety of weapons including AK-47s and SKSs but his preferred rifle was a 375. With the increasing Frelimo and Zanla presence in the area the demand for fresh meat increased and Shadreck became the resident butcher.

Very often he would hunt alone, while other times he would have two

---
[27] Translated as 'Place of the Elephant'. Modern day spelling is Gonarezhou.

or three support personnel. On one occasion, one of his bearers was gored and killed by an elephant and buried hurriedly alongside the Lundi river, before Shadreck hastened back to Mozambique and stayed there for a few weeks before returning on another foray. What fascinated his pursuers was his ability to extract ivory so quickly from the elephant he shot. He did it by cutting off the ears of the animals and wrapping the skin around the tusks to protect them from the heat and then lighting a fire under the head of the animal, which burned the flesh away, loosened the tusks and allowed him to pull them free. He was able to shoot elephant in Rhodesia and be back in Mozambique within three to four hours, where he then sold the ivory to high-ranking government officials.Former SB Inspector John Davey remembers Shadreck well. "He was a truly remarkable individual, slightly built, of humble demeanour, who was surely one of the great elephant hunters of all time. I came to know him quite well and he told me he had learned to shoot as a boy, playing with Portuguese children whose parents were missionaries. They had a .22 mm rifle, and he went on from there to become an incredible marksman capable of dropping elephant from any angle with almost any calibre.

"He claimed to know most of the bulls in the Gona-Re-Zhou, referring to them as 'my cattle…I know all of them' he told me. I had the privilege on one occasion, of visiting his 'office' which was in a hollowed-out Baobab. At a quick or passing glance most casual observers would not have noticed anything particularly strange or unusual about this tree. At the base was a small hole through which one had to crawl to enter. Inside was a cavity which allowed some freedom of movement and above a platform which was the roof where he could stand and survey the surrounds covering a great distance.

"He was a master of the art of anti-tracking and stored his ivory in the sands along the Lundi River. Bearers would come at appointed times to collect tusks and take them back to Mozambique. Because of his skill and expertise, he was the biggest ivory producer in the Lowveld and he supplied everyone who wanted. For Frelimo he was of such stature we were told he was taken to meet President Samora Machel. Apart from ivory, I'm sure he was also supplying them with information on what was happening in Rhodesia. But I knew we could get him on our side and if we succeeded, he had the information to help us swing the war in the area in our favour. Our

CHAPTER FIVE

problem was always getting current and accurate intelligence on the enemy whereabouts, and he knew exactly where all the Zanla camps were at any time. I also came to know his nephew Julius and through him worked with Shadreck on recovering enemy land-mines. When I let them know what the rewards were for the devices they soon arrived with the dreaded TMH 46's which were causing so much death and destruction but I never realised the opportunity to fully recruit this amazing man to our cause because where was not enough support for this from my seniors. To this day, I regret that."

In the course of trying to hunt Shadreck down the rangers identified a former Portuguese administrative post known as Mavue, at the confluence of the Lundi and Sabi rivers as Shadreck's base and also as an enemy facility housing both Frelimo and Zanla. They passed this on to the SAS.

"When the Park's guys came to report this I was ready to go," remembers Darrell Watt. "I had picked up all the chatter about Shadreck and they asked me if I would help them catch or kill him because he was living with and being protected by Frelimo and their Zanla comrades. I was keen, and I knew the area well from having run tracking and survival courses there in my early days with Rob Johnstone. I had also heard all about Shadreck and I was dead keen to have a crack at him.

"They provided us with a young ranger by the name of Angus Anthony – poor bloke he was told to go because he was the youngest on the station. The following night we went in and had no trouble finding the target. The lieutenant with me was terrified and started to make too much noise. He was an officer but I told him to 'shut the fuck up' or they would hear us. We moved closer then he told me he had seen a door open and seen a light! I said, 'it's the new moon you fucking idiot'! We walked back through to Fishans on the Lundi river where we spent the night. I reported back to Bob MacKenzie and told him we must attack immediately. The next day reinforcements arrived. More SAS, an RAR platoon and a mortar section from the School of Infantry."At this time, February 1976, we were up in the northeast of the country at Elim Mission, preparing to do some reconnaissance work," remembers Allan Hider. "I was one of the support troops deployed to help out if the reconnaissance guys got into trouble. This was my first operation – just fresh out of Brady Barracks where I had done an advanced signals course. The recce went into Mozambique in the direction of an extinct volcano and returned uneventfully and we were pretty bored, so we did some practice for 'hot extractions' with a chopper carrying four slings under a cross bar and did a few flights for the pilot to practice flight simulation with four of us slung below. Then suddenly we were told we were being loaded up and flown to the southeast of the country to do a camp-attack. At this point I was new and had never seen any action. I had passed selection but I did not have my colours so it was all very exciting and I looked forward to going into a real combat situation and proving myself. We flew down in a Dakota and landed at Mabalauta. The senior officers did not tell us much apart from the fact that the target was across the border and we would be going in full force with air cover provided by a Vampire ground-attack jet. Also in support was a mortar platoon with 81 mm tubes and the plan was for them to lay down a barrage of bombs on the camp immediately prior to the assault.

"As per our Standard Operating Procedures we formed up into four-man call-signs to form stop-groups to surround the camp, then drove to the Sabi/Lundi confluence about six kms away from the camp. Then under the cover of darkness we walked in with Scotty McCormack and Darrell in the lead and with Bob MacKenzie in command. When we arrived in the area of the target, Bob and Scotty ordered a halt and we sat down and rested for about an hour – Scotty and one other went in and did a close-in recce during this time. We then moved in single-file and call-sign by call-sign we were positioned strategically with orders to kill or capture anyone fleeing the camp. In place, we readied ourselves for action, and waited in the dark for the mortars to open the batting. Just before first light we heard the hollow thump of the projectiles leaving the tubes and then they started raining down but their range was wrong - they overshot, most missing the building and falling in the area where we had not placed stop-groups due to scarcity of troops and the lie of the land – the area between the enemy and the river was cleared with a few small hills with vegetation while the rest was pretty open. Bob and Darrell's guys, being the last two stop-groups to be dropped off, had found a road near open ground, put up some claymores and waited. When the mortars hit, a large group of the enemy, who must have thought they were just getting inaccurately mortared casually walked straight into them; claymores were initiated by Darrel and the fight began – two RPDs and six rifles laying down devastating fire saw those not hit and cut down racing back into the mortars which had found their range.

CHAPTER FIVE

"My group of four under the command of former US Marine Tony Emmerson were positioned above a dry riverbed lined by thick bush and the next thing the remnants of the group that survived their encounter with Darrell was all around us. Emmerson, to my dismay, had told us we were not to fire as it would give away our position – I had been training for seven months and was pretty keen on killing someone so this instruction was not well received. After all the noise from Darrell and Bob Mackenzie's side the first thing I saw was two gooks walking on the other side of the re-entrant – they were 180 degrees from my arc of fire and I could see Emmerson tracking their movement but he didn't come into the aim. I took a bead on the front one and dropped him – the other disappeared into the bush – I must have parted Emmerson's hair with the muzzle blast of my FN. He then turned to shit me out and I was spluttering an excuse about 'preventing them getting away' when I noticed he had suddenly stopped talking – he was looking over my shoulder with very wide eyes – I looked around and right behind me stood a big gook with a white t-shirt and AK chest webbing. He was reaching out to me but as I turned he registered I was white eyed and he then tried to get to his AK – my weapon was pointing in the wrong direction but off safe and ready to go – I swung it around and shot him – he sighed and dropped to my left. My rounds must have gone through him and into a second gook wearing a rice-fleck camo shirt behind him – it looked like he was hobbling away and I then filled him in and he went down on his face. At the same time other gooks were coming around the other side of our stop-group. One of the other chaps who I thought was a real tough guy fell apart completely when the fighting started and, shaking with fear, he cowered behind a large tree he thought was bullet-proof.

"The next thing a terr came around the tree with extended pig-sticker bayonet and the 'tough guy' was virtually paralysed with fear. He brought his rifle around to fire but all he got was a click – stoppage – screamed, dropped his rifle and fell on his back. Fortunately, Dick Lazlett, who was from the UK, turned from his arc of fire and shot the gook three times through the mouth, blowing his head apart and leaving bits of brain spattered all over the quivering soldier's weapon and legs.

"We then heard talking coming from the south, so Dick moved and we ended up in all round defence. I was still kneeling as I could see better but a gook approaching saw me first and opened up on me on full auto. I looked to my right and saw his tracer rounds coming at me – kind of dipping and then going over my head. I got into prone position so fast he must have thought he had nailed me. He then moved from bush to bush closing in on us with an unarmed side-kick following him – he must have lost his bearings and suddenly sprung out of the bush in front of Dick who shot him a few times – one of the rounds going thru the top cover of the RPK that he was carrying. He stumbled through our position and after dropping his useless weapon, cartwheeled down the slope into the riverbed and lay still. His sidekick hit the deck and Dick started trying to pick him off – firing shots here and there (Drake-Shooting) and he kept saying 'there he is'! After my stupid start all I was doing was watching my arc of fire.

"It went quiet and then Emmerson told me to go and collect the weapons of the dead all around us, which I did. He then instructed us to get ready to move but we were not advised that the call-signs to our east were closing in on us. Poor Barry Deacon ran into a bush that Dick was paying close attention to as he was still trying to nail the buddy of the RPK man; Dick fired a burst and then next thing I heard Emmerson say that 'Mackenzie has a casualty'. I then saw Bob Mackenzie stick his head up on the extreme right of my arc of fire and I was moving to shoot when I noticed his US Army issue helmet and held my fire; I was a mere squeeze away from blowing his head off!"

"We prepared the LZ for medical evacuation and I saw the medic attending to Barry on the ground. Afterward Barry spoke to me and said that he was moving from cover to cover as they knew our position from our rifle fire – he had just stopped at his next tactical bound when he got shot in the leg. Blood was gushing from the entry wound which was near his knee – he tried to stem it but it just gushed out the exit wound – the cheek of his arse – his femoral artery had been severed – what saved him was a great medic who cut down into his thigh and tied off the artery immediately. A chopper came in and took Barry out. He later lost his leg.

"We then regrouped on the road to shake out into a long sweep-line. While this was happening, Darrell ordered Emmerson to find a gook who he had shot but wasn't sure whether he was dead or not as the guy had crawled off the road. Emmerson then put me in point position and with him covering me, I moved quite far up the road where I saw heavy blood spoor sliding off into the bush and within a couple of metres I spotted an AK sticking into the

CHAPTER FIVE

ground by the bayonet and went in for a closer look. The wounded terr had turned around to face the expected enemy but could not retrieve his rifle. He had almost expired and barely had the energy to open his eyes. I told Emmerson that I had him and he then pushed past me and aimed at the gook to finish him off but had a misfire. This was the guy supposed to be covering me! He then grabbed my rifle and shot him while I cleared his stoppage.

"We then got into position in the sweep line and swept into the camp. There were a few minor contacts on the way in and we then assaulted with bayonets fixed with Darrell leading us through the complex. Bob Pike with an RPG-2[28] was blasting a few holes in the buildings on the way through the complex.

"While we assaulted the position, an RAR sweep-line was also co-ordinating with ours and stood back on the western side while we swept through. Once we had secured the buildings they started to advance to the north side of the camp alongside the river. We had found a heavy machine gun on wheels so we used that to provide them with covering fire as they moved forward. Some of the gooks must have fled into the thick bush in front of them and we watched the RAR machine gunners march fearlessly forward laying down devastating fire as they flushed the enemy from their hiding places, cleaning most of them up. Some may have buried themselves in the reeds and others may have taken their chances with the crocs and swum for it, but most were killed."

"After securing the position," remembers Watt, "I came out the back door of one of the houses and found Bob Pike and Verne Conchie sitting on a pile of bodies with huge grins on their faces. They had found a store full of booze and there they sat smoking while downing beers looking like a pair of trophy hunters having their pictures taken. I shat on them and told them this wasn't the right time and place for a piss-up and picture-taking.

"We then went back to the killing ground where the initial fight started and gathered together the bodies for intelligence gathering purposes. At the same time we found a couple of gooks hiding in the bush who were very keen to surrender. They were moved on to the BSAP SB guys. They struggled to ID the headless person.

"Bob Pike was a former Brit Para who was a little unstable and I was never sure of him. He and Verne Conchie were good pals initially but then

---
[28] Rocket propelled grenade-launcher.

became enemies. Bob was arrested later for throwing a grenade under a taxi when he was off duty. In court he told the magistrate it was an accident; he said he was nervous driving on a country road and had been fiddling with the pin which then came out and so he threw it just as this taxi full of black civvies was passing. The court must have believed him because he was released but later he was thrown out the regiment. Verne was from New Zealand and a former poacher; an exceptionally good guy except when he had had a few drinks when he became violent. He used to protect the new guys from the old soldiers when they tried to fuck them around and was always up for a scrap. Verne was arrested for shooting at a coloured man in uniform outside some seedy hotel in Pioneer Avenue; he was fortunate to get off with discharging a weapon in a public place. Rumour had it that they were injecting air into the veins of wounded gooks but I'm not sure that was true.

"After the attack, a considerable amount of military hardware was recovered including a SAM-7 or Strela heat-seeking missile. This was the first time this weapon was encountered by the Rhodesians and set alarm bells ringing at the highest level. Sadly, Shadreck was nowhere to be found, and he lived to poach another day. I was really hoping we might take him alive because I wanted to get to know him."

Chapter Six

You are the impartial judge
Of the battlefield
Therefore, I do not fear you, Death, yet.

◆

Leaving Rhodesia

Civilian Life

"At the end of my SAS contract I felt I needed a change. Bob Mackenzie wanted me to stay and offered me a Navy diving course as an incentive to sign on again, but I declined the offer. I decided to go and try my luck overseas and was quite pleasantly surprised to land a job with a company called Burns Security who had a contract with the American government in securing their embassy in Regents Park, London. The ambassador at the time was Anne Legendre Armstrong.

"For the first time I had to work with dogs which I enjoyed but it was all terribly boring and I ended up amusing myself by letting my dog Bruce loose on the rabbits that lived on the lawns. The Polish butler reported me for this and I received a reprimand.

"One of the interesting people I met at the embassy was the singer John Denver, a guest of the ambassador. It was early morning during my rounds at the residence where I was dragging old Bruce the dog past the door when it opened and a suntanned John Denver walked out. I immediately recognized him from his gold rimmed glasses. He saw me walking my old pensioner dog and had a good laugh. We exchanged pleasantries and then I went back to my guard-house.

"My second dog, Candy, was a neurotic bitch who was very nasty and impossible to control. I put her into the bathroom once and this annoyed my supervisor who ordered me to bring her out, whereupon she sunk her teeth into his bicep and he was off to hospital. I worked there for six months, six nights on and one night off and made some money but it was just too boring. I decided to quit and head for the Greek Island of Hydra where I heard there was sunshine, beaches, pretty girls and cheap booze. There I met three mad Rhodesians who had also just left the army and we wasted no time laying into the Retsina and chasing beautiful Dutch girls. Booze rather than warm beds was our priority so we lived rough and holed up in a cave that was sometimes used by a shepherd. It was a bit like being back in the army without having to worry about being eaten by a lion or killed by some angry gook. When we were completely broke we found out money was to be made by selling your blood in Athens at a transfusion centre, so off we went and emptied our veins until we were solvent again. I made enough money to get a ticket to Brendizi in Italy and from there I made it back to the UK with another Rhodesian in his camper van.

"When I went back to England I tried to get work on the oil rigs. There were a couple of Rhodesian SAS guys that were diving off the rigs. Shane Beary, brother of Rory and John Rossier[29] was also working there at the time. I ended up working at Barrow in Furness as a pipefitters mate building oil rigs for the oil and gas industry.

"Although a long way from Rhodesia I followed the news at home as best I could and it became ever more disturbing. While I was safe overseas, innocent people at home, some of whom I knew, were dying and it was the grim news from around my old home town of Umtali that really began to upset me. The situation on the eastern border had worsened dramatically with Mozambique independence and it worried me.

"In June 1976, virtually the entire Botha/Habing family, farmers from Chipinga hit a landmine. She and her three children, looking forward to a weekend home from boarding school, were killed and a friend Shirley Wicksteed had both her legs amputated. Throughout the country, but especially in Manicaland, which was where I felt my roots were, farmers were being slaughtered regularly.

"Two months later four territorial soldiers from Umtali, all respected men in the community, were killed in a mortar attack on their base camp outside the town and Sgt. Greg West, also from Chipinga, who I had been at school with was killed in a contact in November while trying to draw fire from the men in his section. Then the town came under direct mortar and rocket attack in August and again in November. It was a sign the war was escalating to another level. By the end of the war more than 40 children out

---

[29] He would make a fortune as one of the divers to find Stalin's Gold.

CHAPTER SIX

of 160 at Chipinga Junior School had lost at least one of their parents.

"I felt unhappy and uneasy, and then, while in the toilet I was reading a story that had hit the international press. On the 9th August the Selous Scouts carried out a spectacular raid on Nyadzonya, a Zanla camp in northern Mozambique. I discovered later, Uncle Ron went to great lengths to keep Ken Flower out the planning loop and went directly to General Walls. Walls apparently got a hell of a shock when he saw what Ron wanted to do but he was eventually persuaded to allow them to go ahead. The Scouts went in dressed as Frelimo and killed over a 1,000 enemy without losing a man. It was one of the best hits of the war and I had missed it. I realised then I was in the wrong place at the wrong time and it was time to go home and get back to war. I packed my bags almost immediately.

Back to the army.
"After I returned from the UK we heard that PK van der Byl had been fired as Minister of Defence after John Vorster pressured Ian Smith. The Nyadzonya raid had pissed Vorster off because he was still trying to cozy up to President Samora Machel of Mozambique. The sacking of PK was a bad day for us. He was the one guy who understood we would never win the war fighting defensively and was happy to let the soldiers do what they needed to do.

Stannard continued: "Reading a copy of the *Rhodesia Herald* and received an ugly reminder of why I needed to get back into the field and do something. On the 3rd December 1976 there was this report:

'A Zanla gang arrived at a village in the Mount Darwin area armed with AKs and knives. The father in the village refused to give them food so they tied his hands behind his back and beat him almost to death. Then they cut off both his ears, his lips and the flesh on his nose. Then they forced his wife, with a gun at her head, to roast the flesh on an open fire and eat it. She swallowed and vomited but was forced to keep eating until it was all eaten. She was then laid out on the ground with her legs forced apart. Another terrorist thrust a burning branch between her legs and up into her vagina. All this was done while roughly 60 villagers were forced to watch the proceedings. The Village Headman and his brother were then badly beaten, requiring hospitalisation.'

"With my mind in a spin, I decided to head for Salisbury's 'Round Bar', have a few beers and see who was there. I was pretty sure I was going to go back to the SAS but by chance I bumped into Dave Scales who saw me and came over for a chat. He asked me what I was going to do and I told him I was planning to go back to the Squadron. Dave was in the Selous Scouts then and he asked me if I would be interested in joining them. The more he told me about the unit, how much they all loved working for 'Uncle Ron' and how happy he was, the more interested I became. He went on to tell me about a small reconnaissance group which had become known informally as 'Popski's Private Army'[30]. It was initially commanded by Chris Schulenburg, who was assisted when out on operations by Neil Kriel. Dave Scales and Tim Callow were key players in the development of the team. This really got my attention. Dave told me how Schulie was perfecting the art of the 'two-man' recce and he spoke of some of the exceptional black operators including Martin Chikondo and Stephen Mpofu with whom they were working. I asked Dave to check with Neil and Schulie to see if they were happy to have me aboard. The next day I was excited to hear that the answer was 'yes' and not only were they happy to have me, but Uncle Ron said I was also not required to do the selection.

"The physical side of the selection did not worry me too much but I was not looking forward to the cuisine. On the course they were forced to live off rats, snakes, baboon meat and animal-eyes. The idea was to make the prospective Scouts learn how to live almost entirely off the land; to drink from the stomach of dead animals; a stinking yellow liquid and to eat green maggot-ridden meat just before it became poisonous. I was lucky to become the proud wearer of the brown Selous Scout beret without having to enjoy all these culinary delights.

"I felt particularly proud about being a member of the Selous Scouts because my family had a historic association with the regiment's namesake, Frederick Courteney Selous. My great, great uncle was Ted Burnett, a frontiersman in the opening up of Rhodesia who travelled and explored with Selous."

"In a way, my great Uncle Ted had played a significant role in the opening up of Rhodesia and now it was my turn to fight for what they had started.

---

[30] Named after the specialist team commanded by Vladimir Peniakoff that operated as part of the Long Range Desert Group against German General Erwin Rommel in WWII.

CHAPTER SIX

With all this history in mind I was feeling rather pleased with myself until my first meeting with Neil Kriel to better understand what I was going to be tasked to do. To my dismay, he explained his belief that I would be better used as a spy going outside the country masquerading as a journalist, using my British passport. In his view I was wasted as a soldier. This was not what I had in mind at all; reading and writing were not my strong point and I didn't feel I would be able to pull it off as a journalist so I was pleased when Schulie read my mind. He pointed out to Neil I did not have a clue about being a journalist nor did I know much about the media in general. He was much of the opinion my cover would be quickly blown. I'm sure he was right. As it turned out many of the reporters involved in writing about Rhodesia were in fact British spies who had been well prepared for the role and I'm sure they would have picked me up in no time at all.

'Schulie'

"From the moment I first met Schulie in the SAS I knew I was in the company of a remarkable man who had an aura of quiet invincibility about him. He had joined the Rhodesian Light Infantry from the South African Army after being spotted on the rugby field by Ron Reid-Daly who suggested he join the Rhodesians. He became a sergeant and was then commissioned into the RLI before transferring to the SAS where he was awarded a Silver Cross for gallantry. When his contract was up he went back to South Africa looking to do something in civilian life but I think he missed Rhodesia and the army and came back. He wanted to re-join the SAS. Brian Robinson was the boss then and did not respond well to Schulie wanting to sign up on his own terms. Brian told him to get lost and that's when he went to speak to Uncle Ron. Ron was a more flexible thinker than Brian and he was prepared to listen carefully because he wanted him in the regiment. But I think even Ron was a little taken aback. Schulie did not want to be tied to any contract or have to do any sort of administrative work officers are normally asked to do. He said he only wanted to do reconnaissance and wanted to work on his own. In the Scouts at the time the minimum was three in the recce teams so this was quite a big ask.

"Schulie argued his case. He was adamant that the one-man concept was a winner. He was convinced the enemy would never expect anyone to come close to their locations alone. If they saw tracks of one man, he was sure they would ignore them. He felt three was too unwieldy; it was far easier for a man alone to hide and being without a companion brought his senses to the fore. He promised Ron, if he let him have his way, he would never need to be hot-extracted. Ron listened and eventually agreed to all his demands except that he be allowed to operate on his own. They then agreed that Schulie would operate with one other but he insisted on making the choice himself. They shook hands and he was back in the army but the jam-stealing officers at Army HQ were not so pleased. When Ron took Schulie there to sign him up the pencil-pushers refused to formalise his re-appointment. They were shocked at his appearance. He was always dressed like a tramp; his hair was long and so was his beard. No socks, he normally wore sandals made from car-tyres and torn denims. The snooty HQ officers looked at this lot and wanted nothing to do with it. This was just another example of the divide in the army that existed between fighting soldiers and the Staff Corps who worried more about how a man dressed than how effective he was as a soldier. If they had had their way, one of our greatest soldiers would not have been allowed back into the army. Ron eventually had to call General Hickman to tell him he was having a problem. Hickman wiped the floor with one of the majors there and they fell into line.

"Once he was in the Scouts, he really set the pace for all the other recce operators and took this aspect of soldiering to a higher level. He did it all by example because he was not a man of many words. He had also tumbled to the fact that no matter how hard you try to disguise yourself in Africa, there are some places only black people can infiltrate without being noticed and he realised he would be far more effective if he had a black soldier along with him.

"Ron told him to pick anyone he wanted, and they decided on Rangararayi Hungwe who had just received the Silver Cross. He had been one of the early pseudo-operators in the northeast of the country and on a few occasions infiltrated terrorist groups posing as 'one of them' with just one other Scout. They were always in danger of being compromised but he was very calm and cunning and always seemed to manage to get these terr groups to do what he wanted them to do. On several occasions he walked them into ambushes and traps. On one occasion, thanks to him, they managed to kill or capture a whole group and eventually cleared a whole area out in a few weeks.

CHAPTER SIX

"Because our helicopters had a limited range it was Schulie that went to Uncle Ron to suggest a change. Because he wanted to go deeper and further into enemy territory, he knew the only way to do that was by parachute. Ron was easily persuaded and free-fall training commenced almost immediately with Schulie leading the way, jumping out at 18,000 feet with oxygen. There was no limit to what the guy wanted to do. From then on most of his operations were free-fall insertions and he was seldom home from the warzone. All these ops were with one of the black Scouts.

"He was a very selfless guy in so many ways and he was well aware that the Rhodesian war machine, small by world standards, was badly stretched. This worried him, and he suggested the recce teams be tasked to carry out their external tasks without the benefit of direct helicopter support. If they got into trouble he wanted jet-strikes to break up enemy formations if need be and then it was up to the guys on the ground to make it out of there. It was a very brave suggestion from a very brave man.

Schulie in Full Flight.

"It was soon after I joined the Scouts that we listened to Ian Smith explain to the nation that after meeting Henry Kissinger in Pretoria he had agreed to a transfer of power to black majority rule. We all knew Smith had been placed under severe pressure by the South African Prime Minister John Vorster but the news rattled us and there was a slump in morale, but not for long. Uncle Ron, ever aggressive, was in no mood for worrying about what the politicians were doing, he knew we were under increasing pressure from the enemy moving into the country from the southeast and in October 1976 he decided on a big assault using flying columns that would focus on the bases at Jorge do Limpopo and Massangena, to force Zanla to look elsewhere to infiltrate the country. Schulie and Stephen Mpofu were to play a major role in this operation and their actions would see them both highly decorated."

For armour, it was a typical Selous Scout 'can-do' story using homemade 'Pigs', which were Mercedes Unimogs armed with 20 mm canons from old Vampire jets. For early warning, two reconnaissance teams were to freefall in, one to the north of the target which was Schulie and Stephen and another group to the south including Paul French, Dennis Croukamp and 'Wings' Wilson. Their first task on landing was to make their way to the railway line, lay charges and derail the first trains passing their positions. Then to mine the roads and cut telephone lines. Once that was done, they were then to wait and watch and send word to the main attack-group under the operational command of Rob Warraker if they spotted reinforcements moving in.

Unfortunately, Paul French and his group were dropped a long way away from their intended Drop Zone (DZ) and three days later, fatigued and low on water they had still not cut the railway line. Paul ended up having to drink his own urine to keep going and they were barely on their feet when they eventually reached the railway, laid their charges and cut the phone lines. Not long after, they heard the sound of an approaching train but their excitement turned to dismay when it rolled by unscathed. The charges had been incorrectly prepared and had failed to detonate. Later, another train packed with Frelimo troops passed them by, again without the planned result. On the Saturday, the three moved their position and faced up to the fact that they could soon die of thirst. Even if the column arrived on time, French and Wilson were not sure their bodies could stand the anticipated lack of water.

Schulie and Stephen were also dropped a distance off target but made their way safely by foot and performed their initial tasks of setting the charges, cutting the lines and mining the roads. But then with nothing happening, boredom setting in and with lots of activity nearby, Schulie decided that he would seize the opportunity to attract attention away from the main group under Warraker to the south. He decided to place a claymore mine in a tree while making sure that the villagers in the area could see him because he knew they would immediately race off and call the army. As expected, a Frelimo Land Rover arrived in a cloud of dust, packed with troops, travelling at great speed. Schulie watched this with great glee and just as the vehicle passed under the tree he detonated the mine, blasting the passengers and sending the vehicle hurtling into a ditch.

He and Stephen then moved quickly away to an elevated feature from where he could watch as Frelimo reinforcements arrived and they immediately started looking for tracks. Anti-tracking all the way, he and Stephen headed further north and heard another vehicle approaching which they correctly assumed was carrying more reinforcements. He was very pleased to note that these were Zanla and immediately set up another

CHAPTER SIX

claymore close to the road. Watching and waiting as they passed into the zone he blew them away too, killing or injuring all the occupants. This really pissed off Frelimo and they came in big numbers, causing the two Scouts to run like hell under heavy fire which ultimately ended up in them losing one another and splitting up.

Meanwhile, the main column was on the move. Crossing on the night of the 30th October, they drove into Chigamane where they were warmly received until one of the Zanla men realised he was looking at a white man. The column opened up and killed everyone they saw before moving on to Maxila where, since the defenders had fled, they had to content themselves with destroying vehicles. All this slowed them up but with the target in sight they set up a mortar barrage and then, using the 20 mm cannons plus machine guns, attacked Jorge de Limpopo destroying a troop train carrying Zanla troops. When that was on fire and all the enemy dead, they moved on, blowing up a dam, destroying all the vehicles they could find in the town, and then blasting the railway control station.

To the north, much to Schulie's dismay, when he had finally shaken off his pursuers he tried to call Warraker on the radio to ascertain where they were, only to find that the battery was flat. But Rob had heard all the shooting and blasts to the north, so he knew he and Stephen were in trouble but had no way of knowing much more than that. After dark, when the firing had died down, Rob sent Richard Passaportis north with a patrol to uplift them but he had no joy. Frustrated and angry, the patrol shot up the train that had brought up the reinforcements. Then Rich went south to look for Paul and his guys.

Back home, when he heard the teams were lost, Uncle Ron contacted the air force and they immediately dispatched a Canberra to overfly the area and try and pick up a radio signal. Somehow Schulie managed to squeeze some life out of his battery and when he saw the aircraft he started calling. The pilot picked up a faint transmission which he knew was one of the guys in distress. Schulie did not have a 'loc-stat'[31] but he managed to explain to the pilot where he was in relation to a pan[32] that the pilot recognised from an aerial photograph he had to hand. Once that was known the pilot confirmed

---
[31] Location State – a map grid-reference.
[32] A pan is normally a dry lake, sometimes with salt. When it rains a pan normally fills.

a chopper would be sent in to collect him at first light the following morning. Schulie also told the pilot that he had lost his partner and feared he had been killed or captured.

Meanwhile Rich's patrol were searching in vain for Paul and his blokes and were just about to give up when they too heard a faint voice on the radio. Just in time, because Paul's group had had no water for two days and were on their last legs. Unbeknown to Rich and his team at the time, there were only two to be collected because Dennis Croukamp had left the group and walked to the Limpopo in search of water. He would eventually make it back to Rhodesia under his own steam after a long, lonely walk.

Schulie lay low that night and the next morning, as promised, the chopper arrived over his position but it was under fire so it was a hasty hot extraction but they got airborne safely. He was very emotional about losing his friend and he warned the pilot that on the course he was flying, he was heading for a Frelimo position which was heavily defended. But the pilot was pissed off about being shot at on the way in and the gunner told Schulie he wanted to go and 'fuck them up' on the way out. Just as they were about to engage the enemy position, the pilot shouted through the intercom and pointed downwards excitedly. He had seen someone below in obvious distress, standing on the railway line, waving something and he went into an immediate orbit to get a better look. Schulie quickly confirmed it was Stephen and they went in fast and picked him up again under fire. Afterwards the pilot spoke about the way the two, one big Matabele and one big Afrikaner, hugged and cried when they came together again, both having been thinking that the other was dead.

Meanwhile, the main column still had to attack the town of Massangena and they were running late. Out of the blue, a Frelimo Land Rover suddenly raced towards them until it was shot to pieces, killing all the occupants but there was much cheering when they realised the vehicle was stuffed with cash. Closing in on the town, an abandoned bus was seized. One of the Scouts donned the driver's uniform, peak-cap and all, and set off to press home the assault with the bus leading. A friendly local stopped them on the way to tell them that a Frelimo ambush lay ahead. Sure enough, nearing the airfield, a Frelimo officer stepped into the road, to stop the bus and as planned, the bus pulled over and the 'Pigs' roared past, blasting everything that moved. Frelimo were in complete disarray running and shooting in all

CHAPTER SIX

directions while the column bore down on and past them. One soldier, trying to let rip an RPG-7[33] rocket was actually run over by one of the 'Pigs' just as he loosed off a missile into the heavens. All the defenders were wiped out before Rich Passaportis took some guys across the Save River where they attacked a Zanla base, returning with captured weapons and equipment. The next day the column crossed back into Rhodesia having succeeded in destroying the transport and logistics systems between Jorge do Limpopo, Malvernia and Massangena.

The railway line, already blocked and clogged between Malvernia and Jorge do Limpopo by the wreckage of two trains with another wrecked in the railway station of Jorge do Limpopo, was unusable between those points. Additionally, all the roads travelled by the column had been heavily seeded with landmines. At both Massangena and Jorge do Limpopo all motor transport had either been destroyed or captured by the Selous Scouts.

The immediate effect was that the Zanla troops in the Gaza Province, who had until then been able to truck or haul unlimited tons of war equipment to the border at will, now had to tramp the last 90 kms on foot. This gave them added logistical problems for they had to now find porters, normally women, and set up soft-target transit camps on route line to accommodate them. Listening into enemy transmissions Rhodesian Intelligence learned of the serious blow to enemy morale as they realised how vulnerable they were in what they thought were sanctuaries.

Two weeks later, Schulie and Mpofu did a freefall back into the area landing some 20 kms south of Jorge do Limpopo. The railway line had been laboriously repaired and trains were again running between Barragem and Jorge do Limpopo. Zanla groups would detrain at this point and commence their long walk along the Nuanetsi River though thick bush to the Rhodesian border. But to their fury this arrangement was not to last long; the two Scouts quickly derailed a train travelling at speed, wrecking it completely. Frelimo had now lost four locomotives plus the attendant rolling stock and this proved to be the final straw. They made no further efforts to use this line again until the later stages of 1979.

---

[33] Soviet designed and supplied, shoulder-launched anti-tank rocket-propelled grenade launcher.

Leopard Encounter

"My first operation was to be a two-man recce with Corporal Aaron Jele in Mozambique," remembers Stannard. "It was to be one of quite a few close encounters I would have with a different kind of danger. Four days after deployment all was quiet and we were resting up on the leeward side of a mountain about 30 kms from the camp we had been tasked to check out. For once, we had time and there seemed to be no imminent danger so we were pretty relaxed. It was afternoon and I was enjoying the view as the shadows lengthened and the long grass shimmered in the sunlight. I heard nothing but maybe I smelled something because, for some reason I turned my head to look behind me and almost soiled my pants. I found myself looking straight into the sullen, yellow eyes of a large leopard that bored into me with indescribable intensity. I was shocked, breathless, helpless and speechless. The stand-off seemed to last forever but then suddenly the cat spun around and was gone. Startled by the rustle of the grass, Aaron heard him go and turned to me looking very frightened.

'What was that Kafupi?' 'Ingwe[34],' I said, still wide-eyed, while I tried to breathe properly again. Looking back, I'm pretty sure that cat was hunting and had one us been alone he would have attacked and that could have been very unpleasant.

Martin Chikondo

"When I arrived at the Scouts the guy about whom there was a lot of talk was Martin Chikondo and I was very keen to try and work with him. He was in the thick of the Rhodesian war right from the outset. Below are some of his early citations:

'Corporal Martin Chikondo, a serving member of the Selous Scouts, volunteered for operational tracking duties in the north-eastern border area in 1973. In September 1973, Corporal Chikondo was in command of a section of men attempting to locate a group of some four to five terrorists. After making suitable arrangements with the local terrorist contact man a meeting was arranged for the following night. At the appointed time Corporal Chikondo and four others approached the kraal and were met by the contact man who then called the terrorists. As the terrorists approached the group they became suspicious and opened fire. Corporal Chikondo,

---
[34] Ingwe - leopard

CHAPTER SIX

although under heavy fire from close range and with complete disregard for his own safety, immediately opened fire. Under cover of his own and his machine-gunner's fire, he was able to extricate his men from the open area to a more favourable position. He quickly regained control of his men and saturated the contact area with fire. Later it was discovered that two terrorists had been killed; one of the terrorists being a section leader. As a result of this contact and subsequent interrogation of locals involved much valuable information in respect of terrorist presence in the area was obtained.

In October 1973, Corporal Chikondo was once again in command of a small patrol attempting to make contact with a group of approximately ten terrorists. A suitable rendezvous was arranged for the following night. At the appointed time Corporal Chikondo quite brazenly approached the terrorists to make verbal contact and attempt to lure them into the planned killing ground. However the terrorists became extremely suspicious and Corporal Chikondo, with complete disregard for his own safety and showing a high degree of personal gallantry, opened fire killing two terrorists and wounding one other. Several weapons and other equipment were recovered.

Later the same day the captured terrorist indicated a terrorist base. In the ensuing contact security forces eliminated a gang leader and wounded two others.

In November 1973, Corporal Chikondo was in command of a patrol trying to locate a group of terrorists. As he approached the rendezvous the terrorist leader came out of the thick bush to meet him. During the initial conversation Corporal Chikondo saw a further terrorist nearby with a machine-gun trained on him. Realising he was in fact in an ambush he opened fire killing the terrorist leader. The patrol immediately came under heavy fire from close range. Remaining perfectly cool and using his tactical skill to best advantage, Corporal Chikondo extricated his men, without casualty, from a most precarious position.

During all these actions Corporal Chikondo displayed great personal gallantry, outstanding leadership and devotion to duty far beyond the call of normal operational requirements.'

Having emerged as one of the best soldiers in the Rhodesian army, Chikondo was one of the first black Selous Scouts to be called upon to do reconnaissance outside the country when the SAS were tumbling to the fact that being white in a foreign land, not matter how good you were, was an inhibiting factor.

Early in 1974 Reid-Daly was approached and asked by the Central Intelligence Organisation (CIO) for the loan of troops to do a reconnaissance of a Zambian village called Chiawa, suspected to be the site of a Zipra camp. He declined to detach any of his men but agreed to perform the task with the help of the SAS who then had to provide men and equipment to infiltrate into enemy territory across the Zambezi river. After attending a CIO briefing, it appeared the intelligence people did not know where the camp was, nor did they know much about enemy activity in the area.

When Ron asked what personal identification they would need if questioned, he was told such documentation would not be needed. Troubled by the lack of information to hand he resisted demands to deploy immediately, but under pressure went to work on a plan.

He tasked Sergeant Chikondo, along with Corporal Able, a former Zipra insurgent, trained in the Soviet Union and Cuba, who had been captured and imprisoned before sending word that he wished to switch sides. He immediately established a rapport with Reid-Daly and quickly established himself as an excellent soldier. Able knew his way around the Chiawa area.

Reid-Daly's plan was simple. The men would cross the Zambezi river at last light with the help of SAS crews in two Klepper canoes. The landing party would beach in the reeds downstream from where the Zambian army was based and look for one of the many well used game-paths in the area in order to make their tracks less conspicuous. Once ashore, their instructions were to keep a low profile, move only at night and try to locate the suspected camp by means of a physical reconnaissance. They were also told to keep away from the locals unless they were certain it was completely safe. If they did converse, they were to pose as businessmen from Lusaka investigating the possibility of buying fruit and vegetables.

Two emergency rendezvous sites were selected in the event something went awry and they discussed and rehearsed the necessary drills in fine detail. The river crossing took place with no hitches on a weekend because the planners knew that there would be a number of weekend beer drinks and dances which would be well attended by Zambian Army personnel.

At twilight the following evening, Martin and Able emerged from their hiding-place and moved cautiously in a wide half-circle towards high

CHAPTER SIX

ground, from where they hoped to carry out observations on the suspected area. Unfortunately, a band of honey-seekers walked right into them. To avoid arousing their suspicions, Able, who had learned the local dialect during his time as a Zipra insurgent based in the area, told the people they were traders looking for produce and that they were lost. The honey-seekers were friendly and unsuspecting and insisted on guiding them to the chief's village, advising them that he would assist them.

There was nothing the two Scouts could do without arousing suspicion and accepted the offer. At the chief's village a beer drink was in full swing and they were warmly welcomed by the chief. Chikondo and Able were happy to join in the fun but just when all seemed very settled the chief suddenly demanded they produce papers to prove their credentials. Chikondo had to think fast.

'Chief,' said Able, taking a gamble, 'we did not tell those people the truth. We haven't come to buy produce. We are Zimbabwean freedom fighters from the camp. We sneaked away without permission to look for women.'

The chief laughed and expressed happiness at discovering their true identities but still insisted on seeing a pass from their camp commander. He explained that this was a Zambian Army instruction to identify spies following the deaths in the area caused by landmines planted by the Rhodesians. Adding to the Scouts' woes, he then despatched one of his men to ask the Zambian army to send troops to check the visitors out. The pair watched apprehensively as the messenger mounted his bicycle and departed. It was time to commence emergency escape drills.

One of these was for Martin to make his excuses and go off to relieve himself in the bush. Shortly afterwards, Able would follow him and they would both slip away to safety. The signal for this to commence was for him to smooth his hair in a particular manner, which he promptly did. Unfortunately, Able was engrossed in conversation and he missed the signal. Martin did not realise this at the time, stood up and excused himself, but as he left the circle by the fire a villager stood up to accompany him.

Assuming that Able was following, he walked into the bush on the fringe of the village, followed by his escort. On finding cover he pulled a pistol from his waistband, told the escort to clear off before he killed him and shouted for Able to run for it. He then took off for the second emergency

MEN OF WAR

Rendezvous (RV) but still no Able. At dawn, Chikondo radioed for a hot-extraction and was lifted out of Zambia by helicopter. Later, it was learned that Able had been overpowered by the villagers and handed over to the Zambian Army. He was never seen or heard from again and it is assumed he was summarily executed. So, apart from confirming the presence of a Zipra camp in the vicinity of Chiawa, the operation was a disaster.

This led to a bitter argument between CIO boss Ken Flower and Reid-Daly, with the latter pointing out that he was appalled at the lack of information coming from the CIO while reminding them that it was on their assurance that the two men had entered the country without needing some sort of documentation to validate their presence in the country. He concluded the meeting by telling Flower that, while he was happy for the Scouts to continue with external tasks, he would not in future allow his men to be in any way involved with operations planned by the CIO alone. All future external operations would be planned by Selous Scouts intelligence personnel. This was the beginning of a bitter feud that would plague Reid-Daly and the Selous Scouts throughout the rest of the war.

Life with the Scouts

"Life with the Selous Scouts was a pleasure. Uncle Ron created a wonderful camaraderie among his men," remembers Stannard. "Quite remarkable when you remember we were from different races, religions, political persuasions, ethnic groups and social classes and also in the mix were ex-terrorists who had only recently been the enemy. And yet everyone seemed to get along with one another so well.

"Ron loved to laugh and he had a wonderful sense of humour. We had a 'Prick of The Week,' the winner of which would get a 'Certificate of Merit', for

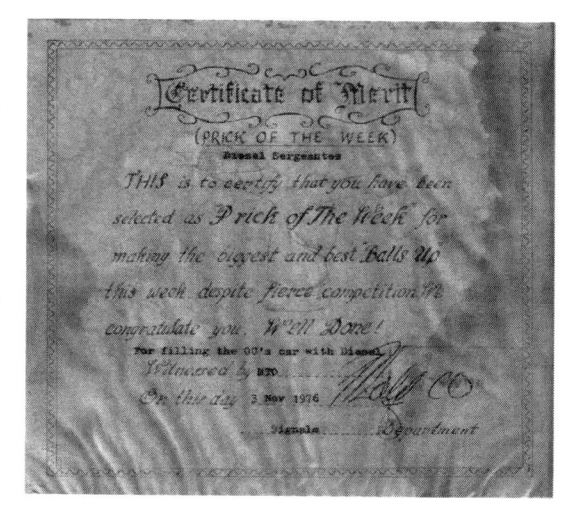

CHAPTER SIX

making the biggest fuck-up of that week. It was pinned up outside the pub and the winner had to buy a lot of beer to get himself out the shit.

"Ron's personal 'butler' was an ex-gook by the name of Chigango. He had been a very senior terrorist who Ron had 'turned' and he loved Uncle Ron like a father. When General Fritz Loots from South African Special Forces came on a secret visit to meet Ron and stay a few days, he damn near shat himself when Ron told him the guy serving their evening drinks was a former terrorist.

"Chigango used to take Ron his tea and a newspaper every morning. On one occasion Ron was on 'days-off' but had stayed in camp for some reason and because he was off duty he got pissed in camp, which was rare. When Chigango went in in the morning with his tea he couldn't wake him. This had never happened before and he panicked and came screaming out the quarters, shouting that 'Ishe[35] is dead …. Ishe is dead!' There was immediate pandemonium and one of the majors came running out of the Ops Room to investigate. They found Ron lying there with his cup and paper looking pissed off.

'Ishe!' Chigango shouted. 'You are supposed to be dead.'

'Well I'm fucking not…. you dumb cunt!' Ron said.

"Ron was no authoritarian; he was the boss, but he was always ready to listen and learn from his juniors. He was extremely innovative and always up for new ideas on how to win the war. He wanted a mounted group so with help from the TF[36] guys horses were brought in. We then did quite a bit of riding in the paddocks. I ended up doing a few mine-laying operations into Mozambique on horseback which was different, but I was not great on a horse and ended up spending a lot of time on my feet.

'The Osprey' all-ranks mess was always a lot of fun and cheap beer flowed freely. Joe Bresler and I used to get pissed then take his Ford Capri on to the dirt runway and try and roll it doing hand-brake turns and 'wheelies'. I was also back with my old friend Noel Robey who I had approached at Mukumbura when I first wanted to join the SAS.

'One Saturday we were sitting there hammering the beers with the sun beating down when boredom set in. Tim Callow dared me to roll a smoke grenade into the ladies' toilet which was a little way from 'The Osprey'

---

[35] Ishe – lord or master.
[36] Territorial Force or Reservists.

pub. He had one ready and this seemed like a good idea so I waited until I spied two Rhodesian Women's Services (RWS) ladies going in the toilet, snuck up and rolled one under the door. I had not taken account of the fact it was a temporary structure made out of treated wood and a huge cloud of purple smoke soon billowed out the windows and out of the cloud came two shrieking ladies at speed in a state of undress with their camouflage denims down near their knees. The yelling was heard throughout the camp and the HQ staff came streaming out the building to see what was going on. By this time, much to my dismay, the whole toilet was smouldering and then burst into flames needing a reaction from the campfire-brigade. They were also in the bar getting pissed so they used beer to douse the flames among much laughing and shouting. I stopped laughing when I heard Tim shout.

'Kafupi, RSM Pretorius is coming and he's going to fuck you up!' That was all I needed to hear. I sped off to my VW Beetle, fired it up, hurtled out the main gate and headed for Salisbury and relative safety."

"Not being able to play sport was missed," remembers Stannard. "Most of the white Scouts were rugby players and because of the war we were seldom able to play which was a real pity because some of the guys had been capped for Rhodesia and were in the prime of their playing days. Against this background, Noel Robey was instrumental in organising the only time the Selous Scouts managed to get a rugby team together."

Noel remembers. "One Monday our orderly room Sergeant Joe Lewis arrived for duty at our base, André Rabie Barracks, with major head wound bandages. When asked by his Warrant Officer what had happened we discovered Joe had gone to the Forces Club at King George VI Barracks on the Friday and got into a 'meaningful discussion' with members on rugby. An argument ensued as to who had the strongest team within the Forces. Joe was ex-RLI and also played rugby so he knew what he was talking about. He promptly announced that should the Selous Scouts ever have the opportunity to field a team we would thrash any team around including the first league teams. The argument got out of control resulting in a free-for-all against Joe. In the ensuing punch-up he had the top part of his ear bitten off and it was now dangling by a thread. He managed to escape with these minor injuries but his honour had been wounded, hence the beehive wrapping around the head.

"Uncle Ron, who was a rugby man, decided to restore Joe's pride and

CHAPTER SIX

sort out these Forces' loud mouths. He gave orders to Neil Kriel and Piet van der Riet to put a team together using any Scout TF and regular members to whip the Forces team. Quite a number of the pre-war regular players were deployed on operations. But with these urgent orders issued, operational call-signs were summoned home and the war stopped for a week. Territorial Scout members needed for the game received a 'call-up' for a week.

"We got back to barracks and I was surprised at how many members were back early from our deployments. Needless to say, speculation was high that we were finally going to sort out Zambia or Mozambique in some massive operation. We never gave any thought to the possibility of a grudge rugby game till we went to the mess, where we were enlightened about the pending task, much to the delight of the chaps brought back from operations.

"I don't know how or where we got our jerseys and socks but they were in the regimental colours and we were very proud of our kit. What happened to it later is also a mystery to me; maybe Uncle Ron had it stored for later use, which never materialised. We had a fair sprinkling of active Rhodesian, Mashonaland, Matabeleland, army and Midlands players gracing the team, true to Joe Lewis's argument that we could have taken any team. I think we practised twice during the week with Saturday as match day. Captain Golightly and the Motor Transport (MT) crew had buses laid on for the African troops and families with orders from the Boss that all members of the unit would go support the team.

"There was an amazing atmosphere at the grounds with our soldiers supporting us. I think the Forces team were totally aghast when they saw who was in the Scouts team. We won the game before the kick off. We totally overran them and restored Joe's honour. When the game was over, we went and had a piss-up and that was that. Next day my call-sign was re-deployed and we were back to war."

"When we were based at the training camp at Wafa-Wafa," remembers Stannard, "the nightlife was in the holiday resort town of Kariba and Caribbea Bay, with the casino, was the favourite spot. I was there with Piet van der Riet, Tim Callow, Martin Chikondo, Mick Hardy, Willie Divine, Rory Beary and Schulie was our boss. The days in the sun tracking and training were tough, so a trip to town to have some fun was something we all looked forward to but while the rest were getting permission to go, Rory and I kept getting night duties. Eventually I went to Schulie and asked him what was going on.

'You and Beary are staying here because if I let you go in there, one or both of you will fuck someone up!' I wasn't happy to hear this, but I had to admit he had a point. Rory had been in a lot of shit throughout his military career.

"I was a damn nightmare," remembers Rory. "In 1968, after only a year in '2 Commando' RLI, I had a string of 13 charges against me, ranging from AWOL to insubordination to assault. I did not co-operate with the Regimental Police (RP) and flatly refused to go on CO's orders. I was driving RSM Robin Tarr absolutely nuts. Basically, they didn't know how to cope with this kind of behaviour and abandoned me in the Guard House while they figured out what the solution was. Whilst languishing in my cell one morning in the Guardroom, I was surprised to see the then Captain Reid-Daly, who was then the Training Officer, enter my cell. I immediately leaped to my feet and showed the respect I sincerely felt for the man. The fact is he was probably the only man in the army that I looked up to for some reason. He proceeded to crap all over me; told me to pull my finger out, cut out all this rebellious bullshit, behave like a real soldier and accept my punishment like a man. I really believe it was at that point that my life changed; I'm sure I saw a glint of something in his eye and a wry smile. I took his advice, went on orders, and was given 28 days in Detention Barracks at Brady for my troubles. I am sure that if Uncle Ron had not entered my cell that day I would have been dishonourably discharged and thrown out in disgrace."

"Finally, Schulie took pity on the two of us," remembers Stannard, "and he gave us permission to go into Kariba. On the way there I spoke to Rory.

'For fuck's sake Rory, try and keep it clean tonight and let's just have some fun.'

'Yeah Kafupi, don't worry,' he said with a smile.

"He had such a gentle demeanour and soft voice, so it was hard to imagine him hurting anyone. We went into the main pub at Caribbea Bay and established ourselves at the end of the bar where we were drinking furiously but with no problems until a bunch of Grey's Scouts came in and took up the space where we were sitting. Rory told them to fuck off and drink elsewhere because there was no room for them where we were sitting. Well this one 'Donkey Walloper' told Rory to go fuck himself and that was it; a switch in his head flipped and he went berserk, laying into these guys with some of the fastest fists in Rhodesia. More of them piled in but

CHAPTER SIX

we eventually flattened them. They were rolling all over the place when security guards with dogs came charging in and Rory then fucked them and their dogs up. The manager then came to the rescue. This was a bonus for Rory because he hated this guy and so the manager got fucked up badly too. Eventually RPs and Police arrived and we were carted off. I was allowed back to Wafa-Wafa but Rory spent the night in jail. Schulie was furious and needless to say, that was our last night out in Kariba."

"While I did not know all the details at the time, throughout my service in the Scouts, Uncle Ron was engaged in an ongoing feud with CIO boss Ken Flower and Colonel John Redfern, the Director of Military Intelligence (DMI). Both men hated Ron and would share none of their intelligence with the Scouts. The reasons given by him (Flower) at the time were ridiculous and should never have been accepted by ComOps[37] but he was, by all accounts a very persuasive man. The real reason, we now know, is Flower was actually working for the British and he was doing everything in his power to hamstring the Selous Scouts. Ron was undaunted and simply resolved to use his own men and resources to gather the intelligence they required to continue to operate successfully. This frustrated the CIO and MI who then went out of their way to frustrate the Scouts. People like Winston Hart, Peter Stanton, Ken Bird and Ken Milne played an important part in filling this intelligence void."

"I knew that Ron was having a hard time with his own people in Military Intelligence," remembers BSAP SB Superintendent Keith Samler. "They were accusing him of poaching and gun-running and all manner of things, designed to destroy his credibility and that of the Selous Scouts Regiment generally. His telephone had been tapped and strange as it may seem a police enquiry into the allegations against him concluded irrefutably that there was no base whatsoever to the allegations. Much later I discovered that my home telephone had also been tapped and I was also subjected to a lot of malicious allegations. In his book, *'Serving Secretly'*, Ken Flower briefly alludes to this period of time in relation to the Selous Scouts and reading between the lines leaves no doubt of the Government/CIO hierarchy's intent to distance themselves from the regiment. The CIO had decided to sideline Selous Scouts' operations."

---

[37] Combine Operations. Supreme decision-making body that combined heads of all the services making up the Security Forces.

Madulo Pan.

In January 1977, Schulie and Stephen Mpofu were briefed on the existence of a large transit camp situated in the vicinity of Madulo Pan, some 80 kms south of the Rhodesian border and west of the Maputo to Malvernia railway line. A photographic reconnaissance was run by a Canberra, but when the film was developed all that could be seen was an extensive path pattern leading into a thick belt of trees and bush.

To avoid detection, Zanla transit camps had become little more than resting places. Stocks of ammunition, food and supplies were concealed in wide areas of the surrounding bush. There were no huts or grass shelters, and the camping areas were generally sited amongst thick bush or under large trees to hide their presence from our aircraft. The transit camps were normally manned by a small garrison that lived in nearby villages. Their function was to ration and resupply the groups passing through *en route* to the war and to provide guides to take them to the next staging post. It was known that the infiltrating groups rarely spent much time in these camps so there was a need to move quickly and to strike effectively.

When 'hot int'[38] was received indicating the camp would be occupied by a large number of terrorists between the 10th and 12th January, Reid-Daly and his team immediately got down to detailed planning. In the absence of a pinpoint target they reluctantly concluded that a conventional attack by ground forces would meet with little success as it was known from experience that the enemy would swiftly melt into the flat but thickly wooded terrain and escape. Because of this it was decided to put in an air strike using newly designed flares.

The Rhodesian Air Force, ever innovative, had produced a device which, when attached to a flare, enabled a Canberra to ignite it by a radio impulse. This gave them the much-needed capability of accurately bombing targets at night. After much trial and error, a system involving the use of two flares had been devised leading to pin-point accuracy. The first flare would be positioned by ground forces a maximum of 800 metres from the target. The other had to be placed about two to four kms farther out from the first flare, which gave the advantage of not alerting the enemy too early by the ignition. This allowed the bombers those extra few but vital seconds to correct their line of approach in case they were not bang on.

---

[38] Hot intelligence

CHAPTER SIX

The drill was simple; the navigator having been told the precise distance which the flares were from the target, would offset his bombsight accordingly. As his aircraft approached the target he would initiate both flares, pass any course corrections to the pilot, and release his bombs on the forward flare. If this had been correctly positioned and the distance from target accurately calculated, the bombs would straddle the target. The major problem was that a team had to locate the target and place the flares before they could be activated.

The Air Force had also perfected a bomb known as the Alpha bomb of which dozens were dropped at one time. It was cylindrical in shape and designed to bounce and explode just above ground and thus it had an awesome killing capability as an anti-personnel bomb.

Three Canberra bombers could carpet an area a kilometre square with ease and there was little likelihood of anyone walking out of the target area unscathed. Like most innovations designed for specific purposes the technique did have limitations, the most dangerous of which was that the bombers had to run in at 300 feet for their bombing runs to be effective.

Rob Warraker had by this time fostered a close working relationship with the Rhodesian Air Force Photographic Interpretation Section and they produced an enormous blown-up photograph of the transit camp area. An unusually large tree, some 400 metres from the camp, was selected as the site for the first flare. The position chosen for the second flare was a large, isolated clump of trees. It was two kms from the first flare and on the required compass bearing.

A comprehensive joint planning session took place with the air force and all necessary details for the mounting of the attack were worked out. It was scheduled for dawn on the morning of the 12th January when it was almost certain the majority would be standing upright when the bombs fell. After the bombing, the plan called for Captain Richard Passaportis to take in a heliborne force of 15 men shortly after first light, sweep the camp area for wounded, and to gather up any weapons or documents which might be useful. The Scouts were allowed a small-armed fixed-wing aircraft in support, which Major Bert Sachse would use to overfly the area and control the operation. Two Hunter fighter jets were also made available to lend support should Richard and his men find themselves in trouble.

Schulie and Sergeant Mpofu jumped from 17 000 feet just before last light on the 10th January and landed safely 12 kms to the west of the target. There they established a lying-up place (LUP) where they remained for 24 hours, did all their equipment tests and checked to see if they had been noticed. Late afternoon the following day they started moving carefully through the bush towards their target, reaching it after dark. A close-in reconnaissance confirmed activity, and to make absolutely sure, Mpofu crawled in next to the campfires and listened to the many conversations.

Satisfied, the pair immediately set about locating the pre-selected points to set up the flares. But on the ground by the light of a weak moon, while trying to avoid outposts and sentries, Schulie found it challenging and being unable to identify the points he seriously pondered a postponement of the attack. Then, just as he and his partner were about to give up the search, they located the unusually large tree. Working swiftly, they set up the first flare, and walked on a back-bearing for two kms until they found the other flare point, the clump of trees.

In the early hours of 12th January, they set up their radio and settled down to make contact with the incoming flight of bombers when they would come within range. Towards H-Hour, a Canberra, with its bomb bays full, arrived in the vicinity and circled at extremely high altitude, well away from the camp area. Lying in the nose cone, wearing many layers of warm clothing to keep out the icy cold, was Rob Warraker who soon established communications with Schulie and confirmed that it was all systems go. This was relayed to the other bombers which were flying towards the camp.

A few minutes out from target, the pilot leading the strike force called for light. Schulie immediately initiated the most distant flare manually and gave the pilots a final in-flight briefing. The pilot of the lead aircraft initiated the second flare by radio, then raced in at 300 feet and released the bombs. They were on the button and the reconnaissance team lay quietly listening to the screams and shouts that erupted from the camp area. Quickly and silently collecting the remains of the flares to remove any sign of their presence, the Scouts left the area and walked to their pick-up point.

At first light, Passi and his men arrived over the target area in their helicopters. To their astonishment, a hail of gunfire met his force and he initially concluded that the bombers had missed the target. The two Hunters, loitering nearby on call, screamed in angrily with their rockets and cannons, but the return fire did not diminish.

CHAPTER SIX

Looking down from his aircraft, Bert Sachse suddenly realised a heavily armed Frelimo column had arrived and Passi's force was too small to tackle them. Sachse quickly cancelled this part of the plan while the Canberra carrying Rob Warraker was tasked to attack the column. Quickly reversing course, the pilot brought the aircraft out of the clouds over Malvernia and immediately took heavy flak followed by a direct hit which caused it to bank steeply then plummet to the ground, sending a cloud of black smoke swirling aloft as it exploded. And so perished Rob Warraker, 29 days after he had been presented with the Silver Cross of Rhodesia for outstanding gallantry. Along with Rob, the Canberra's crew, pilot Flight Lieutenant Ian Donaldson and navigator Air Sub-Lieutenant David Hawkes, were both also killed. Enemy casualties were reported in the hundreds.

A 'very gallant soldier'

By GRAHAM BROWN

CAPTAIN Robert Warraker, the South African killed when a Rhodesian Air Force plane was shot down on the Mozambique border this week, was known as a very gallant soldier.

In 1975 Captain Warraker joined the crack Selous Scouts commando unit and was awarded the Silver Cross of Rhodesia last October after action in Rhodesia's north-eastern border area.

A letter of congratulations from his commanding officer says: "This is an outstanding achievement and you may wear your decoration with justifiable pride.

"Your exemplary work, particularly your leadership and personal gallantry in the recent brilliant raid, will one day make most graphic reading. It is a pity that all the details of this cannot be fully revealed.

"You can be assured, however, of the esteem of your comrades who are aware of the role played by you."

Mrs Elizabeth Gunselman, his mother, said at her home in Sandown, Johannesburg, yesterday that Captain Warraker loved Rhodesia and was devoted to its army.

"He came down here on business last month and asked me to frame the letter from his commander. I took it to a picture framer yesterday and just after I returned I was told by a Rhodesian Army padre of his death," she said.

Captain Warraker matriculated at Milner High School at Klerksdorp and moved to Johannesburg with his family seven years ago.

After earning his mine captain's ticket he worked on the Free State Goldfields. In 1967 he visited Rhodesia on holiday and liked it so much he decided to stay.

Captain Robert Warraker.

Burnett and Selous

Pieter Oberholzer. First white murder victim of the Rhodesian war.

PM Ian Smith inspecting an RLI Guard of Honour before UDI.

Peter Walls and PK van der Byl. (Craig Fourie)

Schulie, Ian Smith, John Hickman

Stannard as a District Officer in Mtoko.

Two-toed tribesman with policeman.

Sandy MacLean, Peter Walls, Peter Rich.

Selous Scouts Recce Group. Callow, Chikondo, Schulie, Scales.

Watt standing far left and Tracking Team

Ken Bird with Kelly the hunting dog.

SAS Sergeants Mess. Watt standing rear far right.

Neil Kriel.

Stannard front left. Chikondo front right. Callow centre rear.

PK with Pete Simmonds flying.

Major Bert Sachse

Ron Reid-Daly

'Fireforce' rising at Grand Reef.

Watt receives Wings on Chest from President Wrathall.

ZANLA Training camp

SAS selection mud-fight.

Shadreck the poacher

Officer Cadet Stannard and his father Assistant Commissioner Peter Stannard.

Tim Callow. Op Vodka

Martin Chikondo

Stephen Mpofu

Hunter pilots before attack on Zambia. L-R Dave Bourhill, John Blythe-Wood, 'Baldy' Baldwin, Tony Oakley, Brian Gordon.

PK van der Byl, Tim Callow, Dale Collett.

SAS before raid into Zambia.

Chapter Seven

Whether the widow weeps
In a Salisbury mansion
Or in a rude grass hut
The tears
The hole left in her life
Are still the same

◆

The War Escalates

Pafuri with Chikondo. April 1977

"My opportunity to work with Martin came when it was decided to place landmines on the road to Pafuri from Chicualacuala," remembers Stannard. "Although I was under the command of Neil Kriel, I was briefed by Bob Warren-Codrington. He explained that Zanla was crossing into the country at Pafuri, close to the Limpopo River, where we shared a border with South Africa and we needed to do something to close the route. To this end, I was tasked with crossing into Mozambique to lay Anti-Personnel (AP) mines and two anti-tank mines on the road. Bob was emphatic about getting some results from the anti-tank mines so he instructed me to lay them carefully and get it right.

"I then asked if Martin was available to partner me and was very pleased to hear he was. By this time he was the recipient of a Silver Cross. Quietly spoken, thoughtful and very intelligent; I used to think he should have been a lawyer rather than a special force soldier.

"He was not scared of much but the Limpopo River got his attention.

'Kafupi, how are we going to get across the river?' he asked. 'I'm not a very good swimmer, these mines are very heavy, and I'm scared of crocodiles.' I explained to him that we were going to float across on two inner tubes used in tractor tyres. This did not impress him, but he had no better ideas so off we went.

"We moved by vehicle to the drop-off point where we inflated the tubes and loaded all our weapons and equipment for the night crossing. We were quite low in the water because the mines were damn heavy and when we started across the current was strong. Martin was tough as they come but I could see he was not at all happy.

'Kafupi,' he whispered to me, 'if I fall in the water and a crocodile eats me you will have to tell my wife please.' I was also nervous because the water was crawling with crocs but tried to be nonchalant. I reassured him, telling him to stay calm and that we would make it across. Once we had stabilised the tubes and got our rhythm going we made good progress and beached on the other side without incident. We immediately hid the tubes, cleared our tracks and organised ourselves and our equipment for the move to the target zone. We walked hard through the night and then laid up quietly the following day.

"That night we went to work. I laid a dozen AP mines which was relatively easy and then got busy on the big ones while Martin kept an eye open for anyone approaching. I used an old parachute with a hole in the middle over where I dug so the soil removed was deposited on the fabric and not on the road where it would contrast with the lighter coloured sandy soil. Once set and buried we sprinkled twigs, grass and leaves around the area where we had been working, cleared tracks with a light brush from a branch and then surveyed our work. Under the moonlight it looked good and we then moved off to lay the second one.

"This was tougher, the ground below was harder and the mosquitos arrived in their millions. It was a warm night and I was sweating heavily while the insects relentlessly attacked me to the point where I wanted to scream. They were in my eyes and ears making it really tough to concentrate on a tricky task where one little slip could spell disaster. I had to make sure the base was absolutely level. The anti-lift device was placed under the anti-tank mine and then the pin was pulled. The bottom of the mine held the lever in place so the moment it was lifted the mine below would explode. Martin and I then carefully covered the devices and swept the area clean. We wasted no time in walking back to the river, inflating our tubes and floating back to Rhodesia with no problems.

"A week later Bob Warren-Codrington called me into his office.

'Just to let you know,' he said, 'we have a report that two of your AP mines were detonated.'

CHAPTER SEVEN

'Oh Ok,' I said but I was a little deflated. Then he continued.

'They then sent a convoy of vehicles to collect the wounded and one of the anti-tank mines was detonated.' That brought a smile to my face but then he looked at me slightly strangely.

'After that they brought a Russian engineer up from Maputo to help them clear the area.

He found your second one and was busy lifting it when he was vaporised.'

Then he went back to his maps and I left the office.

"As I walked away, I was then approached by a sombre looking John Murphy who brought me the terrible news that my friend Andy Chait had been killed during a camp attack in Mozambique. This knocked me hard. Andy was such a great soldier, and I struggled to understand how anyone had managed to get the better of him. But they did; maybe he was just too aggressive, but he was one of the best I have ever worked with.

"I remembered the first time I met Andy soon after joining the SAS when we were deployed to Macombe in Mozambique while the Portuguese were still in control. The Portuguese kept changing their minds about whether we were allowed to engage and kill the enemy or if we had to limit our activities to surveillance. This irritated the hell out of Andy who was itching to kill any terrorist he could get near. When we were told we were going out on a 14-day patrol but we were not to kill anyone, Andy came over to me.

'Well Kafupi, he said, 'if we can't shoot them let's just run them down and grab some of the bastards and fuck them up.' I just looked at him in disbelief, but he was deadly serious."

Darrell at School of Infantry October 1977

In the middle of 1977, Darrell Watt was summoned before SAS CO Brian Robinson and told he was being dispatched to the School of Infantry on a three-month Potential Officers Course (POC). The SAS was critically short of commissioned men and Darrell would help fill that deficit.

"Through my years in the army I had worked under a lot of officers who I thought were pretty useless," remembered Watt, "so it was with mixed feelings that I packed my bags and headed off to Gwelo and the 'College of Knowledge' as it was jokingly referred to in the military. I expected to listen to a lot of hot air and to be lectured at by instructors and officers who had not gained a lot of operational experience. It would be a time of traditional soldiering with all the normal spit and polish routines and time on the parade ground which did not interest me much.

"The moment I arrived there I hated it and wanted to be back in the bush. Because I was from the SAS and known as a seasoned combat soldier, they went for me in order to humiliate me. RSM Collier seemed to have a special vendetta against me. On the parade square, he would just look at me and shake with anger. Then he started poking his pace-stick hard in my ribs while he had his sidekick, Sergeant 'Fundie' Hatfield, who was the course senior NCO, screaming in my ear.

"I had just come from fighting the enemy and been dealing with serious hardship and was in no mood for being called a 'useless, hairy-back SAS gorilla,' and a 'useless cunt' by people I had no regard for. If I had been a recruit it would have been different, but I was not a recruit. I was already struggling with my temper when Collier told Hatfield to march us 'on the double' but my mood worsened when Hatfield was told to halt us. I came to attention as ordered and then Collier singled me out for more abuse and came right up to my face, screaming at me while jabbing me in the ribs again with his stick. I'd had enough. I broke ranks, closed with him and stared him in the eye.

'If you poke that stick in my ribs one more time Sir, I'm going to take it and break it over your fucking head!' I warned. There was a complete silence; nobody had heard the RSM spoken to like that before and Collier got such a fright he was also lost for words. Then he recovered his composure and ordered Hatfield to march me off the square and to bring me before the CO to be disciplined.

"I was marched off quickly and ordered, under Hatfield's supervision, to stand outside the office of Major Pat Hill. Hatfield, again, tried to impress the RSM by ordering me to double. I stopped in my tracks and turned to Hatfield.

'Listen,' I said, 'you're a fucking jam-stealer who has never heard a shot fired in anger, and if you carry on like this, I am going to give you a very severe beating any moment now.' He knew I meant it and went very quiet.

"At the Major's office, in went Collier and Hatfield first to tell Pat what a bad boy I was, and they came out looking very flushed. I then went in and could see the Major was in a difficult position, but I had had enough. I was very frank.

CHAPTER SEVEN

'Sir,' I said, 'I am sorry about this, but these people have no respect for operational soldiers, and I mean what I say. If they don't stop harassing me, I am going to fuck them both up. It's just that simple.' The Major told them both to leave me alone, and that was the end of their nonsense.

"Not being a man who reads or writes a lot, I did not enjoy being back in the classroom listening to a lot of theory, some of which I did not understand and most of which did not seem to apply to the war that I was fighting, so I became even less interested.

"It was against this background of boredom, that I was excited to hear there was a real emergency as a result of a Zipra attack on the town of Gokwe and there were not enough troops in the area to react to it so we were called upon to do the follow-up. There were 15 of us on the course and among that lot were some excellent soldier's including Ant White, Piet van der Riet and Bruce Fitszimmons. They were just as pleased as I for the break in listening to the lectures. Also involved were all the Admin and Stores NCOs and officers; most of whom were overweight, unfit and pretty useless as combat soldiers.

"We grabbed our weapons and equipment and drove through the night arriving in Gokwe in the morning. Soon after sunrise, I found the tracks we needed to follow almost immediately. With Bruce, Ant and Piet in support, I knew it was just a matter of time before we caught these guys and was looking forward to giving them a good hammering.

"Once on the tracks, it was pretty easy to read the spoor, I was in a hurry for action and set a fast pace. I knew the 'jam-stealers' were not going to be much use but even I was surprised to see them peeling off before we had even left the outskirts of the town. Absolutely useless. And some of these guys were supposed to be teaching us how to fight and win the war!

"It was not that long before there were only seven of us who could stay the pace and we left the rest of them to eat our dust. The guys from the Selous Scouts were all in good shape and up for the fight. We were on fresh tracks of 15 Zipra, led by a tough guy by the name of Wilfred Masoja, a Tonga, who we had tried many times to kill or capture on raids into Zambia. To their credit, the Zipra guys were fit and strong and they kept up their pace heading towards Lake Kariba. After two days of tracking we were close, but we had still not engaged them. I was happy to keep tracking for as long as possible to stay out of the classroom back at the School of Infantry.

However, the line of flight was well plotted and choppers, including a 'K Car[39]' carrying RAR troops aboard, intercepted, spotted the group and went into action. Unbeknown to me at the time, my cousin Roger Watt, a chopper pilot, was about to get involved and Wilfred, the Zipra commander, was going to rally his men and stand and fight with courage and skill. This is Roger's story."

"On the morning of 18th May, my flight engineer Rob Nelson and I loaded everything into the chopper and set off for our new base in Chirisa National Park. About ten minutes out, we heard that an RAR follow up group had contacted the terrs and was calling for more trackers, as well as a casevac for two slightly wounded men. I acknowledged the call, landed at base, refuelled, unloaded our personal gear, and took off with four game rangers who were to be relief trackers.

"We arrived, dropped off two of the Rangers, but the third told me he had spotted something in the bushes as we were coming in to land, so the four of us; two trackers, Rob and I went back to check. Suddenly, as we were climbing, the bush beneath us came alive and the sky was filled with green tracers. I could feel the aircraft taking hit after hit as I desperately pulled power to get out of range, and at the same time tried to bring our twin Brownings to bear on the enemy.

"I remember seeing the altimeter at 1,200 feet then suddenly the aircraft filled with white smoke which turned black and was pierced with flame. I closed both fuel controls and started an autorotation. At this stage, everything seemed to slow down. It seemed I had all the time in the world to make decisions.

"Firstly, where to land? There were two obvious places, the dry riverbed or a ploughed field close to a deserted village. I chose the ploughed field. Secondly, I saw that the flames were being affected by the rotor-wash and were passing through the interior of the aircraft in a clockwise direction. In operations we always flew with both rear doors and the front left door off, the pilot's door being the only one fitted. I decided to jettison this door to enable me to exit faster when we got down. As I reached for the lever, I saw that both trackers had climbed out to escape the flames and were standing on the step outside my door so I didn't jettison the door. I believe this decision

---

[39] Normally the controlling helicopter on fire-force deployment carrying the operational commander and armed with a 20 mm canon.

CHAPTER SEVEN

actually saved our lives, as the flames were blocked by the door. I undid my seat belt. I could feel the back of my neck and my left arm being burnt and by unstrapping I could move forward away from the flames. Looking back I could see that the rear wall of the chopper had been burnt through and I knew that just behind that were the control rods to the main rotor. If the rods were burnt, then the controls would be useless and I would not be able to land the aircraft. I was either going to die on landing or survive and be trapped in the burning wreckage. I remember my left arm burning but I knew that if I took it off the collective there would be no chance of putting it back into the flames in the final moments. As it turned out, I made a near perfect forced landing in the ploughed field, with just slight forward speed. The nose wheel dug in and the aircraft tilted forward and then settled back on all its wheels. The burning fuel then washed to the front of the cockpit and my hands, face and legs were burnt. As the aircraft nosed in, I was in a detached frame of mind. I heard someone screaming (which must have been me) and from then on I do not remember anything else until I was rolling on the ground outside the aircraft to put out the flames. I then stood up. The two rangers had survived the landing. I moved towards the chopper to fetch Rob but one of the rangers said he had jumped from the aircraft while it was about 300 feet up.

"We stood a moment, pulling ourselves together and then realised that the ammunition was exploding so we moved away taking stock of the situation as we went. We had only one rifle and one full magazine among us and we knew that there was a fairly large group of terrs nearby. We decided to try to reach the village, which was on higher ground. We would have some shelter there if we needed it. At this stage, the shock began to wear off and the pain came in great waves. There was not much shade from the sun, or cover from the terrs. After about 15 minutes we saw, to our horror, that a group of men with black faces, was approaching the still burning wreck. We prepared for trouble but they were game rangers.

"They didn't have any morphine but they went and fetched water from the river for me and for one of the rangers whose arm was also burnt. I spent the rest of the time pouring water over our burns. Rob's body was also found and brought back to the village.

"Forty-five minutes later, the two Hawker Hunters that had been scrambled from Thornhill arrived overhead. Using the RAR corporal's radio, I told Rob MacGregor, who was leading the flight, what had happened. After a wait of about five hours, which seemed forever, a chopper arrived, having come all the way from Wankie. We were flown to an airfield nearby, where we were met by an Norman-Islander fixed-wing with a doctor on board and flown to Salisbury.

"I spent just over three weeks in hospital, where I was really well cared for. I declined a skin graft on my left arm deciding that I had had enough pain already and that I would rather live with the scar, which is now barely noticeable. The game ranger had a skin graft on his left arm. The three of us were very lucky."

"Wilfred Masoja, the enemy machine-gunner, had done what the Russians had taught him to do and Roger was on the receiving end," says Darrell. "He had spaced his men out in a triangular formation, told them to stand their ground and let rip on automatic despite the K-Car pounding them. We were lucky there were not more like him.

"Only after we arrived back in Gwelo, after this contact, did I hear that my cousin Roger had been shot down. I decided immediately to go and see him. The officer commanding that day was irritated when he heard about this and asked why I had not sought permission to leave the barracks. I replied that I'm not going to ask permission because I've just seen just how useless he and the other course officers are and I'm not going to bother myself. He said nothing because he knew I was right. I had had enough of them all and I have no doubt the feeling was mutual. Despite all the problems I was commissioned in October 1977."

Enemy capture.

Robson continues: "Following my first deployment and our lucky escape from the Rhodesian enemy we were very relieved to be back in Zambia and somewhere safe and to meet up with some of our comrades who had also survived being in enemy territory. We were well fed and well looked after and we did some retraining to prepare us for our next deployment.

"Three months later we were taken by vehicle to the border town of Siavonga near the Kariba Dam wall. From there we moved to a small staging camp called Nyamumba Farm. At that point the river is narrow and across the river in Rhodesia the country is rocky and mountainous. Our group of 40 crossed the first night then found a secure position to hide the following

CHAPTER SEVEN

day. Then the next night another group came through and from there we split up again into three groups and started moving south into the Vuti and Urungwe Tribal Trust Lands. I was the officer commanding our group of 40. Our task was to politicise the people and explain to them what we were trying to do. We were also ordered to mine the roads used by the police and military and we were told to plan an attack on the convoy that moved daily from Salisbury to Kariba.

"There was plenty of *dagga*[40] available in this area, so I had to be strict with my men to stop them smoking too much. We carried radios but at this stage we did not use them. Unlike our previous deployment, the local people were very friendly and very supportive of our cause so we felt secure in that we knew our informers would warn us if enemy troops came into the area looking for us and give us time to move to safety.

"We had some successes with our mines and several vehicles were destroyed on the road to Binga. We also spent some time watching the main Kariba road preparing to ambush it and do as much damage as possible but on the day that we got into position, for some reason, the convoy never came past us so that was a failure. But then more reinforcements arrived and we were tasked to move closer to the bigger towns and show our forces to the local people so that they could see that we were growing in number and would soon be in a position to take over the country. At this time, we heard that groups were coming into the country with anti-aircraft missiles. Eventually I was told there were six groups that had the weapons.

"The town we were told to focus on and attack was Gokwe. A successful attack on the town would send a message to the people that we were strengthening our position in the field. We set off, moving mainly at night. I was happy to have with me, my machine-gunner, Beans, armed with his PKM, Tokarev pistol and RPG rocket launcher. He was a big strong guy and very brave under fire. We wore our green fatigues but also carried a pair of blue jeans to wear when we wanted to avoid being too obvious.

"One night on the journey, we slept near a village and listened to the dogs barking then in the morning we heard the cocks crowing. We stayed in our position for a day and then the next morning I sent Shumba and Fani to go and approach the people and ask them to help us with food and water. They never returned. I never saw these two men again and have never

---

[40] Cannabis

discovered what happened to them.

"Near Gokwe, we were met by another group led by Richard Ngwenya whose numbers had been reduced through contacts with the enemy but we were all happy to meet up again. That night, with food and beer from the villagers, we celebrated seeing our comrades again and sang some 'Chimurenga songs' but maybe we made too much noise and were heard by the enemy?

"The basic idea, after discussions with our commanders on the radio, was to demarcate the zones each group would operate in and increase our numbers to move closer to the towns. The plan was to get all the different groups in the area together the following day, to discuss our future plans. We were awaiting the arrival of the third group led by Assaf that morning, and waiting for some young girls to bring us water when suddenly the terrible sound of helicopters approaching was heard, and then gunfire and we were again under serious attack.

"The war started, and we returned fire as soon as the helicopters and Hawker Hunters appeared on top of us. A Lynx was circling and putting in strikes while we saw paratroopers being dropped in two positions. The bombing continued and suddenly I was hit by a blast and went flying. I was shot and received shrapnel, one between the ribs near the heart, one in my hand and one in my leg. Everyone else around me was killed or captured but I and my friend Lameck Gondo managed to hide until nightfall in a cave and then that night we walked about 20 kms non-stop until dawn. I was in a lot of pain, but I knew we had to get a long way away from the scene of the action or their trackers would have time to follow and find us and probably kill us.

"Two days after being wounded, we were very hungry, I had lost a lot of blood, my wounds were infected and swollen and I was in agony; I did not feel I had the strength to carry on much longer. We laid up on a small hill which was near a village. In the morning my wounds were so bad that I could not walk so I sent Lameck to a village that was close to the hill to look for food and medical attention. Unfortunately, Lameck's Shona was bad and the people there were Shona speakers so when they heard him talk they were not interested in helping and the Headman ran away. Lameck returned with the bad news and we worried that these people were going to report us to the police or army. We had no option but to move to another location

CHAPTER SEVEN

immediately. By this time, I was desperate and together we approached another village and aggressively demanded assistance. On seeing my blood-soaked clothes, the old man there was very sympathetic with us and took us to a hiding place in a hill which was near his home.

"However, the treatment I got was 'traditional African medicine' made up of leaves and bark soaked in water. This mixture was inserted into the wounds and it was very painful. Unfortunately, this only made my situation worse and my wounds became badly inflamed and lots of pus came out of them. I felt sure I was going to die of my wounds and lost consciousness. I vaguely remember seeing a white man with a big red beard before I passed out.

"When I awoke, I saw I was in hospital on oxygen and a drip. Because we had intentions of going back to Zambia, I thought I was there. Then I noticed I was in leg-irons and shackled to the bed, so I was alive, but also in trouble. I did not know it then, but I was in the Selous Scout Fort in Bindura. Selous Scouts trackers, led by Pete Clemence, had caught up with us and I had been captured and taken by helicopter to Bindura."

Op Virile

By the end of 1977 Selous Scouts commander Ron Reid-Daly was lobbying hard to have the RLI, SAS and most of the Selous Scouts switched from internal operations to permanent deployment in Zambia and Mozambique and tasked with the reconnaissance and destruction of externally-based insurgent camps. He knew all too well that using the country's best troops in a defensive role was a recipe for failure.

The enemy build-up across the Mozambique eastern frontier was continuing apace and the border town of Espungabera had become a very effective launching-pad for Zanla insurgents. To the south there were large concentrations of enemy personnel on the coast at XaiXai, from where they were being transported north by road or rail to Barragem. From Barragem, the Frelimo Brigade HQ for Gaza Province, they had been compelled to move on foot to Malvernia or Pafuri following the successful sabotage of the railway.

Reid-Daly was a frustrated man. As early as 1975, as Frelimo was preparing to take power in the country, he had dispatched Major Bert Sachse to Umtali to do an appreciation of the looming threat along the country's eastern flank.

"Unlike the *Operation Hurricane* north-eastern border area, good roads inside Mozambique ran parallel to our border along the eastern flank," remembers Sachse. "Logistically it was ideal for the development of enemy activity and it was a golden opportunity for them to open a new front, stretching our defensive capability even further. I recced the whole area after the Frelimo take-over in 1975. It was obvious that this part of the country would soon be in the forefront for Zanla's attention as some of the richest tea estates, farms and forestry enterprises in Rhodesia were situated there. And close by were heavily populated tribal areas; prime targets for subversion and recruitment into enemy ranks. Our view was that as it was impossible for us to protect the border so we should therefore decide which areas were vital to our survival and which offered the best killing grounds. Having reached a decision and selected the best localities for this purpose, we should then work to funnel the infiltrators into them. The best kill-zones were, without doubt, the Mtoko area and the areas around Umtali where we had had good successes. Both consisted of savannah country, dominated by hills that offered good Observation Posts (OPs) for locating guerrilla groups and for guiding in fire-forces.

"I proposed we immediately 'freeze'[41] the areas around most of the potential entry-routes north and south of Umtali so we could deploy our pseudo-teams and give them time to get settled in with the populace. By the time the enemy started to infiltrate we would have our informants on the ground, and we would be ready for them. Ron was fully supportive but the war in the east of the country was still in its infancy and the police were still under the mistaken impression that they alone could control the growing threat. Added to this, there was some resentment towards us in the army and particularly towards the Selous Scouts. The police felt we were treading on their turf.

"I eventually ended up having to seek support for this move from Angus Ross, who was then the senior BSAP Special Branch officer in the Manicaland Province. The SB man felt our methods might alienate the population. He was also naively of the opinion that Frelimo would now act responsibly and avoid any conflict that would be to the detriment of the people and the country. I could not convince him that with only a few

---

[41] A 'frozen' area was cleared of all other military activity to allow Selous Scout 'pseudo-groups' to infiltrate the area and gather intelligence.

CHAPTER SEVEN

men, whose pseudo identities would be revealed to only a few selected contact-men, we could successfully study the whole area under the guise of being Zanla commissars preparing the way for the insurgent onslaught and acquire the intelligence we needed to plan ahead. I hit a brick wall with him. He was adamantly opposed to the idea and insisted this was a police matter and the police would be handling it. Basically, we should mind our own business. Ross was supported all the way up the police chain of command and unfortunately the military hierarchy were not assertive enough. Looking back, this decision was a watershed moment in the war. As a result of it, the enemy soon entered the country in large numbers and by the time we were called in to react and address the problem, they were too well established and organised. We had lost the all-important initiative and we never really regained it.

"Somewhat strangely, Ross, who was said to be headed for the top in the BSAP, suddenly resigned his position and left the country to settle in the UK. I strongly suspect he was a British agent and his frustration of our tactical plans was deliberate and carried out on orders from his spymasters in London. All this happened at the same time as Mugabe and Tekere were being safely seen out of the country to safety in Mozambique by Dan Stannard. Looking back, I wonder if maybe Ross was needed by MI6 in London to manage the political rise of Mugabe and summoned home for the task immediately at hand?"

Thus it was, by late 1977 the situation demanded an immediate and effective response to the flood of insurgents into the country. Reid-Daly wanted to mount a large operation to inflict as much damage as possible on Mozambican road and rail communications, causing a major disruption to the enemy logistics infrastructure while trying to force them to infiltrate north of Umtali up to Mtoko. His plan was to retake control and force the enemy to react to Rhodesian initiatives rather than the other way around.

In his view, the first step was to neutralise the road from Chimoio to Espungabera by sending in a column to destroy five bridges and to this end he approached General Walls directly because Reid-Daly knew all too well that ComOps, with Flower at the fore, would block him on the basis that these were economic and not military targets.

When General Walls was told the action would put the Chimoio road out of commission for over a year, he threw his weight behind the plan and gave Reid-Daly a thumbs-up. Named *Operation Virile* it was scheduled to commence on Sunday 20th November 1977 with Bert Sachse in command.

Captain Charlie Small, a Cambridge University-trained engineer, was given the responsibility for blasting the bridges. From information he gathered from air photographs he was soon able to determine in advance, and to calculate with great accuracy the precise quantity of explosives required to demolish each target. The total figure was calculated at six tons. Scouts, all experts on demolitions and detailed to assist Charlie, included Chris Gough, Jim Lafferty and Rich Stannard.

Prior to the incursion, a mortar troop was to be pre-positioned on the slopes of Mount Selinda inside Rhodesia. Their task was to keep the 400-man Frelimo garrison at Espungabera occupied for the duration of the crossing. Air support was to consist of two helicopters, a single K-car and one G-car to be used for casevacs. In addition, two Hunters were on standby and two Lynx spotters were made available.

The plan called for the column to be broken down into three separate groups. First was the advance guard commanded by Major John Murphy, the main force under Sachse while another American officer, Captain John Early, would take charge of the rear-guard.

"About a month earlier, having no knowledge that *Operation Virile* was being planned I had been summoned to the office of Major Neil Kriel," remembers Stannard. "He was poring over maps and air-photographs. Without going into too much detail he ordered me to hook up with Dennis Croukamp and prepare to do a recce of the road from Espungabera to the town of Dombe some 60 kms south and report on all enemy positions and movement. It was urgent and I was told to be ready to go the following day.

"Dennis and I were then taken to a point on the border near Mount Selinda where we were met by a guide who led us to the border into enemy territory through a series of rolling hills towards the road. I remember it was deadly quiet on the way in and we anti-tracked all the way. The only sounds came from the grasses whistling in the wind and the call of the occasional nightjar. We reached the road and walked south noting it was rutted in parts but looked fine for four-wheel drive vehicles.

"The only excitement occurred while moving carefully off the road to adjust my pack I was suddenly confronted by a large figure approaching with a huge sack on his back. I was getting ready to shoot or hide when I

CHAPTER SEVEN

realised he was unarmed and simply a thief carrying stolen tea from the tea-estates in Rhodesia. We stayed still and let him pass us by.

"Two days later we had covered some but not all the road, but it appeared to be in good enough shape for our vehicles and we headed for home. On getting back to HQ, Dennis submitted the report indicating the road was fine.

"When orders were given, I was placed in the group commanded by Captain John Early tasked with blowing the bridge over the Buzi River as one of the first objectives to be achieved on the incursion. John was a Vietnam veteran where he had served with Special Forces and been heavily decorated. He was also an expert free-faller and had been my instructor on my recently completed course. I had made life a little difficult for him at the closing stages when the officer commanding the training school came to check on our progress. He was a very serious guy and was watching Dave Berry and me very closely to see if we knew what we were doing. Approaching the door of the old DC 3 at 12,000 feet I whispered to Dave.

'Let's jump out of this like hooligans and give him something to think about.' Dave smiled and out we went acting like clowns much to the dismay of the OC who immediately admonished John. John was quick to tell him we were competent and that he intended to pass us.

'But did you not see how they left the aircraft?' he asked. 'It's completely unacceptable,' he huffed and stormed off leaving John with a wry smile on his face.

"Another great American, 'Big John' Murphy would lead the vanguard. He was an ex-recon Marine, who had recently transferred to the Scouts and he was very popular. He had already become well known for his 'recce by fire' tactic. He liked to lead from the front in his armoured transport and lay down heavy fire into likely cover and flush the enemy.

"In overall operational command was Umtali-educated Bert Sachse who I respected, having worked with him only a few months previously on a mine-laying task south of Malvernia. On the Malvernia mine-laying operation Bert and I went with Rory Beary who was also from Umtali and a tough operator. Our task was to lay anti-tank and anti-personnel mines alongside the railway. We approached our target at night and placed the APs first, then got to work on the big TMH 56 anti-tank mines and it was tough going because the ground was like rock and I really battled to dig

MEN OF WAR

deep enough. I eventually buried them but ran out of time to attach the anti-lifting devices and booby-trap them. Once done I made my way back to the main group just as dawn was breaking.

"Job complete?" Bert asked.

"Yes, completed Sir," I replied.

"No sooner had we had this exchange than the earth shook and there were two ear-shattering blasts, followed by furious machine-gun fire and screaming soldiers. Their reaction was extremely quick, and Bert quickly had us on the run, humping our packs, 'legging' it out the area with all possible speed as they tried to outflank us. Somehow, we escaped their clutches. God knows what they would have done to us had they cut us off as they were very angry!

"Bert had been commissioned at Sandhurst and had then come back to Rhodesia to join the RLI. He was awarded a Bronze Cross for bravery during *Operation Cauldron* where he silenced a machine-gun nest that was pinning his troop down by using a rifle grenade and then routed the enemy in a very successful contact. He had gone from the RLI to the SAS before joining the Selous Scouts where he was held in high regard.

"Charlie Small was a lovely guy with a sharp wit and unassuming way about him. He was a real expert when it came to demolitions and I sought his advice before the operation. When I asked him to help me calculate how much explosive I needed for the Buzi Bridge he listened carefully. 'How much have you worked out you need for your pier-footing and abutment charges?'

I gave him a figure, he looked at me, adjusted his glasses, deep in thought.

'Okay, double it,' he said.

"I immediately followed his advice and increased my load to 12 tons which I would carry in my vehicle. Prior to the attack the Motor Transport Yard had been a hive of activity with Cecil Link managing the men hard at work on getting the vehicles armed and ready. Cecil was a towering figure with his big, bushy beard and beaming eyes, and he directed much of the mechanical work. The key guys in sorting the vehicles were the TF Scouts who came from an engineering background who came up with all sorts of clever ways of arming the trucks and improving the protective pieces. A home-grown Stalin Organ was produced, and the Mercedes Unimogs

CHAPTER SEVEN

were fitted with 20mm Hispano cannons poached from the air force after decommissioning of some of the old Vampire jets. Not a pretty sight, they were known as the 'Pigs'. John Murphy's vehicle was a Berliet that had been stolen from Frelimo, known as 'Brutus'.

"There was also an old passenger bus which had been modified to accommodate a 12.7 mm machine gun on the roof. It was hidden behind camouflage that had been disguised as suitcases. A 50 mm Browning heavy machine-gun was mounted at the rear and the windows had sliding screens. The bus inside was crammed with hairy Selous Scouts kitted out in Frelimo uniforms armed with AKs, RPDs and RPG-7 rocket launchers. Because of the economic sanctions, equipment and weapons available to the military were in short supply so captured materiel was badly needed and used extensively. 'Uncle Ron' would pop in every now and then to survey the scene and encourage the guys. The excitement was palpable.

"We loaded up at night and the entire column left in darkness and motored through to the former Hot Springs Leisure Resort. Hot Springs had been a popular holiday destination, visited by thousands of Rhodesians but had been forced to close because of the war.

"The men were pumped for action and excited but not for long; soon after arriving we were told the operation was postponed. It came as a big blow and in a sulk, we took to sitting in the shade of the vehicles brewing tea. What we did not know at the time was a big combined RLI/SAS attack was about to be launched against the main enemy base at Chimoio. It appeared ComOps were worried that if we went ahead it might cause the enemy to vacate Chimoio camp or alternatively put the camp and Frelimo on a higher state of alert and endanger the attackers.

"Once the attack, *Operation Dingo,* had commenced on Wednesday 23rd November, we were told what was happening. It involved 88 men of the RLI, 97 men of the SAS and every aircraft the Rhodesian Air Force possessed, including some of the old Vampire jets which were brought out of retirement for the occasion. The operation was a big success. One thousand two hundred guerrillas were killed for the loss of one Rhodesian soldier, SAS Trooper Frans Jacobus Nel. One Vampire pilot, Flt Lt Phillip Haigh, was also killed when trying to crash-land his jet in a field after his aircraft was damaged by ground fire. Twenty-four hours after this attack the Rhodesian forces emplaned and flew north to launch another attack, this time on the Zanla base Tembue located north of the Cahora Bassa Dam, 225 kms from the Rhodesian border. Unlike Chimoio, kills there were very disappointing. These two raids caused havoc with enemy morale and their desertion rate rocketed as a result, throwing them into a state of massive administrative chaos.

"We listened in to the action on our radios and I imagined my SAS mates fighting hard through the thousands of enemy troops. I must confess I was envious and a little frustrated. I occupied myself by checking all my lines of Cortex and the detonators.

"It was therefore with much relief that Captain Early came to tell us we had received permission to 'go'. To confuse any enemy informers, and they were all over the place, we left Hot Springs on the 26th November and moved to Chipinga before going to a launch point 12 kms from the border. Having done the original recce, I moved ahead of the main column with a guide to help me. Before we approached the frontier, the engineers cleared a passage through the minefield. Then, at first light, the column gingerly picked its way through and took an old disused track for some 12 kms until it cut into the main road leading from Espungabera to Chimoio.

"The risks remained high; not only because of the strong Frelimo garrison at Espungabera but also because there were many pocket-sized Frelimo detachments based along the road we were taking. We knew that Frelimo at Chimoio were in a high state of readiness after the recent attack and, since they had not been touched by the Rhodesian forces this meant that their Russian-supplied T-54 tanks were intact, ready to range out and maul us at will.

"Our concern was that if the Frelimo at Espungabera launched a speedy follow-up and chased us up the road before we had knocked out the first bridge over the Buzi river, and the garrison at Chimoio got warning in time to move their armour south to intercept us, the column could find itself trapped between two numerically more powerful forces, and with no escape route available to get them back to Rhodesia. For this reason, it was vital to the plan that the Buzi river bridge north-east of Espungabera was demolished immediately after entry into Mozambique. Having achieved this, a strong rear-guard would be left in position to hold the escape route open while the column advanced at best possible speed to grab the northernmost bridge, which crossed the Mabvudzi river just south of Dombe. This was the

CHAPTER SEVEN

approximate half-way point on the Espungabera-Chimoio road. Once there, they would launch the advance guard north of the river to hold Frelimo at Dombe while Captain Charlie Small and his demolition team got to work on the bridge. Then, as soon as the bridge was ready for blasting, the advance party would cross back and then the bridge would be demolished. This tactic would be followed at each of the remaining three bridges in succession as the column withdrew to Rhodesia and safety. We expected to be operational for two days.

"Having joined the main road, the advance guard and main column went into defensive laager while we, under Captain Early and consisting of six vehicles, drove off at best speed to blast the bridge over the Buzi. On the move, we signalled the 10 RR mortar-team to commence 'stonking' Espungabera in order to draw Frelimo attention away from us, a job that they did very effectively.

"As we approached the bridge, we came under very heavy fire but our 12.7s and 20mm cannon went to work and the sentries were either killed or put to flight running for cover in the dense riverine where they continued to fire on us. Ant White and his guys got busy and dealt with them and we were able to get on with our task. Most of our force then took up defensive positions on the northern side of the river.

"We then set about the heavy lifting and carried the tons of gelignite from the vehicles on to the bridge. I waded into the river and set about attaching explosives to the pier in the middle and John did the same on the other side. The water was deeper than expected and adding to our problems, machineguns opened up on us and rifle grenades exploded nearby. It was not a nice feeling being up to your chest in water with bullets splashing close by. Some of the surviving sentries had looped behind Ant White and had opened up on us from the other side, but it was not long before Ant got his cannon going in their direction and that silenced them.

"Having completed the laying of the charges, Captain Early then joined me in rigging up Cortex ring mains from one pier to the next. Word then came over the radio from Major Sachse telling us to get moving and get the hell out of there. Once all the vehicles were across the bridge on the north side, we quickly offloaded about two tons of explosive which we placed on the surface of the bridge close to where it joined the road. With everything in place, I readied the fuse while John headed north at speed. As soon as

I was a safe distance, I let it go and the explosion was incredible, sending a shower of stone and concrete high in the sky that rained down on us for about 30 seconds. The Buzi Bridge was down and there were four to go.

"We quickly joined the main column and Major Murphy continued further north to Dombe while we in the rear-guard took up defensive positions along the road to await their return. We halted in the vicinity of a small business centre and I happened to spot a fuel depot so went to investigate and was pleased to find plenty of fuel waiting to be turned into a fireworks display. I quickly set about laying explosive charges among the drums and holding tanks, then warned the rest of the guys that there was going to be an explosion telling them to take cover. All went quiet and then it was like man-made thunder with the blast providing an amazing spectacle as a huge black mushroom cloud billowed skyward, darkening the sky. The loud bang had our ears ringing for a good five minutes. Then there was a silence, followed by the loud booming voice of John Murphy over the radio.

'What the fuck was that?' he asked. I quickly explained it was just a couple of old fuel drums that needed attention and he went quiet.

"At this time he was heading towards Chimoio with the civilian bus in front packed with heavily armed 'hairy armpits' in disguise trying to look like friendly black civilians while some of the guys were lying spread-eagled on the roof hiding behind fake suitcases just itching to start firing. Unfortunately, the bad condition of the road made speed impossible and John was unable to maintain a decent distance ahead of the main column. Standing by overhead were the two Hawker Hunters if the column got into serious trouble.

"The first enemy response was when an RPG-7 rocket exploded on the road in front of the truck carrying the explosives. The men on the luggage-laden roof-rack of the bus pulled the flaps back and let the ambushers have it before pulling to the side of the road to allow the two 'Pigs' to pass and neutralise the ambushers with their Hispano cannons, which they did with ruthless efficiency.

"Once through the ambush area the column was re-formed. No casualties were reported but Bert Sachse realised they had now lost the benefit of surprise. Frelimo were angry and in aggressive mood, so the Hunters were summoned and they belted any targets that presented themselves.

"That afternoon John Murphy moved close to Dombe town after the

CHAPTER SEVEN

Hunters had battered it and stood vigilant while Charlie Small went about his business. As soon as Charlie was done, he signalled and John and his group moved back over the bridge. When they were clear, Charlie 'hit the tit' and the bridge crumpled into the river. They then headed back to Gogoi with John taking up position to the south and Bert to the north.

"Soon Charlie, Bert Sachse, Chris Gough, Jim Lafferty and their teams were back at work and it was hard physical stuff because over three tons of explosives had to be moved. They toiled until the early hours of the morning, hampered by the fast-flowing waters below, and just after sunrise the biggest bridge ever blown by the Rhodesian army was reduced to rubble.

"That afternoon, 30 kms past Gogoi, the column reached a road construction camp. Bert and his men went to look and found a fleet of large United Nations supplied vehicles that were being used for Zanla transport. Bert called Uncle Ron up on the radio to tell him he had found a total of 17 five-ton tipper trucks, two monster D-8 bulldozers, three similar-sized road graders, three CAT construction tractors, and two road rollers as well as a parts store containing at least a quarter of a million dollars-worth of spare parts.

"The place was completely deserted. Due to the United Nations' sanctions, we in Rhodesia were unable to source this sort of machinery and equipment and our country's Roads Department was making do with vehicles which would often have been better suited as museum exhibits. This stuff would be a bonanza for them.

"Bert asked for guys from the Rhodesian Corps of Engineers to be flown in to check the vehicles and equipment and decide what best to do with it, but permission had to be obtained from ComOps. They turned the request down initially so we went to work laying charges to destroy the equipment when Ron came back on the radio. ComOps had changed their minds and a team of technicians was being flown in to help with the 'liberation' of the vehicles. All that could be moved was taken, and it was all much appreciated back in Rhodesia. Unfortunately, the almost new bulldozers were deemed too slow and had to be destroyed along with everything else left behind.

"With all the newly 'acquired' equipment, the convoy now stretched over a distance of some five kms, making it considerably more unwieldy, slower and a lot more vulnerable. Ron asked Salisbury for the Hunters to be sent back to provide air cover but this was turned down because they said their ammunition was in short supply. Ron was furious so they relented and sent the jets which was a huge relief. On the last leg of the operation on the way out another bridge was dropped and more graders were 'acquired' for the Department of Roads at home. We crossed the border back into Rhodesia on the morning of the 30th November.

"As a result of this raid, Espungabera was totally cut off from its support base at Chimoio and would henceforth be supplied by porters bearing loads. It was also reported by our signal interceptors that the armoured brigade at Chimoio, despite frantic pleas for help from Espungabera, had declined to assist. The Chimoio raid had sent them scurrying into cover and they had decided to stay there.

"In accordance with the plan, Bert left two separate 'stay-behind' groups to monitor the aftermath. Slowly, hidden vehicles showed themselves again and the teams went back on the offensive and destroyed them. The bigger targets were strafed by Hunters and soon the bewildered enemy were back to walking. What came as a surprise to the guys left behind was the arrival of local tribesmen who appeared, uninvited, carrying food and gifts to express their delight at what we had done to Frelimo! They told the blokes they missed the Portuguese and hated their new government under Samora Machel.

"Our guys were also asked to give the people medical attention which they did, using what little medical supplies they had. It was not long before people started trekking in to see them with all sorts of ailments, begging for treatment. There had been no doctors or medical facilities available to them since the Portuguese had left. Considering that the Selous Scouts were all white men it seemed incredible that all they encountered was friendship and kindness. Clearly the local people were ready to take on Frelimo and it's a pity our superiors did not seize on this opportunity earlier than they did."

Working with Schulie

"During my time in the Scouts, I only did one operation with Schulie. He was a perfectionist and he expected the same from the people that he worked with. One mistake with him, it did not matter where you were, he just sent you packing. On this occasion, I went with him into Mozambique to monitor enemy vehicle movement coming out of Mapai and to call in air-strikes. He gave me all the heavy stuff to carry so it was hard going all the

CHAPTER SEVEN

way and the simple mistake of making too much noise when you stepped on a dry leaf could get you into a lot of trouble.

"We went in at night after a very short briefing and after that no more talking. We made it to a position on top of a hill from where we had a clear view of the road and waited for traffic. All was quiet when he whispered in my ear about going to look at a bridge and I thought this was to be a quick look at something but he slipped away very quietly and three days later I was still sitting there, picking my nose, contemplating the rancid smell of my body odour. I must have missed the sound of his bird call or something but he suddenly appeared out the bush and I nearly soiled my pants I got such a fright. I was too nervous to say anything to him.

"Finally, the monotony was broken by the appearance of a vehicle convoy and I was very excited about the immediate prospect of calling in the Hunters which were on standby to put in an airstrike. But not Schulie.

'Can you see weapons?' he whispered.

I looked hard but could not, but I was thinking what the fuck does it matter? We've been here a week, been driven nuts by Mopani-flies, and these must be gooks or people associated with them, so let's blow them away.

Schulie was unmoved. He studied the potential target through his binoculars, then he spoke.

'Richard,' he whispered, 'I think they are civilians and God will not be happy if we kill them. I will only kill people carrying weapons.' And that was that. I looked on forlornly, my finger aching on the trigger, as the vehicles passed us by and went back to swatting flies.

A few days later, another vehicle approached and appeared to break down in front of our position. People clambered out the cab and went to work on the engine. In a flash Schulie was gone. He said nothing to me; just one moment he was there and the next he was gone. A few hours later he returned and reminded me that wherever you position yourself the first issue you must sort out is an escape route. He had already done this, and that was the route he followed the moment he felt there was a chance of being discovered.

"He was extremely fastidious and I became too frightened to move for fear of doing something that would anger him. On one occasion he saw me turn a leaf as I took a step and he gave me a serious dressing down. At night

I did not move from my sleeping position if I needed a piss. I just rolled over where I lay. When the rain came down, rather than move to a sleeping position, I just lay down right where I was in the rain and got drenched rather than make a wrong move. Although we did no damage I must have done alright in his eyes because when we arrived back at base he spoke to me.

'Rich,' he said, 'you should be an officer. I think you must go back to get your commission now. Just stop fucking around. I'm going to speak to Uncle Ron and tell him I think it is time for you to go back to Gwelo.' This he did, and sure enough, I was called to Uncle Ron's office and told I was being sent back to the School of Infantry.

"Meanwhile, my schoolmates from Umtali Boys' High were dying. 'Spider' Webber was a good friend in Crawford House and had a wicked sense of humour. His mom lived in Chipinga where she had a trading store. He was probably twice my height with the longest legs in the cross-country team but I used to give him a damn good run for his money, although I never actually beat him. He became one of the best long-distance runners in the country. Like me, after school he went to join Internal Affairs, and again like me, he grew restless and went to the army but straight onto SAS selection, which he passed and was 'badged' in June 1973.

"He joined the regular army, married his schooldays sweetheart, Jodie Smallman, and then went on an officer's course which he passed, being commissioned early in 1976. From there he was posted to the Rhodesian African Rifles as a 2nd Lieutenant, where he served with distinction.

"While on operations in the south-west of the country, Spider and a small RAR section were on tracks of a Zipra gang who had abducted a soldier from his village during his leave. They followed them relentlessly for four days until the spoor took them into a village where they were ambushed by the gang they were tracking, and Spider went down in a hail of bullets. He was only 23 years old. He left his wife and two young daughters who would never get to know their father. It was 7th September 1977. A very good man died that day.

"A few days after Spider was killed near where his family lived, Mike and Marinda Glenny of Melsetter were ambushed. They were in a vehicle on the Highlands tea estate near Silverstreams when they came under fire but they escaped to a nearby factory. They survived, but unfortunately, they arrived

CHAPTER SEVEN

home too late to save their six-and-a-half-month old baby daughter Natasha. She was murdered by a group of 20 Zanla. When the child's nanny saw the group approaching she immediately put the child on her back and tried to cover the head in an effort to conceal the child's colour. When they saw the baby was white she tried to convince the men she was an albino but to no avail. They ripped baby Natasha from her nanny's back and bayonetted her to death. The maid then received a severe beating and needed to be hospitalised. Just after this happened, the Reverend Andrew Young, who was the United States Ambassador to the United Nations and the man appointed by President Jimmy Carter to deal with Rhodesia, spoke in glowing terms about Mugabe. He described him as a gentle person, incapable of killing and totally incorruptible. It was sickening reading how anti-Rhodesia all these politicians were."

"A week after the Glenny murder, 'Sokkie' Barnard and Jopie Coomans, two much-loved members of the community who farmed nearby, were

Bravery award recommended for nursemaid

ONE of the most heart-warming things about the recent tragedy when a baby, Natasha Glenny, was bayoneted to death at her Chipinga farm home 10 days ago was the outstanding bravery of the nursemaid who tried to save her charge—and now women leaders in Salisbury hope that she will receive recognition.

Mr Mike Hogg, an advertising executive involved in planning the Harmony campaign, and leaders of the Women's Institutes and the Women's Voluntary Services of Rhodesia all consider that this largely unsung African heroine deserves the highest praise.

A Chipinga resident last week telephoned me to ask what was being done for the unnamed nursemaid.

"Fortunately she has been taken to safety by the authorities. She had to receive medical treatment after the injuries she suffered during the beating. But so far few people seem to realise what her brave action might mean for her and her family or can guarantee that she will not suffer for it later," said the Chipinga caller.

"Naturally her identity must be kept secret at present. But surely her name should go forward for one of the civilian decorations for bravery, on the same lines as Karen Hughes was given an award for her actions during the Woolworths bombing?"

According to all reports, the nursemaid left in charge of baby Natasha, only child of Mr and Mrs Michael Glenny, rushed to save the baby when terrorists appeared on the Chipinga farm.

She risked her own life by strapping the child on her back, threw a cloth over its head and pretended that Natasha was her own baby. She even went further and risked more by telling the terrorists that the baby had been born an albino, when the terrorists discovered it was a white child.

That took cold courage and was a tremendous risk for her.

After the terrorists snatched the baby and bayoneted it to death they beat the nursemaid so severely that she had to be taken to hospital, said the Chipinga resident.

VERY LUCKY

"All of us in this area hope she will receive special recognition. She couldn't have done more if it had been her own baby."

Mrs Jean Smith, president of the National Federation of Women's Institutes of Rhodesia, agrees.

"She was very lucky to escape with her life. She was a very brave girl because she could simply have disappeared when the terrorists came instead of trying to save the baby," said Mrs Smith.

"I personally think that she deserves official recognition of her very brave actions."

Mrs Phyllis Ovenden, secretary-treasurer of the Women's Voluntary Services of Rhodesia, said: "It would be a wonderful idea for her to receive a civilian award for bravery and I am sure all WVS members would agree that something should be done to see that she gets one."

Mr Hogg said he believed there was an "incredible" amount of latent goodwill among races in Rhodesia, as this brave action showed.

"I would think it a very good idea to give some recognition to her deed, even secretly if necessary," he said. "If she was so brave she has the same right as a soldier to be awarded a decoration. This is a positive aspect of harmony between races here that should not be overlooked."

Decorations of this nature take a long time to go through official channels and if one is awarded to this African nursemaid it might not become publicly known for a long time.

INVESTIGATED

But a spokesman for the Prime Minister's Office said: "This matter is being investigated. We are conscious of what is going on in these circumstances."

The only other African woman in Rhodesia to receive a decoration for bravery in 1974 was elderly, widowed and crippled Mrs Herene Motsi. Mrs Motsi lived with her sister and nine grandchildren in the Mrewa area when their village home was struck by lightning and set on fire. Although she had lost both legs below the knee she dragged six of the children to safety and was later awarded the Meritorious Conduct Medal for bravery.

– 147 –

ambushed and killed travelling back from Umtali. Sokkie and his wife Daphne had been ambushed in the same vehicle a few days before but they refused to give up and leave the farm they loved. Sokkie was old Rhodesian stock; his family having come to the Eastern Highlands with the Moodie Trek in the 1890s. I was at school with the two sons, Jannie and Andre."

Back to School of Infantry

When I got there the only people that were happy to see me back were the batmen. They had grown new hairstyles in the fashion of the gooks and were very pleased with themselves. I heard from them and other people that most of the instructing staff were of the view that I was simply not officer material and they would be very happy to fail me. It was not a great way to start but I told myself I had to do the best I could because I didn't want to let Uncle Ron down. I also wanted to prove something to myself.

Initially I was back on the regular officer's course and really struggling with going through pretty much all the stuff that I had done before. With the war raging, I couldn't help but think it was such a waste of time having me off operations doing stuff I had already done. So it was a great relief when a request came through from Ron asking that the process speed up and that I be placed on the shorter territorial officer's course. This was agreed to and two months later I was commissioned a full Lieutenant into the Selous Scouts. It was a very proud day for me and life was good because I was in love with Sylvia and we were planning on getting married.

Chapter Eight

We have ridden the wave of destruction
Known combat's wild free power
Fed on the drug of life renewed
Amid the smoke and the flame.

♦

Pseudo Operations

Tembue.

"Martin must have been one of the hardest-working of all the Selous Scouts and his tasks were always tough ones," recalled Stannard. "July 1978, we received word of another big enemy build-up in far northern Mozambique and Schulie, Martin, Tim Callow, Sergeant Aaron Jele and a fifth Scout called Newton, were tasked with being dropped in to do the recce. By this time, as a defence against attacks, the enemy had learned to spread out widely and avoid concentrating in numbers where they were more exposed and vulnerable."

"With this entry," remembers Tim Callow, "we could not drop our normal safe distance of about 30 kms from the large target due to time constraints. We were always concerned with patrols from the enemy camps hunting for food, which the gooks were always short of. All we knew was that the then Prime Minister, Bishop Abel Muzorewa, was due to meet President Carter in America and for some reason known only to ComOps the timing of this attack was tied to that meeting. As a result, we were instructed to jump as close to the target as possible, move to the target ASAP, as intelligence was very limited on the camp and area, which the planners needed for the planning of the attack. We usually had aerial photographs of the target and drop zone (DZ), and we normally were able to speak with any capture (related to the target), that the BSAP SB held. This was imperative to each operation that we executed, as we needed target intelligence that affected us on the ground and not just SB strategic intelligence requested by ComOps. Unfortunately, in this deployment this was not to be, due to the 'hurry factor'. Each day, once deployed, we were updated on this meeting date, as it kept on being delayed which under the circumstances was certainly exposing us to a greater risk each day,

"On the night scheduled for the drop the moon was not sufficiently full to give the pilot enough moonlight to navigate accurately. Freefall entry had been rejected because any navigational error would have made it tougher for us to reach the target and get the job done in time. We decided to use a low-level static-line parachute entry, just before last light. Aerial reconnaissance had tentatively pinpointed a total of seven camps dispersed over a large area.

"Schulie's team, with Newton, went out the door first and Aaron and I a few minutes later after ensuring that we were not jumping into kraals or any populated areas. After landing, we concealed our reserve rations and radio batteries, then moved across country to take up our different positions. Two days after insertion, we were in our positions overlooking the base area. I was with Aaron, but Schulie, Newton and Martin operated singly so as to spread the eyes over the biggest possible area. We were soon disappointed in that we did not see the enemy numbers we expected. However there was activity and we noticed all the anti-aircraft guns were manned and ready for action. Because we did not locate the large number of enemy we expected, ComOps decided to delay any attack and we were ordered to stay where we were and just keep observing.

"In the meantime, we noticed that enemy patrols were frequent and that they looked aggressive so we were on top of our game making sure we were not picked up. But they bumped us. Ten days after landing in the area a large, heavily armed patrol flushed us out and we had to move fast. We took up another position 150 metres away to the north but on checking my kit I realised I had left my radio behind. I waited a while, then slipped back to recover it but as I came over a rise I was greeted by a hail of hot lead. Aaron and I pinned back our ears and legged it straight down the side of a virtually perpendicular mountain. By the time I met up with Aaron later that night at our crash-RV, my ankle was the size of a football. I thought it had been broken and I had to use a stiff stick to hobble along. Moving to the RV with Aaron we happened to walk through another camp complex, which was deserted at the time, with sign of recent occupation. We also met up with Newton who would return with us. Having linked up, we moved out of the

CHAPTER EIGHT

area at speed and radioed for a hot extraction which came the following day. With the enemy alerted to our presence, choppers were prepared to extract Martin and Schulie, but they decided to remain in the area.

"The camp returned to its normal activity very soon after we had extracted. They must have assumed that we had all left the area and had no eyes on them. The reports indicated the enemy was still there but dispersed all over. Campfires at night and smoke from early morning cooking fires enabled them to pinpoint the bigger concentrations of fighters."

After 11 days alone, the two Scouts were running low on food and water and decided to meet back at the original drop zone to replenish supplies from the cache they had left there. They met in the dead of night, had a quick exchange of news, grabbed what they needed and moved back to their observation points.

Three weeks later, the two were still there and, although ComOps found it hard to believe, so was the enemy. After much deliberation an attack was finally ordered that would follow the normal form of an air strike followed by the para-dropping of stop groups and assault troops immediately afterwards. André Rabie Barracks was used as a staging post for this operation, which saw the whole of the RLI and the SAS living in bivouacs next to the airstrip to preserve security.

The attack went in early the following morning but confusion regarding radio frequencies in use led to a breakdown in communications between the two Scouts on the ground and the air force. This led to missed targets and paratroopers being dropped too far from the camps which reduced the number of enemy casualties but once again the enemy had received a bloody reminder that nowhere in Mozambique was safe for them.

"After the operation," remembers Tim, "Winston Hart (BSAP SB), informed us that our entry had been compromised from the beginning as we had been seen parachuting in by a hunting party. He learned this from a capture. Thereafter, unbeknown to us at the time, the majority of the camp inmates immediately moved out and camped by the side of a major road about 20 kms from the target.

"After our return I had to attend a debriefing at ComOps and just in case Schulie and Martin needed another re-supply, I was tasked to do some HALO training jumps with Newton following a 'supply-box'. If it was called for Newton was going to be the man going in. With my ankle still in a bad

MEN OF WAR

way my boss Neil Kriel organised a staff car to be left at my house which I could use until I could walk properly. I was then called in to see Uncle Ron who told me in no uncertain terms that I was not a Lt Colonel or indeed a unit commander and I was to return the car. I said, 'yes sir' and carried on using it like any good soldier would. I was then told by the Scouts second in command to return 'that fucking car or my other ankle would be broken'. Guess what? It was done!

"Finally, Jake Harper-Ronald, our intelligence bloke at Neil's forward HQ, who was quite an artist, drew a cartoon with the caption 'Them not baboons, Comrade, them Rhodesians'. This was because Aaron thought that he had heard baboons just before we were whacked.

Good friends die.

On 30th April 1978, a 16-year-old schoolboy Derick Hattingh fought off a gang of terrorists at the family farm Watchfield in Glendale not far from Salisbury. The attack, by a big group of heavily armed terrs, began in the early evening. Unfortunately, his 13-year-old younger brother Johan

CHAPTER EIGHT

was outside at the time and he was killed as the firing began. Derick then armed himself with an automatic weapon but before retaliating, he carried his aging grandfather to a place of some safety in an alcove. He then saw some terrs outside a window and accurate fire put them to flight wounding at least one in the process.

A PROUD Derick Hattingh (17) is congratulated by the Prime Minister's wife, Mrs Janet Smith, soon after being awarded the Meritorious Conduct Medal at an investiture ceremony at Government House, Salisbury, yesterday. Derick received the medal for fighting off a gang of terrorists which attacked his family's farm homestead earlier this year. Looking on is Derick's mother, Mrs Lslie Hattingh, and younger brother, Ronald (10).

"The following month in late May 1978 I heard about the death of Charles Olivey who was senior to me at school but well remembered as one of twins," remembers Stannard. "His dad John was a one of the legendary Rhodesians who turned the Long Range Desert Group into the incredible fighting force it became in the Western Desert in WWII. He was a founder member, captured and escaped from the Germans, being operational from 1939 through to 1945 and awarded the Military Cross.

"After the war, he returned to the family farm in Melsetter and as a lay minister, he helped build the first Anglican Church St George's - in the mountains near the village. Charles was a prefect and being a big guy, played lock for the Umtali 1st XV before going to the army. He did a Leadership Course and became a sergeant based at Kariba. When he went into the Reserves he was commissioned as an officer in 4th Battalion Rhodesia Regiment. After doing a course at Gwebi Agricultural College he returned to the family farm with his girlfriend Shelagh Page, a Rhodesian hockey player.

"Following a spate of land mines on the road to the farm, Charles went to assist a mine-clearing team when he hit a mine and died instantly. Another sad loss of a great Rhodesian.

"In June 1978, we were told almost 40 missionaries throughout the country had been killed by terrorists. None of us could really understand this because most of them were supporting the terrorists and yet they were being murdered for their efforts. On the 23rd terrorists killed all eight missionaries and their four children at Elim Mission in the Vumba. Before becoming a mission this was Eagle Preparatory School, where many of my friends went to school. Another missionary would die of her horrific injuries a few days later, making it 13 deaths in total.

"When I heard of these killings, I always wondered how my friend John Bradburne was getting on near Mtoko which by this time was riddled with 'gooks'. Most of the farmers in the area had been forced to leave but old Jack Tarr who I knew from my time there, refused to go. Almost 70, he remained there with his black dog, Judy. He knew they would come for him and they did. When he heard Judy barking he called her but she went for the gooks and they shot her. They had already killed all his sheep before coming to the house. All Jack had was an automatic shotgun but he took them on and killed one and wounded at least one other before the army arrived.

Peter Bouwer 13th July 1978

"Mid July 1978 I heard about the death of Pete Bouwer, another great school-friend. He came from Rusape and was a world-class athlete, breaking all the records at school and in the country. He was particularly brilliant over 400 and 800 metres. Unlike me, he was conscientious and clever but we got along so well and he used to chide me for being badly behaved. While I was not as good as him on the track, I was doing well as a swimmer and hoping to represent Rhodesia. Pete used to urge me on, saying if we keep training, we'll both get to represent the country; him on track and me in the pool. Unfortunately, I was chucked out of school before we could achieve that. Pete was there to say goodbye and wish me well when my dad

CHAPTER EIGHT

came to collect me. But Pete made it into the Rhodesian Athletic team in 1971 and there's no doubt, if he had lived in a different time and place he would certainly have been an Olympian.

"After some time in the army he married his childhood darling, Sharon Mason and they went farming in the Tengwe area near Karoi. They had had two sons when a Zipra gang arrived and Pete was murdered.

Going Pseudo

"Back in the Scouts as an operational officer I was anxious to try my hand in pseudo-operations. While I had always enjoyed doing reconnaissance work, the Selous Scouts had really come to prominence in the field of pseudo-operations and I was itching to give it a go so I was really excited when given permission to join Jim Lafferty's 'Nine Troop'.

"Jim was ex-SAS who had come across to join the Scouts soon after the unit became a reality and he was a highly respected operator. Known as 'Pops', he was Rhodesian born but of Irish extraction; calm and quiet when sober, but when on the booze he liked a lot of trouble. Invariably, he would select the biggest man in the bar and then diligently set about antagonising him until a fight started. Unfortunately, Jim always ended up in a bad way but he never learned. Once, after having been thrown bodily down the stairs of a nightclub by the bouncer, he still picked himself up, dusted himself down, then painfully but gamely climbed back up the stairs to start the next round.

"The other problem with Jim was that he spoke in whispers, so you had to listen carefully and after a few beers he went even quieter to the point where we gave up trying to hear what he was saying. He was an RSM's worst nightmare; he took bad dress to the highest level and was averse to any limitations on hair growth. When it reached a totally unacceptable length, even for the Selous Scouts, Uncle Ron suggested that he go and get himself a handbag and that seemed to get his attention, but his hair was always unruly.

"On operations he became a totally different character. Imperturbable, brave, cunning, he had a tremendous rapport with his African soldiers and although it seemed alien to his basically aggressive nature, he never raised his voice to them. They viewed his drunken escapades with much amusement, but they were always genuinely sympathetic when he appeared back at barracks, battered and bruised after another night on the town.

"The Selous Scouts pseudo-groups were, in the main, led by European NCOs and officers, while the men they led were a mix of regular African soldiers and former terrorists (TTs) who had been 'turned' in one way or another and integrated into the regiment. This was always a tricky manoeuvre but one that, with few exceptions, was carried out successfully. Without these guys the Scouts did not have sufficient knowledge of how the enemy was operating and this would have been a major constraint in ongoing covert operations. In order to successfully 'turn' these men to the Rhodesian cause it was imperative that, from the moment of their capture they were afforded the best medical care and were treated fairly. Mac McGuinness, operating out of Bindura Fort ran this important part of the recruitment process. Once these guys were successfully recruited, they were rigorously interrogated by the Special Branch officers who would squeeze every drop of information out of them.

"It was mid 1978 when we were ordered to deploy into the Chiduku Tribal Trust Land about a hundred miles (160 kms) due east of Salisbury. This area bordered on European farmland where farmers had been suffering a spate of terrorist attacks. On arrival, I was extensively briefed by BSAP Special Branch Inspector Ken Milne who was then one of the intelligence officers based at the Selous Scout Fort in Rusape. Ken went into great detail explaining to me what they knew of the enemy *modus operandi*; which Headmen were collaborating with the enemy; how they were transmitting messages; where the drop-boxes were; and which villages were feeding and supporting the enemy. He had a lot of information at his fingertips but the bad news for us was that most of the population in the designated area was totally supportive of the enemy and this was the reason it was proving so difficult to find the terror groups operating there. Added to this, information to hand indicated a large group of about 50 well-trained, heavily-armed, aggressive terrorists had recently moved into the area and they needed to be found and dealt with as a matter of urgency. The only way to flush them was through the successful deployment of Scouts disguised as terrorists who could establish their whereabouts and then call in a fire-force to kill them. I found all the background information most interesting and did my best to digest and retain all that was passed my way.

"The Selous Scout contingent at the Fort was under the command of Bruce Fitzsimmons who was another early member of the regiment and

CHAPTER EIGHT

also a very experienced pseudo-operator. The other Special Branch man in residence was Gordon Buck but the most commanding presence within the Fort was Gordon's pet pig which pretty much ran the show. A massive porker weighing in at about 300 lbs this sod had the run of the place and woe betide anyone who got in the way of that damned pig.

"After a few days preparing at the Fort we were ready to go. I had seen quite a lot in my time as a soldier but these black Scouts or 'Skuzapo' as the locals called them, were a very scary sight indeed. Most of them were big men, heavily bearded, swathed in grenades, rockets and ammunition pouches, their long black hair hung off their heads in unruly dreadlocks and their wrists were ringed with big bracelets. Wearing a mix of blue denim and East German standard issue camouflage they were armed with AKs and RPDs and each section had a rocket launcher and mortar. But what set them apart from anything I had ever encountered was the smell! These guys stank in a league all of their own and I wondered if just scent alone would betray our presence in the area but was assured I need not worry.

"With Jim running the show on the ground, we deployed in two sections at night under a bright moon into rugged country broken up by black granite hills shrouded in beautiful Msasa trees. Small streams flowed out of the hills. On the walk-in we made good, uneventful progress into the target area until we reached a pre-determined point where I was tasked to peel off from the main group with two TTs and climb a high hill topped with trees from where we would commence our observations at first light. Jim's two groups would then proceed to start infiltrating the local community posing as 'comrades' in order to try and gather the intelligence we needed to locate the enemy in the area.

"My two TTs were Sam and Nelson, both former Zanla terrorists trained in Tanzania and Mozambique. Sam was a little taller than me, quite a bit older with a relaxed demeanour and he liked to talk. Almost immediately, he set about telling me about African customs and how the rural people live their lives which I found very interesting. While I had lived in the country all my life, like many of my white compatriots, there was a lot we didn't know about African culture, their spiritual beliefs and their basic way of life so it was a good time to learn.

"Nelson was much younger, more boisterous and spirited and less thoughtful than his counterpart. He was quite cocky and I wondered if he might become a bit of a handful but that all changed when I asked him how he had been captured. He immediately went very quiet and became a little sheepish. A little lost for words he looked away and I watched him gazing at the hills in the distance when I heard Sam chuckling behind us and this got Nelson's attention.

"The fact is, the life of the Zanla terrorist was not all blood, sweat and guts. These guys were masters of the domains in which they operated, and they were treated like kings. Some of this, I suppose was due to the fact that they were seen as heroic fighters, but it also boiled down to the power of the gun; they were armed and dangerous and would not take no for an answer. While the young males, the *mujibas* in the area concentrated on surveillance of the area watching out for Rhodesian forces, the *'chimbwidos'* the young females, were there to provide the fighters with water and food and to provide sexual pleasure on demand. Nelson had obviously been too busy having his sexual needs satisfied when surprised by a patrol and captured literally 'in the sack'. He was not at all proud of this fact and was visibly embarrassed in the telling.

"When the pseudo groups went into the villages they would very often do so when the light was failing, particularly if there was a European as part of the detachment. Bad light would make it harder for the locals to notice the different facial features that would give a white man away and blow their cover. Very often the European commander would carry the radio they would use to transmit any important information. At times this had to be done very surreptitiously and no call-signs or formal identification was used. So, as it turned out, it was about 10am on the second day that we had been in our position when I heard a blowing sound come through on my radio. I pressed the switch and whispered, 'go ahead over'.

There was a whispered reply from the call-sign commander:

'We have had a contact and one Charlie-Tango killed, unknown number wounded.' He told me that they had been opened up upon by a group of Zanla but none of his guys had been hit. He told me they were on tracks and trying to re-engage the enemy, but I was to keep an eye out for any movement below. He gave me a grid reference which I noted and went to my maps to plot the position of the contact. Once I had established where they were, I summoned Sam and Nelson and told them I wanted to go and investigate.

CHAPTER EIGHT

"We did not have far to go before we found where the contact had taken place and the body of the dead terrorist. We relieved him of his weapon and ammunition and I then told my guys we needed to get back on to higher ground again so we could look for any enemy movement.

"The three of us quickly climbed a nearby hill and no sooner had we reached the top than I heard an urgent whisper from Sam behind me and was motioning to us to get down quickly and hide. No sooner had I hit the ground than I looked up and saw a large group of about 30 terrorists in extended line sweeping the area searching for us. I brought my rifle to my shoulder and took aim at one of them and was sorely tempted to squeeze the trigger when I saw Sam slowly shaking his head indicating to me that I should not fire. I eased off the pressure, it was obvious they were too many of them for us to deal with and it was better that we let him be in the hope we would be able to find them later and then call in the fire-force. After combing the area for about 30 minutes the group abruptly changed direction and disappeared. We remained very still, and as soon as the sun went down, I moved our position to another nearby hill with a panoramic view of the valley below. Despite the best efforts of another section of Scouts operating below us they lost the tracks and the Zanla group disappeared into the foliage and, to our great disappointment, vanished, at least for the time being.

"A problem then arose when one of the sergeants in the pseudo-team reported sick, needing to be casevaced with tick-bite fever. This was an unwelcome development because calling in a chopper would compromise us, so I had to make another plan. I checked with him and he said he definitely wanted to be extracted. I contacted Bruce at the Fort and they said they would send in a civvy vehicle at night so as not to attract attention and we arranged for the sergeant to be picked up at a point on the road into the Tribal Trust Land (TTL). Travelling at night in those areas was extremely dangerous. The chance of hitting a mine or being ambushed was high. But Bruce was not frightened of much and he said he would be coming in. With the help of three others they helped the sick sergeant to the road, being careful to try and hide tracks on the way and to my relief the vehicle arrived safely. But after all the effort, the sergeant suddenly changed his mind and decided he did not want to be uplifted after all. After all the risks that had been taken on his behalf, I was absolutely furious and when I arrived back at our position I lost my temper and slapped him. This was completely out of order for an officer to behave in this way, but I simply lost control of myself. I was under a great deal of pressure as it was, and something flipped that I could not control.

"When the situation simmered down I decided there was nothing for us to do but simply stay static on our kopje and keep watching for signs of enemy movement. The tedium was broken for me by Sam who took the time to help me identify and understand the different behavioural patterns of the people in the villages below us. And this is where I realised that black troops were able to perform at a level that was beyond the soldiering skills of most Europeans. They alone knew the nuances of everyday life in these communities and only they were discerning enough to notice when something unusual was taking place which demanded further investigation.

"Five days later, despite our best efforts, nothing was happening and I was bored stiff when Sam suddenly gave me an urgent but gentle nudge, handed me the binoculars and pointed out a small village complex which he wanted me to have a closer look at. I knew he had seen something but had no idea what. I aimed the binoculars, looked and searched and hard as I tried nothing caught my eye. A little irritated, I returned the glasses with a blank stare and a dumb shrug but I could see in his eyes he had seen something that I had missed.

'Look, Kafupi' he said urgently, 'look at that *chimbwido* who is carrying that can of water on her head. She has just gone into her hut and changed her dress and is wearing something brighter and prettier. She's getting ready for her lover. And look at that other woman who is going in a different direction; she is carrying food in that bag, I saw her fill it. They are going to feed and please the 'comrades.'

He could barely contain himself.

'Kafupi my friend,' he said with a triumphal flourish, 'the *gandangas*[42] are there now. That group is back and I tell you they are hiding in those trees near that hill.' With that he pointed to a dense thicket, in amongst the rocky outcrops, about a kilometre away from the village of the girl in the bright dress.

"Excited, I watched carefully, and as predicted the girls, following different routes, went into the thicket but did not reappear. Then we saw *mujibas* in groups of two fanning out of the village going in different

---
[42] Shona word for terrorists.

CHAPTER EIGHT

directions, clearly in search of any sign of a hostile presence. All the pieces were falling into place and I became convinced Sam was right, but I wanted to see an actual weapon on a man to achieve the certainty demanded by the hierarchy. Our forces were financially strapped and anyone calling out a fire-force based on an erroneous observation was harshly dealt with. As a result, I was reluctant to make that decisive call that would trigger the dispatch of aircraft and men from Grand Reef Airfield roughly 40 minutes away. I looked to Sam and Nelson for reassurance.

'Are you blokes 100% sure they're in that thicket?' I asked.

'Yes Kafupi, they are definitely there. There is no doubt.'

"I looked them both in the eyes and I was convinced. Now, it was time to get my head around all the questions I would need to answer once the fire-force was unleashed.

I checked my maps, took compass bearings and prepared the exact loc-stat. I estimated the number of enemy at 40 and then checked the wind so as to give them the best angle of approach. I then studied the terrain again and tried to work out the best drop-zone for the paratroopers, where the assault line should form and where to best position the stop-groups to block their lines of escape. The enemy position was well concealed, but the topography also provided opportunities for us to box them in and kill them.

"Once I felt I had covered all the tactical questions that I would have to answer I pressed the pressle switch and commenced my transmission.

'Two-Five Alpha we have a positive sighting', I announced with feigned confidence.

'How many?' came the quick reply.

'About 40,' I answered.

'Have you a positive ID,' he asked.

'Yes,' I lied.

'Standby,' he said.

But I did not have to wait long when word came through that the fire-force was on its way.

With that I started to sweat again.

'Sam, are you bloody sure they there?'

'Yes Kafupi, don't worry they are there and it's a big group I tell you!'

"I looked at him with interest; he had not stopped staring through the binoculars and he was getting more and more excited. I thought to myself, funny how allegiances can change so quickly. Only a short time previously these were his mates and now he could barely contain his excitement as he waited to watch them being killed by the very soldiers that he, Sam, had recently tried so hard to kill.

"I was on the radio talking to the fire-force commander when I heard the unmistakable thumping sound of the Alouettes approaching and knew battle was about to commence. But I was not alone. Almost simultaneously I saw terrified women running out of the trees into the open and racing back towards the villages. They had also heard the sound of approaching aircraft and knew that deadly danger approached.

"The normal complement of a fire-force was three 'G Cars'[43] one K Car (helicopter gunship) with the fire-force commander aboard, one 'Lynx' (fixed wing ground attack aircraft armed with rockets and bombs), and a Dakota carrying 16 paratroopers. The paras had perfected the art of low altitude drops into action but I worried a little about the low rolling hills they might land on and hoped the pilots and dispatchers got their altitude right so the jumpers had enough time for their chutes to open.

"As the choppers became visual, heavy fire commenced from inside the thicket. I could hear people screaming hysterically below and then I heard the 20 mm cannon open up from the K Car. Loud explosions followed as bombs went in and smoked billowed from the trees as I saw the parachutes open and the choppers dropping the assault troops who charged towards the trees with little regard for their own safety. It was a truly amazing spectacle which I thoroughly enjoyed but couldn't help thinking I would have liked to get off the hill and join in the action.

"Then, with the battle in full swing and the excited reports from the stick-commanders as they started the killing, I was suddenly surprised to hear a chopper closing in on our position from behind. Literally out of the blue, it was suddenly on us and no sooner had it been expertly landed on a piece of rock than RAR Major Andre Dennison jumped out with the rotors still spinning. A handsome, swashbuckling, action-man, my eye was immediately caught by the ivory-handled Smith and Wesson 44 Magnum in his holster. But my surprise quickly gave way to annoyance because his landing on our position would likely compromise our position but I had no time to remonstrate with him. He simply looked at me and my two

---

[43] Troop carrying helicopter with four fighting men aboard.

CHAPTER EIGHT

colleagues with some disdain, then turned away, jumped in the chopper and they were gone. It was a damn silly thing to do because our cover was now blown. I think he was just curious to see who had called in the attack and that was very unprofessional.

"Andre was loved and hated and he and Uncle Ron did not always get along. Ron got it in the neck frequently because the Scouts preferred to use the RLI but it was actually the black Selous Scouts who complained bitterly when RAR shock-troops were used. They preferred the RLI which they insisted was a more efficient killing machine than their counterparts. What is beyond doubt, is that Dennison's 'A Company' was an excellent fighting unit and he was a very brave and capable commander but he did piss a lot of people off.

"The good news for me, however, was my first pseudo-operation turned out a big success. I never discovered how many kills but it must have been a substantial number along with a few captures who were taken back to the Fort. We had struck a telling blow in the area and set them back but sadly, not for long, the enemy recovered their numbers and continued to inflict casualties on the farming community right through to the end of the war.

"On getting back to the Fort Ken Milne was all smiles.

'How did you enjoy going pseudo, Kafupi?,' he asked.

'I loved it Ken,' I replied, 'and I so enjoyed my TTs but it's a lot more complicated than I realised. I learned a hell of a lot from these guys and I'll get better at it.'

"Unfortunately, my elation was short-lived. News of me striking the sergeant had spread and there was a very hostile reaction to me. Probably deserved, but worse than I expected. Back at barracks in the pub, I was ostracised by the white officers. A testament I suppose to how close they were to their black soldiers and NCOs. Throughout the Scouts there was an undercurrent which made me very uncomfortable. I went and apologised to the sergeant but he refused to accept the apology. Then the word was that on the next deployment the black Scouts would kill me and call it an accident. I was in a quandary when Uncle Ron called me in to his office.

"'Kafupi,' he said, 'we've got a big problem here I'm afraid, and I don't think it's going to go away.'

"I know Sir, I have tried to apologise but it looks like I'm not being forgiven and it's very uncomfortable out there." Ron looked at me very thoughtfully and spoke softly.

'Kafupi, I think you're a bloody good soldier and a good man. I'm not holding this against you, but I think you must think about going back to the SAS.'

"A lot of other COs would have had me on the carpet, but this was the measure of the man and what made him such a great leader. I knew he was right and accepted the advice.

Last Op with Jim Lafferty

"Before leaving the regiment, I did one last operation with Jim Lafferty in the Mtoko area which was then heavily infested with gooks. I liked being there because I knew the place well from my days in Internal Affairs. Also along were Joe Bresler and Terry O'Leary. We deployed with no problem but Jim, as was his wont, was in a state of utter depression and completely dysfunctional. We moved onto a hill where we settled down while another all-black pseudo call-sign was tasked to move through the villages below and try to gather information on the whereabouts of the enemy. It was ridiculous but we all had to sit there doing nothing until Jim came out of his funk during which he did not say a word to anyone. Eventually, he emerged from his stupor and we were able to go to work.

"The group on the ground were under the command of a pock-marked Ndebele fighter by the name of Merimeri who I was wary of as he had a reputation for being ruthless and distant. He started sending in reports of suspicious activity with lots of *mujibas* moving in a particular area. Jim was on the OP while Merimeri was on the ground trying to pin-point the enemy position. Eventually Merimeri said he had established their position and sent in a loc-stat which was sent on to Passi with a request for a fire-force. Passi explained the fire-force was busy elsewhere, so all he could do was send in Canberra bombers to stonk the target. Very soon the aircraft were airborne and we looked on with interest as they came in on their run and out the bays came the deadly bouncing-bombs. But no sooner had the first blasts been heard, than there were screams on the radio. Merimeri had screwed up his map-reading and our own chaps were being bombed. Miraculously, nobody was killed but it was a terrifying moment and Passi was understandably furious.

"It was the end of my days in the Scouts and it had not ended on a very high note. I was going to miss Jim. One of a kind, the black Scouts

CHAPTER EIGHT

absolutely adored him; he was as close to a white African as I ever saw. Truly a legend of the Rhodesian war."

Catch and release.

"After I was captured near Gokwe," remembers Robson, "I was taken to the Selous Scouts Fort near Bindura, I received excellent medical attention, but I was in a lot of pain and had stitches all over my body. As my condition improved, the guards kept telling me I was going to be executed by hanging. This troubled me because I thought why bother to help me recover from my wounds if all you are going to do is kill me. I kept asking for my friend Lameck Gondo who was also captured with me, but they just told me he was in the cells under interrogations. After about three weeks when I was stronger and able to walk, the interrogations started.

"They never minded the wounds had not healed. In fact the interrogators used those injured places to hurt more so that I would talk. What I was not sure was what Lameck had told them. As it turned out, he had lasted three days, before he broke and told them what they wanted to know, so by the time they started on me I was already compromised. The people questioning me were both black and white, some were hard on me, some were very gentle, but they were relentless, and I was kept hungry and short of sleep. Ken Milne and Mac McGuiness were the two white SB men I saw the most of. I was amazed at how much they already knew about me and us in general, but I refused to talk. At one stage, I heard them talking and someone said, 'this is a tough bastard'. Then they told me that Ethan Dube, one of our senior commanders had been captured and he had explained everything to them. They now knew too much, and I decided there was no more point in trying to lie to them. I then told them my whole story.

"My wounds were still healing when I was flown with McGuinness to Gokwe Rest Camp where the District Commissioner had his office. They had information from other captures, and they wanted to compare it to what I could tell them. We looked at maps and I had to point out the routes we had used, where we had rested, what villages gave us assistance, where we had cached weapons. Then we flew to Bumi Hills and I had to show them every base we had occupied, how we had moved in and out and what locals had supported us.

"Major questions were: 'What was the Zipra mode of operations? How would Zipra approach a village? How do Zipra base up? What was their security codes? Where were they trained? Who were your instructors? Were there any Russian instructors? What doctrine did you learn?' I received a shock when they produced photos of us at Francistown Police Station. They knew a great deal about what we were doing in Botswana and where everyone lived. They seemed to know all about the main people in Zambia and Mozambique.

They had photos of Zipra people which they wanted me to identify and they wanted to know all about the people from the organisation that I knew. We stayed in the Bumi Hills, operating in Chief Mola's area for a month.

"After we returned I was very surprised when they then asked me if I would like to meet their commander, Ron Reid-Daly. I was quite shocked. We had all heard about this fearless man who commands the Selous Scouts, but I never thought I would ever meet him. I was very nervous when being taken to him by McGuinness, but the moment I met him, I knew he was a good man. He was very relaxed and I was asked to sit down and we had a good conversation. He wanted to know more about me, my family, my background and why I had joined 'the other side'. He knew about my training in Russia and wanted to know all about it. He told me the story about Ian Smith being shot down in his Spitfire in WWII and how he had escaped capture by the Germans, thanks to the help of the Italians and become a guerrilla fighter. He commended me on by bravery, and reminded me that we were both soldiers at heart, that we should not be enemies and that we actually had a lot in common in that we both wanted our country to be prosperous and peaceful. I felt very relaxed with him and told him all he wanted to know.

"When I agreed to co-operate I was returned to the Fort at Bindura. We were confined there and told we would be shot if we tried to leave. I was with some other recent captures including Lazarus Hamadziripi, who I remembered from Morogoro Training Camp. But none of us felt we could talk freely about what had happened or what we were doing. There was still a lot of mistrust between Zanla and Zipra and we were all very concerned about what was going to happen next. We were put to work doing menial jobs, like laundry, sweeping the camp, cleaning vehicles and helicopters. For someone who had passed a Russian Officers' Course this was not very pleasing to me, but I did what I was told to do. Then we were told that we were going to Inkomo Barracks outside Salisbury, which was the Selous Scouts HQ.

CHAPTER EIGHT

"We were taken there by Major Neil Kriel to start a new life. We were labelled 'TTs' - 'Turned Terrorists' - and given service numbers along with $40 for toiletries and other essentials. My number was 123477. The fact that I was so fluent in English was pleasing to the officers who were watching us and assessing us. There we started training and I met up again with Peter Clements, who had captured me but also saved my life. Because if I had not been caught, I would have died in the bush and been food for the vultures and hyenas. Because of my good English and the fact I was an officer I was put in charge of all the other TTs and it was my task to report to RSM Mavengere, the Selous Scout Regimental Sergeant Major. From there he would report to the white officers and the SB personnel. Most of the other TTs were Zanla people so it was difficult to get people working together but Ron Reid-Daly had a special way of making us all feel like we belonged there as if we were joining a family.

"Peter and I got along very well and I asked if I could start operating with him. He sought permission and was given the go-ahead and we started planning for my first operation which was to be in the Binga area which I knew well.

"As we prepared to be deployed for the first time, I checked my weapon and was shocked to find the firing-pin had been removed. I immediately pointed this out to Pete. I said we are going to be in a contact soon and you expect me to fight without a firing pin. This was a trick they used on TTs to take them out and watch them in the field first before giving them a weapon that could actually fire. I refused to go without the firing pin and permission was granted for it to be replaced.

"When we deployed to an OP to look out for enemy movement it was a tense time again because of all the mistrust. It was hot and we needed to refill our water bottles. Each one had a turn to go down to the river, but I was forbidden to go alone in case I tried to run away. I assured them I was not going to do such a thing and eventually permission was given to go. I went down to the river and while filling the bottles I looked back up the hill and there was Robson, also a TT, but by this time a veteran. He was watching me quietly and had I tried anything he would have killed me. We soon became good friends.

"Maybe my biggest asset was my command of English and as a result, I was used more and more on the radio which was unusual for the black troops. Then Pete started to teach me the radio procedure for calling in a fire-force which was nearly always done by white NCOs and officers because loc-stats and other details had to be precise and the pilots had to understand what was being said perfectly.

"Early in 1978 more Zipra comrades were captured. These were Vinje Magwadla, Siganacha, Sydney Mlambo and Terrence who was a teacher. They were turned and trained then the four of them joined me for deployment with white and some other black Scouts. We masqueraded as Zipra and went into the villages in search of information. This was highly dangerous work because often the locals would bring out real Zipra men to check us and if there was any doubt, we stood a good chance of being eliminated so we had to be very cautious. The moment we knew where the groups were, we then called in the fire-force to attack and kill them.

"In May 1978 we ran into a serious problem when Terrence disappeared from Inkomo Barracks. All the Zipra TTs were then under suspicion as they tried to find out where he had gone to. I was taken back to Bindura to be questioned and we were all confined to barracks while the investigation was underway. But eventually, I was cleared and back on operations."

The turning of terrorists

"When a capture was brought into a Selous Scouts Fort," remembers Ron Reid-Daly, "the first priority was to give him the best possible medical attention available, for he was often wounded and this sometimes meant immediate surgery. Until this time the only things said to him were concerned purely with his health and physical welfare. The captive was usually astonished to see that everything had been done to ensure his life was saved. And because of this, whether consciously or unconsciously, a feeling of gratitude would begin to permeate his mind. As soon as possible after this, the BSAP SB men attached to the Selous Scouts, both black and white, would get down to talking to the prisoner. This was psychologically the perfect moment for them to commence their interrogation and in nine cases out of ten the information just poured out, almost as soon as they began. The only thing captures were generally reluctant to admit was their involvement in any murders which their group might have committed, but where people in the group other than themselves had committed the murders, they were usually only too happy to speak out. After the interrogation, depending

CHAPTER EIGHT

upon the importance of the man in the enemy structures, his knowledge and his potential 'asset value', a decision was taken whether to recruit him into the Scouts or not.

"We found that the best recruiting method was to send another former 'comrade' to visit him in hospital. He would draw up a chair by the hospital bed and have a long conversation, dwelling in particular upon the hardships they were experiencing in the bush. He would make a point of covering the whole gamut of misery from the harsh environment, the bad food and the harassment by the Security Forces to the hard fact that the latter always won in battle. The savage punishments meted out by their leaders to their own men was emphasised, and also that while the comrades fought and died out in the bush, the leaders lived off the fat of the land in Mozambique and Zambia when not jetting around the world. We tried, if possible, to use a recruiting agent who was already known to the captured insurgent. Often, to complete the initial softening-up process, I would be brought in if available and introduced as being the commander of the Selous Scouts – *'Skuzapo'* – the people the insurgents feared more than anyone. But, astonishingly, I would appear to be a nice friendly chap. The turning itself comprised no magic formula. No one was ever beaten up by his SB interrogators. In fact, the interrogation technique was quite the reverse. It was vital that a trusting relationship be quickly established between the prisoner and his questioner.

"The first weapon in the interrogator's arsenal was that by co-operating and joining the Selous Scouts the prisoner could cheat the hangman. The carrying of arms of war in contravention of the Law and Order (Maintenance) Act, let alone being responsible for murder, carried the penalty of death by hanging. Having allowed him to tentatively distance himself from execution, the next step was for the insurgent to be openly distanced from his old loyalties.

"But first he faced an unenviable inquisition, for no Selous Scout call-sign was ever ordered to take a particular captured guerrilla with them on deployment. He had to make an all-out effort to convince a group that he was trustworthy. If he could not achieve it, it invariably meant a return to custody and the gallows. In pursuing this process, we relied to a large extent on our friends from Special Branch."

"I personally interrogated scores of captures and their response to capture was nearly always the same," remembers Keith Samler. "With few exceptions, one thing all captures had in common was their inability to describe what they were fighting for. In nearly all cases came the parrot-fashion answer, 'We are fighting for our land.'

"When asked what a capitalist, a communist or a democracy was or for the name of their political leader the answer was always 'I don't know'. It was very easy to spot the psychopathic type and these would be handed over for charging and incarceration. Others, especially the wounded, could be turned quite easily. There was no need for brutality although the occasional boxing of ears would be good just to get the issues clear to one and all.

"Wounded captures would be taken to the medical tent and attended to by a doctor, an army medic with a stethoscope and given an immediate injection of a saline drip. They loved injections; the instant cure for all ills. I would give the capture a cigarette. His eyeballs would pop out. 'Where is the noose or firing squad' you could almost hear them thinking. Depending on his injuries, a white waiter would then appear with the biggest plate of food imaginable and a Coke. Questioning would begin a few minutes later and the answers would flow like a torrent. Within 15 minutes I knew if the capture would make a good inductee. Once he had been fully debriefed a couple of black members of the call-sign, both 'TTs', would talk to him. His mouth would drop open when he discovered we were 'Skuzapo' and that he had not been summarily tortured and executed. His turning had started.

"On one occasion a capture from a local contact had been blindfolded and brought in by truck. He was taken to the medical tent and attended to by one of our black 'TTs'. While he was receiving superb medical attention, I was lighting and holding his cigarette for him so he could puff on it. I was wearing East German camouflage kit and a Cuban Forage Cap as were the others in attendance. He was comfortably lodged in a tent for four days where he was debriefed thinking he was back in Mozambique with his 'comrades'. The information we received had a significant impact on internal and external operations. When he subsequently discovered he had been the victim of a gigantic hoax he simply would not believe it. We had to bring in other captures and 'TTs' to convince him. He went on to become a Scout."

"If a 'turned terr' or TT was successful in convincing his future colleagues of his *bona fides*," remembers Ron Reid-Daly, "he'd then be taken out on deployment to prove them. This proof lay in showing the will

CHAPTER EIGHT

and ability to set up his erstwhile comrades for the capture or the kill. Once that had happened, he was compromised and whether he liked it or not there was no going back. Added to all this, the new TT had a sweetener; a cash lump sum for joining the Scouts, and thereafter a good salary. Throughout the process no political question was ever put to him. He was never asked if he supported Nkomo, Mugabe or Smith, for it was a question better not asked. Once in the field the answer was taken for granted, as each man's life was dependent on the others. In truth, his motivation could be compared to the old British military call for loyalty. Not King, not Country, this man, nor that man, but for something irresistible; for a band of brothers and comrades known as a regiment. In our case it was the Selous Scouts.

"The 'turning' was a life-and-death issue for the Scouts in the field, for if they made an error in character judgement and the TT turned yet again, then it would likely cost them their lives. To their lasting credit, only a few mistakes were ever made in those tumultuous times.

"Whenever possible, after an insurgent had turned, we endeavoured to uplift his entire family and bring them back to live with us in the barracks at Inkomo. This had the two-way effect of binding him even more closely to us, and also giving him peace of mind so he could devote himself to operations, secure in the knowledge that the 'comrades' were not exacting bloody reprisals against his loved ones. His family, once they were with us, received free rations, housing, medical treatment and schooling while the 'TT' himself drew the identical salary to a regular soldier, the only difference being that the Special Branch paid his salary instead of the army.

"I think one of the best illustrations of the bonds that developed between these tame insurgents and the regular soldiers, particularly between them and their white group commanders, was the occasion when I discovered that Bruce Fitzsimmons had carried out a cross-border operation into Mozambique, taking with him two African soldiers and seven TTs. I sent for him and dressed him down, pointing out how simple it would have been for his tame insurgents to capture him and use him as their passport to rehabilitation with Zanla.

'Sir,' said Bruce growling through his beard, 'they are my men and I have total trust in all of them.'

"There were occasions when we detected something was not quite right with a tame insurgent. During the early days, one particular TT led 'Stretch'

Franklin right past an enemy camp on three different occasions, which, when we found out, looked very suspicious indeed.

"When an investigation was carried out it was discovered he had been responsible for the murder of two police constables, whose bodies he had disposed of by stuffing them down antbear holes. He had not mentioned this to the SB during the initial interrogation and he had been walking around in perpetual dread, wondering what they would do to him if they found out.

"Winston Hart took him aside and told him that we were aware of what he'd done, but that as far as we were concerned it was all water under the bridge. The Selous Scouts were concerned only with what occurred in the future. He immediately brightened up, changed his attitude and notched up kills.

"We did not succeed with all of them though. A notorious individual by the name of Mabonzo was captured. He had made a big impact in the Op Hurricane area and was becoming a bit of a legend with the locals, who were petrified of him. He was known to be particularly hard on any villagers suspected of collaborating with us. I wanted to see if we could turn him and spent some time with him, but he was totally unrepentant and had no interest in compromising his cause. I respected his commitment to what he believed in and put out some feelers to see if I could save him but to no avail."

"Mabonzo was in a class of his own," remembers Winston Hart. "I was heavily involved in the 'turning' of captured 'gooks' and one must understand by the time it was all over, two thirds of the Selous Scouts were former terrorists so we were pretty good at it. I got to know Mabonzo well and found him fascinating. Formerly a petrol attendant in Shamva, he had come into the country from Zambia initially and his group was decimated by our troops but he survived to fight another day. When he came back into Rhodesia later as part of a second incursion he was a hero. He had the run of things in the Shamva area where he let it be known he was bullet-proof because bullets would turn to water if they struck him. This was thanks to a magical spell that had been cast over him.

"A pal of mine, Hugh Gundry, a vet, was vaccinating cattle in the Madziwa TTL on 17th April 1974 when suddenly the herd parted and there appeared Mabonzo who promptly gunned Hugh down and killed him, so I had an axe to grind with this guy.

CHAPTER EIGHT

"I called in Dale Collett and told him to get to work on finding this bastard. I told Dale I was going to grow a beard and would only shave when Mabonzo was dead or captured. Dale got close but missed him several times but then there was a sighting and a reaction force came in to attack. Mabonzo stood his ground and fired a RPG rocket into one of the choppers killing Major 'Dumps' Addams[44] in the process. However, in the ensuing firefight he was hit in the leg and captured before being brought back to us at the fort in Bindura. On this occasion the bullets had obviously forgotten to become liquid!

"Our doctor, Kavin Staff went to work on him and battled to save his life and he made it after having had his leg amputated. Eventually he was back to good health again but minus a leg when I had him brought to my office. He came in on crutches and we got down to business. I was keen to see if I could 'turn' him. He freely admitted to all the murders he had been involved in and was quite relaxed about it all. He was unapologetic, believing it was all for the cause and perfectly justified. This was very unusual. I then explained that he would hang if we handed him over to the police but he might have an option if he accepted an offer to work for us. He was outraged. 'Not a fuck,' he said, would he work for us. He was quite happy to die. Sod that he was, I had to admire his commitment and courage; he was a rare bird indeed. Ron and Mabonzo used to play lots of Ping-Pong and really got along well. He was one of the few Ron could beat at the game, mainly because he only had one leg. He went off to the gallows undaunted."

"Over the years a considerable number of these tame insurgents approached me with a view to becoming regular soldiers of the Selous Scouts, with a number that did not indicate they were former enemy," remembers Reid-Daly. "They wanted that part of their lives scratched from the record. Our African soldiers were chary about this but eventually I agreed to it. Some turned out to be absolutely first-class soldiers.

"I liked Robson from the moment I met him," remembers Ron Reid-Daly. "The poor bloke had been through a rough time, but I could see he was tough and also very bright and erudite. For him, as with all the chaps we 'turned', it was a tough call but I always tried to relate to them man to

---

[44] Known to his family as 'Damps" and to his military colleagues as 'Doomps'. Other sources state Mabonzo was sniping from a tree and Major Addams died from a stomach bullet wound.

man; soldier to soldier, to get us on to the same wave-length and it normally worked. Thanks to the Russians, he was also very well trained and I thought he had all the qualities of an officer but being a TT, I knew this might be a problem with the African soldiers and so I called in RSM Mavengere to run it past him.

"He came to my office, came to attention, and saluted. I told him to sit down as I wanted to run an idea past him and seek his opinion. He was all ears.

'RSM,' I said, 'I have been watching this guy Robson. He's done damn well in the field, he's bright, he's not slow to take command when asked to and he's popular with the men; black, white, TTs and soldiers. I'm thinking of commissioning him. What do you think?'

His face dropped; he was horrified.

'Ishe,' he cried, 'you cannot do that! If you do, there will be a mutiny among the soldiers! He's a TT and he will never be accepted as an officer by most of the men. Please do not do it. You will destroy the regiment.'

"I wasn't expecting him to agree but I was taken aback by the vehemence of his reaction.

'Mr. Mavengere,' I said, 'the number of TTs in the Scouts is growing all the time and they are doing bloody well. I think it is time for us to show them that really are in this together and they must know, if they shine and have the ability, they too can aim at becoming officers?'

He went very quiet and looked at me thoughtfully. He shook his head slowly.

'I don't think this is a good idea at all Ishe.'

"I thanked him for coming and told him I would think about it. I did give it a lot more thought and it was one of the rare occasions where I decided to ignore Mavengere's advice; I decided to go ahead and do it. I called some of the key NCOs and officers in, told them I had made my decision and asked them to respect it. Robson was duly commissioned into the Rhodesian Army and went on to become an excellent officer."

Chapter Nine

When the war drums rolled and the dark clouds gathered.
Was the time when we ran,
Through the smoke as it rose from the burning huts.

◆

Back to the SAS

Booze and marriage

"The first time I ever saw Sylvia was when I went into 'Petals'," remembers Stannard. "It was a very well-known florist on First Street in Salisbury. I was just one of a long line of soldiers, back from the bush, who had upset his girlfriend and needed to buy some flowers to make amends. As I discovered later, she had met and sold flowers to most of my mates, for the same reason I was in there. She was damn pretty, had a lovely twinkle in her eye and I thought I'd like to get to know her better, but the shop was not the time or place.

"Early 1978, it was a Saturday afternoon at the 'Round Bar' at Le Coq d'Or in Salisbury. It was a complex on the corner of Baker Avenue and Kingsway and a favourite meeting place for the troops back from the bush. Entrance was up a flight of stairs where the poor bouncer positioned himself. From there you turned left to go into the Round Bar and to the right, at night, was a dance floor, where the band played. Another flight upstairs was the Sahara Bar which was a little fancier and a lot more romantic. 'Round Bar' was built around a pillar and on a Saturday lunchtime those were some of the busiest barmen in the country. A buffet was served but most of us were too busy getting pissed to eat.

"This was the 'Swinging Seventies'; we were a bit behind the times in Rhodesia, but it was the era of bell-bottoms, blue-jeans, Elton John boots, mini-skirts, Abba, and The Eagles, *Hotel California* blasting through the speaker in the bar with us all trying (and failing) to sing in tune.

"It was a bit rough at times but hell it had atmosphere. It was also the main watering hole for every SAS, Selous Scout and RLI troopie when back in town. We all meshed together in a boozy mix generally. The Selous Scouts with their mammoth beards looking all grizzly, bronzed and steely-eyed. No missing the RLI troopies; a lean, tough bunch of suntanned teenagers, always up for a fight, some with tattoos badly done by their mates. They had their own jargon, almost their own language; a concoction of ChiShona, Afrikaans and slang from the south, mixed with some Cockney.

'My China,' was my friend. 'My China plate,' was my best friend.

"Howzit ek sê my China?' If you heard those words you knew you were safe. If not, and someone mentioned something about 'cruising for a bruising', it was time to get to battle-stations. They had some serious brawlers including Ray Mordt, who never lost a fight in his life and went on to play Springbok rugby and scored three tries in a test against the All Blacks. A Friday or Saturday invariably ended in a punch-up involving the RLI and bodies would be seen tumbling down the stairs into the streets; then the wailing of the 'B-Car' sirens, attack-dogs would be unleashed and general mayhem followed.

"The SAS blokes generally kept to themselves; keen to be with their chums and chase the girls. They tried to avoid confrontation with other guys but if it came calling, there was never any backing down. Andy Chait and Darrell Watt were two hombres with lethal reputations.

"I'm not afraid to admit, I ran like hell to get away from Chait once. He was a charmer, when he wasn't killing people; the girls loved him, and I suppose we were all a little envious; I know I was. On this particular occasion, he was at his smoothest, chatting up some girls in the 'Stagger' when I decided to be a clever-dick and stuff it up for him. I think the only reason I survived was that he was wearing slip-slops (plastic sandals) which slowed him down and I made it to my old VW banger, fired her up and rattled out in a roar and a cloud of black smoke before he could strangle me.

"On this particular day, the afternoon wore on, I and the rest were getting drunker and hornier and there were lots of good-looking girls around but as they saw it getting rowdier some decided it was time to slip away before the fighting began. I noticed the pretty girl from 'Petals' with shapely legs and a short blue skirt and kept a blurry eye on her. The big chat-up line then was; 'I'm going back to the bush tomorrow and I'll probably die so any chance of a snog?' That hadn't worked for me, so I thought I had better up my game.

"I saw some guy from 3 Commando RLI that I vaguely knew, who

CHAPTER NINE

had been shot in the legs and was on crutches. He was nervous, thinking I might run off with them, leaving him stranded but after we settled on three beers and a packet of chips, he agreed to lend them to me. Somewhere I found a bicycle bell to help attract maximum attention. Then I took off on my crutches into the circle of girls, ringing my bell furiously but stopped in front of 'Petals'. Only up close did I notice the pert button-nose, her auburn hair in soft curls and the blazing brown eyes; she was gorgeous, and I was in love. My chat-up line was I had broken my right ankle doing a night freefall jump deep in enemy territory and needed love and attention. Then being a knob I referred to her as 'Shorty.'

'Who's your shorty, you little prick,' she said; and I loved her even more. But the ice had been broken, she gave me her details and thus began out courtship.

"I was madly in love and we were getting along marvellously when Neil Kriel invited Darrell Watt and I to dinner at the Monomotapa Hotel. The '12 000 Horsemen' was very smart, one of the best restaurants in town, and we were asked to bring our partners, so Darrell brought Gwen and I asked my darling Sylvia. Also invited was Chris Schulenburg but he was single. This was a rare break into refined dining and we were all pretty excited about it. We arrived, decked out in suits and ties and the ladies in their long dresses looked radiant and lovely.

"In those days they said Rhodesian beef was some of the finest in the world and Darrell and I ordered huge rump steaks which were delicious, and the booze flowed fast. Plenty of beer then we got stuck into the wine; Rhodesian wine was not in the same class as the beef, but we drank the stuff like water. Neil was a pretty sober-minded guy and I think he sensed this wasn't going to end well, so he excused himself, paid the bill and left. We had a few more drinks with Schulie and because he was staying in the hotel that night, he invited us up to his room for an ABF (absolutely bloody final). The ladies were not too keen, but we ignored them and dragged them upstairs.

"Once in Schulie's room, the nagging from the women worsened and the more they moaned, the more we drank. I'll never know why, but I suddenly decided to dispatch the furniture out the window starting with a heavy chair which went flying until it smashed on the roof of the Explorers Bar some 12 stories below. With the ladies now screaming, Darrell decided it was a good time to drop his trousers and present his bottom to the world. To get his arse high enough he had to stand on a small table and being so drunk, he wobbled lost his balance and damn nearly went bum-first out the window. Had he not been so strong in managing to grab a hold and claw his way back in, he would have killed himself. Not the best ending for one of the country's greatest fighting soldiers; to die baring his backside to the world outside a hotel window. Schulie just sat there and watched us fools. The women wailed, hugging each other for support while I grabbed a service-bell and started ringing it loudly out the window while shouting 'Ice Cream…Ice Cream!' Then Schulie spoke very icily above the din.

'Kafupi and Darrell, drink up now - fast,' he said calmly, 'because I've called the police and they're on their way.'

We both knew he wasn't bullshitting; we quickly gulped down the remaining liqueurs and Darrell shouted 'run'!

"Out the door at speed we went with Drambuie liqueur running down my chin. We headed for the fire-escape with our poor ladies bringing up the rear, knowing the cops would come up the escalator. Darrell shouted to the ladies to drop their high-heels for increased speed during this real time 'escape and evasion' exercise. We ended up in the basement where we split from Darrell and Gwen, and then with Sylvia holding her red dress high, fled through the kitchen with chefs and staff looking on in astonishment. Coming out the back of the hotel, we rounded the building and into the car park where my trusty 'Beetle' banger was parked. We jumped inside and raced off to safety. Darrell and Gwen peeled off in the other direction and also managed to avoid the coppers.

"At home, poor Sylvia was speechless and understandably furious. I wasn't frightened of her at that stage or the police, but I was terrified of Schulie. The next day, I received a serious warning; stay away from Captain Schulenburg because if he sees you, he's going to kill you. I knew that was for real and did just that.

"Despite this fiasco and a few other shenanigans, Sylvia, in a moment of temporary insanity I suppose, accepted my offer of marriage. The date set was 30th September 1978. My mom and dad were delighted, thinking marriage might calm me down and make me a better person. I don't think my future father-in-law was exactly over the moon but he very kindly agreed to allow his daughter to marry me.

CHAPTER NINE

"At this point in time my dad had left the police with the rank of Assistant Commissioner and joined Military Intelligence. Unlike me, he was held in very high regard by all his peers and in the community. When I approached him about the possibility of getting married in the Police Officer's Mess he was reticent. He knew the possibility of bad behaviour was a very real one and he was not prepared to take the chance of us smashing the place up and embarrassing him. Instead, he and mom suggested a garden wedding at our home. The setting, on the front lawn under the trees near the rose garden was ideal.

"On my big day, while I behaved myself at home there was a pre-wedding piss-up at the pub down the road from the church. Along for the celebration, were my uncles Dan and Major Richard Stannard. He was referred to as 'Big Dick' in the army and I was 'Little Dick'. This caused much confusion in the military and on a few occasions, I received his pay cheque and he got mine. Later, when I got into trouble, he also got it in the neck due to mistaken identity. While we were related and shared the same name, we had very little else in common. He was a tall, refined, well-mannered man with a very smart accent; a pretty smooth operator, unlike me and he loved women.

"While the rest of the blokes were happy to get pissed Big Dick was looking to get laid.

'Where's the girls," he asked, 'we need some company.'

Just then, in walked Sylvia with bridesmaids and friends. 'Big Dick' brightened up big time. He spied Linda, the senior bridesmaid and made a bee-line for her. From that moment on he did not take his beady eyes off her. But the ladies had obviously decided, if the men were going to get pissed before the wedding even started then so were they and they were 'flying'. My father had already given them a warning about too much drink too soon, but I think Sylvia had already been around me too long and taken on my bad habits."

"When my wife Irene and I left the pub to go to the church," remembers Tim Callow, "Schulie at the last minute asked us for a lift in the Beetle that I had borrowed from an SB mate in Bulawayo, as he couldn't find a taxi. I explained that there was nothing behind the front seats and I mean nothing at all, not even floor-boards. So poor Schulie had to spread his legs and ride to the church standing on the axle in the back of a Beetle."

"My best man was Themi Themistokilis, who I had had much fun with in Greece," remembers Stannard. "I pulled on my formal dress 'Greens' along with Sam Browne, sword and beret. The service was held at Christ the King Catholic Church in Highlands with Father Mark, an American parish priest conducting the ceremony. I arrived nervous and a little jittery; the booze had helped calm my nerves but I was still shaking. My dear mother and father looked relaxed, but I don't think they were. Standing at the altar waiting I kept fidgeting and having to keep hiking my sword up my side as it kept touching the carpet. Thirty minutes later, I was still standing there without a bride and everyone, including Father Mark, was beginning to think Sylvia had done the sensible thing and done a 'runner'. My mates were sitting there pissing themselves, watching sweat pour off my face. In the church, hoping like hell I was going to be jilted were Tim Callow, Chris Schulenburg, Mike Smith, Torty King and James Hayden.

"It was hard to believe anything had gone wrong because the distance from the house, where the bridal party was leaving from, was about a kilometre to the church, and they were using my dad's new Citroen. These were the days of sanctions so new cars were a rarity and to be treasured.

"The car was driven by my uncle Don Pike. He was a real man of the bush who had an almost mystical relationship with birds and animals. As a boy his pet crow would fly with him to school while he rode his bike. It would then perch on the school fence and wait for him all day until he had finished his studies and then fly home with him. After school he joined Internal Affairs and was an Agricultural Adviser helping the Africans improve their farming techniques, but his hobby was animals and always had the strangest of pets. For a long time he had an ostrich which nearly died when it swallowed something that stuck in its neck. No problem for Don, he took out a knife, had his gang hold the bird down, sliced the neck open, took out the offending object and the ostrich lived happily ever after. He also had a pet lion which he kept for years but on one particular day the lion made its way to a bus stop in Wankie town and caused such a riot he had to get rid of it.

"All was quiet in the church when suddenly there was the sound of a car driving up. I gave thanks to God. All heads turned to watch the bridal party make its grand entrance. The first person through the church door was my father-in-law, who staggered forth with blood pouring out his

CHAPTER NINE

head looking like he had just been in a gunfight. He was closely followed by Sylvia who couldn't walk straight because she was pissed and looked like she had just been dragged through the bush. As it turned out, my uncle Don, who must have had his mind elsewhere, had collided head-on with another car on the short trip to the church and had written my dad's new car off, so the wedding was off to a spectacular start. Don and Sylvia, amazing given the state of the car, only had a few bruises and scratches. Once the wounded had been attended to and a little calm returned, we proceeded with the nuptials and managed to get married without any further drama.

"We all then made for the family home and the reception. Dad, having been an esteemed member of the community, had invited some of Bulawayo's leading lights including the Mayor. My mom had made a huge effort and everything was beautifully laid out. Set up under the trees was a bar which was manned by Sam our cook. Sam was a tall, slender bloke and when I arrived I took a second look at him because he wasn't looking too steady on his feet and he was jumping around like a lunatic. Helping him was our new gardener by the name of Blackwell. It turned out our previous gardener, Nelson, had been moonlighting as a very proficient burglar and had broken into a number of homes in the suburbs. He cunningly and correctly deduced that being in the employ of the most senior policeman in the city he would never be a suspect. He was right but his career in crime came to an abrupt end when my Mum caught him selling fantail pigeons from a cardboard box at the bottom of the garden and called the police. They arrested him and laughed the rest of the week.

"We got through the speeches without too many problems and I managed to say all I was expected to say but it was tough keeping a straight face looking at my poor father-in-law who was still having to use a handkerchief to mop up drops of blood popping out of his face. What did concern me a little during my address was the irritating sound of Sam singing in the background. Clearly, he was now very drunk.

"Once the formalities were over, Sam took his singing skills to a new level and this went down well with all the Selous Scouts in attendance. They knew the Shona songs and joined in with him. As did Linda, the chief bridesmaid, who was not going to be left out. She had a powerful voice, set herself down on Father Mark's lap and started singing:

'EAST IS EAST AND WEST IS WEST
BUT I LIKE SEX THE BEST...
AND HERE IS TO THE HOLE THAT NEVER HEALS...'

And with that downed another huge Cane and Coke. By the end of her song, the poor priest was soaked in booze. And the Mayor, a conservative God-fearing gentleman, bade mum and dad farewell and left in disgust.

"Meanwhile, Big Dick, eyes on Linda, decided it was time to pounce when she left Father Mark's lap and made her winding way inside the house. He arrived just in time to see his 'date' crash face-first into the carpet and commence furious vomiting. The rest of the bridesmaids came running and hauled her off into the bathroom to retch.

"Big Dick cut a disconsolate figure when he reappeared just as I was about to cut the wedding cake with my regimental sword. By this time Sam, the erstwhile barman, had fallen down unconscious and was curled in a heap at the top of the driveway so there was no noise from him. Just as the blade cut through the icing there was a massive thunderclap, the sky looked like it was on fire and the heavens opened. Clearly the Gods had a problem with what we were doing because the lightning shorted the lights outside and everyone ran for cover inside the house.

'With the demise of 'Singing Sam', the DJ for the night, my cousin Rob, took up the slack and tried to get the bedraggled guests dancing but he appeared to only have one record; *'Staying Alive,'* by the Bee Gees. He played the same song so many times someone went and tore it off the turntable and hurled it into the night. He later apologised to me for the lack of variety but explained he had an obsessive-compulsive disorder. I said, I'm sorry for you, but what the fuck has that got to do with playing the same song 50 times in a row.

"When I went in search of Linda, I found her groaning loudly, lying on my parents' bathroom floor, spread-eagled, spittle and vomit dribbling from her lips; the lipstick was long gone and one false eyelash was clinging to her left eyelid. The drinking continued at a ferocious pace and the general behaviour just got worse and worse. The only chap who kept his senses was Schulie. He liked his booze but was never one to make an idiot of himself like the rest of us. He took to the lounge and watched the rest of us clowns getting wrecked. We eventually ran out of booze, but as always my darling mother had stashed a secret reserve supply for this event so we drank until dawn.

CHAPTER NINE

"The next day I could barely walk or talk but managed to stagger to the steps of the Air Rhodesia Viscount with my beautiful bride as we prepared for our honeymoon in Victoria Falls. We were soon airborne but in order to dodge heat-seeking missiles, the pilot, with great skill, first flew low following the contours, then climbed quickly and it was too much for me. I vomited on my wife's new going-away shoes and felt like I needed to be hospitalised when we arrived there. I took to my bed at the hotel and felt like death for days. The honeymoon was a disaster. I couldn't wait to get back into the bush with my mates.

Second SAS selection

"After my honeymoon and my return to the SAS I was told I would have to be assessed again before going operational. So early in November 1978, I and four other young officers were sent on a bush-craft assessment exercise under the supervision of Darrell Watt. Very little happened under Darrell that was not tough but I was to receive a very unpleasant surprise when we went into the area and I realised how infested the place was with groups of heavily armed and very motivated Zipra troops. I was a little horrified when Darrell insisted on taking us out into the field in broad daylight where we stood out and were an easy target but this was his way of inviting the enemy to attack us so he would have an opportunity to watch us under fire. It did not take long and we were walking into repeated firefights which were brief but vicious with an enemy that seemed to be watching us constantly. It was all very unsettling and I kept thinking to myself that if this was just an exercise then God help me when the real thing comes along!

"On the second day a young African male walked nonchalantly into our lying-up position where we thought we were safe. This really rocked me because I knew he was lying when he said he had accidentally walked onto us while looking for firewood; we all knew he was a *mujiba* who had been sent by the enemy to establish our position. Nearby there would be a big group ready to react to try and kill us. Darrell told me to interrogate the guy and find out who sent him and more about what was going on in the area. I was furious and a little scared; he lied and lied and I lost my temper and almost killed him trying to get the truth out of him. On two occasions I thought he was dead and had to work hard to revive him. Looking back I salute the man; he was very tough and despite my best efforts he would not reveal any information at all. We knew we were now in danger and Darrell ordered us to withdraw to a new position. No sooner had we relocated ourselves than a sustained attack commenced on our old position with small arms, rockets and mortars. It all happened at dusk and it was a spectacular sight watching the rockets explode and the purple tracers that ripped through the trees against a blood red sky as the sun slipped over the horizon.

"By dawn the following day we had moved to another position and clearly we had the jump on the enemy because an armed terrorist came into view walking jauntily along with an RPG, carrying a radio and one of the Bee Gees song was playing loudly. The sound of this song again did not endear me to this guy. This was well and truly a liberated area and this guy did not seem to have a care in the world. Darrell shot him in the head and that was the end of him. The Bee Gees carried on playing.

"After several days of hectic combat and lots of ducking and diving a message came through for me to prepare to return to Bulawayo as I was required to do another SAS selection. I was absolutely mortified; I had really done selection and felt it was unnecessary and unfair to expect me to do another. I looked at Darrell and asked him if he thought this was reasonable and fair and he simply shrugged his shoulders and said 'orders are orders my mate'. The powers that be had decided this and he explained there was nothing he could do. I was furious, I knew then as I know now, that this was punishment being meted out because I had left and gone to the Selous Scouts. But there was nothing I could do; in their minds my loyalty was in question and they were going to check that out. Petty politics bedevilled the Rhodesian army; in the same vein, RAR troops that failed Selous Scouts selection were not allowed back into the RAR. Sometimes I felt we were busier fighting amongst ourselves than we were the enemy.

"I was also sorry to be missing out on an opportunity to go after a gang that may have had something to do with the shooting down of the Viscount Hunyani and subsequent killing of the survivors in September 1978. Darrell, Andre and two of the other blokes stayed, went after them and killed them, but it has never been confirmed that the gang they eliminated was actually involved or not.

"I arrived back at Llewellin Barracks where I had started my army career and I was about as unhappy as I was when I first walked through those gates. The troops, about 30 of them, were waiting to start the last part

CHAPTER NINE

of the course. All, like me, were trained soldiers but from different units and different countries around the world. I braced myself for one of the toughest selections in any army in the world. I had been spared the preliminary phases but the most arduous part of the course awaited me.

"Captain Rob Johnstone kicked off by asking me to stand up on a stool and explain to the men why I wanted to be an officer in the SAS. The audience looked on in silence.

'But I'm already in the SAS Sir,' I replied. We were in a hangar and the place went dead quiet. Colour Sergeant Masson, one of the senior instructors frowned and looked at Johnstone, searching for answers. They both knew I was right.

'Bullshit Lieutenant Stannard,' Johnstone shouted, 'just answer the question!'

I then gave them some pretty bland answer about wanting to be an elite soldier and fight for my country and was waffling on when he shouted at me again.

'Why have you a hole in your sock?' I looked down and sure enough my big right toe was sticking out my sock.

'Just been on operations Sir – Rhodesian army wool socks are the worst on the planet when wet and they turn into hairy caterpillars.'

'Officers don't walk around with holes in their socks even if they've just come off operations. Is that understood?'

Suddenly a light went on in my head. This wasn't about testing me physically; this was all about finding out if I had learned to control my temper. My short fuse had gotten me into trouble before and this was clearly of concern to them, so I was pleased to know that I had to be careful.

"Once the speeches were over, we had to start boxing and we had to pile in and punch like hell. We all had to have a go at each other, until battered and exhausted. Then the 'pre-rev' as it was called, began, with the idea being to destroy us physically and mentally. The instructors were like hunting dogs; searching for weaknesses and when found, working on them until you gave up. Sergeant Paddy Giblin ran all of us up and down the rugby field carrying two iron balls each, stopping on command to do push-ups, 'burpees', then pick up the balls and run again. I was exhausted and lay on the dry grass gasping for air.

"To my surprise, Paddy came to me, knelt down and whispered in my ear: 'You're pushing yourself too hard Sir, you will burn out by nightfall – pace yourself as we have a long way to go.'

By this time I thought my throat was going to crack from the dryness; we had not had any water for hours and all of us were about to collapse. Then they ran us to the pool and made us swim lengths. I remember drinking pool water by the pints as I swam. By this time half the chaps had given up. The rest of us had passed the point of no return. The blokes who had given up sat looking dejected in one corner of the hangar. It was a sad sight.

"The instructors took it in turns to run and scream at us until they could see we were about to collapse, then they would back off and allow a brief recovery period. As an officer, while the others had the chance to catch their breath, I had to prepare a set of orders. I was told to draw up a comprehensive plan for an attack on an enemy camp that consisted of buildings and I was told how the base was defended and what weapons were available. I had two hours to make up a model of the camp and come up with a workable plan of action. Having done two officer's courses at the School of Infantry I was well practised at this sort of task. I did as asked and my orders appear to have been well received.

"Next morning we were loaded onto vehicles with our packs and driven to our camp in the Matopos National Park. For scenic magnificence the area was hard to beat. Grasslands, broken up by a mass of weathered, granite hills, sculpted into fantastic shapes that dominated the landscape.

The range of hills ran for over 50 miles (80 kms) and the slopes were covered in dense bush. This whole area was regarded as sacred by the Ndebele people as it was reputed to be the home of their ancestral spirits. Their King Mzilikazi was buried at Entumbane nearby, along with the country's founder, Cecil John Rhodes, whose final resting place was at World's View. Also buried near Rhodes was Dr Leander Starr Jameson and some of those who fought to the last man alongside Major Allan Wilson at the Battle of Shangani in 1893.

"Our packs weighed a good 30 kgs and we started out with two iron balls, each of which weighed five kgs along with our FN rifle, extra magazines, ammunition, and water-bottles. It added up to quite a load. Each member was issued a map, compass and given specific grid references to make for, each about 30 kms away. The main roads were patrolled by the staff, and if they caught you breaking any of the rules you were given more

CHAPTER NINE

iron balls to carry. The pain from the pack straps biting into our shoulders was excruciating.

After the third day another ten individuals dropped out due to horrible blisters that burst and left the soles of their feet bleeding and raw. The combat-medics did their best to relieve the pain but in most cases to no avail. I didn't escape the ordeal; blisters popped up on the balls of my feet but luckily mine weren't too bad and I was able to keep going. With morale low, desperately tired and in lots of pain, we were split into groups of four and issued with an ammunition box filled with sand. One of my teammates was Mike Skoropski a former French Legionnaire. Together, we cut a large branch from a Mountain Acacia and using para-cord we hung the box from the pole. It was an absolute bitch to carry and we took it in turns at different ends of the pole with plenty of swearing and bellowing in between. We had a quick five-minute break every 30 minutes and managed to keep the iron bitch moving over rough granite outcrops, through rivers and in and out the valleys. To add to my woes I was given an extra two iron balls because I fell on a slope, lost my Bergen down a rock face and my iron balls fell out. I received a lecture about officers not lying but was so exhausted I just said nothing and took on four balls rather than the two I started with. By this time there were only 12 of us left. By the fifth day 25 had fallen out. The final day was a speed march up a steep mountain. I cannot begin to explain how relieved I was to finish and put this behind me. The ordeal over, I was passed and accepted back into the SAS as an officer.'

Operation Vodka.

"While I had been sweating my guts out on selection, my two pals, Tim Callow and Sergeant Aaron had been off on an exciting recce that would set the stage for one of the most daring Selous Scouts raids of the war and when I heard what had happened I wondered if I had made the right decision to leave.

"It was known that a Zipra camp existed 140 kms north of the Rhodesian border at Mboroma in a remote area of Zambia," remembers Tim. "Information received also indicated that the camp accommodated a prison where captured members of the Rhodesian security forces were being held along with political dissidents who could be of use to us. We heard the inmates were being given a very hard time. At that time it seemed that Zipra was building its forces in Zambia in preparation for a major conventional attack on Rhodesia so it was decided it was time to give them a good smack, recover some of our own people, and let them know that if they were coming for us they had a big fight on their hands."

"Aaron and I went in by parachute end of November 1978, after a detailed briefing and having studied all the aerial photographs. As planned, we landed about 30 kms south of the camp, then moved very slowly and carefully, taking three days to reach the outskirts of the complex, before moving to a hill feature to establish an OP close to the camp. There we got our radio up and running. This was an excellent area to work in; the Zambezi escarpment, no locals to compromise us, clean water and fairly thick vegetation with rocky outcrops making it easy to hide. On our walk in to the target we came across one hunting camp which was vacant. In the early morning we could hear the slightly mournful sound of the prisoners singing from quite a way off. Some days it rained quite heavily but we established exactly where the prison complex was and that there were over 100 inmates inside the enclosure within the camp. We watched them as they went through their daily routines which appeared to include lots of chanting and political indoctrination. We counted over 40 heavily armed guards who appeared alert and they were supported by 14.5 mm anti-aircraft guns which were dug in. On at least one occasion we saw them open up on some arbitrary plane flying overhead. We then went looking in the area for an airfield not too distant from the camp to be used if and when an attack was launched and troops and captures had to be recovered by Dakotas.

"At the end of the recce after two weeks we exfiltrated back to our cache at the entry point, as Uncle Ron wanted us to stay in the area as long as possible, with the aim of us leading in the attack team who would parachute into the area. We now had enough food and Neil Kriel communicated with us using a Telstar light aircraft every afternoon, as the High Frequency (HF) set was not usable. ComOps was taking too long for approval, and eventually we were extracted back to HQ when our rations and Very High frequency (VHF) batteries had run down.

"Ron was champing at the bit as he always had troubles with ComOps. We heard later that their concern was the possibility that British-supplied Rapier anti-aircraft missiles might be available to the defenders, so Walls and the top guys wanted to hit the camp with Hunters first and then send in the paratroopers.

CHAPTER NINE

"Eventually approval was given and the air and ground attack went in just before Christmas. The assault group, which had been practising hard at Inkomo Barracks was led by Rich Passaportis. The plan called for the Hunters to strafe the camp just before Richard's guys hit the ground. The jets were bang on target as usual just after first light and then Richard's assault group of about 40 was on the ground and charging in for the attack with back-up provided by a mortar section. They killed all the armed defenders that presented themselves and had little problem in overrunning the camp."

Cde Steven Mathanda (Biko), a Zipra combatant but under suspicion of being a Rhodesian spy remembers:

"On that fateful day my team was the one on duty in the kitchen, cooking for other comrades. In fact, the previous night I had dreamt the camp was being attacked and comrades running away in all directions and I told that dream to my fellow comrades I was working with. So after 8am while we were still working in the kitchen there was a sudden noise of aircraft followed by loud explosions. It then became every man for himself. I quickly dashed out and went straight to a tree where I momentarily hid under. Our comrade, Umfana kaDaggie returned with rapid fire using a Zegue and then there was a lull in attack by the aircraft. It was at that moment that I ran across the camp and hid where there was a small cave, it was not even a cave, but an opening at a rock. I can tell you three of us, myself, Benjie and Mabaleka fitted there. While the Rhodesians were making their comb-up after dropping paratroopers, we were there seeing everything, it was frightful."

"Unfortunately, on the day of the attack, quite a few of the prisoners were absent," remembers Callow. "It turned out the guards had shot an elephant that day and taken a whole lot of prisoners to butcher it and carry the meat back to the camp. About 30 inmates were taken in almost immediately. It was during a sweep of the camp that ventilators were discovered and these indicated a system supplying air underground to what were almost certainly bunkers. With time running short the order was given to drop bunker-bombs down and blow them but when screams were heard that was changed. On closer inspection, it turned out these were underground cells for more prisoners and the tunnels were opened to allow them out. Some of these poor guys had not seen sunlight for months and were completely bewildered when brought to the surface. When they were told they were being rescued by Rhodesian soldiers they could not believe it. Some of the prisoners could not be enticed out of the dungeon as they simply did not believe that we had come to rescue them. Fortunately, many prisoners did return with us, but some flatly refused.

"After torching the camp, grabbing documents and destroying what could not be taken the troops and all the freed prisoners walked to the strip we had identified as a mission station. The recovery went off without a hitch and everyone was back in Salisbury that night.

"The next day there was a huge celebration back at the barracks with the press in attendance. It was one of the most emotional scenes ever witnessed with the Scouts singing and the freed prisoners being reunited with their families. The prisoners regaled the journalists with terrible tales of floggings and torture. Some had been underground for four months when we arrived. Some had been in the dark so long they had been blinded by the light and required medical attention. The international press had a hard time trying to find a way to spin the story that did not make the dreaded Selous Scouts look like the bad guys. This was a really good one for us with a good result. For a change, it was less about killing and more about saving people; a mercy mission that made us all feel good and a reminder of how cruel people can be to their own kind."

Aaron Jele

"Not long after the successful attack on the Mboroma Base," remembers Ken Bird, "I was sent to Brady Barracks in Bulawayo to join the Selous Scouts 'Three Group' and take the fight to the low level echelon Zipra groups operating in Matabeleland. Corporal Aaron was one of the experienced pseudo operators we were happy to have with us. At that time, the local BSAP Special Branch was having little success in capturing or killing the resident tribal area groups. They did, however, enjoy urban success, with the use of captured and turned Zipra gooks. They were deployed in a spotting role, to follow familiar heads bobbing through the municipal beer halls. My liaison with the local SB, CID and uniformed branches was excellent and I would always supply the SB office with a copy of our top-secret reports. In turn, they would share their intelligence with me. This was essential to create cover stories to authenticate Zipra pseudo operations. However, there was a major personality problem with the Scouts Group commander and the

CHAPTER NINE

SB man on the spot. This culminated in much hurry up and wait; stop and go operations, with tittle-tattle tale wails on the scrambler phone to Selous Scouts HQ. The response from the SB was reciprocal; almost to tell the Scouts to get fucked. Ultimately it meant endless cross-provincial flights, liaison pub dinners and submitting pseudo plan after pseudo plan tailored to suit particular districts and then being disregarded when the sulking took over.

"So, I was pleasantly surprised when a miracle happened one day and all parties agreed to a pseudo op into the Kezi district of the province, where there were, what we thought, a couple of renegade Zipra terrorist groups, intent on robbing and raping and yet hero worshipped by the locals.

"Aaron was tasked to lead one of the two groups we planned to deploy. Just when we were about to commence the operation, he was given a very highly unusual instruction; to carry an air to ground launcher and warhead missile from a captured SAM-7 series. I must admit I was confused. The local Kezi population, a simple subsistence people, didn't even know or concern themselves with the difference between an Alouette chopper and an armoured car. Things became a bit more incredulous when I was asked to have the anti-aircraft weapon facilitated onto the late afternoon Air Rhodesia passenger flight from Salisbury to Bulawayo. The obvious question about detonating in mid-flight was brushed off with an assurance that the warhead would be separated and it would be disguised as a spare part for a truck. So SB Salisbury airport facilitated a spare part for a truck on the flight as a favour to Selous Scouts and, on its arrival, I collected a fully loaded up one-piece SAM-7, with warhead in position. At least it was Scotch-taped in brown wrapping paper and I pointed it gingerly at the traffic behind me as my open Land-Rover jarred its way back to the Bulawayo Fort without downing the local bus service, seen in my shaky rear-view mirror.

"The two four-man groups sent into the field were indistinguishable from the real Zipra, except for the SAM-7. I doubt there had ever been any flight over the Kezi tribal lands, so I left that part to a highly pissed-off group, who had to carry the heavy tube and whose evil eye seemed to swing towards every heat source. I bid goodbye to my sections and arrived back in town in time to go for a few beers at La Gondola pub.

"The following day Aaron's group made their initial pseudo approach as new arrivals, ex-Zambia and Botswana, on the border of Kezi BSAP district.

The response was predictable, they received a message that the local terror group of four would be popping along to greet them. So the pseudo group chose a good spot, lots of good cover and when the real gooks arrived, with their local sweethearts in tow, preening and pouting, they gave them the 'Hands Up' order and captured three, but one made a break and was taken down in midstride by a burst from Aaron's AK. Being like a wounded animal the gook continued to make ground, until Aaron pounced on him, wanting to take him prisoner rather than kill him. The gook pulled the pin on a grenade but Aaron, now on top of the guy, showing immense strength, held his fist closed over the grenade's striker lever and ordered his brother soldier to stand clear, then drew his knife and stabbed the gook through the heart killing him. Then, unable to find the pin, flung the grenade to explode among the 'sweethearts' who had stopped flirting and started screaming. Aaron rounded up the captures and called for uplift having left the body of the dead gook behind as a keepsake memento of a day's 'pop-a-long outing' for the ladies!

"Leaving the body and the ladies in waiting behind did not go down well with the police who had to then go out and collect the body and look for the ladies to get statements from them. They probably reported that the new guys were carrying a spare part for the District Commissioner's John Deere tractor!

"Corporal Aaron was killed in action a few months later by the Botswana Defence Force, when a crossing point had not been secured for their re-entry into Rhodesia after a cross border operation. This was a loss of a good man and should never have happened."

Chapter Ten

How many
Will be unable, or unwilling
To be shackled again to cutting the lawn
And visiting Auntie on Sunday.

◆

Assassinations

Maputo

With Pieter Willem Botha, better known as PW Botha, taking over as South African prime minister from John Vorster early in October 1978, military support for Rhodesia was ramped up. Botha was strongly of the opinion that South Africa should do all it could to ensure that Robert Mugabe would not assume power in the event there was a change in government. When a plan emerged to eliminate the Zanu leader, Botha was all ears. Informed of the SAS involvement and the need for naval assets to facilitate such an operation, he did not hesitate to give his consent. At this time Mugabe was residing in the Mozambique capital of Maputo and his home there became the focus of attention.

The first attempt, scheduled for November 1978, was to involve landing eight SAS men and a former Frelimo soldier who had defected, from a submarine supported by men of 4 Reconnaissance Commando South African Defence Force (SADF) who would land the raiding party in two Zodiac inflatable boats. The SAS team, known as 'Zebra Group', was commanded by Major Grahame Wilson and commenced training for the operation at Langebaan north of Cape Town where 4 Recce were based.

During rehearsals for the raid it was realised that it would be preferable to launch the SAS men from a Strike Craft which would then leave the area after discharging the raiding party. The raiders would then be recovered by submarine under cover of darkness and sail to safety. The submarine selected was *SAS Johanna van der Merwe* under the command of Commander Evert Groenewald. Although the intelligence to hand was detailed it was decided that Wilson and one other would do an actual reconnaissance so as to gain first-hand knowledge of the whereabouts of the house and how best to approach it.

SAS Johanna van der Merwe, with Wilson and partner aboard went ahead, while the rest of the Zebra Group boarded the strike craft and followed from Durban. They deployed into the city, walked to the residence, established the route of approach and returned to the submarine without incident. The sub then dived and made its way to a rendezvous with the strike craft late the next day, whereupon Wilson transferred to the surface vessel.

That evening a signal was received from intelligence that Mugabe was in residence and Wilson was set to go. Zebra Group then boarded the Zodiacs with the 4 Recce crews aboard and headed for the beach while the strike craft headed out to sea and out of sight and headed home to Durban. But the mission was aborted as a result of structural problems with the Zodiacs that would have delayed their landing on the mainland and this was deemed unacceptable to the mission commanders. Zebra Group returned to Durban disappointed.

The second attempt commenced mid-December 1978 when the SAS team under the command of Major Grahame Wilson along with the support compliment from the Recces departed Durban harbour on 26th December in a strike craft. The following night the harbour defences were breached without incident. The Recce escorts went some distance out to sea and waited. By midnight Wilson's men were outside Mugabe's house but were disappointed to see all the lights were off and nobody home. A decision was made to abort the mission and the Raiders returned to the strike craft.[45]

Operation Inhibit.

Stannard: "Within two weeks of passing my second SAS selection and soon after Grahame's guys came back from Maputo, I took part in *Operation Inhibit* on 17th December1978. Captain Bob Mckenzie briefed me at Mabalauta. My mission was to lay anti-tank mines on the road to Malvernia to stop the Frelimo convoys transporting men and supplies for Zanla. I parachuted in with 18 guys but they dropped us way off target and we had to walk hard for two days to get to where we needed to be. By this

---

[45] 'Iron Fist from the Sea'. Arne Soderlund and Douw Steyn. Delta Books. 2018.

CHAPTER TEN

time we were desperately short of water. The river we expected to drink from was bone dry and the men were carrying heavy loads of mines and mortars. I knew heatstroke was a distinct possibility. I sent Willem Ratte off to look for water in the direction of where we heard what we thought were frogs. Unbeknown to us, it was Nightjars mimicking the sounds of frogs so Willem's search proved fruitless. We were now pretty desperate and we had cut Frelimo spoor so we were ready for action but the heat and thirst was debilitating. I could have called for an air-drop but thought this would invite derision from my peers who were watching me closely after my return from the Scouts. Many were pissed off with me for going in the first place. I just told my guys we would have to tough it out and hope we found water soon.

"Arriving close to where we were supposed to be Billy Grant and I went ahead to have a look down the road and saw about 40 Zanla coming towards us. We went back to the rest of the guys and prepared to ambush. The main killer group was positioned with two four-man early warning sections north and south and Billy laid the Claymores.

"Then suddenly I heard Dave O'Sullivan on the radio from his 'stop' position saying the 'gooks' were visual and filing past. It was nerve-wracking because he was counting them as they passed him by and the number just kept getting bigger. I think the 'gooks' were quite relaxed because they believed the area had been cleared by Frelimo. The road they were on was a mere 20 metres away. When I heard Dave say 80, I looked at Billy next to me in the 'killer-group' and searched his face for guidance. I saw Billy nod meaning – let's hit them."

"My heart was pounding so hard I was sure they could hear it," remembers Grant. "I will never forget the moment when I broke from cover and saw the look of sheer terror on the faces of those people as I fired that initial volley and the claymores detonated. Before they hit the ground the rest of the 'killer-group' was attacking.[46]"

With half the soldiers armed with RPDs the fire was a solid sheet of lead followed by grenades and the group of terrorists crumpled, but not without some return fire, and in the initial exchange Lance Corporal Maurice 'Mo' Taylor, the popular Englishman, was killed.

Grant remembers. "Some of the terrorists sprinted over to the other side of the track where they were afforded some cover. Unfortunately for them

---
[46] Pittaway and Fourie: "SAS Rhodesia."

their heads were still exposed so Dave O'Sullivan put his sniper training to good use and was bowling them over like at a coconut shy."

"All credit to Billy," says Stannard. "Once the initial attack was over it was Billy who jumped to his feet and shouted to follow him which we did and we ran over the rise to find the enemy cowering in cover whereupon we got busy again and a lot more of them went down. This was Billy at his aggressive best and close to 50 were dead and blood-trails provided clear evidence that a lot of the survivors were 'leaking'. No sooner was the shooting over than we were ripping water bottles off the bodies and guzzling the water. Incredibly, just after the shooting, two Frelimo suddenly appeared coming to have a look. We let them get close and then Willem Ratte shot them.

"This may have been the most successful rifle ambush of the war. Unfortunately 'Mo' Taylor never made it; he was a wonderful guy. Just before he was killed, he had given some of his water to one of the guys who he felt needed it more than he. That was an act of incredible kindness."

Third Maputo Attempt January 1979

"In January 1979 I went on my first operation to try and kill Mugabe in Maputo with Grahame Wilson. We sailed from Durban and deployed from a SA Navy strike-craft in three Zodiacs. We landed on the beaches of Maputo while the Recce guys in the Zodiacs waited at sea. By midnight we were outside Mugabe's house having had to calm a drunken watchman down. I was so excited about the possibility of blowing that house and occupants to pieces but again it was not to be. The place was absolutely deserted. I'm sure Mugabe was tipped off., probably by Ken Flower?"

Attempt to capture Tongogara. Late January 1979.

"I had just returned from the Maputo assassination attempt when Martin Pearse told me I was needed to have a crack at capturing Josiah Tongogara who was reported to be operating from a camp near Tete. After the failure in Maputo I, and almost everyone else I knew, was becoming a little despondent about the quality of our intelligence. Our 'spooks' seemed to be letting us down all the time. I know the Scouts had been having the same problem and Uncle Ron was fighting an ongoing battle with Military Intelligence and the CIO. Both outfits had it in for Ron and seemed to spend

CHAPTER TEN

more time making life difficult for the Scouts than they did for the enemy.

"It was also a very tough time for us frontline soldiers from a morale point of view. Politically, the tide appeared to be turning against us and none of us knew if we could fight our way out of the jam we were in. The troops were full of fight however, so we officers had to be careful not to say or do anything that caused any alarm or despondency.

"I knew ComOps were desperate to pull an ace out the pack and pull off something that would shock the enemy and attract a lot of media attention. We had not managed to nail Mugabe or Nkomo so their attention switched to the senior Zanla military commanders and top of the list were Josiah Tongogara and Rex Nhongo. Martin Pearse gave me the background but told me our Intelligence Officer (IO), Dave Padbury, would brief me.

"I listened carefully and I was unimpressed. The overview and recent intelligence was vague. He was reported to be based near Tete but by this time Zanla had learned the hard way about concentrating too many people, so this was a large camp spread out over a large area. To find him in there was going to be almost impossible. The only way was to nail him on the road. I was told Tongogara used Land Cruisers of different colours which wasn't much help. Then he told me he used different routes which came as no surprise at all and so that wasn't much help either. At the end of it he had actually told me little I didn't already know and nothing to lessen my concerns. It turned out all they were saying was go in, recce, find a road, ambush and try to capture Tongogara. If you can't capture him then kill him.

"What they did not elaborate upon was the fact that my men and I were going to be dropped at night into an enemy camp complex roughly 60 square kms in expanse containing over 10, 000 enemy fighters who were on high alert for lunatics like me who were going to try to infiltrate their lines and kill their top general. Making matters worse, Tete had just been attacked from the air and lost an arms/ammo dump so Frelimo were also on the warpath.

"I walked out the briefing room feeling underwhelmed, thinking these guys were really doing little more than throwing the dice in a bid to kill or capture this guy and actually had little clue as to how to do it. What I found out about afterwards was that Schulie had been tasked to do the job but when he heard the crap intelligence he told them to fuck off. I should probably have done the same but only Schulie could get away with behaviour like that.

"I called my team for the operation together to brief them. I felt torn; their lives were going to be on the line too and was it fair on them for me to follow this order? I had to find a fine line between being assertive and confident so as to keep their spirits up and being dead honest. Foremost on my mind was the size of the camp complex and my focus was on how not to get trapped in there. I told them I was not pleased with the quality of the intelligence but we were soldiers who followed orders. I also told them that I was well aware of the risks and I was not planning on getting bogged down and overstaying our welcome. The numbers we would be up against were pretty scary but I reminded them we had all been there before and with speed, aggression and straight-shooting we would all be coming home. As always, with these wonderful guys, we ended the briefing with big smiles, laughter and a keenness to get there and fuck them up. I was happy to have Rob Cuthbert, Mike Peens, Rob Riddell and our troop medic Barry Skinner in the group.

"That night 16 of us loaded into the Dakota. Some serious firepower with 12 RPDs and four RPG-7 rocket launchers. We were dropped south of Tete not far from where the main road from Chimoio runs northwards. I knew the terrain from previous visits and my immediate concern was landing in one of the many big baobab trees that covered the landscape. I left the aircraft and was surprised at the brightness under a clear sky and a full moon, but I had little time to enjoy the view because my main parachute took too long to open and I quickly realised I was falling too fast. I just had time to pull my reserve which slowed me thankfully but reduced my control over the point of landing and sure enough I crashed through the canopy of a large tree. I remembered the drills drummed into us at para-school about keeping your legs tightly together when going through trees to stop your 'nuts' being crushed. After much crashing around through the branches I eventually came to rest dangling from the tree. I let my pack down first then let myself down slowly. Using low whistles we found each other and everyone was in good shape. All equipment was intact. Then we marched swiftly away from the DZ until we found some open country near the main Tete road. I wanted to be hidden near open ground so we might see anyone coming to look for us.

CHAPTER TEN

"When I saw the first light of the sun, I dispatched the two 'early-warning' call signs to their respective positions north and south of the spot I had selected to place my main 'killer-group'. It was close to the road, so we had a good view of what was coming and going but I was concerned about the lack of cover. However, I didn't have much time to ponder our whereabouts when I heard an urgent, but clearly audible whisper on my radio from the call-sign north of me.

'Land Cruiser approaching ahead of convoy with heavy troop transports.'

No sooner was the message complete when the lead Land Cruiser came into view carrying Frelimo armed with AKs and RPDs looking very alert and ready for action.

There was absolutely no time to hesitate and I gave the signal to open fire. Any hopes of a capture coming out of that vehicle who we could snatch and take home were quickly dashed. The machine gunners were deadly accurate and although the occupants managed to fire back at us briefly, their aim was high and they were quickly ripped to pieces by the bullets that tore into them. The lead vehicle careened off the road and there were no survivors.

"The sustained and accurate fire from the killer-group was devastating. The troop carriers had wooden sides and splinters flew high in the sky as hundreds of rounds raked though them and into the troops inside. The first truck crashed into an embankment on the other side of the road amid screams from the wounded. As it came to rest, survivors poured out but they were quickly cut down. It was complete carnage as mixed Zanla and Frelimo ran in all directions while trucks crashed and burned. There was no escape. Those running north ran straight into the early warning group and ones that went beyond us were blasted by the group to my south.

"After 10 minutes of intense action I called for the men to stop shooting and the screams of the wounded and dying were horrible. There was some sporadic but aimless fire from the enemy but they were on the run. Barry Skinner, being the good man he is, went to try and help some of the enemy wounded but I had to order him back; there was nothing we could do for them; I knew time was very short and there would be a rapid reaction of a large enemy force that I had no wish to tangle with. We had expended plenty of ammo, so any lengthy engagement was going to be very testing for us.

"I checked again to make sure we were all there, then told the guys it was time to get the fuck out of there. We headed west at pace while I got on the HF radio and requested immediate uplift. About five kms away from the scene I spied a suitable LZ and sent in a loc-stat.

"As always the 'Blues' were top of their game and soon the sound of two Bell helicopters was like music to our ears. The soothing, thumping sound of their rotors brought smiles to our faces. We had all survived and soon we would be home safe. We arrived back at Grand Reef outside Umtali and got stuck into the cold beers! Then a Dak took us back to New Sarum and from there back to Kabrit and a massive piss-up.

Debrief at ComOps

"The morning after I was lying in bed, drowsy, gazing out the window at the bright red light from the rising sun, streaking though the emerald green leaves of the mulberry tree outside my window. It took my mind back and I remembered the panic the day my brother and I raced off to our mother and pleaded with her to take our beloved Alsatian, Chaka, to the vet immediately because he was bleeding to death. We had seen the 'blood' splashed along his flank, matting his sleek black hair, his tongue was out and the saliva dribbling from his muzzle was a reddish purple. We were both in tears, thinking this was the end of the dog we loved so dearly. Mom got a hell of a fright and we loaded Chaka up in the back of the car and zoomed off to the vet at high speed with me blubbing all the way. Frantic on arrival, we pushed and carried the dog in to the surgery and to the vet. The next thing, the vet was shaking with laughter and we all looked on in horrified disbelief. I actually felt anger welling up in me when he spoke.

'The dog has eaten a lot of mulberries boys, he's as fit as a fiddle. Go home and wash the juice off.' In silence and a little embarrassed we bade our farewells and made our way, happily home.

"My mind was still miles away; then I heard the familiar raucous cry of a pair of pied crows squawking outside on the driveway fighting over a frog I must have flattened it in the night when I drove up the driveway. I was careful not to move too fast in any way or direction; my head throbbed, my tongue felt like it had grown hair in the night and my breath smelled of stale booze. I was nursing a hangover from hell.

"Then the damn phone rang, jarring my senses, forcing me to lift my broken head off the pillow. Who the fuck is calling me at this time I thought?

CHAPTER TEN

I put the phone gingerly to my ear and instantly paid attention. It was the crisp, calm voice of Martin Pearse.

'Rich,' he said sternly, 'the 'Brass' want you at ComOps. They want a full report on your last operation.' This took my breath away.

'What?' I blurted out in disbelief. 'Isn't that Dave Padbury's job? He's the Intelligence Officer? He can tell them what happened!' There was a short silence, then the measured tone.

'Well Rich, they say they wanted you to go in quietly and capture Tongogara and bring him home without too much disturbance. You went in there and obliterated a convoy, blew the place to pieces and killed a shit-load of Frelimo and Zanla, right in their base complex. This is not what they had in mind and they want to hear from the guy who disobeyed their operational orders. Good luck,' he said, and I heard a chuckle as he out the phone down.

"At this point I was still not sure if ComOps or my wife posed a bigger danger to my survival. I had come back from the bush and headed straight to the bar to drink myself dumb. I still had to say hello to Sylvia. Then I heard the 'voice'.

'What! You in trouble again?' she shouted. The sense of irritation in her voice was clear and I had no doubt she wished the worst for me.

'Yes, I think so,' I replied rather meekly. Then there was silence.

"The fact is, I felt for her, but the same scenario after every bush trip was being repeated. Most normal men, away from their wives or partners for a long time would be happy to go straight back to them but we were different. Getting pissed with our brothers in arms, was, I think an essential part of our decompressing process; like deep-sea divers coming to the surface after a long spell underwater. A sort of familiarisation phase as we came back into a world of relative normality; it mellowed us for the next step. The cold beer, the music, soothed and calmed us; helped us forget the hardships of where we had just been.

"Unless you have done what we were doing, very few understand how sounds and habits are amplified when living under extreme stress, in close proximity to your mates over a long period of time. What might be ignored in normal life becomes obvious and sometimes annoying in the bush.

"It may be the way your mate brews his tea, or how he eats his tinned sausage and baked beans. So when you look at your buddy and you love him and are ready to die for him, but his eating habits are driving you crazy;

he may be only six metres away but the sound of him hoovering his meal with a small wooden spoon out of his mess tin, lights you up. Anger comes in waves and crawls under the skin, sending shivers shooting through the body. All the while ants are biting you, pesky Mopani flies are in your eyes, in your ears, up your nose and then the Tsetse flies attack in waves, like miniature fighter-bombers, they strike and suck as much blood out of you as they can carry away.

"With your senses hot-wired you become sensitive to trivia. Not helping the mood is almost continual pain and discomfort of some type. An itchy crotch causing severe scratching leading to irritating abrasions was common. Our feet stank and sweated in our boots so the skin peeled off our toes causing 'foot-rot', veld sores suppurated and brought the flies to feed on them. We invariably got the 'runs' and had sore bums.

"That first night back with our arms around our fellow mates and our shrunken belly full of Castle Beer was like a ritual for us; a time to heal the mental wounds of war and remind one another that we loved each other; because only with that special, brotherly bond, we were going to survive what still lay ahead. This war had changed us all forever, for better or worse, we were living in a different world that was shaped by a closeness to violence and quick death that we knew could be coming our way soon. Although we had survived, we had all killed and we had seen, very vividly, how quickly life can end. We had won the last round but there was another coming soon and sudden death could well be our destiny.

"Our poor wives and girlfriends did not understand why they came such a distant second in our range of priorities. Inevitably there was anger when we arrived home but, although we were hungover, we were calmer and better prepared for being partners again.

"One must remember this was the Rhodesian Army; nobody knew too much about post-traumatic stress syndrome, (PTSS) nor cared. We had no professional counselling to help us with our nerves, what we had seen, or our carefully hidden fear of dying. Anyone looking for a shoulder to cry on was told to fuck off and stop being a baby. We only had our mates really for solace and support and I believe the best medicine for fear and trauma was laughter. Somehow, often with wicked humour, and no matter how bad it was, we managed to laugh at one another and that helped us dump the demons that were lurking around our senses. The ones that made it through

CHAPTER TEN

into the dungeons of our subconscious; we just drowned the miserable bastards in beer and good cheer and got on with enjoying being alive.

I approached the bedroom door with caution.

'Honey, I'm sorry about last night. I just have to go and tell General Walls and the rest of ComOps some war stories over their tea break.' This made no sense to her. She knew lowly lieutenants didn't speak to General Walls.

'Jeez you're so full of shit, Stannard,' she replied and promptly went back to sleep.

"I leapt in the shower and tried to get my head around why the heads of the Air Force, Police, CIO, Army, Internal Affairs, along with the 'Supremo', General Walls, wanted to see me so urgently. After all, the war was in full swing and I had initiated an ambush in Mozambique. There were plenty of those going down at the time so why me? I was also angry because this was Padbury, the IO's job, and if he wasn't to be called in then I thought he could at least prepare me for what I was to say. I had no maps, no aerial photos; not even a bloody pointer. What I did have was a world-class hangover.

"I left Kabrit in my old VW Beetle, smoke billowing out the exhaust, down the road into central Salisbury, looking as smart as I could. On arrival at Milton Buildings, I cut the engine and made my way up the stairs towards the inner sanctum of ComOps; a place we all knew about but never dared think we would visit because it was only for the Gods of War and not us mere mortals.

"Ushered upstairs, I stood outside a door and then a green light flashed and in I went. The first person I saw was General Walls himself. I saluted him and he welcomed me in warmly. Then, for all to hear he spoke.

'Congratulations on being mentioned in various dispatches Lieutenant Stannard, you have done some good work out there.'

'Thank you Sir,' I said, very relieved we were off to a good start. He introduced me to the assembled heads of services then motioned to some maps that had been set up for me. There was a strong smell of cigarette smoke and many empty tea cups lying around. It was all very quiet as I studied the maps. The grid references of the operation plus relevant stickers for destroyed vehicles were all accurate as far as I could tell.

"Then I launched into the debriefing, outlining my plan of attack and why I did what I did. I felt it was not the time to bring up the fact that the intelligence briefing prior to the operation was pathetic; I was given three different Land Cruiser colour possibilities, so my target was obviously changing vehicles and routes daily; no mention as to how many Zanla and Frelimo bodyguards he moved with; no information on road blocks or what reaction forces I might have to deal with. This had troubled me at the time but there was little I could do about it.

"I was blunt with them. I acknowledged my orders were to capture and extricate with Tongogara, but I also explained I was not going to get my men killed recklessly just to boost national morale. I told them when I gave my operational orders to my troops I told them what the objective was, but I also told them if we found ourselves in a situation where there were too many of them to carry out a swift snatch we were going to go in hard, whack them with everything we had, and get the hell out as fast as we could. How, I asked my audience, was I supposed to flag down a Land Cruiser and pluck some person out of a vehicle which was closely followed by an escort of three truck-loads of heavily armed enemy soldiers. There was no answer. I don't think any of them had a clue what to say.

"The room went very quiet as I explained I did try but when the situation revealed itself, I had no option to order my men to let rip with everything they had because we came under heavy fire and had to hit back. I was happy to report we could shoot straight and they couldn't or we'd probably all be dead. The fact that we had killed over 60 people and come out unscathed was a testament to the quality of my men and their skills and I was not going to apologise for my actions.

"I finished and looked at my interlocutors and they all looked at me and did not say a word. Nobody asked any questions. I looked at Ken Flower and he looked at me. I was wary of him and expected questions from him, but he remained silent. Little did I know it then, but I was looking into the eyes of a traitor, who had probably told them I was coming.

"General Walls broke the silence.

"Thank you for coming Lt Stannard,' he said, and showed me to the door. I saluted and got the hell out of there, then raced back to the bar for more beer.

"After I left, General Sandy Maclean reported that I was too aggressive for sensitive operations and the task of capturing Tongogara was given to Lt Andre Scheepers who then went in but he was also compromised. Probably by Ken Flower.

CHAPTER TEN

"What we fighting soldiers did not know at the time, was the bad blood between Generals Hickman and Walls was muddying the waters at the top. Hickman was an aggressive forward thinker, but Walls disliked him and marginalised him, to the detriment of the war effort.

"A big flaw in our structures was the absence of a single Special Forces Headquarters to manage both the Selous Scouts and the SAS. It was attempted in July 1978 but unfortunately the SAS and Selous Scouts couldn't put their rivalries aside and work under a centralised command structure. I can bear testimony to that fact; I had to undertake a second SAS selection which almost finished me off because I was effectively been 'punished' for having defected to the Scouts.

"In my view, looking back, the Selous Scouts, probably using one of their black guys to infiltrate Zanla, were better placed to pull this particular operation off than we in the SAS were. But the SAS guarded its tasks jealously and hated the thought the Scouts could do something they couldn't.

"I had a few days off and was then told I was needed for a recce back in Mozambique and I would be going with a new Territorial Force (TF) officer by the name of John Jordan who was also schooled at Umtali Boys High. I was a bit edgy about his lack of experience but once we met up I relaxed.

John 'Jungle' Jordan.

"Having recently passed my SAS selection, as one of the older candidates to do so, plus being a Territorial Officer and not a Regular Soldier, I was pleased to be included on my first full-blown operation. My performance on this task would be evaluated before a decision was taken as to whether or not I would receive my 'colours'. I was also excited because I would be going with Rich Stannard to test a new concept of a lightweight, mobile, two-man recce team that could move fast through the bush. Rich had recently returned to the SAS from the Selous Scouts where he had honed his reconnaissance skills working under Chris Schulenburg. He wanted to carry on using the same tactics in the SAS and managed, after some hard work, to get Captain Martin Pearse to give him permission.

"Immediately after selection, in February 1979, I had gone on a 'training Op', with several experienced operators to find routes being used by terrs into the country and to try to identify some of their local contacts. Rich was one of these operators, we had both been to the same school, we got along very well, and I feel sure this is why I was chosen to be in the two-man team with him. As a new operator, no belt and beret, but very enthusiastic it was a huge honour for me. I must confess that at this early stage of my SAS career I did not fully understand what was in store for me.

"In order for the plan of a two-man team to work there had to be backup in the form of a normal, fully equipped, four-man fighting-stick with medical supplies, machineguns, radios and other equipment we would not have immediately to hand. Our only comms would be an A63 ('small means') radio to relay messages back to base via the stick on their TR48 ('big means'). Without them within range we would have no way of contacting Rhodesia.

"After the normal full briefing and delivery of orders we all moved from Grand Reef airport via Lake Alexander north of Umtali into Mozambique and the Chimoio area. We knew there had been terr bases in the area we were going into but no close-in recces had ever been done. All the reconnaissance had been done from the air.

"To carry out our reconnaissance mission we had selected a large hill in the area. After drop-off by chopper and selecting an area for the support stick, we set off in the direction of the target which was about 40 kms away. The walk in was going to take time as we planned on moving with extreme caution and anti-tracking all the way. Our plan was to take three to four days' rations and work from there regarding future intentions. We could only walk at night so as not to compromise ourselves with the locals. On the second night we came across paths and the odd abandoned hut, which slowed us down but created no problems. As our designated feature came closer into view the less it looked like a 'hill' and the more it looked like a bloody great mountain. We decided to scale it on the steepest side in the hope that there was less likelihood of habitation. It was in this move around the mountain that we came across bivouacs which we presumed to be occupied by their camp perimeter sentries. This was a little alarming because we had to move towards the mountainside but avoid the camp and its inhabitants and get there before dawn.

"With little time to spare, we managed to find the rock face and immediately commenced the ascent. In true Hollywood fashion it had to get worse before it got better. Tired and struggling upward through rocks we stumbled upon a beehive and had to make a wide detour around them to minimise the number of stings. Anyone who tells you bees sleep at night

CHAPTER TEN

is talking rubbish – these were wide awake and not at all pleased to see us!

"We were exhausted, and my brain kept telling me the end was in sight but just as I had experienced climbing the Matopos mountain on selection, that one last rise ahead just kept on going and going. However, I shall never forget the breath-taking view that greeted us when we finally crested the mountain as the first rays of golden light streaked up on the horizon. We stopped, drew breath and gazed in awe at a view that went on forever. But there was not time for enjoying the vista, we quickly looked for good cover and went into hiding for the day. As we had been taught, we secured ourselves and ensured that we had 360° visibility, but it was completely open so we did a lot of crawling and crouching. Amazingly, there appeared to be no enemy presence atop the mountain. Their commanders had missed a big tactical opportunity and we were blessed.

"All we had been taught about 'Shape, Shine and Silhouette' became very important for us perched on top of our mountain right on the edge of a camp complex housing thousands of armed men preparing to terrorise the people of Rhodesia. Strips of hessian hung over our telescope and over our faces while we tried to make use of whatever shade there was available. The view below us looked like something out of a military textbook.

"In daylight the path network was very visible to us but the bivouacs were well hidden under trees and shrubbery. The task of carefully plotting and mapping out the camp occupied us for several days. As we gathered the information we transmitted it to our support-stick who then passed it on to ComOps in Salisbury.

"Despite being mentally occupied we were physically inactive because we had to move as little as possible during the day and avoid the creation of any silhouette. I had done isometric exercises when swimming for Rhodesia and thought that it could be useful in this situation. Basically I had learned to use certain muscles to exercise other muscles. By extending my arms out straight in front of me, palms together, I squeezed my hands together. My outside arm muscles were thus exercised. I then reversed the pressure and put another set of muscles to work.

"We soon realised that what had started as a short two-day observation was developing into a much longer task as our work was nowhere near finished. However, we faced two problems. Drinking water had been limited to four or five bottles because of the lightweight and fast-moving concept plus we were not moving across open ground to replenish from any rivers. Secondly, our radio used dry cell disposable batteries and we were running low on them. Again, selection course came to mind – '…. don't tell me the problem; give me the solution!'

"The weather had been hot and dry so we looked wistfully into the blue sky and saw dark clouds forming. Hidden from view under a tree we hung a poncho to collect any possible rain, drizzle or dew. Looking at the batteries I worked out that if we could connect them together somehow, collectively, they must be able to produce enough to power the radio. I had to try to remember schoolboy science about wiring in 'series' or 'parallel'. I worked it out and managed to stitch together a power generating system with four used batteries out of their cardboard casing connected with wire that allowed us to continue transmitting in short bursts twice a day – 6am and 6pm.

"A mounting mental challenge that I had not anticipated nor prepared for, was the sudden need to converse only when absolutely necessary. Being a TF soldier and a banker by profession I came from a busy work environment that was constantly humming with human interaction. Every day was filled with banter about our goals, wishes, dreams, families and always lots of sport. In the SAS, I had to make the sudden switch to being a loner and this did not come easily. The only time Richard spoke to me was when he absolutely had to, otherwise his lips didn't move. The fact was that sound could get us both killed and conversation was a luxury we could not afford. Initially, I really struggled with this forced silence and did a lot of talking to myself but grew used to it as the days passed us by.

"Eventually, after days of intense scrutiny, we felt we had the target comprehensively assessed, that the information we had passed back was absolutely correct and that it was now the time to mount an attack. We strongly recommended they use maximum firepower; heavy bombers, strike aircraft, and paratroopers supported by helicopter gunships. The size of the camp and the number of occupants certainly justified this call. We could not be sure of the number but estimated several thousand terrs, several light and heavy vehicles and three anti-aircraft batteries.

"Verification of the facts was called for once or twice and exact grid references given of the above items. Although we were never told I am sure there were aerial photographs by the Canberra bombers done late at night.

CHAPTER TEN

After some time, unfortunately, the decision was taken to limit it to an air strike only. My first reaction was one of disappointment, because this was my first operation and I wanted it to be a really good one. What we didn't know then was that all the available shock-troops from the RLI and SAS who were needed for this operation were too busy on other tasks so it was a critical shortage of manpower that made it impossible for them to put boots on the ground.

"We were excited but ComOps was in no rush, so we had to play a waiting game while they asked for additional information. I was becoming more and more concerned. Lack of food was a growing problem, and I knew we were soon to going to run out of battery power and that would leave us lost to the world. We had planned on two days and were now into our sixth. Our teabags had been used so many times they had been squeezed of every last bit of flavour. Finally, on our seventh day word came that the attack was coming in in the morning.

"As always we were wide awake at dawn but this time we were nervous. I was concerned about the anti-aircraft guns. Had we positioned them correctly? Would the jets be able to pick them up quickly and nail them before they did any damage? The big bang was about to go off and we had better have got our facts right. If not, we were going to be in a lot of trouble and my SAS career would be over. The other question was, would we be compromised? What would happen to us after the aircraft turned for home?

"Waiting has never been one of my strengths and this was agonising. So close but still anything could happen. There was total silence when suddenly the radio crackled into life and we heard the voice of a very calm squadron leader.

'Roger – we have target visual ... and keep your mouth open all the time.'

"The Canberra bombers with their 1,000 lb. bombs would be first in. 'Whispering Giants', they were known as, because on the approach to target, they seemed to glide in so quietly.

We lay on our backs looking skyward for any debris that might drop from above after the bombs hit. Being so close to the actual blast we had to keep our mouths open to try and equalize the displacement of air in our lungs immediately after the blasts. We blocked our ears with our fingers then saw the aircraft before we heard them and watched as they angled in towards an unsuspecting enemy.

"Two bombers dumped their loads; the ground shook and a shockwave went through the air. Shaken, I looked down to see the vegetation no longer existed; nothing, absolutely nothing! It was as clean as though a giant razor had shaved the face of the earth. Full grown Mopani trees completely gone without a trace. The silence after the noise was what I remember more than the actual blast. Nothing; no birds, no wind, no sound, just a deafening silence. I worried I had gone deaf.

"Still trying to gather my senses, I was relieved to hear from the cockpit of a Hawker Hunter, the casual drawl of the pilot telling us they would be on the target soon as the dust had settled to strafe the target after the Canberras were done.

"Travelling at such speed, and as low as they did, we heard nothing and did not pick the planes up immediately. Then they came into view and we watched the pair dive, then slow roll into a climb, back up with engines screaming, onto a 'perch'. There, they poised like hungry raptors, while picking their targets then swooped back down at supersonic speed with cannons firing and rockets blasting off the wings in puffs of smoke before streaking downwards. The missiles flew so fast it looked like the jet had come to a momentary halt. As the one Hunter climbed away, I studied the mangled wreck of a huge pantechnicon truck through my binoculars then saw a large sheet of metal like a huge silver feather fluttering back to earth.

"Then there was a flash from the ground and one of the Hunters came under fire from a Strela heat seeking missile that raced into the sky in search of the jets. We looked on anxiously but the pilot flying top-cover saw it coming and warned his wingman who took immediate evasive action and dodged the rocket. Rich then spotted the team who were operating the missiles, called the pilot to give him a target identification and like an angry eagle the fighter screamed down and let rip with his cannons, blowing the gunners to pieces.

After taking out the main static targets that we had identified, the Hunters picked off anything else that looked worthy of their attention and raked it with fire. We noticed that at all times one aircraft went high and circled while the other fired at anything that moved or looked threatening.

"We watched the whole show in awe and like every soldier in such a situation, we asked ourselves why we joined the army rather than the Air Force! After a few more passes their leader, in the usual languid tone said

CHAPTER TEN

'cheers guys', they were heading back to their Thornhill base near Gwelo where he said they would toast Rich and I over a cold beer. Then as quickly as they had come, they had gone. Bloody hell, we thought, we hadn't had a meal for days let alone a cold beer, and these guys would be having both within an hour.

"But the show was not over. We heard the drone of a piston-powered aircraft and a Lynx came overhead carrying our commanding officer, Captain Martin Pearse, who congratulated us on a job well done and briefed us on what had happened and what was ongoing. Several helicopter gunships then arrived and were picking off any targets they could see. Any movement gained their attention and was dealt with. This was a scorched earth approach and sitting there observing, I concluded the decision to use aircraft alone was probably the right one. Martin instructed us to remain in position for a few days to observe and report back anything that happened or moved. The good news was that we would be resupplied with food and batteries by the next chopper passing over the mountain but for the meantime we were going nowhere.

"He had barely finished talking when coming up behind us, very close to the ground, one of the helicopters was looking for us without drawing attention to us. It was so well done – the chopper dipped briefly, the gunner dumped a box on the ground, and they were gone again. We were delighted, we had batteries, rations, water and best of all; cold beers wrapped in newspaper. Also, fresh bread rolls and some hot food in boxes. The Rhodesian Air Force - best delivery service in Mozambique!

"For the whole of the next day nothing moved. We looked for anything, some movement, but nothing. By late afternoon vultures were circling above and started to drop from above for the bits of bodies scattered around. This added to the eerie feeling we had. The following day a Frelimo patrol came into the area. They drove through, in a Russian half-track vehicle, without stopping but slowing down to have a good look at destroyed items. We reported this immediately but were told to continue to observe.

"The following day it was a similar situation except that several half-tracks came. Again, we reported immediately, more from our eagerness to have more aircraft activity than anything else. Instruction was to report any further activity in an hour or so at which time a decision would be made. Exactly an hour later we were on the 'blower' reporting on many vehicles in the area and what they were doing. After a short time, it was decided to send aircraft to 'look and see'.

"Soon the Hunters were back overhead circling above looking for targets, but the vehicles disappeared and hid under the foliage well away from the attack site. Sensibly, they did not open fire. Having seen nothing to go after the pilots announced they were heading home, and it all went very quiet again. That evening we received our orders to withdraw.

"During the following day we packed up and prepared to move out, being careful to ensure our presence was well concealed. Later that afternoon we started moving off the top, possibly a little complacent, because there was nothing around that we could see. We used the same route down as we came up but being daylight wondered how we had managed without being heard or investigated. Because of the slope we did move further around the top of the hill heading in the direction of where we aimed to descend. Once we were on flat ground, we took a compass bearing and walked slowly, separated by several metres, observant for booby traps or anything unusual or unexpected. We were careful to avoid open spaces, stopped occasionally under shade to look and listen and I kept a backward eye wide open for anyone following us while Rich watched the compass. Then a low whistle and Rich was pointing ahead, indicating a path. He crouched down to cover and I moved forward, low to the ground, to check it out. I halted in the long grass and looked left and right warily then rose up very slowly to check out the path for any spoor. Alarm bells began to ring in my head when I saw fresh, clearly defined boot-tracks and I sensed that we were very close to the enemy. Despite the wind blowing I noticed the prints were unaffected. Using hand signals, I passed the information back to Rich who immediately indicated we move away in a different direction. Gingerly I started to move off when my world exploded – a noise I am at a loss to describe but it was mind shattering.

"It has always amazed me how fast the mind works. How so many images can pass through the brain in what must be micro-second? Was it a landmine, bomb or cannon-shell? I reminded myself I am still here and living so it cannot be a bomb and I am moving so it cannot be a landmine and the elimination process establishes that it was RPD machineguns ripping through belts of ammo. Basic training and well-practiced drills came into play and we reacted like automatons without deliberation.

CHAPTER TEN

"Rich was lightning fast in returning fire while I hit the dirt and started crawling backwards wanting to get the hell out, but I knew I had to take up the firefight immediately and help him hold them off. Scrambling for cover behind a tree that was thinner than my leg I opened fire on the moving grass and dust cloud ahead of me. I felt, rather than saw, Rich moving back, changing magazines smoothly, while continuing to shoot into likely cover. As we were trained, we were both mindful that ammunition was precious and not to be wasted so we were both keeping a mental note of how many rounds we were expending.

Almost automatically, our contact drills were coming into play - move, magazine, stay down, return fire. Totally focused on the people trying to kill us, we were oblivious to all other dangers. The key to the buddy/buddy system working is timing and Rich and I were quickly in sync with one another as we manoeuvred back away from the path into thicker undergrowth. Once we were in cover we stopped, listened and looked around. Where were they? How many of them? Were they still coming for us?

"Rich calmly indicated a direction of flight with a hand signal and we moved off as quickly and quietly as possible while he fired off a quick transmission to our support team telling them we were in trouble and needed help. The urge to simply cut and run like hell was huge but he displayed astonishing calmness under fire and this is what probably saved our lives. This was an SAS officer doing what SAS officers are trained and expected to do.

"Then we heard the unmistakable metallic clicks as they tapped their magazines with bullets so as to let one another know where each one was. Now we knew they were in extended line sweeping slowly towards us to flush us from our hiding place and kill us. But the tapping was a Godsend for us because we could gauge how far away they were and the direction they were moving. But during the momentary lull I suddenly realised I had a sharp pain in my leg and that my denims were wet. At the time I didn't give it much more thought because I was more concerned about where the enemy was and when they would hit us again. There was a feeling of slight relief when the tapping sounds seemed to have become more distant and we moved away confident that now we had sent the signal, and that help in some form would soon be on its way to us although I wasn't at all sure what they would do for us. What I do know was that I started praying. Over and over again I repeated the 'Lord's Prayer'. It sure helped and gave me comfort."

"I saw him get shot," remembers Stannard, "and heard the slap as it hit him. Funny, but I knew he was hit before he did. The problem was that before the operation I had told Jungle that if he got wounded I would kill him with a white phosphorous grenade so there would be only charcoal for the enemy to play with. I said this in jest but he took it very seriously so this was the first thought that entered his mind! I was going to kill him!

"After he was hit, there was a break in the firing while they tried to figure out where we were hiding and I used the lull to radio a distress signal back to the relay team requesting an immediate 'hot extraction. But 'Jungle', realising he was wounded, remembered my warning if he was hit, took off like the wind. I raced after him but despite his wound and all I could not catch the poor bastard! He was not running from the 'gooks' but from me! I screamed at him to stop and eventually he did, but I was exhausted. When I got to him, I told him to relax, I had been joking and I wasn't going to kill him."

"On the run, and to make their task as difficult as possible we started to concentrate heavily on anti-tracking," remembers Jungle. "The difficult art of moving through the bush without breaking or disturbing nature in any visible way. Prints in the sand are obvious but undergrowth disturbed, or a leaf detached from a branch lying at the wrong angle so the underside is upwards facing the sun could be a death-sentence. Much easier to do with time on your side. Our flight direction was no longer the main focal point, it was more a case of looking for the hardest ground; rocks preferably, over which to move. Often, we would travel at 90 degrees to our intended direction so as to walk over rocky outcrops or in a running river and then out again over rocks. Anything to slow down the trackers following us. If the trackers had to stop to look for a clue it was giving us potentially life-saving time to put distance between us.

"We were making good progress but the pain in my leg worsened and it started to throb. I whistled softly to Rich and we moved to an area on hard ground. I told him why I needed to stop and only then realised the wetness was caused by my blood and not water from grass or river. My denim was a dark shade of red. I tore open the trouser leg and saw the wound just above my knee. The dirt and blood covered it and made it difficult for a close inspection. I had a drink of water and poured some onto my leg. This, of

CHAPTER TEN

course, caused a stinging sensation but showed two wounds on either side of the leg. Luckily, we both had a 'first field dressing' with us so we placed a dressing on either side of my leg and bandaged it tight. But we did not really have time, and the pressing need was to start moving again and worry about wounds later, so we were on the move again.

"Meanwhile, Rich had changed channels on the radio and contacted our backup stick to find out if help was on its way. We were told they had been told to pack up and standby for uplift in roughly 30 minutes. A separate chopper would be coming for us. A message was relayed telling them I had been shot in the leg and we were told a medic was aboard the chopper. This was all wonderful news, but we still had our work cut out to stay alive long enough for them to collect us.

"Rich set a more definite course of march so that we could relay to the incoming aircraft our location. Basically, a case of moving as far away as possible from the original contact area. The problem was going to be a landing zone for the chopper. Vegetation in the valley was mostly Mopani trees roughly all the same height. We had to find an open area; a rocky outcrop or a dry pan; somewhere with enough space for the chopper-blades to spin without hitting anything hard.

"Our ears were tuned in and when we heard the thumping of the rotor blades we could barely contain our joy. The pilot called us up and asked for a directional signal. This was done by holding down the transmission switch on the radio hand piece. Within the helicopter is a receiver that indicates on a direction finder the source of the signal. The pilot then flies on that line and straight toward us. As soon as troops on the ground have the aircraft 'visual' they then talk the pilot on to their position after telling him roughly how far away he is.

"Because we had been unable to find a suitable LZ, making it impossible for the chopper to land, we would be 'hot-extracted' by grabbing hold of a trapeze-bar slung below the aircraft on a steel cable which would then be winched aloft.

"With great skill the pilot stopped overhead just above the trees while we climbed on the bar sitting either side of the cable. Typically, this is when the chopper lifts straight up until the bar with the occupants is clear of the trees and then moves off but our machine was losing power and the pilot had no option but to drop the nose and maintain forward momentum to gather the speed needed to get lift and fly away. This meant we would have to be dragged through the trees until he was able to gain altitude, and in the process, I crashed into a tree losing my pack and my seat on the steel bar. Rich managed to hold on. As the chopper gained height and flew away, I was left alone clutching on to a branch looking forlornly at the helicopter flying away and then below me for sign of our pursuers. I had to ask myself if my fate was to survive two gunshot wounds in my leg, run and avoid the terrs for close to 10 kms only to be left to die in a tree?

"It all went very quiet and I was alone, sad and scared, thinking of what limited options were open to me if I had been abandoned. Capture terrified me. I prayed and was thrilled to hear the approaching rush of rotors signalling the return of the helicopter. To make sure they saw me and to make it easier for them, I clambered higher up the tree to where I had a stance and stood and waved furiously at the pilot. He came in slowly and carefully to a point where I could almost touch the open door. I was not going to take any chances with being left behind again and I reckon I could have been chosen for the Springbok rugby team as a lineout jumper the way I leaped up and grabbed the back wheel of the old Alouette. With both arms wrapped around the wheel the sudden weight on the one side of the chopper caused it to rock violently but the pilot managed to hold it and lifted up and away. A very short distance further on, when we were out of danger we landed briefly, I let go the wheel, arms aching, and leaped back into the aircraft. Finally, we were on the way home with the medic having a close look at my wound.

"The original idea was to fly direct to Umtali General Hospital and drop me off for observation and treatment. However, being dressed in terrorist uniform, still covered in camouflage paint, and being one foul-smelling mess it was decided that we go direct to Grand Reef base to get cleaned up and then return to hospital by road later.

"In view of the success of the operation I was awarded my SAS colours and the Military Forces Commendation (Operational) for bravery. The official commendation dated 3rd July 1979 reads: *To bravery and determination on active service.* One of the shortest citations in the Rhodesian SAS but what an adventure for a rookie on his first operation. I was, and still am, a very proud man."

CHAPTER TEN

Stannard concluded: "This was very much an evaluation exercise and at the end of it I had to report to Martin and decide whether, in my opinion, 'Jungle' would cut it as an officer. The SAS troopies and NCOs were very prickly about officers and so for a TF guy it was a tough call. But I told Martin that I thought he had performed brilliantly and had no hesitation recommending him for his colours. I was awarded the Bronze Cross of Rhodesia."

Chapter Eleven

The politicians strut pompously
To yet another conference table.
For the umpteenth time bellow and strike a pose
What care I for all this?
Their babble rolls on
We continue to die.

◆

Beginning of the end

Bastille

"It was not long after the recce with Jungle when I got wind of the fact that Martin Pearse was involved in planning an operation into Zambia to kill Joshua Nkomo. The whole country at the time was in a fury following the downing of the second Air Rhodesia Vickers Viscount, the Umniati on 12th February 1979. When I heard I was to be included I was thrilled. We all wanted to have a crack at the 'Fat Fucker' at that point. I assumed it would be airborne and was surprised when I heard we were going to go in by vehicle. Once the decision had been taken to go right into the heart of Lusaka I think they decided to do as much damage as possible so I was told I would not be involved in the actual attack on Nkomo's house but would attack the Liberation Centre. Mac McIntosh would hit the Central Government Stores. I would have Billy Grant as my 2IC and a complement of eight men in two Land Rovers.

"We expected a lot of action. President Kenneth Kaunda of Zambia lived very close to Nkomo and he was protected by the Presidential Guard very close by. No more than two kms away at Arakan Barracks was the Headquarters of the Zambian army. We also knew they had MIG jets at the airport and quite sophisticated anti-aircraft batteries supplied by the Brits. We also expected the police to react but everyone was very excited and keen to get going.

"The first crossing, which was across Lake Kariba, was aborted but we

CHAPTER ELEVEN

made it on the second attempt where we were met by 'Snake' Allan and his group who supervised the unloading off the ferry, then we hit a bush track and we were on our way to Lusaka. A major worry was crossing the Kafue Bridge which was always guarded but for some reason, on this particular night, there was nobody there and we crossed without a problem.

"On the approach to Lusaka, I was surprised at the amount of traffic and we all tried to look as nonchalant as possible, hoping there was no white skin showing through the black camo-cream we were covered with. At the Kafue roundabout on Cairo Road at the entrance to the heart of the city centre we parted company with the main group under Grahame Wilson and Martin Pearse which carried on up Independence Road on their way to where Nkomo lived and close to the Zambian president.

"Our orders were to attack as soon as we heard the noise coming from Wilson's bunch. In the meantime Billy and I jumped on top of a wall to have a look and were surprised at how lightly guarded it was but there were plenty of vehicles there, roughly 30 or so, and I was excited about using the explosive set-up I had put together.

"As soon as we heard the shooting start up the road Billy flung a bunker bomb through a window into the Operations Room beneath him causing a massive blast and sending the roof of the building twisting in the air above us. Then we brought the two 'Sabre' Land Rovers through and machine-gunned the place before Billy and I went to work laying all the charges. I had everything worked out in advance, and all we had to do was lay the ring-mains and blow everything to pieces. Within the complex were the offices of the South African ANC, SWAPO and Zipra. All beautifully equipped, the filing cabinets were bulging with documentation. We took what we could then laid charges before moving on to the armoury. I was pleased with myself in that we got the job done very quickly. With the magazine stuffed with enemy explosives I knew it was going to be a big bang. While we were doing the explosives, the blokes in the Sabres were letting rip at anything moving that came close to us. Just before ignition I grabbed a Zambian flag off the pole and then we let it rip. That blast was one of the sweetest sounds I ever heard; the city shook and I thought surely one of these buildings here is going to collapse. Soon after the blast, Grahame, Martin and the other guys arrived back. There was this big building right opposite us and I badly wanted to take it down but Grahame told me to behave myself. I thought we've come all this way, let's fuck the whole place up while we have a chance.

"Sadly, the 'Fat Fucker' was not there; someone tipped him off I'm sure; much conjecture but almost certain now that the Brits knew what we were up to and sent someone a signal. But on the way home it all seemed to catch up with me and I felt terribly tired to the point I could not keep my eyes open and this was no time to nod off; we were still deep in enemy country and had to be alert. We were still expecting the Zambian Air Force to do something so an attack from the air was much on my mind and that would have been an interesting challenge because we had not a lot to defend ourselves with. Bless Bruce Laing, our medic; he always seemed to come up with the answers no matter what was needed; he saw I was fading and produced some concoction that re-energised me immediately; it was like rocket fuel and my eyes nearly popped out of my head! We arrived back at the bridge just before dawn, collected the other guys and headed for the border and home.

"Soon after we returned from Zambia there was a medals parade at Government House where Jamie Scott, a 15-year old Churchill schoolboy received Rhodesia's Conspicuous Gallantry Decoration, the highest civilian award for bravery. A couple of months before, he and his friend Piet Visser were on their motor-bikes in the Beatrice farming area when they ran into a group of terrs. Jamie opened up but he was hit twice in the opening exchange. Running into cover as his weapon jammed, he was hit a third time before hunkering down with his friend Piet who was also hit. Thinking the two were dead, a group of terrs advanced on them but Jamie cleared his rifle and charged into them firing at close range. He was hit again and went down but the terrs fled. He had been hit in the back, thigh, calf and heel and a fifth bullet grazed his chest."

The end of Uncle Ron

On the 31st May 1979 Ian Smith, who by then had been at the centre of the Rhodesian political storm for 15 years, finished his last day in office and handed power to Bishop Abel Muzorewa. They bade their small staff farewell and left for their new house not far away in the suburb of Belgravia.

The following month Ron Reid-Daly's career came to a sorry end. In June 1979, as a result of his public verbal attack on General John Hickman,

CHAPTER ELEVEN

IN good company... 15-year-old Jamie Scott being congratulated by the Commissioner of Police, Mr P. K. Allum (left), and the Commander of Combined Operations, Lieut.-General Peter Walls, after receiving the Conspicuous Gallantry Decoration from the acting President, Lieut.-Colonel H. B. Everard. Jamie, a Churchill schoolboy, received the nation's highest civilian award for bravery after putting to flight a gang of 10 to 15 terrorists despite being wounded four times. Full story and citations on

REID-DALY RESIGNS

Defence Reporter

THE Commanding Officer of the Selous Scouts, Lieut-Colonel Ron Reid-Daly, who has instituted a civil suit against several senior officers and former members of the security forces for invasion of privacy, has resigned from the Army.

A spokesman for the Ministry of Defence, confirming this yesterday, said Colonel Reid-Daly had "submitted his resignation".

He could not say when it would become effective but unconfirmed reports said this would be on November 1.

Colonel Reid-Daly said yesterday that as a soldier he was unable to comment to the Press.

It was not until late 1974 that the decision was taken to form the Scouts. Since then they have become a household name in this country.

Colonel Reid-Daly was with the School of Infantry before joining the Rhodesian Light Infantry, with whom he served for 13 years.

As he was going on retirement he was asked to take over the newly-formed unit.

Born in Rhodesia, he spent two years with the British Army and the Special Air Service in the Malayan campaign.

Colonel Reid-Daly is the central figure in a civil action in which he is

COLONEL REID-DALY

claiming a total of $53 000 from eight members or former members of the Army.

This follows the alleged bugging of his office at Inkomo Garrison in August last year.

All eight, including the former Commander of the Army, Lieut-General John Hickman, intend to defend the action. The Prime Minister, Bishop Abel Muzorewa, is also being sued in his capacity as Minister of Defence and Combined Operations.

Colonel Reid-Daly, who is commissioned as a Territorial officer, has to give three months' notice, like all other officers.

Press reports in Britain have said he might move to South Africa and that an Army major has been selected to take over from him.

But Army sources said yesterday this was "pure speculation".

– 221 –

he was found guilty by a Courts Martial of insubordination.

Before sentence, the Judge-Advocate General, Lieutenant-Colonel J.P. Reed, took an unusual position on the question of sentence and summed up the tragic series of events with sagacity and clarity.

"Mr. President and Gentlemen," he said. "In whatever sentence you decide to impose will be reflected your reaction to and your assessment of this case overall. It will reflect on the army as a whole and, perhaps beyond the army, the considered opinion of a general court martial comprised of high-ranking officers – the highest military tribunal in the land – as to this wholly disastrous affair.

"While having regard to the tenets of military discipline your sentence will, I am confident, be the measure of your contempt and disgust towards this whole disgraceful bugging affair. But above all, it would demonstrate your condemnation of the outrageous irresponsibility displayed by those concerned in the bugging of the telephone of someone of Colonel Reid-Daly's position as CO of the Selous Scouts. You all know, far better than I do, the role and tasks carried out by this unit. It is, in my judgement, incredible to the point of being bizarre and grotesque that his 'phone should have been bugged on such a flimsy, tenuous pretext, based only on rumour and suspicion, totally without any foundation of fact, particularly over something like poaching or ivory-running, which seemed to be the main object of the ridiculous exercise, and which, when viewed against the backdrop of the war and the security situation overall, are, in my submission, mere trivialities.

"The actual and potential prejudice to top security operations and the tragic consequences which could or may have resulted from the ill-conceived actions of those concerned, are, in my submission, quite mind-boggling".

In response, the court handed down the most lenient punishment available to them, which was a reprimand. Events had taken their toll; the damage was irreparable, and an illustrious military career ended badly and sadly.

"It was only many years later that I learnt of CIO's distrust at this time of the Selous Scouts," remembers Keith Samler. "And the possible political consequences of Rhodesia still maintaining such operations in view of the political positioning and doubletalk that was going on. I knew that Ron was having a hard time with his own people in Military Intelligence accusing

CHAPTER ELEVEN

him of poaching and gun-running and all manner of things, designed to destroy his credibility and that of the Selous Scouts Regiment generally. His telephone had been tapped and strange as it may seem a police enquiry into the allegations against him concluded irrefutably that there was no base whatsoever to the allegations. Much later I discovered that my home telephone had also been tapped and I was also subjected to a lot of malicious allegations. In his book, Serving Secretly, the Director of CIO Mr Ken Flower briefly alludes to this period of time in relation to the Selous Scouts and between the lines leaves no doubt of the Government/CIO hierarchy's intent to distance themselves from the regiment. CIO had decided to sideline Selous Scouts' operations.

"For some reason I shall probably never ever know, although the dirty politicking taking place must have had some bearing, there was certainly a planned, high-level decision taken to sideline senior BSAP SB and army personnel intimately associated with the Selous Scouts. Perhaps because of the political shenanigans taking place, and the probable presence in the army, police and CIO of people not totally committed to the welfare of Rhodesia, it was considered that we were a 'threat' to their plans to hand the country over to the nationalists."

Op Carpet.

"We lived in the suburb of Mandara on the outskirts of Salisbury," remembers Jungle Jordan. "The house was just off Salisbury Drive, a road that completely circled the greater municipality of Salisbury. Our house was a spacious three-bedroom suburban home with an acre of land, swimming pool and clay tennis court with a small pavilion between pool and court. Weekends were wonderful with kids swimming while the adults played tennis.

"Frequent guests were Martin and Mo Pearse with children and Bob Warren-Codrington. Martin was then OC C Squadron and Bob was a captain involved more in intelligence. Years earlier, while doing a routine training jump Bob had got the static line strop wrapped around the fingers of his one hand. As they went out of the Dakota door, the strop, being made of nylon, severed his fingers; actually burnt them off. Stories have it that he screamed all the way down and the normal green silk canopy of the chute was covered in blood. Despite this Bob did not consider this a handicap; he was an incredible tennis player and had his Rhodesian Colours for shooting.

"It was on one of those weekends, after a few sets of tennis that Martin took me aside and said there was an operation being planned and asked if I wanted to come on it. Being in the reserves and a busy banker, I was not compelled to accept but I was immediately amenable to the idea. I brought my wife Maureen into the conversation. She reminded me it was our daughter Lara's birthday on 22nd June so her only request was that I be allowed to return to our home for this occasion. Martin agreed immediately because the actual final date of the op had not been fixed and it was intended to have a week or so training. Martin offered no details; just that there would be a week of intensive training at Darwendale Dam, prior to the operation.

"Monday morning early Martin collected me and we drove, together with the convoy, out to Darwendale. I was pleased to see Rich Stannard there, all smiles and raring to go. Our training venue was a beautiful old farm house, with outbuildings, now the scene of a hive of SAS activity as chaps went to work setting up an ops room, kitchen, canteen and sleeping quarters. The trees were teaming with beautiful birds. The main house was in the process of being remodelled with selected walls being knocked down and rooms opened up to replicate a sketch of a similar house in some other country hostile to Rhodesia. But where, we had no idea.

"Training started before sunrise every day with a run in full battle-dress, carrying rifles along the numerous dirt roads on the farm that circled the dam. After a hot shower and shave it was the normal 10 chin-ups on the bar outside the mess hall before being allowed into breakfast.

"The first day was spent in a 'lecture-hall' hearing more about why we were there and what we were going to do. We were told we were going to mount a raid on a house in a residential suburb that was being used as a secret Intelligence Centre for Zipra. An enlarged copy of the 'house plan' was shown to us, plus its situation in relation to boundary walls, surrounding houses, roads and other items like telephone lines and electricity cables. We still didn't know where it was but assumptions were being made because we were told we were going in by chopper so we guessed there was a range limitation compared to a Dakota.

"With a proposed attack plan in place we had to get our heads around the routine of flying in by helicopter, hovering, landing to allowing troops to deplane and then the fast move into the house. We then had to practise

CHAPTER ELEVEN

this over and over with stopwatches running taking the time of each full run though. They had to work out how long the choppers needed to be on the ground, how long they could stay on the road, and if they had to move, where to? How long would we need to do the job and finally how to do it all in reverse so that we could get out of house, enplane, lift-off and go home.

"Morning and afternoon activities consisted of going through the drill of deplaning from a chopper - a couple of boxes upside down on the front lawn of the old farm house - sprinting into the house, and then turning to put backs flat against the house wall and tossing in a bunker bomb. It was not just one stick of men deplaning but four sticks all at the same time; three sticks for the house and one stick of guys to cover the road in front of the house to stop approaching traffic and pedestrians from either direction. Over and over again we ran through the routine with Martin or Rich shouting 'too slow - do it again'. Hour after hour, afternoon followed the morning and one day after another with the basic routine that was expanded, perfected, adding new things and eliminating unnecessary items as we went along. Although we all practised all aspects of the routine, in different positions and different jobs, the final decision as to who would do what was deferred while Martin and Richard watched to see who was best at what.

"At the weekend Martin and I left the training camp and went into town for the Saturday afternoon to celebrate Lara's birthday and spend the night with family as originally promised. An experienced SAS wife does not ask any awkward questions and no explanations were given. Fortunately for me, if asked, much of the detail was still unknown, but for Martin it must have been very different as he was fully aware of the detail, logistics, dangers and possible political implications. I am sure he had many headaches.

"The following week was pretty much the same as the last but we were getting faster and faster at the specific tasks until we were able to do it virtually blindfolded. Very similar to parachute school, when we did the same routine over and over again until it became automatic. The ultimate aim being that no matter what happened we would be able to complete the task. By the end of the second week Martin was satisfied that the men were ready to roll. We were told to prepare for a detailed briefing. The blokes were on tenterhooks, dying to know where the hell we were headed and what our individual tasks would be.

"We discovered the entire raid was based on information received from a captured terrorist who had turned 'state witness.' Just why was not for us to know, we just hoped his information was correct.

"Martin then explained we were going to a Lusaka suburb called Roma to hit a house that was being used as a safe-house and intelligence hub. Our main mission was to recover as much documentation as possible, kill the occupants if necessary but captures were deemed preferable. We were told the property was only lightly defended.

"Once the target had been explained there was silence as we pondered what lay ahead. We were flying in to the heart of a large city in daylight, landing among houses, between telephone lines and electricity cables. I couldn't fathom how the choppers would have the range to get us there and back. And we all knew the Zambian Air Force had Migs just nearby at the main airport. In armament terms, what did we have to deal with them if they were scrambled after we were finished blowing houses to pieces. We knew this wasn't a suicide mission but it sounded pretty close! It was certainly going to be daring.

"I was to be responsible for the group guarding the southern approach road immediately in front of the targeted house. Sergeant Major 'Petrol Pete' was responsible for the party on the northern approach road. Our job was to stop anyone or anything from coming in or going out during the time we were on the ground. No problem if it was an individual or two but it was going to get interesting if a truck-load of troops or APC came trundling down the road – Zipra or Zambian Army.

"I was told our chopper would land on the road running past the front of the house but about 600 metres to the one side. The other two choppers had to land on the road behind the house on a vacant stand, allowing the guys to run in from behind the house we were attacking. The fourth chopper, with Lt-Colonel Garth Barrett aboard in overall command, would hover at the start while men went in then land nearby and wait.

"While the guys ran from the back breaching the walls, 'Petrol Pete' and I would run from our chopper to our roadblock positions. While the noise of four helicopters would be unusual, thus attracting attention, it would also be confusing as it was both front and back.

"The house was surrounded with a concrete panel wall and a double-vehicle gate at the front. The plan was that the two house-raiding parties would have a 'Hulk' with which to breach the wall. The 'Hulk' was 'Made

CHAPTER ELEVEN

in Rhodesia'; a simple but specifically designed, shaped explosive made from a piece of angle iron about 1.5 metres long and packed with plastic explosive in the 'V'. It looked like a long 'Toblerone' chocolate; the open 'V' side had double sided tape on it that would glue the device onto a wall. The shape of the angle iron would direct the blast towards the taped side along the length of it, smashing a hole in the concrete wall, thus allowing the team to run through.

"The day before the raid we flew to the bush strip at Mana Pools with two Dakotas. We would all sleep around the aircraft and under the wings. The Daks would have our overnight kit, but more importantly, they would fly all the documentation we hoped to be recovering back to Salisbury.

"It was very early on 26th June 1979, the morning of the raid that we were up, dressed and ready to go, and well before 4 am. It was winter and even the Zambezi Valley gets cold. We all struggled to stay warm. All kit was checked, and then with someone else, double-checked to ensure you had whatever you required. Each of the choppers had two full 44-gallon drums strapped to skids just behind where the back door would be. There was a pipe from the screw-top plug into the main fuel tank using an electric motor to pump from the drums in-flight. Another 'Made in Rhodesia' conversion. I remember seeing the tech un-strap a drum about half-way to Lusaka and bung it out the aircraft.

"We were heavy on take-off and flew very low most of the way. Unexpectedly we hit crosswinds that blew us off course. Only when Lusaka city was visual did the pilots realise that our angle of approach was wrong. The resultant correction used precious fuel and time so the original plan had to be tweaked. This was all happening as the four pilots communicated with the Command Dakota circling very high over Lusaka.

"We only realised something was wrong when the choppers approached the road from the opposite direction to what we had prepared for in our rehearsals. We would have to do almost the complete opposite to what we had trained for. The other surprise was that the property was far better defended than we expected and we could see machinegun posts around the perimeter. The gunners initially thought we were Zambian Air Force I suspect, and did not open fire. But soon guards were running out of buildings and taking up positions. This was not what we were told to expect. Just as we hit the ground the incoming fire started and it was heavy. One of the chopper pilots almost had his head taken off. The gunners in the choppers were ready for them and got busy while the troops de-planed and started fighting their way forward to blow the walls.

"With our guys, 'Petrol Pete' and I, ran to our allocated areas and did a quick recce of the area. The neighbourhood, their peace shattered, was understandably in an uproar. I looked up and saw a guy hanging over an adjoining wall with a cine camera trying to record a bit of the action. A few rounds quite high over his head got him down and running for cover. Then I heard a car; a small Fiat came screaming around a corner coming straight for us. The only way to stop him was to open fire but not wanting to hurt anyone unnecessarily I shot the tyres out and that stopped them but while one of the occupants ran away, the other climbed out and also started trying to film us. Again a few shots into the car, now vacant next to him, put paid to his activity and he also ran off. I later found out that they were overseas news reporters trying to record one of the most daring raids in modern warfare.

"The noise and explosions coming from the house blocked out everything else but after the initial excitement of neighbours peering over walls and journalists trying to film what was going on, movement ceased. Then I noticed a guy moving down the street from the direction of the house towards us. He looked nervous; anyone would under the same circumstances, but there was something not quite right. With the guys covering me I approached him, and after questioning, he assured me he was a 'garden boy' for No 15 and on his way home to the local township. He claimed he worked two days a week but the ones he mentioned didn't correspond with today. He also had a very smart pair of shoes on so I decided to detain him, which really got him excited and angry. I radioed the command chopper to tell them we had a suspect.

"Meanwhile, events were unfolding rapidly within the compound. The intensity of the noise from gun fire and the thump of explosions was more than expected. Once through the perimeter wall the teams split to the left and right of the house - Martin one side and Rich, the other. Both teams were carrying bunker bombs to neutralise anyone or activity in a room or area. It is a percussion grenade as compared to a shrapnel grenade, really designed for clearing bunkers. Martin got to his mark and pulling the pin, lobbed it into a window, then withdrew back around the corner of the

CHAPTER ELEVEN

building. Tragically the house was of such poor construction that the force of the bomb not only blew the roof off but collapsed the wall that he was crouched behind – killing him. Rich did exactly the same thing on the other side of the house, rushing in after the explosion to eliminate anything still moving. Initially he was unaware of Martin's death but when Martin's radio went silent, Rich called him up. Unfortunately, Martin and his radio were buried under rubble and his men were digging furiously to remove it. Only when they recovered his still body could they respond to the radio messages and pass the grim news.

"Rich spoke to Garth Barrett sitting in the fourth chopper on a school sports field nearby. The order was to bring the body out, back through the hole in the wall but the raid was to continue. Rich automatically assumed command of the raiding party, instructing his men to take control and continue with the original plan to sweep through the house looking for documents and possible prisoners.

"Due to the time lost by being blown off course while inbound and Martin's death the time spent on the ground was reduced to 40 minutes. Radio commands were transmitted to us for all to hurry. Then the red pencil flare was sent up to indicate the withdrawal. The final act was to place four boxes of explosives on the four corners of the house with delay fuses – approximately 20 minutes.

"The choppers came in from their lay-up and we stacked them with documents. So full were two of the choppers the guys had to stand on the skids along the side. On the way out we chucked pamphlets telling people we had no problem with the Zambian people, and that we were coming back to kill more Zipra. Flying low, the civilians below waved at us like conquering heroes.

"One of the choppers ran out of fuel with the Zambezi river in sight but the pilot managed to make it to a safe landing on the river bank on the Rhodesian side. As soon as we landed the documents were loaded into the Dakota and they took off for New Sarum where BSAP SB were waiting.

"It turned out the 'garden-boy' was actually Alexander Brisk Vusa (Russian trained) the Zipra Head of Intelligence based at the Lusaka office. He had been in the house, taken by surprise and tried to get away. He would prove to be invaluable in breaking down the internal workings, command structures and logistics of Zipra. Thanks to him, five days after our attack a new offensive was launched on another camp outside Lusaka where we destroyed over 100 tons of arms, ammunition and explosives from Russia and East Germany that had been imported using Libyan aircraft.

"Also as a result of information gleaned, Allan Savory, who was a former member of the Rhodesian Army and a former MP, was revealed as an enemy collaborator when a letter from him was discovered. For reasons unknown to me, he was not charged with treason but left the country. Forced to sell his house, the chap who bought it called it 'Traitor's Gate'.

"Three days after our return, it was our medals parade and I received my MFC, while Rich received a Bronze Cross. Poor Mo Pearse was there to collect Martin's Silver Cross. One of the Rhodesian SAS's finest officers was lost to us and we all felt a little lost without him."

"Nothing was going to be the same again without Martin," remembers Richard Stannard. "He caused some grumbling among the junior officers because he always gave me the juicier operations. I respected him enormously and there is no doubt he was one of the more brilliant fighting officers of the Rhodesian war. He was also a very compassionate and caring man.

"I so well remember on one occasion Lt Mac Macintosh and I received a tongue-lashing from him for not paying enough attention to the accommodation that was needed for the African staff who would be cooks and cleaners at a forward base that we were setting up. He was extremely angry. Martin always made sure everybody else was taken care of before he attended to himself.

"Just before the operation when he was killed, I pissed him off one last time. I was wearing a button on my lapel which he noticed just before we were about to board the helicopters that would fly us to Lusaka. At the very time I was involved in a very interesting conversation with Lt. Mike Bailey about, of all things, citrus trees. He was from Inyanga and a fruit farmer and I wanted to know more about it. Then Martin approached, looking carefully at the button.

'When I was a USAF pilot in the war, I discovered God was a boiled egg in my lunchbox so I ate him,' it read. I thought it was damn funny but not my Officer Commanding. I'll never forget the look on his face when the words sunk in; like a bad smell had just wafted past his nose.

'Take that bloody thing off, Lt Stannard,' he growled, 'totally inappropriate and out of order. Get rid of it immediately!'

CHAPTER ELEVEN

Mike could barely control his chuckling. I took the button off and pinned it on the inside of my shirt. An hour later, poor Martin was dead."

Attack-Divers Course.

"The South African Navy attack diver's course which was run in Simonstown was something everyone in the regiment wanted to do but only a lucky few were picked every year. Being sent on this course was often used as an incentive to get chaps whose contracts were expiring to sign on for another stint. The deal being you get to go on a course if you sign on again. Operators who had performed well and acquired a lot of experience were invaluable and nobody wanted to see them go, so all sorts of special offers were used to get them to sign up again.

"I was desperate to get picked because I, like a lot of the other guys, knew that the training received on this course would stand us in good stead after leaving the army. The course at the time was rated as one of the toughest but also one of the best offered by any navy in the world. As it turned out that is exactly what happened and a lot of chaps used this qualification to get work after the war. Many went to work on the rigs in the North Sea and did very well there. One of our blokes, John Rossier, did the course and went on to become one of the main players in the search for, and eventual discovery of 'Stalin's Gold'.

"The man who would make the call on my behalf was Martin Pearse and I kept nagging him to send me. I thought that if I irritated him enough, he would relent and dispatch me to get some relief! Not helping my cause was the fact that I was still not forgiven for having joined the Selous Scouts. I was also well aware of the fact that Darrell Watt was far more deserving of being sent than I was. To advance my cause, I quietly approached Martin's wife for help and upon a night Martin, who was meticulous, went to bed and to his dismay discovered a pair of flippers under his pillow which she had quietly placed there for me. A few days later I received a welcome phone call from Martin.

'Okay, for heaven sake, you are on the course, now stop harassing me,' he said, and put the phone down. My tactics had worked, and I was over the moon. To say the other junior officers were angry is an understatement!

"We then flew to Cape Town in July and were transported to Simonstown and shown our accommodation. I was the only officer on the course, so I was given a room in the Naval Officer's Mess. The rest of the guys were billeted out in the accommodation provided for non-commissioned officers.

"We were all very excited. Most of us had recently been on the Russian Front or some other far-flung theatre of operations having the shit shot out of us, and this looked like a much-needed seaside holiday. Six weeks in heaven, or so we thought.

"At the school we then went through quite a lengthy process signing various forms and then taking possession of all the diving equipment we would need for the duration of the course. Once that was done, we were then put through a battery of medical and psychological tests. EE's (electroencephalograms) were done underwater to check our hearts and lungs. It was an extremely thorough examination right down to them checking the arches of our feet. There was much mirth when, suddenly we all started talking like 'Donald Duck' after some time in the dive-chamber breathing helium.

"Physically we all passed with flying colours but psychologically we did not do so well. In fact, we fared very badly. They decided, after careful analysis, we were all mad and dangerously unbalanced and they expressed genuine concern about allowing us to continue. The worried looks on the faces of the psychologists who checked us was a sight to behold. I think they were genuinely frightened of us and looked at us like we were a group of psychopaths. I must say, I did agree with them up to a point. Noel Robey had them worried but I think we were all in a sense 'damaged', after what we had been through. There was much discussion after the tests but they eventually decided to let us continue.

"That came as a relief but then the course started and it became immediately clear that this was not going to be all fun and games. Instructors, known as 'Dickies', made it very obvious from the outset that they were going give us a very hard time. In a way we were all ready for that, but the fact that we were going to be treated like raw recruits just off the streets did not go down well with the guys. We were all very seasoned soldiers who had moved on a long way from being recruits and all of us had seen a lot of action. This attitude towards us created immediate resentment amongst our group.

"The training was extremely physical and the days were long. We did lots of running carrying logs while wearing wetsuits with sand inside

CHAPTER ELEVEN

rough against the skin. All made more difficult by having to run wearing masks and having to breathe through our snorkels. Endless compass-swims backwards and forwards from the Navy Dive Centre. It was winter, the cold wind blew constantly and the sea was freezing. We pissed in our wetsuits to try and stay warm. Much of the training was done in a huge water tank at the school into which we dived regularly, followed by the Dickies who would then do everything they could to make us drown by pulling off our masks, yanking our mouthpieces out and turning our air of. We would be seen thrashing around in the water feeling like we had breathed our last. On reaching the surface, lungs burning and gasping for breath we would hear the screams from the Dickies immediately.

'Get down there you people, get under the water, this is the navy not the bloody army!'

"One of the exercises involved diving down and swimming through a dark, forbidding tunnel which was narrow, lined with barnacles and full of seaweed. The fit was so tight your No. 2 or 'diving buddy' had to swim behind you. The Dickies were tactically placed and they would then attack and cause us much trouble as possible; masks, regulators and hoodies were torn off and we had to fight back and swim fast to survive. But soon we were taking these challenges in our stride and the guys were all performing at the highest standard. Our minds might not have been right but we were doing well in becoming the attack divers they expected us to be.

"As this was a typical recruit's course we were lined up in the morning on muster parade and the schedule for the day was read out in Afrikaans which most of us could not understand so there was a lot of giggling in the ranks. Punishment for the slightest infringements were imposed with gay abandon. Known as 'skinnies', they involved having your wetsuit removed and having to complete the land and water obstacle course. I can remember diving off the pier, hitting the water and being unable to breathe such was the effect of the icy water. The obstacle course involved diving, swimming to the beach, running, crawling, hauling yourself up on ropes then back into the sea and the tiring swim to the 'Admiral's Beach'. From there, a long run around the Diving School barefoot on tarmac covered in small stones that bruised our heels. Very often the circuit was not completed in the right time and we would be sent off again. But no matter what they tried they never came close to breaking any one of us nor could they stop us laughing and I think that is what really puzzled them and pissed them off. With all the physical and mental pressure on us I knew there was going to be trouble somewhere, sometime, and I tried to tell the guys to behave but my warnings fell on deaf ears.

"I knew the fighting had started about two weeks into the course when I noticed Billy Heyns had a couple of nice bright blue 'shiners'. They had gone to 'Raffles', a Sea Point nightclub and true to form, Billy had had a go at the bouncers calling them 'fucking baboons'. Rob Cuthbert got involved with a barstool and there was a huge fracas. They managed to make it to the lift where one of the bouncers took a swing at Billy who ducked a big punch which landed squarely on John Corken's nose breaking it. John had to be taken to Groote Schuur hospital to have it straightened and repaired, so he was not a pretty sight that morning either.

"Standing on muster-parade, Billy was still chuckling and so were the instructors who I think were quite pleased to see him in a state of disrepair.

'Ja, ja, Engelsman; pasop vir die groot manne,' (yes, yes Englishman, watch out for the big men) said one as he passed Bill by on his way to get some of the disgusting coffee they served there.

"Making my life a little tougher was the fact that, being the lone officer, the instructors were particularly keen to make my life even more miserable than the rest. On one occasion in the tank I was attacked by three of the guys and I really did think that they were trying to kill me when they ripped everything off me and did their best to inflict as much bodily injury as possible. All my attempts to find a quiet place at the bottom of the tank and contemplate what was for dinner in the officer's mess that night, ended up in failure. The word from the Dickies to the rest of the course was, '… fuck that little officer up.' Only later, did I find they were giving answers to the other guys so they scored higher than me in the written tests we had to do. There were apparently no rules when it came to making me look like a loser. Then I spotted a new pair of badly bruised eyes.

'What happened this time Billy?' I asked quietly.

'We were playing rugby on the beach at Hout Bay, sir,' he lied.

'Bullshit,' I said.

"I soon discovered they had been in the Lord Nelson bar not far from the Dive School when some of the patrons started giving them a hard time. Having realised they were Rhodesian soldiers the Afrikaners started taunting them.

CHAPTER ELEVEN

'You've lost the war,' they were saying, 'you've fucked up, so what are you doing in South Africa? We will win in South Africa because we don't give up like you people. Go back to Zimbabwe.'

"This speech was really asking for trouble. The fact is, we were under a black government then, led by Bishop Abel Muzorewa, so we were all worried about the future despite overt bravado. Some of us had been fighting hard for seven years against mounting odds and the demands upon us were increasing. We were asking ourselves if our efforts in the past had been for nothing and did we want to get killed when we got home fighting for what was a lost cause. These guys had touched some very raw nerves.

"It was too much for Cuthbert, Corken, Ferreira and Heyns. They launched into these people and did some serious damage breaking bones and putting a few 'lights out'. The police were called and their problems mounted; the blokes they had beaten up were in fact off-duty policemen. They were arrested and carted off to the local jail which was full of 'coloureds'. The cops did not want to mix white and black so to the joy of the coloured prisoners they were told they could go free so that the whites could occupy their cell. Granted bail in the morning, one of the Dickies brought the battered brawlers back to the base and back to work.

"On the course, the instructors made it clear that in order to be a competent attack diver you had to be attacked and they were relentless in going after us. Billy Heyns attracted added attention because they couldn't stop him laughing. On one occasion someone stuffed a small octopus into his mask but that did nothing to dim his spirits. This pissed them off even more. I think the Dickies were a bit taken aback when our chaps thought they would join in the fun and started ripping off each other's masks; it turned into a complete mayhem, the likes of which the Dickies had never seen before. The harder they went at us the more cheek and backchat they got which completely unnerved some of them. One of the instructors eventually had had enough of us, lost control and had to be replaced. They then brought in some really tough guy to try and get the boys to behave but I don't think they realised what they were up against. The fact is, there was really very little they could throw at us that was worse than what we had been through.

"In the final stages of the course we were taken to Roman Rock Lighthouse. Built in 1861 on a single rock, how this little lighthouse lasted all those years in the face of the roaring south-easters that never stopped blowing, as well as the surging seas, was beyond me.

"There we did a free ascent where we removed our mouthpiece which was connected to a hose and then commenced the ascent from about 30 metres. About half-way, one's own oxygen supply is running low and it's time to 'boot' for the surface. This was an exercise aimed at training you to react to a lack of oxygen at depth. I was doing well when I saw the bubbles vanish and panic set in; flippers flayed at the water and I popped out at the surface like a cork out a bottle.

"It was the last week of the course when I went to meet a lady who was a friend of Winston Hart. Winston was one of the BSAP Special Branch policemen attached to the Selous Scouts and he suggested I look her up. It was a nice break from the course and I was happy to meet her. I then asked her to come for dinner at a restaurant which had a smashing view of the Atlantic Ocean. The evening progressed happily and I was so enjoying her company when the subject suddenly switched to the war. She started asking me for details of some of the friends of mine who had been killed. This affected my mood, but I was managing well until she asked me about what had happened to Martin Pearse. Then I felt I was drowning again but this time in a sea of emotion that I could not swim against. All of a sudden, my eyes started tearing up and I couldn't stop crying before I broke down completely. It was terribly embarrassing. I tried to pretend I was using the napkin to extract something from my eye but then I started sobbing loudly. She kept asking if I was okay, but I was unable to talk; I remember feeling so bad about the mess I was making of the beautifully starched white napkin now a sullied, wet mess. Then I started bawling and the entire restaurant saw and heard me and went deadly quiet, but I was not able to stop. It was an awful moment but a whole lot of fears and emotions that I had tried to bury had suddenly caught up with me.

"What I never got to tell her was that Martin had spoken to me just before he was killed and told me that he had decided to leave the army because he wanted to give his family a better life, a safer place to live and he wanted to return to university and complete a degree. He felt he owed it to the family. He was very torn because he loved the SAS and he did not want to let anybody down, but he felt he had done this time and it was time for him to move on. I urged him to do what was right for his family and reminded him he had done more than enough for Rhodesia.

CHAPTER ELEVEN

"All these thoughts and more had overwhelmed me in that restaurant and I asked the lady if she minded if we excused ourselves. We left quietly and I went back to my billet to gather my thoughts. I was in a lonely place, searching for answers and deeply troubled by the fact that this war was indeed taking its toll on my mind. Looking back, we were all combat-fatigued but at the back of our minds we all knew the Rhodesia we loved was slipping away and maybe all our efforts had been in vain.

"Finally the course ended, and we had all passed, mostly with very high marks. We were organised for what was supposed to be a joyous celebratory dinner at 'The Seaforth Restaurant'. All was well until a South African Defence Force rugby team arrived and took up a big table near us. They were very noisy and there was tension almost immediately with lots of mumbling and grumbling going on. Our lot was twitchy and as usual it was left to Billy to speed things up. He did so by grabbing one of the SADF guys by the tie and pulled so hard he snapped it off. The reaction was instant, and a punch up flared immediately with some big men beating the hell out of each other, sending tables and chairs flying and guests fleeing in all directions.

"It was mayhem when we heard the police sirens and in stormed the big 'Men in Blue' of the South African Police. This was not a good thing for sure, but it quickly got worse! My heart missed a beat when I saw the one cop, with a murderous look on his face, had a revolver in one hand and his other arm in a plaster-cast in a sling. One of the other cops had two very black eyes and a badly bruised face. These, I realised to my horror, were the same two off duty policemen that Cuthbert, Corken and Heyns had beaten up at the Lord Nelson bar only a week before!

"The one with the broken arm was way beyond incensed; he was shouting in Afrikaans, revolver drawn, I could see he was itching to shoot and seemed quite capable of killing someone. Having been on the receiving end of these guys' aggression, he knew better than anyone what they were capable of and probably felt fully justified in killing them in the interests of protecting the public. On reflection he had a point! They had cracked a lot of heads in a short stay as guests in the country and most courts would have agreed that the police were justified in deciding on the need to use maximum force.

"In the midst of this chaos I screamed, '... don't shoot ... don't shoot' and went at them waving my arms in the air in a desperate bid to stop them opening fire. The wounded cops saw me and hesitated and held his aim but it was so close. As they yielded, I yelled at my guys to back off and pushed them back and away. With the police still brandishing their weapons, the fracas slowly quietened down but the restaurant was a mess of broken furniture, blood and broken bottles with women screaming in the background. If the police had not drawn their weapons I don't know what would have happened because this was a brawl involving a lot of big men who desperately wanted to inflict as much pain and suffering on one another as they possibly could. Left alone they were quite capable of killing each other.

"The shouts of the policemen to stop were finally heeded and the two warring sides staggered apart as the cops weighed in. In no time they grabbed my blokes who were being dragged out to the waiting vans. They were thrown inside, doors slammed shut, sirens screamed and they raced away to the Simonstown Police Station and the holding cells.

"The next day they were before an angry 'Beak' in Simonstown Magistrates Court. For striking a policeman the mandatory punishment was 12 months imprisonment. They were looking at either Pollsmoor Prison or a return to the Russian Front and I think most preferred the latter.

"Pleading special circumstances, the magistrate was told these were highly trained SAS men, urgently needed back in their homeland to continue the bitter battle to save southern Africa from terrorism. After much persuasion he relented. He ordered they leave SA immediately under escort to the aircraft that would fly us home."

Making of a martyr

"On arrival home from Simonstown, there was a report in the 'Rhodesia Herald' quoting a captured terrorist who had recently attended a gathering addressed by Mugabe. The guy's name was Takesure Mavura and he claimed to have been abducted from a mission school, and then taken to Zambia before being sent to Tanzania for training. He reported that Mugabe instructed them to, '…kill all whites and even the priests. He said you are now going back home to fight the white people especially those on the farms. Whenever you come across a European in a car destroy him and his car. He explained that the missionaries must be killed because they talk politics through the Bible and the Bible had been brought by the white man.

CHAPTER ELEVEN

FRIEND OF LEPERS IS SHOT

Herald Reporter

THE man who dedicated much of his life to working with lepers and the man who was once described as "a poet and a visionary", John Richard Bradburne (58), is dead.

Mr Bradburne, who was a voluntary worker at the leper hospital at Mtemwa, near Mtoko, was murdered by terrorists. He was abducted from the hospital just before midnight on Monday and his body was found by security forces yesterday morning about 20 km from the hospital. He had been shot.

For the past 10 years Mr Bradburne had dedicated his life to working with the lepers at Mtemwa, the country's last leper colony.

From June 1969, Mr Bradburne, a lay preacher, lived, ate, drank and prayed with the Mtemwa lepers until, in 1973, officialdom stepped in and banned him from the settlement.

"I was sacked because they (the Rhodesian Leprosy Association) claimed I was careless with supplies and did not keep proper books," he said later.

But Mr Bradburne was more concerned about helping the lepers than about book-keeping.

His banishment, however, did not stop him. He simply climbed up Chigona hill, at the bottom of which the lepers lived, and from there he watched over the people he loved.

Later, after some Mtoko farmers had interceded with the Leprosy Association, he was allowed to come down and move into a broken-down hovel once used by a leper. From there he continued his work of looking after the physical and spiritual needs of "his people".

When he was not in the Mtemwa chapel or working with the lepers, Mr Bradburne, a former teacher, street musician, stoker in a trawler and soldier in the Gurkha Regiment, enjoyed playing his recorder and writing poetry.

He once said that he had always had a 'horror' about leprosy and, when he first heard about the Mtemwa leper colony, "felt unwilling to come here".

"But my conscience would not rest and I decided I had to do something to help. Now I am very happy here. This is my journey's end."

Last night, Phillippa Berlyn, the writer, said of Mr Bradburne: "He was a complete man of God. He was totally good. The lepers depended on him and, I believe, loved him very much.

"He gave up his total life for the lepers and he was also a very good poet. I am very sad that he is dead but John himself, I am sure, would forgive those responsible."

She also said that she had received telephone calls from people who had known him at Mtoko. "The whole of Mtoko, people of all races, are all angry and sad about his death."

MR JOHN BRADBURNE as he kept watch outside Mtemwa. Behind him in his tin hut are an altar and some of the pictures he gathered over the years.

– 239 –

The Bible brought the wrong kind of politics. He said we must kill them because they are the backbone of the Rhodesian Front.'

"And then, on the 5th September just as we were poised for some of the heaviest fighting of our war I received word that my old friend Father John Bradburne had been found dead on a road near his beloved lepers. The alarm was raised after Father David Gibbs from All Souls Mission was approached by an elderly African who told him, 'A European has been killed'. They went and found John lying lifeless on the main Mtoko road."

"According to the events described in the book 'Vagabond of God,' John became very uneasy in the days prior to his death. His hut had been invaded by red ants and he saw this as a bad omen, so he had moved to live in the chapel. He then climbed his favourite Mount Chigona to pray and seek divine guidance. When he descended, he told the lepers that an angel had told him to stay where he was.

"It appears that *mujibas* had for some time been making plans to get rid of him because he was persistent in blocking the movement of their cattle when it interfered with the welfare of the lepers. The thinking was that if John went the lepers would go too and they would have no more problems. Around midnight on Sunday 2nd September they arrived at his door carrying sticks and grenades. Called outside he dressed in his Franciscan habit, then opened the door and asked the group for a chance to pray. He was told there was no time for that. They tied his hands, grabbed his transistor radio and walked him some miles into the night where they met up with a group of roughly 40 people. Here he was mocked, forced to his knees, asked if would like to eat human faeces and ordered to have sex with one of the girls. When he refused he was forced to dance and ululate. When the merriment ended, his hands were tied and he was taken to another village where he was thrown into a hut. From there he was frog-marched through the bush to the foot of a mountain and placed in a cave to await the arrival of the *'vakomana'*.

"A Zanla commander duly arrived with 15 heavily armed men to hold some sort of kangaroo court. He asked why this famous white man who had helped people had been abducted and the *mujibas* told him he was a spy and produced his transistor radio as proof. The commander said this was nonsense and ordered him to be released but this met with dissent. The commander was reminded that they would all be at risk if this were to happen and John perhaps informed the Security Forces of their identities

CHAPTER ELEVEN

and whereabouts. On second thoughts the commander decided John should remain in custody and be taken to Mozambique. Offered this option, John refused and demanded he be returned to his colony. The commander then invited John to eat with him and after the meal told him he was free to go. John then set off but was accompanied by a crowd of people including two men who were armed. It is understood that they came to a stream where he was manhandled to his knees and shot in the back over 20 times. He was then dragged to the main road and left there.

"At his funeral, fresh, warm blood was noticed under John's coffin by at least two of the priests in attendance and the undertaker said he had never witnessed such a phenomenon before. The body was taken back to the parlour and the coffin opened for inspection. They could see no blood and the bullet wounds were clean.

"This has been certified a miracle and John is to be canonised but at the time I was sceptical. However, years later when I visited John's grave, Father John Dove told me that when John had been at Silveira Mission two eagles perched near John's room all the time he was there. And when they found his dead body a Bateleur was circling above as if in some aerial vigil. There was also a report by the journalist Angus Shaw, a committed agnostic, who visited John's old home to investigate the claims of his special relationship with nature. When he returned to his car it was swarming with bees and so was his apartment in Harare.

"I look back on this death with great sadness. He was a truly holy man, who devoted his life to improving the lives of the people who killed him. He was not the first nor last man of the cloth to be murdered by those they tried to help.

"Coming from a Catholic family the role of the church in the war became an issue of bitter contention within the religious community. While mom and dad were good Catholics, the politics of the day were testing their commitment to the church. Bishop Donal Lamont, for instance, the Catholic Bishop of Umtali, was a strong Mugabe supporter and instructed his subordinates to assist the enemy with whatever means they had at their disposal. He was eventually deported and many of the country's Catholics were very happy to see the back of him. Sadly, John Bradburne was only one of many missionaries and priests destined to die in the Rhodesian war."

Operation Tepid

Days after the murder of John Bradburne, on 10th September 1979, the Lancaster House Conference convened under the chairmanship of British Foreign Secretary, Lord Peter Carrington. One man he specifically insisted did not attend, was former Defence Minister PK van der Byl. Carrington knew that van der Byl knew too much about how the British intended to manipulate people and events to get what they wanted, which was a Mugabe-led, independent Zimbabwe.

Recalling events leading up to the conference and Mrs. Thatcher's breach of promise regarding recognition of the new Muzorewa administration, PK was frank: "Then 'Frau' Thatcher got in and started the whole Lancaster House business. We gave it the 'shotgun treatment' ... we tried everywhere to get some support, but we were totally undermined by the Brits. 'Frau' Thatcher did a complete reversal. She was on record saying she saw no reason why Muzorewa should not be recognized and even less reason why sanctions should be maintained. Twenty million dollars was raised to pay Bongo to recognize the Muzorewa government. I don't know where it came from. May have been the Saudis but I think not. More likely the Omanis and that would have been thanks to Tim Landon. We hoped if Bongo came on board the Arabs would follow. Unfortunately it didn't work."

Leading the government delegation was Prime Minister Bishop Abel Muzorewa, who PK thought little of. "Muzorewa was a windbag with a certain amount of charisma," remembered PK. "He was helped enormously by the British government, starting with the Pearce Commission. Not much of a leader, easily manipulated by others. He had no idea of government and he was given real power despite what our detractors say about him having been a puppet of the whites. Ultimately, he was easily manipulated by Carrington at Lancaster House."

While the politicians convened in London, back in Zambia plans were rapidly unfolding to boost the Zipra strength to prepare for an invasion. Under Soviet tutelage Nkomo's army was effectively split into conventional and non-conventional divisions. The grand plan was to continue the insurgency into Rhodesia thus forcing the security forces to deploy men and resources to contain the threat, while preparing conventional battalions for a full-scale invasion of the country when the time was right. Rhodesian intelligence knew this plan was unfolding and that camps were being established closer

CHAPTER ELEVEN

to the country's borders, but they were struggling to establish their exact whereabouts. So when an air force aircraft flying near the Zambezi River took unexpected heavy fire from a position in Zambia this attracted the attention of ComOps and Canberras were ordered to fly surveillance runs across the border looking for camps.

Photographs subsequently taken over a heavily wooded area north of the Zambian border town of Siavonga caught the eye of the analysts who believed they could identify trench lines running along the high ground straddling a depression. If they were right the disturbing conclusion was that there was a threatening enemy presence being established within easy striking distance of Kariba town with all the attendant strategic implications. But they could not be sure, a closer inspection was required and Bob Mackenzie was called in to organise a reconnaissance and, depending on what he gleaned, a plan to remove the threat. Mackenzie then reached out to his lieutenants.

"It was sometime in October, Bob called me and Lt. Phil Cooke in and told us what was going on, and then showed us the aerial photographs," remembers Stannard. "He had decided we were going to be deployed with 16-man call-signs to go and check out this area, see what was going on, and then we would work out what to do next. I listened to him carefully. By this time I had developed a healthy respect for Zipra. Unlike Mugabe's Zanla people who seemed to spend more time murdering and mutilating civilians than fighting, the Zipra troops were organised, disciplined and far less harsh on the civilian populace. They were also far better fighters and less inclined to cut and run like their Zanla counterparts.

"While lines of what looked like trenches were visible, the photographs did not reveal any tell-tale tracks indicating the movement of a large group of men. It appeared, their troops had been well trained in anti-tracking and had learned to restrict their movement to rocky surfaces only. It also appeared the trenches were well camouflaged by lining the diggings with soil the same colour as the surrounding surfaces.

"I was to be dropped by chopper 10 kms north of the suspected position and Phil to the south. We were then to do a night-march on a compass-bearing to positions atop one of the ridges and lie up there. Then the plan was to launch a full-blooded air-assault on the suspected camp using the Canberra heavy bombers. We would then watch, wait, and try and kill anything that came within range.

"We infiltrated with no problems and waited for dawn. In came the bombers and they pounded the position with HE, Golf-bombs and then incendiaries. This was October, the bush was dry, so starting fires was easy. But despite all the ordnance raining down from above there was absolutely no reaction from the ground at all. It looked like the enemy was long gone. Despite the nil-return, we were ordered to stay where we were for the day and then move to higher ground in the night and get into ambush positions. Regardless of my orders to walk at night I had a gut-feeling this was not a clever move. It was a very dark night and the bush was extremely thick. I knew we were not going to be able to move quietly and if there were any enemy around they would certainly hear us coming. I decided to disobey my instructions and wait until we had some light before moving.

"Meanwhile Phil was in the process of doing what he was told and was bashing his way through the bush, when they walked right into an enemy sweep line and a furious firefight immediately ensued. In the contact, John McLaurin was hit in the stomach but the RPD gunners had the better of Zipra and the enemy fled leaving one dead. They dragged some of their wounded away. Poor John needed help badly. The medic went to work with drips and did his best to make him comfortable but he needed blood and surgery which could not be provided in the field. The word from Kariba was that he would have to wait for casevac in the morning but he never made it.

"At first light we were ordered to advance up the ridge from our different positions and rendezvous at the top. Phil's team was struggling. Apart from a death, two of his guys had had to be evacuated with heat exhaustion. On the climb up the ridge they again came under heavy machine-gun, 14.7mm and mortar fire, Phil was shot in the arse and another guy in the arm as they were pinned down from above. Phil initially thought it was us shooting at them but I assured him it was not.

"I could hear he was in big trouble and I was moving as quickly as I could towards him to help when we heard Bob airborne in a Lynx telling us he was on his way to help with some air support as well as try and establish what was happening. He had sent for the Hunters but was coming in ahead of them to be of immediate assistance because he was concerned about enemy numbers. He was reassured by Phil that it was a platoon strength group they were up against. Unfortunately, Phil was wrong; there were a lot more who had not yet made themselves known and the Lynx came under

CHAPTER ELEVEN

heavy anti-aircraft fire from a fixed position nearby, and I thought they had been shot down listening to the distress calls on the radio. As the pilot rolled in for a rocket strike one heavy calibre shell had shattered the aircraft control panel, wounding the pilot, and causing pandemonium in the cockpit. The pilot called 'Mayday' indicating a dire emergency. He then reported there was smoke inside but they were still airborne and making for home as firing continued at them. Tough for Bob and the pilot but their arrival gave us some relief as all the enemy attention focused on the aircraft giving us a chance to move.

"I was in a rush to get to Phil and we raced through some deserted villages towards the firing. Bob, although under heavy fire and contemplating a crash landing, shouted at me on the radio warning me not to go on to the high ground where the enemy was now known to be present in big numbers. Meanwhile the pilot was trying to get Bob to grab his parachute and bale out, but Bob insisted on staying in the plane. They limped back to Kariba and crash-landed successfully without further injury.

"We were still on the move when I heard the welcome sound of the jets coming and very soon saw them swoop out the blue and dive down on to the target firing rockets followed by bombs. Despite this, the enemy appeared to hold their positions and keep firing. Clearly, they were not going anywhere without a fight. But we were badly outnumbered at this point and were ordered to a pick-up point for evacuation back to Kariba. Phil's group went first and while on the move I caught sight of movement above us. Through binoculars I saw an enemy section watching the air show so closely they had not seen us. I checked the lie of the land and saw that we could approach them from a flank through thick bush and surprise them. Quickly I gave my guys orders and we raced off around them. By the time we emerged from the thicket we were on them. There were only three of them - we killed two at close range and captured the other after he had been shot in the leg. Bruce, our medic, put up a drip and splinted his leg before our chopper arrived. I was very chuffed (pleased) to get on the radio before uplift and tell Bob that we had a capture. He was delighted.

"On arrival, our prisoner was whisked off to hospital and unfortunately for him they had to amputate the leg but he was soon in better spirits and when assured he would be well looked after, he revealed what he knew. He was the logistics officer so he knew all the details. Dug in on the hill were 240 well trained and well equipped soldiers who were going to defend their position at virtually any cost. They were from the 1st Battalion of Zipra's First Brigade and were expecting reinforcements soon. All credit to the Zipra fighters and their commanders who endured two days of heavy bombing and then carried out a classic night-withdrawal without suffering many casualties.

"But that was only part of the story. He went on to speak about the growing number of conventionally trained battalions being readied in the country for the invasion of Rhodesia and told us all about the equipment they were acquiring from the Soviet Union. This included jet-fighters. It was a disturbing picture he painted, and I knew we had a lot more battles to fight."

Bob MacKenzie SAS column attack.

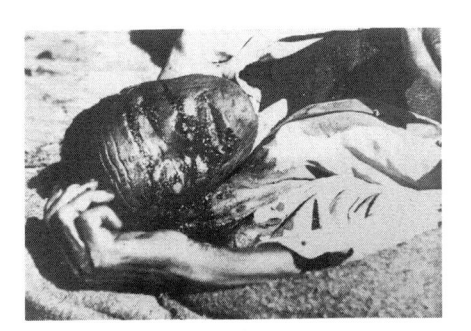

Village Headman beaten to death.

Stannard just after commission in the Selous Scouts.

Rich Passaportis.

Allouette G Car.

Men of the Rhodesian African Rifles. (RAR)

RLI Fireforce Paratroopers.

SAS recce team.

Stannard on right on diving course with SA Navy.

RSM Mavengere

Schulie and Koos Loots standing.

Selous Scouts Recce Group 1980

Stannard receives Bronze Cross of Rhodesia from General Sandy MacLean.

Stephen Mpofu going External.

Peter Walls 2nd from left, Air Marshal Frank Mussell PK.

RLI Paras

Selous Scouts rugby team. Winston Hart standing far left. Uncle Ron middle rear. Tim Callow on his left. Neil Kriel 2nd from right rear standing.

Selous Scouts. Op Virile

Uncle Ron. Mac McGuinness. Neil Kriel.

Koos Loots middle. SAS men leaving Rhodesia after Mugabe election win.

Police Commissioner P.K. Allum and Joshua Nkomo in 1980.

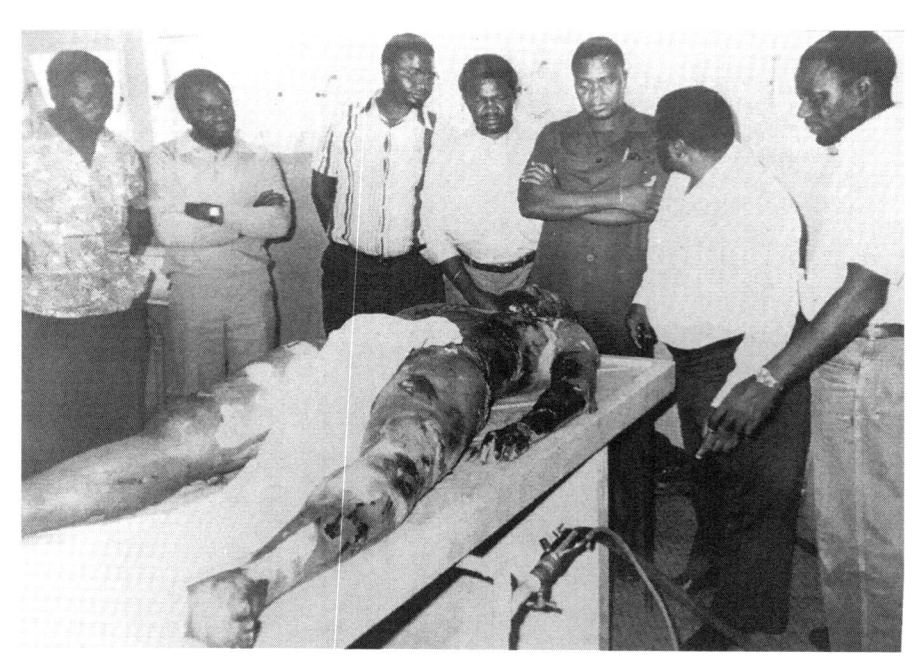

Body of Josiah Tongogara.

SAS Medals Parade. 'Jungle' Jordan

Dave Berry before Matola attack.

Rob Hutchinson just before Matola raid.

Op. Barnacle. Stannard 2nd from right with Schulie far right.

– 261 –

MEN OF WAR

Stannard with Captain Saxena 2nd from right.

Stannard as covert operator; Op. Barnacle.

Chapter Twelve

We believed in destiny, and when ignited
Even by leaders themselves misguided
We moved, we strove, we wrought.
We drossed our metal in the fire of war.

◆

The end of Rhodesia

Josiah Tongogara

As the fighting intensified so did the political wrangling at Lancaster House. Key players at the conference were the military commanders and the British were quick to schmooze General Walls with everything from test rugby tickets to tea with the Queen Mother. But the man who surprised all the attendees with his good nature and constructive approach to problem-solving was the man Rich Stannard and the SAS had tried so hard to kill or capture – Josiah Tongogara.

Having grown up on the Smith family farm in Selukwe, Tongogara told reporters at Lancaster House how kind Ian Smith's parents, particularly his mother, had been to him as a boy. This was not what the British press, British politicians, and particularly Carrington, wanted to hear, nor would it have pleased Mugabe. Spotting Smith at an informal gathering at the opening of the Lancaster House conference, Tongogara greeted Smith warmly and told him how much he hoped all the whites would stay when the war ended. In his initial meetings with General Walls he was even more effusive.

"He said to me, in no uncertain terms," recalled Walls, "that we soldiers needed to sort the problem out and to hell with the politicians. I got the impression he did not have much time or respect for Mugabe."

At all times, self-effacing and humble, Tongogara told the press: "I do not even care whether I will part of the top echelon. I am not worried. But I am dying to see a change in the system, that is all. I would like to see the young people enjoying together. Black and white enjoying together in a new Zimbabwe."

I will work with Walls —Tongogara

LONDON.

THE commander of ZANLA, Mr Josiah Tongogara, said yesterday he would be prepared to work "in any capacity" with Salisbury's top military man, Lieut-General Peter Walls, under a peace settlement.

Mr Tongogara was speaking in an interview with the Africa service of the British Broadcasting Corporation.

He is part of the Patriotic Front delegation at the talks, Iana-Reuter reports.

"If the Lancaster House agreement determines that myself and Peter Walls should work together, there's no reason why I should not work with Peter Walls," Mr Tongogara said.

He said there would be no difficulty in declaring a ceasefire if the talks reached a comprehensive peace agreement.

He insisted that the PF forces be involved in running the country as it moved towards legal independence under a settlement.

He made it clear he believed his men should form the basis of the new force.

He also disputed there was a rift between the two Patriotic Front forces.

"We are now working as one army."

But he said both armies had "thousands of thousands" of men and it was not possible to rule out clashes inspired by "some elements who are against unity".

In his book 'Winds of Destruction', Peter Petter-Bowyer has a detailed account of what was happening away from the conference table and it is clear Tongogara was in a hurry to end the war and bring peace to the country with or without Mugabe. To this end he soon met with the two top Zipra commanders, Lookout Masuku and Dumiso Dabengwa and quickly got their support for a deal that did not involve any of the politicians.

Tongogara's plan was for a military alliance of the three warring armies under the command of General Walls with Tongogara and the two Zipra leaders forming a command council. It had become clear that the Zanla commander had quickly warmed to Walls and believed he could trust him,

CHAPTER TWELVE

as did Joshua Nkomo. On the other hand he was suspicious of Ken Flower, who he had noticed, was cosying up to Mugabe.

Tongogara then wanted a 100-seat interim Government of National Unity represented in equal part by the parties currently headed by Muzorewa, Smith, Nkomo and Mugabe. The non-executive President of the country would be Sir Humphrey Gibbs and he wanted this structure in place for five years before elections would be held. Interestingly, Tongogara, like Ian Smith, did not trust Carrington or Thatcher. He did not want any British involvement at all in the new dispensation and he was solidly against the appointment of a British governor. Some of those close to Tongogara suggest he preferred Nkomo to Mugabe as the future leader of the country.

Under Carrington's chairmanship Tongogara was sidelined and the wrangling continued. On the 14th December, Mugabe's spokesman reflected their belligerent and uncompromising mood: 'Thatcher can go jump in the Thames' and 'Carrington can go to hell,' was their word to the world but everything suddenly changed when a blunt message arrived from Maputo. With the SAS, led by Darrell Watt and Renamo under Luke Mhlanga, running rampant in central Mozambique, Samora Machel had had enough of the Rhodesians and realised the insurrection they had triggered might spread south and threaten his grip on power.

On 16th December, he wired Mugabe saying if he did not sign, he would be welcomed back in Mozambique where he would be given a beach villa and he could write his memoirs. In other words, as far as Mozambique was concerned, the war was over and failing an agreement Mozambique would withdraw all support for Zanla forces. 17th December saw Mugabe, Nkomo and Gilmour quietly and obediently initial the conference report and ceasefire agreement. On the 21st December the final agreement was signed.

Six days later, Mugabe, on the Voice of Zimbabwe radio station, conveyed 'an extremely sad message' to 'all the fighting people of Zimbabwe': The 41-year old Tongogara was dead, killed in a car accident in Mozambique on 26th December 1979. Mozambique and Zanu released a Salisbury undertaker's statement (Ken Stokes of Mashford and Son) saying his injuries were consistent with a road accident, but no autopsy results or pictures were released. He was buried at the National Heroes Acre on 11th August 1980. The cause of death was given as a car accident but speculation persists that Mugabe arranged a Stalinist solution for his charismatic and moderate general. According to Lookout Masuku, an East German assassin who specialised in 'vehicle accidents' was hired and arrived in Maputo ten days before Tongogara's death.

'Tongogara was murdered'

Sunday Mail Reporter

A LETTER smuggled out of a maximum security prison in Mozambique has given British and local authorities the first real evidence that Josiah Tongogara, Commander of ZANLA, was murdered.

Written by Comrade M. Mahluru, the letter is an account of the operation.

It is addressed to the British Ambassador in Maputo, and dated February 14, and reads:

"Your Excellency. May it please Your Excellency to give this letter your urgent attention. My life here is now in great danger and is in your hands. You managed to force the release of those comrades who were prisoners of Mugabe, yet I am now in a cell on my own here at the SNASP (Mozambique secret police) Administration Block in Beira.

"I am sure even Comrade President Samora Machel does not know why I am here. The reason I am kept is because I saw why Comrade Tongogara, Commander of all ZANLA forces, was killed."

He claims that a trusted colleague, a candidate for ZANU (PF) in this week's election, "is the one who caused me to be arrested and has told SNASP that I am a spy for Muzorewa and mad, and must be kept on my own. Yet they will never release me.

"Comrade Tongogara was killed on the day after Christmas when he was quarrelling about unity with Nkomo, which he said was the best thing for the reconstruction of Zimbabwe.

"Then after the discussions they had to go for some refreshment." Mabhuru supplied the names of senior party officials present, and writes that he was "guarding outside the door" when Tongogara was shot "in the stomach".

He names the man who fired the shot—a prominent personality in both ZANU (PF) and ZANLA.

"They then hit him on the head with a short axe and cut open his stomach and damaged his body because ... (a senior official) wanted to tell the comrades it was an accident on the road.

"We then managed the accident 50 kilometres toward Beira. We made the Land-Rover to roll over and then reversed a truck into it. I became sick and Comrade . . . made me to be arrested.

"I can tell you more when you come to fetch me, but please do not first speak to President Machel. Simply come here to the Administration Block at Beira and ask for Mr Pinto. He will not refuse you to see me.

"Comrade Dukai Fambayi who was released will know me.

"My name is Comrade M. Mabhuru."

Sources within the British delegation in Salisbury confirmed yesterday that their Government office in Maputo had received the letter.

Said one official: "It has been investigated, and all we can say at the moment—unofficially of course—is that it checks out.

"We are going to try to get this chap out of jail and see what else he has to say. You must appreciate what a delicate political and diplomatic question this is, however. It has to be handled very carefully."

Josiah Tongogara's death was announced on December 27 and caused widespread controversy.

ZANU called for a commission of inquiry into the alleged Boxing Day car crash, and officials of the UANC have called for the body to be shown to prove it had no bullet holes.

Tongogara, who became commander of ZANLA in 1977, played an important role at Lancaster House and openly advocated unity between Mr Robert Mugabe and Mr Joshua Nkomo.

Stannard back to Maputo

Following the Lancaster House agreement there was official acceptance but thoughts of Mugabe taking over presented a major problem for the South African government and it was decided that another attempt should be made on Mugabe's life. It was planned for January 1980.

It would follow the same plan with the strike craft doing the launching near Inhaca Island and *SAS Johanna van der Merwe* doing the recovery the following morning. The initial attempt was again aborted for mechanical reasons and the raiding party returned to the mothership.

"On the fourth attempt, in January 1980, we approached Maputo further north from our previous effort," remembers Stannard. "Again, we came in on Zodiacs but time was short so this was when we decided to grab a car to get to the house quicker. Unfortunately, the car we waved down was driven by someone who had no wish to 'lend' us his car and a tussle developed. He was from one of the communist countries and shouted at us in some strange language. We were all carrying silenced .22 pistols in the use of which we had been instructed by Dave Westerhout who was then Rhodesia's

CHAPTER TWELVE

World Champion shottist. I was trying to turn the lights of the car off when policemen approached. We let them come in very close before we fired and they went down but not quietly. One ran off into the bush screaming. We knew we were running out of time if we were going to make it out of there alive.

"There was a brief silence while our OC gathered his thoughts and assessed the situation. Again, it was a bitter disappointment. We had come so far and put so much into this exercise, and this was probably our last chance but our options were very limited. With the commotion we had caused it was not only our safety at stake, there was also a huge potential political problem if we were captured and compromised. If at that stage the world had discovered we were in Maputo trying to kill Mugabe there have been a tremendous fallout.

"It was with heavy hearts we went back to the beach knowing we had missed, probably our last shot at the man we all wanted to kill so badly. Only when we got out to sea looking back did we realise what sort of uproar we had caused. The city was a blaze of blue lights.

"Subsequently a Soviet spy[47] was uncovered in Simonstown who may have known about our movements, but again I had the feeling that someone had let it be known we were coming."

Taffy (Alan Brice)

Other ways of killing Mugabe were pursued when he returned to Britain for further discussions. Alan 'Taffy' Brice, ex British SAS, was quickly dispatched to London to try and kill him with an explosive device on his way to his hotel room but there was a leak. The British security services went on full alert and Taffy was quietly called home. This was the first of several attempts that would be thwarted by double-agents within the Rhodesian intelligence network.

Another plan was drawn up for an SAS team to kill Mugabe on his first return drive from Salisbury airport. It was presented to Mac McGuinness at 'Red Bricks', the CIO HQ. McGuinness, to the disappointment of the plotters, turned it down flat on the questionable grounds that it would trigger rioting.

---
[47] Commodore Dieter Gerhardt of the SA Navy, arrested in 1983, sentenced to life imprisonment, and released in 1994.

Meanwhile, the plan within Rhodesia was for all guerrillas to report to designated Assembly Points where they would be neutralised and managed by troops and personnel from a Commonwealth Monitoring Force. This was fine in theory, but in reality, thousands remained outside the designated points and in the field where they went to work amongst the people who would soon vote. The message was quite simple; vote for us or we will go back to war and we will come back and kill you. It was quite simply, an electoral slam-dunk.

On 27th January 1980 Mugabe made a triumphant return. He met Jim Buckley, Governor Soames' secretary, to confirm his forces were in place to enforce electoral victory and later met Soames who merely told him not to overdo the intimidation. For his part Soames promised to maintain the deception that Britain sought a Nkomo/Muzorewa/Ian Smith coalition and would never accept a Mugabe victory. Walls persisted with the 'intelligence-driven' view that the anti-Mugabe forces would prevail and hoped for the best.

Fort Victoria assassination attempt

Within the SAS, there was no doubt, urgent and decisive action was required and Darrell Watt was summoned early February, along with Mike West to take the action that might yet save the country from disaster.

On the 10th February "We knew he was going to address a rally in Fort Victoria," remembers Watt, "and we planned to get him on his way out at the end of the event. I wanted to lay an ambush to ensure success but ComOps did not want our involvement to be that obvious. So Mike and I placed an explosive device under a culvert on the road which would be detonated following the end of the rally as Mugabe's entourage returned. Another officer was airborne monitoring events from the air and he was to give us advance warning of the approach of the convoy. But I think they were tipped off because the convoy returned early and at very high speed. The charge was detonated but too late and we missed the target.[48]

---

[48] The following report by Trevor Grundy appeared in Scotland on Sunday (2nd February 2003). "In February 1980, Stannard was driving Mugabe towards the Midland town, Masvingo. Suddenly, he swerved off the road. Moments later the highway on which they would have been driving exploded into a sheet of flames. Stannard's actions not only guaranteed him rapid advancement through the ranks of the CIO but, more importantly, earned Mugabe's trust."

CHAPTER TWELVE

"But this was only the beginning of our problems because the fire-force at Fort Victoria was activated and we were now on the run from our own soldiers and airmen. We just ran like hell through the bush trying to stay under tree cover to avoid being spotted from above. We were very fit, lightly dressed and carrying pistols only so we moved fast. When we saw the K Car go into an orbit we stood stiff against a tree and held our breath. As soon as they were gone from above we ran again as fast as we could. Eventually we made it to the road and were picked up by a pre-arranged getaway car which included two girls as passengers to make us look more ordinary. We changed into 'civvies' quickly, washed the grime off us, changed number-plates, and dumped all the evidence then took off.

"Just when it looked like we were out of there and safe we came to a roadblock manned by BSAP and Monitoring Force people. Mike and I had our pistols ready. There were a few personnel milling around the car then finally a big BSAP man put his head through the window to see who was inside. He looked at the driver then looked in the back seat where I was sitting. I knew him and he instantly recognized me because we had been to school together. He knew who I was and what I had been doing. I waited anxiously to see what he would do then saw him smile, then a wink of his eye and he waved us on with a cheery 'Carry on Sir.'"

Another plan was hatched involving a black Selous Scout who acquired press accreditation masquerading as a journalist for 'Drum' magazine so he was able to attend a press conference to be addressed by Mugabe. He fitted an explosive device to the microphone that would blow up in his face when he spoke but Mugabe abruptly aborted the conference.

Waiting on board a flight to Bulawayo an air hostess, whose husband had been killed while serving with the SAS was waiting to poison him. He

---

While Ken Flower was almost certainly working for British Intelligence for a considerable period of time Dan Stannard appears to have switched later. He received the Gold Cross of Valour from Mugabe after independence for amongst other actions, passing on a warning to Emmerson Mnangagwa of another plot to kill his principal through the detonation of at least five roadside bombs. Disguised as electrical sub-stations and traffic light control boxes they were placed along the route Mr Mugabe was due to follow in April 1980. Stannard continued to serve Mugabe at a very high level in the Zimbabwe CIO for many years after independence enjoying a comfortable and close relationship with Mnangagwa, Whether Stannard was also the source of the other leaks remains uncertain.

walked up the steps and just as he was about to enter the aircraft there was a call and he stopped. Moments later he turned, descended the steps, and walked away.

Operation Quartz.

"The ceasefire was in place but we were hearing about massive voter intimidation throughout the country and there was huge frustration within the SAS as we had to sit on the sidelines and watch this all happen," remembers Stannard. "The guys were itching to get back into action. With the concentration of the enemy political and military hierarchy in various buildings in Salisbury, *Operation Quartz* was initiated at the end of February and we were allocated different targets.

'A' Squadron was tasked with killing Mugabe at his home in Mount Pleasant suburb.

'B' Squadron was to deal with his deputy Simon Muzenda at his new home on Enterprise Road as well as 'taking out' about a hundred Zanla officers at a nearby Arts Centre.

'C' Squadron was to attack a University of Rhodesia facility accommodating about 200 officers along with senior commanders Rex

CHAPTER TWELVE

Nhongo, Dumiso Dabengwa and Lookout Masuku. Depending on the state of the political play Masuku and Dabengwa, along with their men, were possibly going to be offered an 'out' and taken into custody rather than being killed.

"We were going to attack the Audio Centre near the university. My Uncle Danny had got me into the facility earlier disguised as a cop on a routine courtesy call so I knew exactly what was going on inside and where we needed to go. On that visit I actually met Rex Nhongo and I had an opportunity to look at all the rooms and the general layout of the building. I was struck by how incredibly ugly Nhongo was. I was tasked to assess their morale and what sort of fight they were likely to make of it. I saw no weapons, but I have no doubt they had them.

"We knew there were British Monitoring Force officers inside but it was decided they would just have to pay the price for being in the wrong place at the wrong time. There was not a huge amount of sympathy for the Brits then and a lot less even later. After going in there I reported back to Wilson and MacKenzie who wanted to know my assessment of their morale as well as their capacity to defend themselves. There was no question that we had the firepower to do the job because we had six tanks with us as support if we needed them. But the initial assault was just going to be us on the ground.

"The tanks we had at our disposal had been seized by South African customs when a ship *en route* to a port in East Africa had been intercepted by the South African Navy. They were on their way to Uganda, the papers were not in order, and they were seized. The South Africans had no pressing need for them so they gave them to us in Rhodesia.

"Polling around the country got underway on the 27th February 1980. We were in position at Mount Pleasant School on the sports fields where I once played rugby. It's hard to describe how excited the men were; in a sense this was in all likelihood going to be our finest hour. We had rehearsed this assault so many times and we knew we were going to pull it off, all we needed was the signal and we were all certain it was coming, we just didn't know when. It was now all up to General Walls to make the call.

"I'll never forget, it was around midnight, and we were poised to strike when Bob MacKenzie came to me with a mournful look on his face.

'Richard, I got some bad news for you and the men; we've lost the election and the attack has been called off; I think it's all over for us.'

MEN OF WAR

SECRET

cc Mr Powell FCO
PM has seen
2.3.80

Reply sent.

[initials] 3/3

Salisbury
1 March 1980

The Right Honourable Margaret Thatcher, MP
Prime Minister
10 Downing Street
LONDON SW1

Dear Prime Minister

I am exercising the right conferred upon me by you personally that I have direct access to you when the situation warrants it. I believe it is my solemn duty and responsibility to now report to you directly and make an appeal on behalf of all freedom-loving and law-abiding Zimbabwe Rhodesians. Many of these have trusted you and your Government because of my colleagues and my own example, assurance and encouragement, and in the case of the security forces, our command. We have now completed three days of voting as part of the electoral process agreed at Lancaster House and await announcement of the results on next Tuesday morning. I therefore judge this to be the right moment for me to take this action. I must first explain the background. Despite your assurance to me that Lord Soames would measure up to the grave responsibility delegated to him, I must confirm reports sent to you, through intermediaries, that he has proved to be inadequate, lacking in moral courage, lacking in ability to listen and learn, and above all incapable of implementing the solemn promise, given by yourself and Lord Carrington, that he would rely on us for advice on military and other situations, and act in accordance with the interests of survival of a moderate, freedom-loving and anti-marxist society. I will not accuse him of being unwilling to do so, although many in their bitterness think this to be the case. He has often treated us as if we had no special status in your eyes and certainly not as people who, at great political sacrifice, had agreed to go to the conference table after militarily forcing the other parties to agree to do so. It is true his task has not

-2-/...

SECRET

CHAPTER TWELVE

SECRET

- 2 -

been made easier by your Government insisting on unrestricted entry of hundreds of observers and journalists, many of whom are avowedly left wing orientated and definitely anti-Muzorewa. Many of them, and some junior monitors, have been arrogant enough to set themselves up as instant experts on this country, and Africa generally, and have made pronouncements accordingly, contributing greatly to the emotional and hysterical wave of hostile propaganda levelled against us. Had the Governor acted resolutely and effectively in the early days of the pre-election period, his task would have been much easier, and our survival as a democratic nation would not now be so seriously imperilled.

Although it is possible the moderate parties may achieve acceptable results in the election, I must say to you in all sincerity and gravity that it will be a miracle if it happens and in spite of intimidation, breaches of the ceasefire, and sheer terror accepted pathetically by your representatives. Although I have sufficient faith in God to hope that the true wishes of the people in this country will be manifested some day in some way and may be even now, I must take the precaution of making contingency plans for the worst case on this occasion, especially as reports from all around the country indicate that massive intimidation makes a victory by Mugabe the most likely if not inevitable result of the election.

I should add that many of the affidavits about intimidation, in the hundreds being forwarded to us today, have been sworn by your British policemen and other visitors. I wish you could see the sullen hurt and misery in the eyes and faces of our black people, who are normally so cheerful, good-natured, and full of goodwill.

My appeal to you must be on the following basis :

    (a) If Mugabe succeeds in gaining a simple majority by winning 51 seats or more, or if he is able to attract sufficient defectors from other parties, it is vital to our survival as a free nation that you declare the election nul and void on the grounds of official reports of massive intimidation frustrating the free choice of the bulk of the people

-3-/...

SECRET

SECRET

- 3 -

(b) If Mugabe gets less than 50 seats but has more than any other party, our present efforts to form a coalition based on the tripod of Muzorewa, Nkomo and Smith must be given every opportunity and help, however overt or devious as may be necessary, to succeed in governing the country and resisting the efforts to overthrow them of Mugabe, and anybody who supports him

(c) In the event of the election being declared nul and void, or the moderate parties failing to form a viable coalition with a working majority in the House of Assembly, it is essential from my considered point of view that you maintain a British presence in ZR to run the country with a Council of Ministers, thus allowing us to provide, if necessary, the military conditions for an orderly and safe withdrawal of those people of all races who wish to take refuge in South Africa or elsewhere. This will be preferable to my taking unconstitutional action which would be fraught with snags and dangers, apart from being loathsome to me as a professional soldier, and almost certain to result in much bloodshed and damage to property, and embarrassment to your Government. However, if you are unable to see your way to honouring the bond between us I must reserve the right to take whatever action is necessary in the interests of the majority of people whom I am pledged to serve.

It must be without precedent or at least abnormal, for a person like myself to address such a message as this to no less than the Prime Minister of Britain, but I wish to assure you I do so only in the extremity of our possible emergency, with goodwill, and in the sincere and honest belief that it is my duty in terms of the privileged conversations I had with you and Lord Carrington. I don't know how to sign myself, but I hope to remain your obedient servant,

PETER WALLS

SECRET

CHAPTER TWELVE

I felt like I had been kicked hard in the guts. The word spread quickly among the troops and there was just a sad silence. It was an incredibly emotional time for all of us and the blokes were close to tears.

"Then the sound of engines firing up, the tanks were turned around and they disappeared back to their barracks. It's impossible to describe how angry and upset we were. After all we had been through, with so much at stake and to be so close to decapitating the enemy we despised, the instruction to walk away was devastating. I must confess I misbehaved on the way home, which was unprofessional, but I was furious and the sight of thousands of ululating Mugabe-supporters was too much for me to handle and I lost my temper.

"We arrived home absolutely crestfallen. Nobody spoke, nobody knew what to say. This was it; we were within an ace of a strike and a win but now we had lost. We had lost our country. Later, we would discover that General Walls had been rebuffed by Governor Soames and then by British Prime Minister Margaret Thatcher when he tried to get her to honour her commitment to annul the election if there were electoral abuses. Despite this, Walls took the decision to cancel the military option and that was the end of our country."

Darrell Watt reflects.

Reading the letter from General Walls to Mrs. Thatcher will always trouble and sadden me. Where he writes, "...militarily forcing the other parties to agree to do so..", I now know that it was in a large part, due to our efforts at the end of '79 and early 1980, when just a handful of us from the SAS, campaigned so effectively with Renamo against the Frelimo government and threatened Zanla in their sanctuaries. We had so much momentum and were gathering so much popular support from the people who hated the ruling party, Samora Machel feared losing power if the war continued. This was why he forced Mugabe to the conference table and forced him to compromise. We had given our military and political leaders powerful negotiating leverage, but they squandered it. Given the chance, I believe we could have finished the job, overthrown the government and saved our country. But it was not to be. Ian Smith warned General Walls not to believe the promises made by the British, but he ignored him sadly and walked us into a political trap.

MEN OF WAR

Looking back, I also feel angry about the slowness of some of our senior officers to recognise the changing nature of our war and adjust accordingly in what they decided was important for young military leaders to know. The time I spent at the School of Infantry may have been better spent if they had sat down at the desks and listened to me and other experienced operational soldiers.

I could have tried to tell them what went through my mind every day I was out on operations from the time I awoke until I closed my eyes. What alerted me, from smells to sights and sounds, just how careful every move I made was and how important it was to be constantly on the alert. How much I relied on bird sounds as an early warning. How I came to know the different alarm calls birds make. Some birds only make a particular call when disturbed by humans and I would listen carefully to the change in pitch. Like honey guides which will only use a certain call when taking someone to honey.

Nothing missed my eye, and I was always on the lookout for any unusual change in the natural world that surrounded me. A sudden surge in the number of flies would get my attention. I knew which flies were likely to be seen near humans rather than animals. I always felt more comfortable when monkeys or baboons were near. They too change their bark for humans and they were incredibly alert; nothing passed them by without them knowing about it. Leopard and bushbuck too; they were loud, so their barks often provided me with an excellent early warning system. Thanks to the birds and the animals I could accurately plot the direction and distance of approaching humans. Frogs were an invaluable help at night. Their croaking was soothing and reassuring but the moment it stopped I knew there was human activity out there somewhere and I would have my men on full alert. The same with the crickets; the moment they went quiet I knew we were threatened. I could hear them in my sleep and awake when they went silent. Whenever the bush went quiet, I expected trouble, whether night or day. As a result, I was never taken by surprise. Living creatures were my eyes and ears and I and my men survived because of them.

So much bushcraft that our soldiers did not know enough about. Unlike the Africans who learned from a young age about tracking and bush-craft, much of it through herding cattle when they were children. If a cow was lost they would have to track it down so they learned early and always had a natural advantage over most white troops.

CHAPTER TWELVE

I remember on the Mapai railway line waiting for first light and being always a light sleeper it happened, the crickets went quiet. I was unsure what it was, then I could hear the sound of dry leaves being crushed very slowly and coming from two different places not far from us. I got the guys up quietly and told them to hide their sleeping bags then led them away from our sleeping position. We walked about 10 km due east and did a dogs-leg around and back over an open area on the opposite side of the waterpans. Along the way we connected tripwires to Claymores. From a distance we could see them; trackers in front and about a 100 troops behind them. Soon as there was enough light they attacked the place where we had been sleeping, but we were long gone. They followed again and walked into the tripwires. We did not fire a shot so while they were blowing themselves up they still did not know where we were.

Everyday I considered what were the likely opportunities that might present themselves and how best I may position myself and my men to take advantage of that opportunity. I knew my group of 12 or 16 could take anything on no matter how big the group or how heavy the weaponry. I did not ever take air support for granted apart from when we needed casualties evacuated or to be resupplied. I think some of the blokes became lazy and were too quick to call in airstrikes. The best way to kill the enemy was on foot on the ground. On a bigger scale I think the Americans rely too heavily on airpower. They will never defeat an insurgent enemy from the air alone; they have to have good shock troops on the ground who can close quickly with the enemy and kill them.

I far preferred to fight the enemy on the ground using my own special tactics to outwit them, outfight them and kill them. Eleven RPDs in a group of 12 provided devastating fire. We always ran right at them firing from the hip. Good well-trained machine gunners, we were there for serious business and used skill and controlled aggression to win the day. We were like a pack of wolves, motivated by one thing and that was to kill as many of the enemy as possible and to never lose a battle. We hunted them, day and night and the guys I had were just so motivated I had to put ropes and dog collars on them to restrain them. We were well oiled machines with lots of courage and firepower – they were just mad and fearless. I told all my men to stand when the shooting started and to stay on their feet rather than take cover. It intimidated the enemy enormously, and they almost always would cut and run.

There was never any thoughts to run that crossed our minds of being frightened or scared of the enemy. They completely trusted my judgement and tactical choices, believing in everything I did or told them and I'm happy to say we never lost a fight.

My group of 12 went where the RLI and other troops had failed in the Matibi Tribal Trust Land and chased every gook there that survived our attacks back into Mozambique where they licked their wounds and stayed away. They were operating with Frelimo then and Frelimo went back to tell their seniors the Matibi was a good place to go if you wanted to die fast.

I seldom walked during the heat of the day and when there was heavy dew I was reluctant to move in the mornings until the moisture had disappeared. Too easy for the enemy to follow us when displacing moisture. My men were never allowed to wash and never allowed to brush their teeth. I did not like them taking their boots off. Navigation at night – I used the stars whenever possible.

Some days we were so fit and feisty we could fight several battles and still cover 30 km. We were fitter than the enemy and this was a critical factor; we used skill, good bushcraft and surprise. We appeared when they least expected us to. Sometimes, I liked to bide my time when I knew where they were and let the enemy relax. Best time to hit them was when they were settling down for nice long lunch. The moment they could smell the food they lost concentration and their senses dulled. By then we would have them at very close range and they had no chance. I would work out where the sentries were and plan my approach accordingly. We would creep in on our bellies as close as possible. As soon as one of us were seen that was the trigger for everyone to open fire. By then we were almost on top of them. We would then get into extended line and charge in at speed. They would just run for their lives and we would take them down.

The big mistake many soldiers made was being dropped too close to the target by vehicle or aircraft. Forty kms from the area of interest was ideal for me. Then you have to get into the target area without the enemy or their *mujibas* knowing it. That was the toughest challenge. Every single man in the call-sign had to be tuned into anti-tracking, and one mistake from a man was enough to compromise the whole operation. Rocks and rivers were a Godsend as was the rain. If it came I would hurry the men up so we could

CHAPTER TWELVE

cover as much ground as possible. Soon as the rain stopped we would stop too. Soft, sandy ground to be avoided at all costs. That is why it was so tough on the 'Russian Front' in southern Mozambique.

Once in position, the next problem is to find a place where you can hide but where you still have a view. I used to try and be like the Kudu antelope; I studied how they moved virtually unseen on the sides of hills. I never liked laying up on flat ground. With some height, I could hear more and see more but we had to keep our movement down to an absolute minimum.

Key to cleaning out a heavily infiltrated area was spreading fear through the populace by hitting the enemy hard repeatedly. The more entrenched they were the more confident in their presence in the area. I never involved myself or my men in beating civilians but I was happy to intimidate them so that they knew who was in charge.

I would call villagers together and tell them all that we know the name of the Sectoral Commander and we know he's in command of several hundred well armed men. I would deliver an open challenge by pointing out my 11 men and ask him to bring as many as he could to fight us if he wanted the respect of the people he claimed to represent. On some occasions I wrote letters, giving the reference point of where we could be found and asked the *mujibas* to deliver them to the enemy commanders inviting them to a showdown but nobody ever responded.

Chapter Thirteen

We were a strange quarrelsome folk
We were many. We were all the peoples
Of this troubled land of many names.

◆

Southbound

Joining the Recces

"With the die cast and no hope of turning events around I found myself in a quandary," remembers Stannard. "I loved Rhodesia, it was my home, my friends and family were there, and I did not want to leave it. The harsh rigidity of the *apartheid* system had never appealed to me or to most Rhodesians and we had developed a very different sense of national identity in our short history so I knew nothing would be the same again for us but I felt we had been betrayed and this was a chance to continue the fight for what I thought was right. With Rhodesia passing into the hands of the militant black nationalists the only remaining chance for us to resist and possibly turn the tide against a hostile world lay in continuing the fight from South Africa. After talking to Darrell and some of the other chaps I said to my guys that my mind is made up, I'm heading south and maybe we can carry on the fight from there.

"Unbeknown to me wheels were already in motion to take the whole squadron to South Africa. Also unbeknown to me, the scheming Brits were already in the mix and a British major arrived to try and explain to the guys that all would be well and they should stay in the country and in the unit and help with the building of the new Zimbabwe.

"This split the guys between the 'leavers' and the 'stayers' and caused quite a lot of bitterness which remains to this day. Darrell said he was going to stay and see along with quite a few of the guys. I was not one of them. The Brits approached quite a few of us, myself included, and offered us an opportunity to join the British Army. I was not interested. It was actually quite sad watching this division emerge amongst guys who had been recently

CHAPTER THIRTEEN

so united and it actually got quite nasty. A silenced pistol disappeared out of the armoury and I was accused of having taken it but it certainly was not me. A South African Air Force C130 had landed at New Sarum air base and because there were such strict currency controls in place the guys tried to load up stuff they might be able to sell in South Africa. Bob MacKenzie and a few of the other officers had purchased a boat and tried to get on this plane but the pilots refused to load it.

"For the guys leaving, some went on the plane while others, including Koos Loots, left in dribs and drabs with the plan being to eventually meet up in Durban. Most of the foreigners in the SAS immediately accepted the South African offer but a lot of the Rhodesians, particularly the guys who had come off farms, were reluctant to leave the country.

"Those of us who went were all initially accommodated in an apartment block outside Durban and we were quickly issued with residency papers to make us legal. From there we went to what is known as the 'Bluff' and joined 1 Reconnaissance Battalion (1 Recce). There were about 50 of us under the command of Garth Barrett and the next thing we were all dressed in drab brown fatigues and back on the parade square in an unfamiliar place and in the very unfamiliar role of quasi-peacetime soldiers. For guys who had so recently been in the thick of war it was a culture shock and a bit of an anti-climax and none of us were terribly happy. Our mood did not improve in the days ahead as we tried to come to terms with life in a very orthodox military environment where everything was very structured. There didn't seem to be many happy faces about and religious dogma began to play a big part in our lives. The Padre and his wife were very involved in the unit and this was something we had never experienced before.

"Meanwhile, at home, the final attempt to kill Mugabe was underway. Unfortunately for him, Prince Charles, the heir to the British throne, was also going to be in the line of fire but I don't think any of the blokes involved were too worried about that. The plan was to intercept the official motorcade carrying Mugabe and Prince Charles on their way to Meikles Hotel where a reception was planned to take place just before the official inauguration on the 17th April.

"The operation involved ex Rhodesian soldiers. In the plan, explosives were hidden in what appeared to be traffic control boxes placed along what used to be Jameson Avenue and at the corner, by the traffic lights, where the convoy would turn into Second Street. A lookout, watching from the top of a nearby building would detonate the devices and change the course of history. But with much of the citizenry in a state of super-charged excitement, there can be little doubt absolute chaos and carnage would have ensued had Mugabe been eliminated at this point. And just what the British reaction to the death of Prince Charles would have been is hard to answer.

"We will never know what might have happened because either Mac McGuinness or my uncle, Dan Stannard, or both, got wind of what was about to happen and blew the whistle. The bombs never went off, the operators involved received word they had been compromised, and all managed to exit the country safely. Mugabe was on his way to taking power.

"Meantime, we in Durban, were not happy. Compared to the happy-go-lucky atmosphere we had so recently left behind, we found our new home a pretty depressing place. Although we had got along so well with the Recces when they had come up to Rhodesia that had all changed; now we were in their country and in their eyes, we had lost our war. We were now there at their pleasure and we would have to do things their way.

"In no time there were fights breaking out in the messes and our guys kept getting into trouble in town. I think we were all angry and frustrated and so we lashed out. One of our blokes had a bar in his room in the barracks and we would meet there covertly to let off steam. But then one of the guys brought an RPD and let rip a belt of ball and tracer. I'll never forget watching this beautiful arc of fire drifting slowly in the sky over the Bluff and out to sea. Needless to say, this didn't go down well with the authorities and all weapons had to be handed in. The fact is our guys were bored and unsettled and hungry for action. I worried that we were quickly losing our sharpness and our bushcraft skills and I made this clear to our senior officers who I urged to get us operationally deployed as soon as possible. In the meantime, I exercised my guys hard; we ran up and down the Bluff and trained hard for hours every day. I collared a chap from the Spanish Foreign Legion who was a PT guy and told him to 'work our cases' hard so that we became super-fit.

"Eventually we received word that we were going to be deployed and there was jubilation. We were going to do a raid on Maputo and the guys couldn't wait to get going.

CHAPTER THIRTEEN

Matola Raid.

The operation was under the command of Garth Barrett, code-named *Operation Beanbag* and the aim was to decapitate the leadership element of the ANC's military wing, Umkhonto We Sizwe (MK) which was housed in the suburb of Matola on the fringe of the capital, Maputo. The plan was to drive in, and while we had the support of SA Recces who would block roads and protect our backs, the actual attack was to be done mostly by us former Rhodesians.

We were given three targets:
- A double storey house where we were told Joe Slovo, the MK Chief of Staff and other top ANC guys were living.
- Another house which was the planning HQ for most of the ANC attacks in South Africa. This group was known as 'Sabotage Machinery'.
- A house used by an MK unit tasked with attacking South African Police stations. This group was known as 'Police Machinery'

"I was in 'Alpha Group' under the command of Bob Mackenzie. We had two vehicles armed with 106 mm guns and seventeen men and were to attack 'Target Alpha' and capture or kill the ANC people in there. Some of the other vehicles were armed with 20 mm Hispano cannons that had been taken off old Vampire fighter jets and these were supplemented with 12.7 mm machine guns.

'Bravo Group' consisted of some 20 guys; their target was 'Sabotage Machinery'.

'Charlie Group' was tasked to hit the 'Police Machinery'.

"Garth Barrett was in command on the ground while the operation would be run from the air by an airborne command centre (TelStar) in a C130 Hercules. The plan was to disguise ourselves as Frelimo and infiltrate by road in vehicles painted in Frelimo colours. We intended to obliterate the facilities with the explosive charges we were taking in, recover as much documentation as possible and kill everyone we could not capture. The decision to attack these targets had come from the highest office in the country so we Rhodesians were very much in the spotlight. This was our 'death or glory' moment I suppose.

"Being a demolitions 'boffin' I was very involved in the preparation of the charges we would use and was excited about blowing the shit out of all these buildings. Prior to the raid we trained intensively at Middelburg in the

Eastern Transvaal.

"Initially, the plan was to use different routes to go in and out but that changed and we ended up cutting the border fence south of Komatipoort and driving down bush tracks until we hit the main tar road going to Maputo. This first attempt was a mechanical disaster and so many trucks broke down Barrett got hold of TelStar and told them it made no sense to continue and the attack was aborted. It was all very frustrating but undoubtedly the right decision was made.

"Two months later on the 29th January 1981, we were back at the same spot and ready to roll again. At the final briefing we were told that there were estimated to be about a dozen people at the facility we would attack. We were all pumped up and keen to go when suddenly we were informed we were to attend a church service and listen to a sermon delivered by some *dominee* (priest/pastor). This was crazy stuff and Garth Barrett was furious because this had not been scheduled and the interruption would upset all his carefully planned timings. But there was nothing we could do; orders were orders, and we had to sit there and listen to this guy rant and rave about why God was on our side; the white man was invincible and the enemy was in fact the 'devil'. All total rubbish and I don't think any of the Rhodesians were even listening. We had never experienced anything like this before. Rob Hutchinson, who came from the RLI, thought it was hilarious and started to mock the priest and was told to shut up.

"One of the potential problems that lay ahead was the Frelimo garrison at Moamba which consisted of a motorised battalion supported by armour, so two of the Recce guys were to be dropped near there with RPG-7s with orders to cut the telephone lines and watch the base. If anything moved out they were to use their rockets and report the development immediately. We were also briefed about another enemy camp *en route* which was close to the railway but intelligence suggested they were short on transport and unlikely to be a threat. There were other army camps near the target but the plan was to deploy two teams on the arterial roads into Matola and these guys would handle any unwanted visitors.

"We left behind schedule and made a good start apart from Johnny Masson being knocked off a vehicle and injured, so he had to stay behind. But then navigation became difficult in the dark with all these bush-tracks heading in different directions and when we hit the main tar road we were

CHAPTER THIRTEEN

well behind schedule. We halted briefly and rearranged ourselves in our groups and headed to Moamba where we dropped off the two Recce blokes with their RPGs and bicycles. Just outside Matola a group of Recces was dropped at a bridge to prepare to block any attempt by Frelimo to interfere from the western side and then another group was positioned at a point east of the target to deal with any problems coming from that side. Garth Barrett with John Pearson as his deputy, along with the command echelon, based themselves between the two roadblocks and that was the designated rendezvous point for the assault groups once their jobs were done.

"The plan was for all the attacks to go in simultaneously so having the furthest to drive we hit the road first. We had no problem finding the house and it all looked very quiet on arrival. Adjacent to the house was an orchard which two of the teams crept through while I prepared to launch the actual frontal assault with Frank Vivier and Mike Smith. Frank was a top operator from a farming family in Manicaland who I had worked with in the SAS and I was happy to have him along. Attacking from the rear of the house was another group that included Sergeant Rob Hutchinson, Ian Suttill, Jim Park and Wayne Ross Smith.

"As the attack went in with the other guys tossing grenades through the windows, we blew down the front door with a charge, lobbed a few grenades and a bunch of ANC guys immediately surrendered pleading with us not to kill them. This came as a bit of a surprise, but as we were trying to get the prisoners cuffed and out the way there was a huge blast which almost knocked me off my feet followed by more blasts. To my horror, I could see some of my blokes were burning, our medic Andy Johnston was trying to put out flames covering Ian Suttill and Jim Park was also on fire. I could not see Rob Hutchinson but a grenade had bounced back and exploded at his feet killing him. I broke off the actual assault to go to their aid. Some of the captives seized the opportunity, jumped through windows and ran for it but went straight into deadly fire from Keith Cloete and Mario Vidal who took most, if not all, of them down.

"Just what happened to Ian, Rob and Jim remains unclear but it seems grenades bounced back at them off the gauze windows and maybe they were fired on from the upper level of the building. It was white phosphorous that was burning on Jim and Ian. With Mike Smith and Andy Johnston helping me I tried my best to strip Ian's webbing, dislodge the grenade and douse the flames but to no avail; a grenade in one of his pouches exploded and one arm and a leg were blown off as I held him. I carried him to the vehicle and he spoke his last on the way.

'Did we get them sir?' he whispered.

'Yes Ian, we did,' I replied. Then he died.

Mike Smith and I were lucky to survive but we both took some shrapnel, with one piece going into my eye. Jim Parks, although badly wounded, staggered back to where Bob MacKenzie was with the HQ group. Wayne Ross Smith was also seriously injured with phosphorous burns and shrapnel wounds.

"It was chaotic, and we were still taking fire from some spirited resistance having lost the initiative. The order came to end the assault and load up before I and my guys had had a chance to go in and clear the house out. Rob Riddell laid a charge to blow the house down and we boarded the vehicles. Looking back, maybe Bob MacKenzie and his guys should have gone to the aid of the wounded guys when they ran into trouble, and allowed me to carry on with my assault but very easy for me to say that now I suppose. We boarded the vehicles and moved to Barrett's HQ, meet up with the other teams, and exit from Mozambique. It was pandemonium and sitting in the truck beside Jim, he kept bursting into flames as pieces of phosphorous ignited. While there was a cursory check on bodies, who was wounded and who was alive, it was not done thoroughly enough and only when we were about half an hour away from the target did we realise Rob Hutchinson was missing. In all the years of the Rhodesian war we had never left anyone behind, and some of the guys became very angry when we realised he was not with us. They demanded we return no matter what the consequences were, but this request was denied and this triggered an almost mutinous feeling amongst some of the men. One of the drivers, Tom Oldridge,[49] became hysterical, screaming and shouting while throwing weapons out the vehicle. He had to be sedated by the medic. Poor Jim died on the road home.

'Bravo Group', meanwhile went after the 'Sabotage Machinery'. Corrie Meerholz and his guys were expecting stiff resistance from a well defended facility, but they were pleasantly surprised to meet no such problem. They snuck up to the house and placed a 'Hulk' charge which was expected to

---

49 https://en.wikipedia.org/wiki/Tom_Leppard

CHAPTER THIRTEEN

blow a hole in the wall but damn near blew the whole wall down. Then they tossed grenades and went in firing at the lower level while support fire was directed at the upper storey. Corrie and his guys cleared the bottom of the building and then, after signalling to the support group to cease fire, went upstairs to clear that but most of the occupants were already dead. They killed quite a few people and made a few captures but there was not much of an enemy presence there and as I remember, not much of intelligence value was found and certainly no Joe Slovo. Later we heard he had left only hours before.

"Mike Rich's 'Charlie Group' had a relatively easy time of it. They planted a 'Wreck' charge and obliterated the 'Police Machinery', killing all the occupants. They went in to clear but there was little more for them to do and they made their way back to the HQ position where they had just had to open fire on a car trying to run their roadblock.

"As soon as all the groups were back at HQ we headed home but nobody told Barrett about our missing man until we were about to turn off the main road at Moamba. He asked me what I thought we should do and I told him it was unlikely he was still alive, but I could not be sure and nor could anyone else. The CO passed the message to TelStar so they could arrange a rescue mission if anything was heard from Rob. Like all of us, he had an escape plan and protocols to follow if he was still alive. I would have been more than happy to go back to try and find him if instructed to do so, but dawn was about to break so it was not going to be easy.

"On the way back to South Africa, after picking up the two Recce guys who had had an uneventful night, the column somehow ended up driving into a Mozambique army camp but a Portuguese speaking black guy, who the 1 Recce group had with them, managed to do some quick talking and we got away without any incident. We were safely back in South Africa in the early morning and I was sent to the military hospital in Pretoria to have my wounds attended to along with Andy Johnston and Mike Smith.

"My morale was not good. I felt we had done our duty but losing Rob and leaving him behind troubled me. The next day his body was produced and it looked like he had been shot in the head through the helmet, probably from the firing that was coming down upon us from the upper storey. It is quite possible that he dropped a grenade he was about to throw as he was shot, and that was the explosion that hit Ian Suttill and Jim Parks.

"From somewhere Frelimo managed to find Swastikas and Nazi badges to attach to his uniform and the kit that was left behind. The next thing, gruesome photos of those we killed, were all over the local press and there was international outrage with the UN weighing in to lambast the South African government. General Constand Viljoen held a press conference to explain the South African position and release names of those on both sides who had been killed.

"Lying in bed, licking my wounds, I received an unwelcome visit from some of the hospital staff to tell me that we had basically fucked up, and to deliver a reminder that seeing that we had lost our war in Rhodesia we should actually wind our necks in and do as we were told. In other words, they were doing us a favour by allowing us to serve in the South African Defence Force (SADF) and get killed. This really pissed me off, and I asked Garth Barrett to get me a transfer out of there and back to Durban which was granted.

"More problems awaited me there. Soon as I was out of hospital, I was summoned to see the CO and was completely stunned about what he said.

"What the fuck are you people doing cutting ears off the people you killed?"

Completely unbeknown to me, the press had produced photos of bodies at the scene of the attack that had been mutilated. I was completely lost for words and insisted that was not the work of anyone under my command and that that was the sort of behaviour that had always been completely taboo in the SAS. Hard as I tried, I must have been unconvincing because I was reprimanded and warned I'd be hearing more about this.

"While we had not nailed the 'high value' targets and had lost some very good men the raid sure gave Frelimo and the ANC one hell of a shock. We had hit them hard where they thought they were safe and this had set off a panic. There were sweeping arrests of people inside the military and intelligence services and American diplomats were chucked out of the country. At the funeral for the dead, Oliver Tambo delivered a eulogy warning that all armed white South Africans would now be considered fair targets.

"After this operation, I mulled my future and decided I wanted a change, wanting to get involved somewhere else in the SA military where I would work more closely with former Rhodesians. I knew a little about Neil Kriel and the group he was running and made further inquiries in that regard."

CHAPTER THIRTEEN

lies and bl

By Keith Kiewiet of The Star's Africa News Service who visited Matola, near Maputo, soon after the South African Defence Force raid.

"You see that ... that is South African blood you are standing on. And so is that, and so is that" The Frelimo army major was looking straight at me when he said this. The look on his face was a curious mixture of boasting, anguish and anger.

I looked down and indeed I was standing on a patch of semi-congealed blood. It looked no different to the other bloodstains I was shown at the weekend by angry and perhaps humiliated Frelimo officials.

"An attack by fascist bullies on innocent and unarmed refugees," said the major. Yet, the South African Defence Force has shown the spoils of its daring raid into Mozambique last week, and those spoils included weapons of the nastiest kind.

their sides of the story, journalists assigned to cover the event found themselves in a situation that could only be described as surrealistic.

South African pilots with heavy Afrikaans accents and South African passports were welcomed with open arms at Maputo's airport and at Maputo's hotels only hours after the killing of a number of ANC members by a special South African taskforce. Some South African journalists found themselves in the same position.

Drinking beer in a hotel without water (sic) some of these people must have pondered deeply at the goings on.

The targets of the South African attack were three separate houses, far from each other in Matola. They looked like ordinary houses gone to seed. Inside they looked as

if they had been occupied by squatters. They were dirty and rundown.

They did not look like ANC strongholds. But, who can tell what an ANC stronghold looks like. Certainly, there were lots of ANC posters and booklets there. And, curiously, a Mercedes with a Bloemfontein registration was parked outside one of these houses.

That was strange.

And the questions on everyone's lips in Maputo today is: How did the South African invaders manage to get to Matola undetected and how did they manage to hit three separate targets and then get away to South Africa, again overland, without being stopped.

The South African army is keeping mum and Frelimo, well they're scratching their heads.

Big raid could

The Star's Africa News Service

MAPUTO — There is

about it are the Russians. They must be delighted."

Death of Dave Berry

Meanwhile, a small group of six Rhodesians from the RLI and SAS were making a new home for themselves at Ntabeni, an old forest estate in the Zoutspansberg Mountains. The property had been taken over by South Africa's Special Tasks division under the command of Jan Breytenbach who was going to use it as a launch pad for operations into Zimbabwe aimed at destabilising the new republic. South African intelligence was aware that MK cells were present in western Zimbabwe and they were concerned that Zipra might form some sort of alliance with these groups. The plan that unfolded was to use former Rhodesians, both blacks and whites, to establish an operational link to Zipra which would involve the supply of men and equipment aimed at boosting the movement's effectiveness and provide a solid platform for them to mount a co-ordinated campaign aimed at challenging ZANU-PF rule.

"I was trying to make a go of it in Zimbabwe on the mines," remembers Barry, "but when our son was born with medical issues we came up against the collapsing healthcare services and I became concerned for my family. So, when I was approached by one of the ex-Squadron guys who had already gone to South Africa, with an offer to go back to soldiering, I was immediately interested. Then when I heard the salary being offered was well above the normal pay grade for soldiers, I decided to go and look.

"The base was beautifully situated in the mountains, had a very non-military feel about it and it looked like our families would be well taken care of. There were houses available for the married guys near the old timber mill and separate single quarters for the rest of the chaps.

"I liked Jan Breytenbach, he was a tough no-nonsense guy, and he had a long standing connection to us going back to the early operations the SAS had conducted in Mozambique when the Portuguese were still in control so there was a great deal of mutual understanding. There was never any doubt in my mind that he meant business and if he had his way he was going to cause a lot of problems for the new government in Zimbabwe.

"Already there when I arrived were John Wessels and Bob Beech from the RLI, and Rob Riddell from SAS along with Lawrence , from Selous Scouts. Our first task was to train the black troops that would be working with us. They had been doing pretty mundane, border patrol work and were a pretty unimpressive bunch of ex-Zipra fighters, along with some poorly

CHAPTER THIRTEEN

trained, former militiamen that had been used in the closing stages of our war. I had been spoiled in the SAS, being operational with excellent soldiers, so this aspect of the new job did not come easy to me but we all did our best to whip these guys into shape and get the best out of them.

"When I heard my old pal Dave Berry was unhappy, working as a security guard in Rustenburg, I contacted him to see if he was interested in joining us. He too had started a family, so he was happy to accept the offer and have a decent home for his wife and family. I was also happy to have Dave along; being one of the best NCOs to come out of our war, I knew he would add a lot of experience and operational skill.

"It was quite a surprise to us all when Darrell Watt arrived at the base looking very thin, weathered, and struggling to walk because he had lost most of his toenails. We had had no idea what sort of ordeal he had been through but it turned out he was very lucky to be alive.

"Darrell had left the army and gone into the safari business in Botswana as a guide operating photographic trips close to the Zimbabwe border. While out on a drive his Land Rover became stuck in heavy sand and he left the vehicle to seek assistance but found nobody to help. On his return he saw that his vehicle was surrounded by the Zimbabwe army who appeared to be hostile and looking for him. Not wanting to take any chances he decided to head for safety in South Africa. Armed only with a 9 mm pistol he spent five days walking southwards through Hwange National Park. Most of the time he was tracked by lions and spent the nights sleeping in trees. With no maps in flat, featureless, terrain he was not sure where he was until he picked up human tracks and followed them. Fortunately for him, he caught up with an old poacher who knew the area extremely well. The man shared some of his food with Darrell, gave him some water and directions to follow. Eventually he hit the Limpopo River and crossed into South Africa. Once in the country he contacted Jan, and Jan asked him to join us. It was good to have him on the team and we all enjoyed listening to his latest adventure.

"The only real concern to me was the fact that we didn't really have any experienced officers in our team to lead and assist us. At the time there was a heavy military presence in the area comprising Permanent Force and Army Reservists and these guys did not take kindly to us new arrivals. We were not allowed to wear the regular uniform and they knew our pay and living conditions were better than theirs so there was a lot of resentment.

Making things worse, we could not even speak Afrikaans. Not having any rank, it made it difficult for us to deal with this belligerence and soon the fights started. As a result, Darrell was the man given the task of running our group along with another former Rhodesian, Nick Jooste. They would have to handle matters at a higher level while we got on with the task of turning our group into an effective special operations unit.

"Once we had found our feet and better understood what our aims and objectives were we set off in small groups across the river into Zimbabwe to meet up with the various super-groups with whom we would be working. They seemed motivated and quite well organised but concerned that they did not have the resources and firepower needed to take on the Zimbabwean army. We were there to reassure them that we could and would assist them in strengthening their forces. And we discussed our mutual objectives with their section commanders. They were very anti the Mugabe regime and I felt confident that this plan could work.

"But while we were slowly doing the groundwork, Colonel Breytenbach was growing impatient; he wanted to start making some big hits. Maybe there was pressure on him from Pretoria to produce results, but he told us in no uncertain terms that we needed to start making our presence felt. As a result, we were tasked to blow up the huge fuel storage facility near the border town of Beitbridge, blow the powerlines and sabotage the railway. We were warned not to damage the rolling stock because it belonged to South Africa. A two-man recce went in ahead and came back to report that there was a brigade strength military presence near the town but they looked pretty disorganised and unlikely to present too much of a problem.

"The whites involved were Lawrence, Bob Beech, John Wessels, Dave Berry and me. Along with us we had 15 black soldiers. We had worked hard to get these guys up to a higher level, but I was still not too confident in them when we crossed the Limpopo into Zimbabwe under cover of darkness. Apart from our personal weapons, we had RPG rocket launchers, mortars, explosives and mines so we were quite heavily laden but I was pretty sure we would be able to get the job done.

"The plan called for Lawrence and myself to destroy the train-engines only, not the wagons which belonged to South African railways, while Dave and the rest of the guys did the tanks. They would cut the fence, approach the tanks which were jacketed with water, and fire rockets into them. White

CHAPTER THIRTEEN

phosphorous grenades would be thrown and then mortars would be fired into select areas to add to the general mayhem.

"We crossed with no problem and I went behind the depot with Lawrence to have a good look. All was quiet when suddenly some of the black guys came running to say they had walked past bivouacs and a large number of soldiers who appeared to be asleep, but they were not sure if they had been seen. Dave asked Lawrence and myself to come with him to have a look and assess the situation. I went forward into the encampment and actually looked under some of the shelters but saw nobody. In my mind, all was well and we were well placed to go ahead with the full attack. It was a Saturday night. I was pretty sure most of the army would be drinking in the town and I knew we had surprise and firepower on our side, but the black troops were becoming increasingly nervous about a big reaction that would see us trapped on the wrong side of the border. I know if I had been with my old associates from the SAS we would have got this job done without a problem, but this was different and the general unease forced us to change our plans.

"Leaving the main body, Dave and I first destroyed the reservoir supplying water to the protective jackets that covered the tanks, then we blew the electrical substation before heading to the railway line and the train. By this time there was widespread panic and people suddenly appeared running and screaming. I said to Dave 'let's blow the line', which we managed to do in two different places, but by this time there was too much activity and we decided to withdraw and crossed the river safely back into South African.

"A debrief was convened with Darrell and Jan present to hear about what had transpired and why we had failed to blow the fuel depot. Jan was angry and I didn't blame him. He wanted a big success so that he could ask Pretoria for more men and resources and increase the size of our unit. We also needed to land a big blow to send a strong signal to our new Zipra allies that we were able to supply them with the support we had promised.

"Afterwards, Lawrence came to me and said that he was unhappy with the general professionalism of the troops we were working with and wanted to leave. Being my best friend and a man for whom I had huge respect I ended up agreeing with him and decided that I too, would resign. We told Darrell who was disappointed and he ordered us to Pretoria to explain to Colonel Breytenbach. He was extremely upset by our decision and tried to convince us to stay, but our minds were made up and our resignations accepted.

"We went back to Ntabeni to pack our gear and move on. Saying goodbye to Dave Berry was tough. I felt I had brought him in and I tried to persuade him to come with us but he wanted to stay. Little did I know then, I would never see him again, and the decision we had made was one that saved our lives."

In April 1982 Watt and Breytenbach received information indicating the expected arrival of new locomotives in Zimbabwe from Durban. A decision was taken to destroy them. A plan unfolded to blow a bridge over the Mwenezi River on the Rutenga railway line as the engines crossed. To achieve this, one option, was for 'Mac' Calloway, a South African double agent, still serving in the Zimbabwe CIO, to simply collect the saboteurs at a designated point on the Limpopo River and drive them to the target in his official vehicle. There they would place the charges with delayed detonators, and he would drive them back to a point from where they could cross safely back into South Africa. However, this idea was rejected, and a plan was then actioned to have a group under the overall operational command of Darrell Watt infiltrate the country from the border-crossing at Pafuri and walk to the target. The actual group was under the command of Sergeant Dave Berry, ex SAS and included John Wessels and Robert Beech who had both served with the RLI. The rest of the group was mostly a motley collection of poorly trained black militiamen with a few former RAR soldiers.

Having been moved to a staging point near Pafuri in the Kruger National Park from where they were to cross the border an immediate problem arose when three of the black troops went missing. Despite this Watt and Breytenbach decided to continue with the mission.

On the 16th August the group of three whites and seventeen blacks crossed the border and walked through the night. The going through sandy soils was tough and anti-tracking impossible. What nobody involved in the operation was aware of was there was a census being conducted in the area at the time and this had resulted in an increased security-force presence. On the third day nothing was heard on the nightly Sit Rep and the next morning the alarm was raised and an aerial reconnaissance took place but to no avail. The next day, some of the black survivors crossed back into South Africa with the news of the failed mission.

CHAPTER THIRTEEN

"I spoke to the last guy back," remembers Rob Riddell. "His name was Sibanda and he was a proper soldier unlike most of the rest. He told me they were being tracked by the ZNA (Zimbabwe National Army), probably ex-RAR troops, and they come under heavy fire. Bob Beech was killed in the first volley of fire but then there was a series of rolling contacts during which they expended all their M79 rifle grenades but Dave was killed. He told me John Wessels was wounded in the leg and he tried to help him but John was making too much noise and he left him and made good his escape. Just how long John lasted is not known."

The day after the engagement, the then Prime Minister Mugabe called a press conference at State House, where there were items of captured weapons, explosives and other equipment on display. The bodies were then shown to the press by Zimbabwe Army Commander, Rex Nhongo. In South Africa, General Constand Viljoen told the press that the men were on a 'rogue mission' and acting without official authorisation. Clearly the fall-guy was Darrell Watt.

"I did not act alone," insists Watt. "My orders came from Jan Breytenbach who was taking instructions from General van Rensburg. After the incident, Jan come to collect me and he was looking very stressed. He said one of us was going to be in a lot of trouble. A Board of Inquiry was convened and I testified along with 'Dutch' Huiberts, Mike Smith and Keith Cloete. They tried to give Barry a hard time but he handled it all very well. I was withdrawn from operations and put in charge of vehicles and transport pending a verdict. I was cleared at the Board of Inquiry and offered a job training the Recces but had pretty much decided I wanted to leave the South African army. A lot of my close friends from the SAS turned on me at this point and blamed me for Dave Berry's death. It was not a very happy way to end my days as a professional soldier."

Jailbreak

Project Barnacle was established in 1979 under the command of Neil Kriel. It was formed on instructions from Defence Minister Magnus Malan and aimed at building the capacity to infiltrate and operate inside countries to the north that were hostile to South Africa. The unit would be part of SA Special Forces commanded by General Fritz Loots and based at an old farm near Hartbeespoort Dam north of Johannesburg. The cover for the operation was a company called 'Presidents Security Consultants' with offices in Pretoria, ostensibly doing security work for the private sector. With Kriel at the helm, the recruitment of former Rhodesian personnel with valuable experience in the field of covert operations commenced. An early addition to the team was former Inspector Gray Branfield who had been running the BSAP SB office in Bulawayo, followed by Chris Schulenburg, Peter Stanton, Winston Hart, Dave Scales and 'Mac' Calloway.

"After coming out of hospital and surgery on my eye I knew I wanted to leave the Recces, had heard about Kriel's bunch, but was unsure about what to do. Keith Cloete had opened a gym and we discussed going into business together. But Keith was unstable. He, like the rest of us, was angrier than ever. After the disappointment of *Operation* Quartz being aborted and the losses we suffered on the Matola raid we were all still trying to get a grip on things and more and more coming to the conclusion that we had been horribly let down by our officers and politicians. Keith lost his temper one day and shot the gym up with his AK. Some rounds hit the wall of a nearby prison and he was arrested. Later, he shot himself. An early casualty of Post-Traumatic Stress Disorder maybe?

"I then went to see Neil Kriel who said he was very happy to have me and they organised my transfer immediately. Neil was running the show and reporting to Joe Verster at Speskop.

"It was quite an exciting change from the disciplined structures of the Recces. Although I would be operating covertly, I remained a member of the SADF and was promoted to the rank of captain.

"I was surprised to see my old mate 'Blue' Kelley there. Blue had come from the Australian Army and spent time in Vietnam and then done a spell of mercenary work with the Christian Phalangist militia during the Lebanese Civil War. After that he came to Rhodesia and joined the RLI. Neil was very wary of him and suspected him of being a spy, but I never got that impression.

"There were all sorts of fancy cars parked at the farm and it turned out they were stolen vehicles being used to move agents, mostly black guys, up into neighbouring countries to spy. As I discovered later, the crooks running the car-rackets in Botswana and Zambia, were in many cases, ANC cadres, so there was a rich seam of intelligence to be tapped into in the business. One of the people running the stolen car business was Joe Modise, who went

CHAPTER THIRTEEN

on to become Minister of Defence under Mandela and a primary player in the big arms deal. Unsurprisingly, that deal was riddled with bribery and corruption.

"I was then told I needed to go and find a regular job in civilian life as a cover and I would be called when needed. I managed to get hired by 'Benoni Furnishers'. It was part of a huge company owned by Tony Factor, a very wealthy Jewish gentleman who had built a business empire in the country. The salary was not bad and there was a commission on sales as part of my package. With two pay checks a month, Sylvia and I rented a nice home and we quickly settled into a pseudo-normal life.

"It actually came as something of a pleasant surprise to me, but I started to enjoy the job. Lots of pretty housewives, many of whom were bored, used to come to the shop and I had fun acting the fool, which has never been hard for me, and making them laugh. Once I got them laughing, I always made a sale and I think some of them liked coming in to the shop to see me. My sales just got better and better to the point where Mr Factor himself came to see me to congratulate me. Unbeknown to me I was a born salesman.

"Late 1981 life was good when the phone rang; it was Neil and he told me to report to 'work' immediately. I finished the day's duties and then drove out to the 'farm' in the evening.

"I walked into something almost surreal. Kriel was waving his huge, hairy arms around and yelling at Blue Kelly who was behind him in the kitchen cutting steaks. Neil hated Blue and shat on him all the time.

'He's butchering a fucking cow in the kitchen,' Kriel screamed, while looking to me for some sort of understanding and support. The fact is Blue had been a blockman in civvy-street in Australia, so he knew exactly what he was doing. I told Neil this, but Neil always knew better.

'You fuckers drive me fucking mad,' Neil shouted and stormed out the room. Why Neil never booted Blue out always intrigued me because he could have but didn't. I think Blue had something on Neil.

"Eventually calm returned and there was Neil and Gray explained the background. A South African agent, a chap by the name of Patrick Gericke, was a serving member of the Zimbabwe Army Corps of Engineers and had successfully placed explosives and blown up the huge armoury at Inkomo Barracks north of Harare. It was a big setback for the government and a serious embarrassment. The Zimbos were understandably very angry and it appeared somebody might have fingered him because investigators had searched his home and found reason to believe he was the man responsible. None of our people working on *Project Barnacle* had heard of this guy but he had been arrested and we were tasked to bust him out of jail. Neil and Gray had just returned after having been summoned by General Loots who told them that this guy knew an awful lot about South African covert operations and if he told the authorities in Zimbabwe all that he knew it would be hugely embarrassing. The message was, move quickly and get him back to South Africa by whatever means necessary.

"Gray went on to explain that he was being held at Harare Central Police Station and the Investigating Officer was Fred Varkevisser, an old friend and colleague of Gray's and a very good guy, known to all of us. Fred had been a good rugby player, was well known, and liked by everyone.

"The plan was for Gray and 'Tom[50]' to go up ahead and stay at some holiday resort near Harare so he could try and get a better idea of what was going on but the key guy was Varkevisser. We discussed the possibility of a simple approach to him as old 'comrades in arms' in the hope that he would agree to cooperate but that was rejected. It seemed Fred was happy under the new government and would balk at any sort of betrayal, so that option had to be dispensed with. The only way was to force him to comply with our demands and it was decided the best way to do that was to go to his house and take his wife and kids hostage, which would leave him with little option. Once we had his attention, we would compel him to use his position as the IO, and with easy access to the prisoner, to spring him. A question then arose around who should actually accompany him when he went into the cells to bring him out. All eyes then turned on me.

'Fuck off,' I said, quite emphatically. 'I'm too short to be a cop, they won't buy it!' Then I stared suggestively at the rest of them.

'You are big strong bastards – perfect for the job'! They stared back at me blankly.

'We've got beards, cops aren't allowed beards.'

'Well shave the fucking things off then,' I suggested. I was in a mild panic thinking about what I was going to have to do.

'No, we like our beards,' Neil said, 'and we are senior to you, so I'm afraid you, 'Kafupi', are the man!'

---

[50] A pseudonym

CHAPTER THIRTEEN

"At that moment I wanted to go back to selling mattresses and seducing bored wives, but the wheels started to turn quickly, and Gray left the next day for Harare to get ready for the rest of us. He would be handling Varkevisser; Mike[51] and I were to work together, and Neil was on standby to fly up in our Piper Seneca when the job was done, land at a selected bush-strip at night, and bring us all home to safety.

"I'll never forget Mike and I, dressed smartly in blue blazers with ties, pulling our slacks up and wading across the Limpopo on a moonlit night as we crossed into Zimbabwe with our silenced pistols. We then put our shoes on and walked to the main road, where we were met by an agent who drove us to a farm in the Shangani area where we were dropped at a weir to await collection. From there, Barry Bawden drove the two of us to a holiday chalet near Lake McIlwaine.

"Meanwhile, Gray had lured Fred out to where he was staying, relayed through another agent, using some bogus story about a possible 'source' he needed to meet. Poor Fred got the fright of his life when he walked in and saw Gray and Tom because he well knew Gray was working for the 'enemy'. Gray tried to persuade him to help voluntarily, but he was not interested. An altercation ensued and at gunpoint Fred was told he would have to help or he was going to die. They went back to the family home and Gray told Fred's wife that she and the children were now being held hostage pending the release of Gericke after which they would be given the option of staying in Zimbabwe and explaining themselves or being taken to South Africa where they would be well looked after.

"When Mike and I arrived at the Varkevisser's house, Tom and Gray were waiting. Mike tried to calm Fred and the family down and asked them to just listen to what we were asking them to do and all would be fine. Fred kept saying we were over-reacting to this arrest; that they had nothing on Gericke, and that he would soon be released so best we just leave the man in his hands to sort out. Mike explained we had orders and we would carry them out – Gericke had to be sprung. While they remained with the family, I left with Fred to go to Harare Central to do the dirty deed. It was after midnight when we left, I had a silenced pistol in my pants, and I was keen to get going and get the job done. We went to the car and when the doors closed, Fred spoke.

---

[51] A pseudonym.

'I'm afraid I need to go to my office first,' he said. I did not like the sound of this.

'Why,' I asked.

'There is some important stuff there I need to collect,' he replied.

'Okay, I said,' staring at him as I drew my pistol. 'But if you make one wrong move or sound, Fred, I promise I will kill you.'

"He nodded his head and off we went to the Station which was a hive of activity. He parked his car in his reserved spot and we jumped out. I walked as jauntily as I could up the steps, through the Charge Office and up to the offices. He opened the door and as soon as we were inside, I felt for my pistol while he went to his desk and started rummaging around in his draws. I was watching him like a hawk when he pulled something out.

'Thanks Rich, got them,' he said happily. I was not sure if I was seeing wrong when I saw a small sleeve in his hand containing some darts.

'My bloody darts Rich, I'm not going anywhere without my darts!'

We burst out laughing. It was the most surreal moment. Fred had flicked a switch in his head and we were back to being mates again. We were Rhodesians after all. He had a big grin on his face.

'Okay, let's go and get this bloke Rich.'

"We then went down to the dungeons below where we were met by the guards who looked happy to see us. Fred explained that I was Detective Inspector Smith and I had come to interrogate the prisoner. We signed the register and made our way to Gericke's cell. I was suddenly nervous again when I heard the big steel door clang shut behind us. I thought I'm now trapped, and I might never get out of the place. We walked down the passage, the cell door opened and there was our man. The cell stunk of the dried fish they were feeding him and so did he, the smell being so bad that it actually took my breath away. Fred motioned him toward us but when we put the handcuffs on him, he became frightened and this turned to belligerence and I realised we had a problem on our hands. The guards looked on with great interest to see how we were going to handle this. I was very nervous and I realised I needed to put on a show so I proceeded to give him a few very good slaps in order to subdue him and this was very pleasing to the guards who had a good laugh.

'Ah, he is going to get it now,' one cheered.

"With just a few smacks I had become a bit of a hero in their eyes.

CHAPTER THIRTEEN

With them still laughing, I led him roughly out the cell block and up the stairs, then past a line of policemen who looked on with great interest as we sauntered by. Being outside again in the cool night air was a relief and we bundled him into the car and drove off. Once we were moving, I reached across and took his cuffs off. He stared at me.

'Who are you?' he asked.

'I'm Kafupi,' I answered, 'I'm a salesman from Benoni Furnishers and I sold more mattresses last month than anyone else in the group. Tony Factor thinks I'm one of his best salesmen.'

'You must be joking,' he said, with an incredulous look on his face.

'No bullshit,' I said, 'I'm the mattress-man from Benoni!'

I noticed his eyes go blank. He seemed unable to understand what was happening and I can't say I blamed him.

"Thirty minutes later, we arrived at the bush-strip near Chegutu and a huge sigh of relief to see Neil waiting by the aircraft. Fred's wife and children were also there, looking deeply distressed and my heart went out to them. Soon we were aboard and what a relief to hear the engine roar into life. The pilot wasted no time in getting us airborne but flew low under the radar until we cleared the Limpopo river and were in South African airspace. As soon as I knew we were safely on our way I grabbed Fred's arm and looked him in the eyes.

'Fred, soon as we arrive in South Africa, you will go to see the big boss, General Loots, and you will have to tell him what happened and how much we have upset your lives. They owe you plenty.'

"On arrival at Lanseria airport I was bloody pissed off when told to stay with the plane and babysit the children while the rest of the 'heavies' went off for a briefing. I thought I'm the guy who pulled this off and now I'm the nanny!

"I think the entire South African intelligence community and the political hierarchy must have breathed a huge sense of relief at the unqualified success of the mission. Top army commanders came to congratulate us and then Foreign Minister 'Pik' Botha arrived. He was very interested to know what had happened and how we had pulled the whole caper off.

"Unbeknown to us at the time, it was only late the following day that anyone realised something was wrong back in Harare. A police detail went to Fred's house and when they saw it abandoned, the alarm was raised.

When they realised their prize prisoner was gone the shit hit the fan big time from Mugabe downwards.

"Despite the secrecy surrounding what had happened, there was no fooling my father. I got quite a fright when the phone rang and he was on the other end of the line and sounding very angry.

'What the hell have you been up to?' he said.

'What do you mean,' I answered, feigning ignorance.

'Don't bullshit me; have you seen the papers?'

'No,' I replied in all honesty.

'Well, I suggest you have a look. A spy has been sprung from jail in Harare and the Zimbabwe police have published a sketch of the likely suspect and I'm bloody certain it's you. They looking for a short, muscular individual with blonde hair!'

Later, when I saw the sketch, I was taken aback, but all credit to the artist because he got me pretty damn right.

"What had happened was that my uncle Danny, then head of the Zimbabwe CIO, was very much in the loop and he knew immediately it was me when he saw the sketch and called my dad. Danny was understandably very pissed off. I got messages to say that it was just a matter of time before I was extradited because they knew I was the perpetrator. I was told to lie low for a while.

"It all turned out well for Fred and his family. They were compensated generously and made very comfortable in the Western Cape where they went on to lead very happy lives. Sometime later I received a letter from Fred thanking me. He said it had all worked out well for them and no hard feelings. That made me feel a lot better about the whole episode.

"But I had not seen the last of Captain Gericke. Years later, I was in the process of doing a refresher demolitions course to maintain my certification which was being run by Charl Naude. There was a braai scheduled for the one night and Bruce Laing and I went on a pub crawl and got severely pissed. When we finally arrived, we were in bad shape and for some reason I addressed Charl as 'Commandant' which he did not like.

'Call me anything but for fucks sake don't call me Commandant!' he ordered.

'Okay," I said, 'is it okay if I just call you cunt then?'

"After that I don't know what happened, but I woke up in the morning

CHAPTER THIRTEEN

in the Motor Transport yard, on the grass, in all my clothes. I remembered it was examination day and staggered to a tap to wash my face then stumbled off to the room where we had to write the exam. I slumped behind a desk and then Charl slipped up behind me and whispered in my ear.

'I hope you are as clever this morning as you were last night, Kafupi.'

I then looked up to see that Gericke was the invigilator. He recognised me but never even came over to say thanks for saving him. He was still pissed off about the slaps I gave him in the cells.

"Much to everyone's surprise I managed to clear my brain, write the exam, and pass. And I was the only one in the class to do so.

Chapter Fourteen

We were only human
We bled, loved, laughed and cried
And we laid
The foundation stone
Of the years you live in.

♦

From the Seychelles to the Single Cells

The Plan
"Back from the Harare operation, after all the adrenaline pumping, I was feeling a little bored so it was something of a pleasant surprise when I received a call from Blue Kelly suggesting we meet for a beer and a chat. We agreed on a pub and when I got there, Blue wasted no time in getting down to business.

'The plan is simple, Kafupi. 'We're putting a group together to overthrow the government of the Seychelles,' he explained calmly. This took a while to sink in.

'Are you fucking mad?' I retorted!

'No,' said Blue, 'we're going to do it and you're invited.'

"I then discovered the man we were being tasked to depose was President France-Albert René, a firebrand socialist, educated at Kings College in London, and who was bedding down with communist countries and threatening Western interests in the region.

"When Blue went on to explain that the South African government had given tacit approval for the plan and would be supportive, I became more interested. He went on to tell me that 'Mad Mike' Hoare of Congo fame was to lead the operation and that James Mancham, the recently deposed playboy-president of the country would be lending a political hand. I was pleased to hear a lot of the guys being recruited were former Rhodesians from the RLI and SAS, along with SA Recces and a few of Hoare's guys from the Congo.

CHAPTER FOURTEEN

"Hoare was of interest to me because my Godfather, Ralph Hider, (father of Allan who I served with in the SAS) had soldiered under him with '5 Commando' during the Simba uprising in the Congo in 1964/65 when the rebels aimed at installing a communist government in the territory. One of the Simba rebel groups was led by the Argentinian Marxist guerrilla Che Guevara who Hoare thought little of. Working with Cuban pilots, Belgian paratroopers, mercenaries and the CIA, Ralph and Mike Hoare, based in what was then known as Stanleyville, in the course of *Operation Dragon Rouge*, saved many missionaries and innocent civilians from certain death at the hands of the rebels. Ralph's men were known to be reckless and high-spirited in the face of great danger. The reason for this bravado came out later when it was revealed that the coconuts that were seen being passed around to the troops in large numbers were all laced with rum.

"When I met Hoare a few days later at a briefing I was reminded that men of military fame usually appear smaller in real life and he was no exception. He sported a 'goatee beard' long before it was fashionable and wore glasses. At 62, his disposition was one of quiet confidence and he had a military bearing that was reassuring.

"He wasted no time in explaining the outline. The weapons, we were told, were already cached on Mahe, the largest island of the Seychelles group and the resistance group "Mouvement pour la Résistance" (MPR) formed by Gerard Hoareau, was ready in the wings to rise up alongside us as soon as we seized control.

"It all sounded well planned and achievable until some bright spark at the back asked what the plan was if something went badly wrong and the reply was not very convincing. Unbeknown to me at the time, other former Rhodesian officers had already been approached and declined the offer because they could see the planning was not as good as we believed it to be, and there was no escape strategy in place to deal with a worst case scenario.

"Bearing in mind the fact that the Seychelles is a long way from South Africa, in the middle of the Indian Ocean - a big stretch from the safety of home, but by this time I was sold on the idea and stopped looking too closely at what might go wrong! I took one week of leave from my sales job - my real job at *Barnacle* - and raced off to an Edgars department store to buy my fancy beach clothes for the upcoming seaside adventure."

Also caught up in the excitement was Stan Standish-White. "November

1981, I received a surprise phone call the day I wrote my last exam for 1st year B.Sc. at the University of Cape Town. The previous week had been a nightmare of stay-awake drugs and last-minute cramming. Now was the time to 'ease springs' with copious beers and chatting up any girls who cared to listen to my rubbish. Unfortunately, my ex-C Squadron comrade Japie du Toit had other plans.

"He had heard via ex-6 Recce friends that there was 'a job' of a military nature planned for some Marxist African country to the north and remuneration would be good. Apparently quite a few ex-SAS and other Rhodie chaps were involved. Those interested in finding out more were told to attend a briefing in Durban. In a flash, the promise of action and elevation from the 'penniless student' category peeled off a year and a half of civilian veneer. I reckoned there was no harm in finding out what was up. We got cholera and yellow fever shots, a vague promise of compensation for airfares and jumped on a flight. That our adventure began on Friday the 13th was of no significance till later.

"We gathered in a holiday flat to meet Colonel Hoare. My first impressions were favourable. He did not possess either the crazy eyes of the genuine psychopath or the '1000-yard stare' affected by so many posers. I liked the look of the other guys there, many of whom were good pals from Rhodesia along with some older blokes who were Hoare's associates from the Congo.

"When he told us the target was the Seychelles, we were pleasantly surprised. We had been mentally battening down the hatches for Sudan or Chad or some such dreadful place. The archipelago, which few of us knew anything about, consists of 115 islands spread over a huge area of the Indian Ocean, with the main island, Mahe, home to the capital, Victoria, 27 kms long, with a population then of 62,000 and some 1,600 kms off the east coast of Africa. It had been a British colony until independence in 1976. An international airport had been built in 1971, drastically swinging the fragile economy from fishing and copra harvesting to tourism.

"There had been a coup four years previously. France-Albert René, leader of a socialist party and in fact President Mancham's Prime Minister, had taken power by force (after having lost a couple of post-independence elections) with the help of Tanzanian troops. There was no army at that time so this had not been difficult to do. René then immediately flushed

CHAPTER FOURTEEN

the system of opposition to his communist utopia. There were firings, imprisonments without trial and expulsions. To ensure he did not become a victim of his own methods, René founded an army to be trained and overseen by his Tanzanian bully-boys. He also started conscripting a youth militia that was unpopular with the islanders. He did away with a free press, private schooling, political opposition and nationalised business which crippled the economy. An unusually large Soviet 'diplomatic corps' was soon entrenched and a hostile approach was adopted towards South Africa with the cancellation of landing rights for the national airline. This move saw a dramatic drop in tourism and a further blow to the economy which triggered an exodus of capital and skills. With traditional double standards the UN allowed this usurper to retain the Seychelles seat and vote. Here he supported the 1979 Russian invasion of Afghanistan, the Libyan invasion of Chad and even the demonic Pol Pot regime in Cambodia. The more we found out about this guy the keener we were to take him out!

"All those at the meeting were of a similar mind regarding 'the commies' in general but Mike pressed this point with some glib and erudite talk on what was obviously one of his favourite subjects; 'The Red Menace', ('Rooi Gevaar') which was spreading inexorably through the Middle East and Africa. He had a point; within the previous two years Afghanistan had been invaded by the Soviets, the US hostage crisis had just been played out in Iran and Mugabe had taken over in Zimbabwe. He explained the US had a naval base at Diego Garcia and a tracking station on Mahe. If the Soviets were to assume control the tracking station would be threatened and a 'red belt' spreading across Africa, might well spread across the Indian Ocean. Our judgement was probably a little impaired because we were an ideologically receptive audience. The colonel's fiery address ended with us in a crusading mood and looking forward to fighting the good fight.

"It turned out an expelled Seychellois had approached Mike in 1978 about the possibility of a coup to reinstate Mancham. He was told they had started a resistance movement which many of the exiles had joined. The seed was sown. But over the following years a grand $5,000,000 plan for 200 seaborne troops with helicopter gunships was whittled steadily away by financial constraints to a mere fifty men arriving by civilian aircraft. Eventually Hoare was even restricted to employing only those who would accept the main portion of their pay after the operation. Whoever heard of

MEN OF WAR

mercenaries playing the futures market? Who exactly the financial backers were, Hoare never revealed, but it was probably a consortium of wealthy exiles and a few guys gambling on future business opportunities.

"One tricky situation was that Mancham himself was risk-averse and quite comfortable living the good life being a playboy in London. His participation was vital however to give the whole exercise political legitimacy.

"With all the activity and subterfuge, it's not surprising word of a coup plot got back to René and late 1979 over eighty people were arrested in Mahe, jailed for nine months without charge, let alone trial, and then most were expelled. Weapons shipments onto the island to shore up the regime increased.

"A financial contribution from the SA government has never been proved or disproved but the fact that the SA government was involved and supported the mission is beyond question. What has never been established though is to what level this support went. Senior folk in both NIS and MI (Military Intelligence) had worked closely with Hoare and his PA, Martin Dolinchek. MI had delivered Rumanian AKs (with pistol grip on the front stock), RPG-7 launchers, grenades and ammo for both weapon types to Hoare's house in Howick, KwaZulu-Natal. Kenya, we gathered, was also providing covert support and they were expected to fly Mancham in to the Seychelles along with paramilitaries to maintain law and order after our departure.

"Hoare, we heard, had conducted three recces on Mahe to get the feel of the place and identify tactically important features and installations. He told us that on the previous year's Independence Day Parade he had seen about fifty Tanzanians and two full companies of SPLA (Seychelles People's Liberation Army) all armed with AK47s. In addition, there was reported to be a ragtag reserve force of about 400 armed with SKSs. There was also an 'elite' President's Guard of about thirty men, trained and controlled by the ex-Congo mercenary Bob Noddyn.

"Weapons and equipment on the islands that we might have to contend with, included RPG-7s scattered around and six 75mm recoilless rifles mounted on wheels, six Bofors anti-aircraft weapons, but strangely, no light machineguns. There were twelve BTR[52] armoured cars. There was also

---
[52] Armoured personnel carriers.

CHAPTER FOURTEEN

a navy of sorts consisting of an old French vessel and about thirty crew armed with 9mm sub-machine guns. He indicated that the troops appeared to be lethargic and poorly trained but he had been told that some soldiers had been sent to Tanzania for training. The troops were split between the Pointe Larue Barracks at the south-eastern end of the airport runway and the Unionvale Barracks near the radio station just north of Victoria.

"He reckoned that with about fifty men we could neutralise enemy forces, await the arrival of the interim government and Kenyan paramilitaries by plane from Nairobi and then stand down. Detailed orders could only be given once he knew how many men were available. (Similar meetings were being held in Johannesburg). We were advised to organise international driving licenses.

"The main issue of money had then to be discussed. The deal was R1000 up front and another R10 000 on successful completion. This peculiarly skewed arrangement was perplexing, but we all signed up nevertheless and agreed to meet a few days later for a more detailed Orders Group.

"On reflection, giving a bunch of total strangers this much intelligence and then leaving them to their own devices in a big city for a few days was highly unsound, and showed up the naïveté which characterised Hoare's handling of the operation. As it turned out there did not seem to have been any fatal leaks, but the number of experts and wise men we had to listen to after the event multiplied exponentially.

"As for our personal motivation, we fitted the mould perfectly. The former Rhodesians had left 'unfinished business' up north and many of the professionals had had promising careers cut short. Those who had transferred to the SADF were disappointed with what they found as two different military cultures; the unconventional Rhodesian and the more conventional South African, clashed seriously. Here we had this René guy who fitted straight into the bullyboy gook mould. Kicking his 'commie arse' was going to be a pleasure.

"The mission was to be called *Operation Anvil* involving fifty combatants consisting mostly of former Rhodesians plus South Africans from 2 Recce Commando. Most participants therefore seemed well-trained and current but there were exceptions including a 37-year old opera singer.

"A safe house had already been established on Mahe and weapons were to be delivered by boat. Two advance parties had already arrived there and three more were due over the next couple of days. They were going to be spread between three different hotels to allay any possible suspicion. Their two main tasks were to recce targets and 'create a diversion' if there were any serious problems on arrival of the main group at the airport. We were not to know that serious discord would arise between the NI spook, Martin Dolinchek and the other more boisterous members."

"We were going in as a bunch of tourists representing a charity organisation bringing fluffy toys to the children of the Seychelles," remembers Stannard. "It was known as 'Ye Ancient Order of Froth Blowers' a humorous, charitable organisation to foster the gentle, noble art of froth-blowing amongst gentlemen and ex-soldiers. Ancient quaffers, apparently blew the froth off their pewter mugs in Edwardian times so as to not be cheated out of beer. It was founded by Bert Temple, a former soldier, in order to raise money for children's charities and that was to be our cover, a soft bag full of fluffy toys. Dressed in all our bright floral beach kit carrying bags of teddy bears, I remember thinking this is going to be different, and my God I was right about that! Under the original plan, we would have had some time after arrival on the island, to familiarise ourselves with the geography, including non-tactical targets such as the Beau Vallon Bay topless beach and a tour to the local brewery Seybrew.

"It was stressed at the outset that this was, if at all possible, to be a bloodless coup. The Seychellois were an easy-going, even somewhat indolent tropical island people. We hoped this would make it possible for us to rapidly attain a dominant position, after which violence should not be necessary.

"The plan was to split the men into three assault groups, a HQ group and a couple of 'funnies'", remembers Standish-White.

One group, consisting of eighteen men, mostly 2 Recce guys under former Congo mercenary Tulio Moneta, was to tackle the Army HQ, where the Presidential Guard was quartered, and the State House (the parliament building) where a cabinet session would be interrupted and the top three members arrested. Both these targets were in Victoria. A secondary target was the Presidential palace up the hill.

The second group, which included Rich Stannard as 2IC mostly had three targets: The Pointe La Rue Barracks at the south end of the runway was allocated to a section of twelve men led by Peter Hean (RLI). A couple

CHAPTER FOURTEEN

of houses between the barracks and the terminal, inhabited by Tanzanian instructors, would be targeted by four men led by Simon Willar (RLI & Selous Scouts). The control tower group was to be commandeered by Chas Goatley (7 Sqn, RhAF) and Vernon Prinsloo (RLI).

The third group consisting of seven men under Bernard Carey, was to neutralise Unionvale Barracks just north of the capital and then commandeer the radio station in order to start broadcasting prepared tapes over the local airwaves. It was thought the barracks would be fairly empty during the day, hence the small number of men allocated by the planners.

An HQ group including Hoare and three others was going to establish itself in some offices close to State House.

Martin Dolinchek, who was given no other official role in the operation and was probably working for one of the South African intelligence services, was apparently going to break into the Soviet Embassy and then photograph whatever documents he thought might interest his bosses in South Africa.

The Seychelles Resistance Movement leaders had assured Hoare of both popular and active support. Some of their active members, all in the same colour shirts to help identification, were to assist in the operation.

Weapons would be AK47s and RPG-7s; all in good-condition, supplied by the SADF. Mike had an AK there which was passed around and a couple of the guys showed off stripping and assembly skills. Communications would be maintained with fifteen walkie-talkie sets. Any medical assistance needed could be rendered by the three doctors we had amongst those recruited.

The plan was to carry out a few recces after our arrival and then initiate all assaults simultaneously on Friday (two days after our arrival) at midday when the government executive team would be meeting at State House.

We were shown photographs of René and the two ministers the exiles reckoned were the most dangerous and powerful. Ogilvy Berlouis was Minister of Defense and Youth, James Michel of Information and Education. Michel was also army Chief-of-Staff. Whether specific instructions were given in regard to dealing with these three is not clear, but the tacit agreement was 'if in doubt take them out'. The interim government was supposedly scheduled to arrive within a couple of hours of successful conclusion of the operation. Policing and security duties would then be taken over by the resistance men and Kenyan paramilitaries. The men would then enjoy the rest of their prepaid holiday and scuttle home to collect the outstanding R10 000. It all seemed very simple!

Success would largely depend on simultaneous execution of three assaults, all quite a distance from each other. This involved another large dollop of optimism, of which we seemed to have had a surfeit! The obvious 'what if' question of incomplete success or even complete failure was raised but this was laid to rest with a barrage of comments about the incompetence of the enemy forces and their poor relationship with the local civvies. Failure was not an option!

"There were murmurs regarding rehearsals and training. I seem to remember that Hoare said time was short and the piecemeal nature of the targets would make realistic rehearsals extremely difficult to organise. We were later to find out that 'a friend' in Naboomspruit had offered his property as a training ground. That we did not do any work as a team, be it merely range practice or radio procedure, proved to be a major drawback when the chips were down.

"I don't remember questions on handling of prisoners. That we were to be surrounded by friendly 'resistance men' seems to have satisfied everyone and that was silly. That a small group of operators may have become bogged down securing large numbers of potentially hostile captives does not seem to have been considered. Our previous military experience, where contacts seldom produced prisoners in significant numbers, had not prepared us for this possibility.

"Another concern was whether any of these small teams could remain effective if they sustained any more than a couple of casualties. This was considered such a remote possibility that it didn't merit further study. We would win swiftly and then the hospital would be accessible to us if necessary.

"With the benefit of hindsight, it's easy to see how full of holes the plan was and that was with the weapons already in place on the island. Our previous training in Rhodesia, however, had conditioned us to orders in which there was a large amount of (usually well-deserved) trust and confidence. Plans had been carefully made by those most qualified to make them. We had confidently relied on other sections of our own regiment and other units to help out in some quite serious scrapes. And, quite apart from historical and tactical considerations, we were a bunch of cheeky young buggers dying for a 'dust up'! This strong desire blinded us in a sense.

CHAPTER FOURTEEN

The Attack

"We were duly handed our Budget Tours shoulder bags, 'AOFB' T-shirts and shirt tags, and told to assemble at Durban airport on Tuesday morning. After a boozy weekend with our comrades, we flew from Durban to Johannesburg on Tuesday 24th November 1981. There we met the Johannesburg detachment, who had previously been briefed separately, for the first time. It was good to see Rich Stannard among them. Most of the lads seemed in pretty good shape and ready for the fight. Forty-seven of us then boarded a bus and enjoyed an increasingly festive trip to Ermelo. Old Jerry Puren became ever more nervous of the high spirits, enhanced by various beverages."

"I said goodbye to my wife," remembers Stannard, "and explained that I would be away for a week on a jaunt and waved her goodbye. I then joined up with the guys who had come up from Durban to Johannesburg before heading to Swaziland because it had been decided that leaving from there would be less likely to trigger unwanted interest in us. It was good to see so many familiar and friendly faces and my confidence improved but not for long.

"That night we all had a closed meeting with Mike Hoare and his command element when we received some very unwelcome news; we were going to be carrying our weapons in with us.

'What?' an angry voice was heard, 'you said the weapons would be on the island, now you are asking us to carry them aboard a commercial Royal Swaziland airliner.'

'Nothing to worry about,' said Hoare calmly. We all looked dumbstruck at each other.

'You can withdraw if you want,' he said, 'however if you decide not to go, you have to remain in the hotel until we are on the island.' There was a complete silence. I remember looking around at my SAS colleagues and nobody blinked and nobody spoke. The risks had just increased enormously but we felt we had come too far and we didn't want to let each other down. Many of us had seen combat together over the years and there was a rather naïve solidarity amongst us which was not helping us think very incisively. Unlike the two Recce doctors who were going; they saw this as a risk too far and immediately withdrew themselves."

Standish-White: "It turned out that this had been the plan for us all along

– 313 –

MEN OF WAR

because we all received bags with weapons and two full magazines already fitted in kaylite cut-outs. Customs, we were told, were 'a breeze' because they understood that tourists were the lifeblood of the islands and didn't want to upset anyone. To reduce risk further the resistance had promised to have 'their men' on duty.

"We did not really consider the implications of all this. Would the president, recently spooked by rumours of a coup, really be so relaxed? And how far would 60 rounds go in any sustained punch-up? Now that the weapons were butt-less would the severely reduced accuracy impact on us? How would we now cope with buildings and against armoured vehicles with no rockets? On the other hand we reminded ourselves that we were a fairly capable bunch and taking calculated risks was quite normal for us."

Stannard: "On the morning of departure most of us were nursing bad hangovers when we trooped off to Matsapa Airport in Swaziland, where we were to be the first full flight for Air Swazi's new Mahe run. On checking in at the airport, a security official had a look in my bag where my AK was hidden.

'What is this' he asked and pointed to a torch.

'It's a special underwater torch to look at fish 'I explained a little nervously.

'Oh, that is very good,' said the smiling security man and waved me through.

It was in fact a strobe light. When I told Darrell I was going on this mission, he assured me he would get some guys together and rescue me if we got into trouble and suggested I take a strobe light for signalling purposes. He said he would arrange some mates and a yacht and come get us if necessary.

"Our first stop was the Comoros Islands. On arrival there the plane was kept some distance from the terminal as a couple disembarked and a new passenger embarked. There were plenty of security men in gendarme-type uniform stalking around. Comoros had recently been the site of a successful coup organized by Bob Denard, a Congo contemporary of Hoare. It didn't seem a very friendly place, to be sure.

"I reminded myself what we were supposed to be and concentrated on trying to look and act like a charity volunteer; a friendly, lovable, 'Froth Blower' bringing toys for needy kids but it was not easy. We were all nervous

CHAPTER FOURTEEN

and trying hard not to show it. Having guns on board was like a nagging toothache that just wouldn't go away. I remember gazing wistfully out the window as we were coming in to land on the island of Mahe and wishing I really was on holiday. I couldn't help noticing the bright blue ocean and the rolling white surf breaking on the reef not far from the runway, the hills on the other side of the airport terminal, a vibrant verdant green. Tropical palms waved in the wind. It all looked so beautiful and peaceful. A collective sigh went out among our men as we touched down and an air of anticipation swept over us. Adding to our problems, we were later than scheduled and could expect only an hour of daylight after landing.

"Once outside the moist warm, humid air enveloped us all and sweat started to trickle down my neck onto my bright blue Hawaiian shirt which now looked so damn ridiculous. 'Christ, it's hot,' I thought, as I walked into the terminal building and headed for the 'Nothing to Declare' channel. By this time most of the guys were through and I was behind one of the Recce guys when suddenly I heard the voice of an angry customs officer.

'What is this,' he shouted, in heavily accented English? And there, horror of horrors, he was brandishing the barrel of an AK. I felt my heart jump into my throat.

'I don't know where it came from,' was his limp reply.

"It's odd how in extremely stressful situations one suddenly develops tunnel vision. In this case I was focused briefly on the officer's heavily calloused knuckles. Then I broke out of my stupor, looked him directly in the face, knew the game was up and ran past both of them heading for the exit when the first burst of machine gun fire thundered through the terminal shattering glass in my path. I raced towards the rest of the group already outside who were scrambling in all directions. Standish-White and one other, already on the roof of the bus, were busy hurling bags off the roof rack so we could get to our weapons and prepare for the fight.

"Meanwhile, a police sergeant was dragging Johan Fritz, the Recce guy who had been nabbed, off to an office when a burst was fired at him and the policeman was hit in the shoulder. Unfortunately, a stray round hit Johan in the chest. I ran to where he lay, he had a serious sucking chest wound; his eyes were wide with shock, and he was gasping for air. I stopped briefly to try and help, but we were defenceless and I desperately needed my weapon so after a short while I continued running. We quickly broke through the false bottoms of the suitcases and armed ourselves"

"We on the outside," recalls Standish-White, "were ignorant of developments inside and milling around somewhat aimlessly. Then suddenly the porters and drivers who had been helping with loading gave new meaning to the expression 'mobile swastikas' as they streaked into the jungle never to be seen again! Bob Simms, the 'safe house' caretaker, who had come to meet us with the rest of the advance party, took advantage of the confusion and his jockey training to race from the scene with all haste, taking Dolinchek's weapon with him in the boot of his car. Thus deprived of hardware and not too impressed with the new bunch of unknowns, Dolinchek decided that the Reef Hotel would be a much friendlier environment and duly scuttled off as well. All sixty or so civvies still in or near the terminal were herded out of the way into one of the inner rooms. It was only forty minutes since we had touched down and already 'pear-shaped' was an understatement.

"One point that I must make, in direct contradiction of published reports, was that the situation did not just disintegrate into crazed mercenaries running in all directions and firing at random. Nearly all our magazines were subsequently recovered either by the Seychellois or the South African authorities in Durban and the number of rounds remaining indicated extremely good fire discipline for the circumstances we had found ourselves in.

"Japie du Toit, Bob Jones-Davies and I became part of a group that decided a road block/ambush position at the north-western end of the airport was a good idea to stop any traffic and discourage any reinforcements which might be sent from Victoria. Bob had managed to get hold of one of the walkie-talkies, which proved useful later, but at that stage only provided psychological support because few others had sets and no one had a clue what was happening anyway!"

"Amid confusion, Hoare ordered me to proceed to attack the Pointe Larue Barracks south-east of the airport and 'stop anyone getting out'," remembers Stannard. "I quickly jumped in a Mini-Moke driven by a former Rhodesian ex SAS trooper who looked at me blankly, awaiting instructions. 'To the barracks', I shouted – where else I wondered, did he think we might be going – to the fucking beach!?

"We roared off down the road leading to the barracks but not fast enough and suddenly the hotel bus overtook us with the rest of the group;

CHAPTER FOURTEEN

'Faster, faster,' I shouted as we went at full speed when automatic fire rang out causing panic in the tin shanties alongside the road – barking dogs and screaming civilians adding to all the noise as a bunch of brightly attired mercenaries alighted from their transport and took up positions lining the highway.

"We screamed to a stop in our little car at the barracks gate just as we heard the thump of heavy guns opening up on us and I threw myself down behind a huge coconut tree right outside the security fence with withering RPD machine gun fire coming down to my left and tracer flaring just above me. Dust and dirt from bullets hitting the ground covered my precious 'Hang-Ten' baseball cap that I had stolen from my father-in-law…how I loved that red cap. I remember wondering if it would survive this encounter intact while taking note of the troubling fact that their fire, coming out of a strongly built guard-house, was very accurate. I turned and saw my Aussie mate to my left, also tucked behind a coconut tree.

'Thanks for inviting me to the party, Blue,' I yelled.

'Fuck off,' he yelled back.

Then I head another voice saying, 'Come on chaps – move up on the right,' and there was Mike Hoare. He was standing in the middle of the road, looking very dapper in the twilight, with his royal blue blazer and Wild Geese tie flapping in the evening breeze. I remember thinking this man is either incredibly brave or incredibly mad.

"The fire was intense, the RPDs cyclic rate of fire was so fast it sounded like ripping paper. We had no radios so we didn't know how our buddies were doing on the other side of the barracks but I could hear shouting from within the perimeter. I sneaked forward during a temporary lull in the firing and fired a few shots at some figures amongst the buildings. Then the staccato thud of 14.5 mm heavy weapons opening up with most of the rounds ripping through the trees.

"I think it's our guys," Blue shouted, "they must have broken through on the other side." I was unsure and then came more trouble when first we heard, and then spotted a Soviet BTR 60 eight-wheeled APC roaring towards the gate while shooting off rounds left and right. We were stuffed. With an AK and one spare magazine we had to run for it and I easily cleared a barbed wire security fence and with Blue raced back to the terminal. How I jumped that fence will remain a mystery to me forever but I know my sports master at Umtali Boy's High would not have believed it!"

"Whether the troops at the barracks had been alerted by the gunfire at the terminal is a moot point," remembers Standish-White. "What is not in doubt is that there was a distinct lack of both indolence and good island cheer when four advance party members arrived at the other gate and Roger England suggested to them that surrender might perhaps be a sensible option. One of the three guards adopted aforementioned 'swastika' position and disappeared into the jungle, another opened fire and hit Charlie Dukes in the upper arm and Aubrey Brooks in the back of his right thigh. They fell back and Roger used his T-shirt to stem the copious bleeding from Aubrey's wound. Aubrey was told to return to the main group which had by now arrived a little way from the front gate. He was more seriously wounded than anyone realised, and on the way, he twice blacked out from loss of blood; the second time for some hours, and only came to much later.

"To add to our woes, there was a 20 mm cannon in a gun position up the hill overlooking the camp and runway. This had not been mentioned in briefings and, although it could not be brought to bear directly on the gate area, its very presence and the possibility of HE round fire further disadvantaged us. Some mortars had also been fired but in the excitement the mortar men had neglected to arm the bombs, so they fell into the bush without detonating. In the haste of dispersal from the terminal Jerry Puren had not dished out radios either so there could be no comms between groups that might lose sight of each other. Hoare, who had also now arrived in Barney Carey's hire car and was unarmed, (not by circumstance but by choice), in the 'Lord Lovat of the Royal Marine Commandos' tradition, issued some desultory orders. A flanking attack was attempted by the main group but this fizzled out in the face of vigorous enemy fire. Lack of RPG-7s denied us any effective response and camouflage and concealment wasn't helped by the bright and breezy 'Hawaii Five-O' clobber the guys had on! What put paid to any further action at the barracks was the rapid descent of stygian tropical darkness. A team decision was made to withdraw to the terminal to reorganise. The car Hoare had driven down in was abandoned, along with his briefcase full of details on the operation, all subsequently used as evidence to nail the guys that remained on the island."

"The first guy I met up with at the terminal was RLI Major Pete Hean," recalls Stannard. "I told him we were in big trouble and he said wait for

CHAPTER FOURTEEN

Hoare to make an appreciation. This did not fill me with confidence, and I took off to take cover behind a large embankment as the BTR armoured vehicle was getting more aggressive and being a bloody nuisance. It would speed up to the front of the terminal and spray the building with 14.5 mm rounds that made the building shake and one of the airport towers exploded in a shower of glass and flashing lights as the electrical circuits shorted.

'What was that?' asked a bemused former Congo mercenary who had obviously been out of action for a while.

'A 14.5 mm heavy machine gun,' I replied and ran to where I knew Standish and his guys were positioned. I looked up and saw Tulio Moneta running around the front of the terminal. Wearing white, he had taken his shirt off so as to be less obvious. The sound of a heavy vehicle grinding its gears pierced the night air."

"At the terminal Hoare thought we might give the Air Swazi crew a try to see if they'd like to give us a ride back to SA," remembers Standish. "Since all the phones in the terminal had already been ripped out by our chaps, they crossed over the access road to a nearby garage. There they managed to contact the captain at his hotel but, even after a R10 000 bribe was offered, the lack of enthusiasm for this chore and the colourful terms in which the reply was couched were most disappointing. Air Swazi was going nowhere. A statement emphatically confirmed sometime later when the Fokker sustained a direct hit in the cockpit from a 75 mm recoilless rifle. Jerry Puren was left at the station to try and 'contact the authorities' although what any resulting conversation would have consisted of is a mystery. He subsequently had a fall in the bush while evading 14.5 mm fire and injured his knee so badly that he was virtually immobilised. He remained on the mountainside all night.

"In the meantime our roadblock had apprehended a few vehicles with only a few warning shots. Our leniency had allowed a couple of occupants to flee into the bush, but most were herded off to the 'captive room'. There were AKs in one vehicle. We unfortunately never discovered that the OC of Pointe Larue barracks, one Major Lucas, was one of our captives.

"On the other side of the terminal, three vehicles full of Tanzania troops had emerged and had advanced down the runway towards the terminal buildings. As soon as they were within range they were fired on by our Recce guys. The fire was not particularly intense or sustained but it was sufficient to have all occupants abandoning their various vehicles and conduct 'tactical withdrawals' at speed towards their end of the runway.

"It was now about 8pm. A light rain had started to fall and we had a stalemate. A lone BTR armoured car then ventured out of the Pointe Larue Barracks and trundled down the runway towards the control tower. A good solid burst from both the vehicle's light and medium machineguns put paid to most of the windows and some of the equipment in the tower. This distinctly unfavourable change in the environment encouraged the two or three chaps we had stationed there to temporarily abandon their posts. The Seychellois traffic controller decided that a metal dustbin in the tower was a good bolthole where, with lid firmly on, he could pretend that none of this was happening.

"Satisfied that the tower was now unable to operate, the car moved around to the other side of the building. I'm not sure that the gunner actually saw any live targets due to both the restricted view from his armoured glass peepholes and the highly developed survival skills the lads displayed when confronted with these heavy odds. A group of our guys was making like microbes behind a low wall that was also solidly 'revved' but no one was hurt. Our run of bad luck then took a turn as the vehicle tried to manoeuvre into a better firing position around a couple of the vehicles abandoned at the road-block and slid into a ditch from which it could not be extricated. Some of the boys immediately took advantage of its immobility by climbing on top and smearing the windows with mud so that the crew would thence have zero visibility. The occupants were then given the option of surrender, which they were understandably wary about. I think some pidgin French was yelled at them but *'voulez vous couchez avec moi ce soir?'* was hardly likely to get them in the mood to abandon their steel fortress. To help their deliberations the turret was doused in petrol and I think someone even managed to get some down the main barrel. When this was lit there was an exponential increase in movement and verbal communications from within and soon the top hatch popped open. It appeared that the commander was still not keen on surrender and in those twitchy moments of 'hostile-or-prisoner', he was dispatched. The surviving crew members were herded off to join the other captives in the terminal.

"Roger England then extracted the armoured car from the ditch with the airport tractor, but the fuel-fire had damaged the controls so we couldn't

CHAPTER FOURTEEN

use the vehicle. It was added to the roadblock, which we prepared to defend against reinforcements from Victoria in the morning.

"The army, probably trying to glorify their participation in the action, maintained a sporadic barrage of medium and heavy machine-guns, 75 mm recoilless and the odd mortar. At one stage it sounded like two groups had engaged each other in error down near the barracks but the incoming was largely ineffective as far as our positions were concerned. There were no further contacts and we settled down to wait for 'the command structure' to come up with some sort of plan, indeed any sort of plan!"

"A scheduled Air India flight on its way from Harare to Bombay[53] had apparently started calling the control tower at about 21h30," recalls Stannard. "However the tower had been vacated at this time, save for the traffic controller, and he was hiding in his dustbin so they received no reply.

"At the same time as the plane was coming in to land a 105 mm Soviet supplied anti-tank gun manned by the Tanzanians was ranging in on us and I was ordered to 'take it out'. Then I heard the sound of a jet overhead and to my utter amazement I heard screeching tyres, engines decelerating and saw a Boeing 707 landing. Unfortunately, and no fault of the crew, the plane clipped a wing tip on the abandoned armoured car as it touched down. As it drew up to the terminal, anti-tank rounds screeched over the airport roof and the incoming fire intensified, probably because they thought the aircraft was carrying reinforcements for us.

"Verne Prinsloo and Chas Goatley had been having the shit shot out of them in the tower while the poor controller maintained his position in the bin. The Air India pilot must have been concerned at the temporary silence from air traffic control so he was probably a tad relieved when Chas and Vernon had taken over and spoke to him. Chas, having been a chopper pilot knew the procedures and the protocols so he was able to sound professional even though he was talking over the sound of gunfire.

"I was looking on at the unfolding carnage when someone shouted, 'Get up the stairs and bring the captain to Commander Hoare!' I took off, belted up the gangway and upon going through the door, peered warily into the plane. The stale smell of fetid air struck me instantly. It was deadly quiet in there and in the gloom the passengers were understandably terrified as there was still incoming fire. It was stifling hot and I felt so sorry for the women

---
[53] In 1995 Bombay became Mumbai

and children. Then I moved gingerly into the cockpit and confronted poor Captain Umesh Saxena.

'Captain', I said, politely, 'please accompany me to meet my commander.'

'What is going on?' he asked.

'We are having a spot of trouble,' I replied, and he looked at me quizzically.

'Oh, my goodness gracious me, ' he said in a masterly understatement, 'if I had known this was taking place I would never have landed here.'

"His accent and demeanour reminded me of Peter Sellers and I almost had a good laugh before I handed him over to Tulio who took him to Hoare.

"Making my way back to my position I saw a bleeding Charley Dukes driving a forklift and grappling with a fuel hose. He called for help and a figure appeared out of the dark to help him couple the pipe to the fuel tank. I was truly amazed because earlier I had handed over my morphine syringe to him to help with his pain and I thought he was out of action but, tough guy that he was, he was back at work. I quickly jogged back to the other guys and hunkered down behind our massive tree. I was concerned that if the firing continued the airliner would end up a huge fireball and the passengers would be incinerated. Just as we were about to move, a runner came from Hoare telling me to get ready to move my guys and prepare to board the aircraft.

'Thank fuck,' I said and told the guys to get moving.

"What I didn't know at the time was that Hoare had managed to phone the Tanzanian army commander whose troops were busy shelling the terminal and surrounding perimeter. He had explained to him the ramifications of a commercial airliner being destroyed due to indiscriminate firing by his men. The message got through and the firing stopped. The Tanzanian said to Hoare that the aircraft could go but on condition we stayed behind. We did a check and Aubrey Brooks and Jerry Puren were missing but it was decided a search had to be abandoned in the interests of the main body of men. Bernard Carey decided to take his chances on the island.

"As I approached the aircraft stairs, I saw Hoare and Moneta locked in a heated discussion. Hoare was telling him Moneta that he (Hoare) was going to stay on the island. I bade him farewell and put my AK down on the tarmac but he ordered me to take it on board which I did and moved up the steps when I saw Roger England at the bottom of the stairs.

CHAPTER FOURTEEN

'Hey, get on board Roger,' I shouted.

'No way,' he shouted back, 'that plane's going to get shot down.'

"Considering the fact that we had been told not to board by the military it was not a bad assumption, but I decided to take my chances and found a seat behind Barry Gribben. Then I saw Hoare on board – apparently Moneta had persuaded him to not stay behind."

"Some lucky guys managed to load their baggage, along with Johan Fritz's body, into the baggage hold and forty-five of us clambered aboard,' recalls Standish. "There was some disagreement about taking weapons on board but most of the chaps were not keen to be caught unarmed if we took any fire while taxiing so nearly all of us held on to our AKs. Chas Goatley was posted to the cockpit to 'assist them' with navigation to (by now decided) South Africa. Chas would be there to make sure we went to the correct destination.

"Take-off, accompanied by the South Africans' clapping, and a resurgence of pyrotechnics from our erstwhile unwilling hosts, was at about 1.30am. As we climbed into the night sky, cabin lights went on, we stowed our weapons away and tension subsided. We introduced ourselves to those around us. Who sat next to the Zanu-PF Minister Nathan Shumuyarira's wife is lost in the mists of time but two Romeos amongst us, namely Nick Wilson and Dave Greenhalgh, lost no time in chatting up the young ladies who by good fortune they had sat next to. The bar was opened and in spite of the boys offering bundles of cash, the hostesses, who maintained a professional and pleasant demeanour throughout, refused payment."

"As the jet screamed down the runway in the dark, I remember looking out the window on my left at the arcs of fire lighting up the sky as they opened up on us again," remembers Stannard. "I was in the brace position when I heard the Lord's Prayer coming from the seats to my front. I'm not ashamed to say that I joined them in reaching out to God. I felt guilty because I reminded myself of the number of times I'd gone through this process and I was praying for my life yet again! Suddenly the plane lurched upwards and we were airborne; the acceleration, power and angle of ascent was nothing I had ever experienced before or would again, for that matter. The 'Ancient Order of Froth Blowers' was beating a hasty retreat with our tails tucked between our legs, but at least we were alive.

"The poor passengers were desperate to know what was going on and I went to the back of the plane to talk to the flight attendants. The senior guy wore a smile.

'Thank God you not like the other hijackers who shoot people!' he said.

'No Sir,' I explained, 'we just got ourselves into a little trouble there and you have been good enough to take us home. We will not do anyone any harm.'

He then told me the captain had said I was welcome to some of his special Cognac which I was very happy to accept. After a few good slugs my mood lifted and I decided it was time to lighten the mood of the passengers so I started telling some jokes and was pleased to see the passengers laugh and relax.

"Ironically, there was some ex-Zanla gooks on board who had been wounded in our war and they wanted to know more about what had happened and what was going on. I told them we had come to the island for a big party and then we had run out of beer and we became angry because we had come a long way for the piss-up. A fight had started and the police had been called so we beat up the police and then they called the army in and so we beat them up too. I had them rolling in the aisles listening to my rubbish. The gooks who had been trying to kill me only recently thought this was the best story they had ever heard and I was now their big hero.

'What's your name man?' they shouted.

'Kafupi,' I replied, and this brought more mirth. Little did I know, my bullshit story would soon appear in *The Herald*, Zimbabwe's national daily newspaper."

"Being airborne for me, it was time for reflection," says Standish. "This whole caper could have doubled as the script for a Monty Python movie… but for the dead man in the hold. What had happened to the '7 Ps'? – Proper Planning and Preparation Prevent Piss Poor Performance?

"Hoare's book 'The Seychelles Affair', published five years later, makes many references to troubled gut feelings, misgivings, instinctive aversion for certain people or procedures during the preparations but the moral of the story is that he didn't heed any of them. The rest of us were equally at fault for letting the colourful reputation of the man over-ride the many unanswered tactical questions. I mused ruefully on the fact that we had not even got close to the topless beach; the only diving I had done was behind rocks and the only tan I was likely to get was a striped one."

CHAPTER FOURTEEN

To Trial

"Unbeknown to us at the time, Johannesburg control tower, having detected the warning signal which the pilot had set off, refused landing rights. The fuel situation must have been the reason we were permitted to eventually land at Louis Botha airport in Durban sometime around 5am. After touchdown we waited for hours in the rising tropical heat for 'the authorities' to work out what to do with us. During this time some light amusement was provided by the tardy arrival of the Railway Police Task Force. These guys were supposed to be one of the crack units in the country, specifically trained to handle hijack and hostage situations. They didn't impress us by thundering up and surrounding the plane like an Irish firing squad. If hostilities had been initiated, they would have shot the hell out of each other. We heard later that one of them killed his girlfriend with an accidental discharge from his pistol that same evening.

"Eventually we were allowed to get a breath of fresh air on the companionway that had been wheeled up. The Recce snipers that had been dotted around the aircraft on the verges of the runway had a good laugh when they saw two or three of their erstwhile comrades-in-arms from The Bluff amongst the hijackers through their hi-power scopes. They stood down and started a brew."

Stannard: "Standing outside the cockpit a smiling Captain Saxena turned to me.

'Can you show us Durban tonight? I have heard that they have good curry here and then we can go and look for some girls?'

I looked at him rather wistfully but had to decline.

'Actually Captain,' I explained, 'I would love to be with you and buy the dinner, but I'm afraid I will be in prison tonight.'

"Eventually, we were all escorted off the plane under heavy guard. Colonel Ockers from Special Forces Command was at the bottom of the stairs with a look of utter bewilderment. He recognized many of the faces as we had served under his leadership in the past but he had a job to do. One of the Special Forces snipers told me after the event that he had me clearly in his sights. 'You were one squeeze away from death my friend,' he was pleased to tell me.

"I felt the heavy leg irons lock on my legs and watched my comrades as each one was shackled and chained. Armed guards glared at us, machine

– 325 –

guns at the ready. They looked intense. We told them to relax as we weren't going anywhere when we were barked at;

'Shut Up' and 'Be still'! Then we were loaded into an air force C 130 and flown to Waterkloof Air Base, Pretoria. From there we were taken in prison trucks to Zonderwater Prison east of Pretoria."

"During the journey, Dunlop Paul undid some of our handcuffs with a part from an AK cleaning kit," remembers Standish. "This caused much consternation at the receiving end when we arrived unshackled. Nothing was normal about this bunch of alleged criminals! The bar fighters amongst us were familiar with the procedure of handing in belts and shoes from the bad old days at Salisbury Central Police Station. A glance at the offence cards outside the cells we were marched past was fairly unsettling. We were Sunday School attendees in comparison to these inmates. The guy in charge of the sports equipment was in for murdering his wife!"

"I'll never forget walking into that prison and hearing the metal gates clang behind us as we entered solitary confinement," recalls Stannard. "But in a way, a pleasure – I threw myself down on the prison bunk and the mental and physical exhaustion quickly caught up with me. Soon I was sound asleep. A few hours later I was awoken by the sound of a voice saying, 'Here - Doggy Doggy,' and a metal tray with prison food was shoved inside. It skidded across the floor, spraying most of the contents on the concrete floor but it was food and I was famished. I ate and then went straight back to sleep.

"On the second day we were escorted to the showers. We all stank, a combination of sweat and raw adrenaline. In my shorts and Hawaiian shirt, I felt like a bloody idiot but then looked at my comrades, all similarly dressed, and had to have a little chuckle. Breaking the monotony was the sound of a bent cop a few cells down from me. His name was Andre Stander, and he was awaiting trial. Quite an interesting guy; while on duty as a police Captain in Kempton Park, he would go and rob banks over the lunch break and then be back at work for the afternoon shift to investigate the robbery. Later he would escape and make his way to Fort Lauderdale in Florida where he was killed by the cops. He had a guitar and a sweet voice singing Kris Kristoffersen songs like 'Sunday Morning Coming Down.' The music was definitely appropriate.

"Two days after arrival we were released for our exercise period. It was good to be in the open sunshine even if we just stood around like stunned

CHAPTER FOURTEEN

mullets but at least we were alive. Then rumours started to float around that we were never getting out and I started to get a little worried. Several stern officials from the Fraud Squad descended upon us. Rumour had it they were the only ones in the dark as regards the coup.

'All we need from you lot, is a simple statement so we can help you all get out of here,' they said. I gave an accurate statement to the effect that Mike Hoare had stated it was a covert operation, approved by NIS, so I believed at the time I was recruited, and had been approved by the authorities."

Standish: "We had no clue as to our future, so speculation was rife and the resulting bellowing from cell to cell had the long-term prisoners, used to church-mouse quiet, in a flat spin. The only other event of note was Bob Jones-Davies's twenty-third birthday, for which he got a miniature draughts set made from a matchbox and its contents. They took statements from every man (without first informing us that these would be used in court against us) and three days later released thirty-nine of us without charge. They did however retain our passports. Japie and I stayed overnight with one of the senior cops involved in the taking of statements before catching a plane to the Cape the next morning."

Stannard: "After release, pending news as to whether we were to be prosecuted, I went home but was soon summoned to the offices of my boss, a very angry Major Neil Kriel.

'What the fuck did you think you were you doing?' he barked across his desk.

'I was doing a bit of moonlighting, sir.'

'This operation was blown from the start, you fucking idiot!'

I told him I was sorry and he booted me out his office after more abuse, but he did tell me to keep quiet about *Barnacle* and they would look after me and my family. I was to stick to my story about being a furniture salesman. I went off to have a cup of tea with Darrell Watt who thought it was hilarious.

'Another one of your nine lives gone my mate,' he said and we each downed a mug of sweet tea.

"Angus Highland-Smith, a good friend and former SAS officer was working at IBM at the time and organised an interview for me. I went before a panel and they said you're a 'bit rough' but you have potential and we're going to send you on a course. So off I went learning about computers and was actually top of the class when I was suddenly summoned to their legal department. There was a red-faced gentleman staring daggers at me when I walked in. I could see I was in trouble and sat down nervously to look into the angry eyes of the company lawyer.

'You are a hijacker!' he blurted out and looked at me as if he was staring at a serial murderer.

'Well not exactly,' I argued, 'I'm accused but not convicted'.

Being a lawyer, he knew I was within my rights and he softened a little, but explained I had become a huge embarrassment for the company and they would pay me two months' salary to go quietly. I accepted but on condition I could re-apply when I came out of jail. He agreed and off I went."

Standish: "The international hullabaloo following our release was both intense and sustained. Hypocrisy and double standards were widespread. It was interesting to see India amongst the most vociferous. They had recently openly consorted with terrorists from Pakistan who had hijacked a plane and murdered a passenger. The UN decided to set up a commission to investigate the whole issue; something they had not considered when René had forced his way into power through a coup four years previously. At home, five National Party cabinet ministers were falling over each other in attempts to explain their innocence. The resulting statements were often hilarious and Foreign Minister Pik Botha joined the chorus.

"The press obviously had a field day. It was a rude awakening for those of us used to the supportive line churned out by *The Herald* in Salisbury. Idiots become experts and all manner of hearsay and blatant lies become accepted fact just because they appeared in print. In addition, any reply from us was effectively muzzled by the *sub judice* rule.

"Such was the international pressure, and there was no way South Africa was going to get off the hook without charging us so eventually, four days after the New Year, we were reeled in to police stations around the country and charged with four counts of contravening the Civil Aviation Act.

"Mandatory minimum sentences, if convicted, were five to thirty years. We were all of a sudden in rather deep trouble. Japie and I were understandably disappointed to get no recognition or gratitude from our comrades-in-arms when we turned down the offer of state witness in case we blew it for them in the witness box. As it turned out, the State sewed up their case tight enough without ever having to call the two Recce guys who

CHAPTER FOURTEEN

leapt in after our refusal."

"I was fast asleep when I heard this knocking on our townhouse door at 4am in the morning," remembers Stannard. "It got louder and louder and I went to the door to see lots of policemen.

'We have a warrant for your arrest, get dressed, and come with us immediately.' His weapon was at the ready and he stared at me under the light of the door. I quickly got dressed. The house was completely surrounded. Soon I was back in chains."

Standish: "The case kicked off in the Pietermaritzburg High Court in early March 1982 with Chief Justice James and two assessors on the bench. The press were teaming like piranhas on the first day; so much so that Blue Kelly, the big Australian, had to discipline one by punching his camera. The victim squealed and bleated off into a corner, nursing a prize shiner. Other interested parties included the Traffic Department who had sent two officers to collect hundreds of Rands worth of unpaid tickets from John Mackay. Armed guards were everywhere and we were told later that the Natal Attorney-General Cecil Rees had worn a side-arm for the first week of proceedings. All this activity provided abundant material for the cartoonists, one of whom was our own Simon Willar, who produced some hilarious caricatures to liven up the endless haranguing in court.

"Hoare hit it on the nail when he described Rees as 'no oil painting' and 'of markedly porcine features'. The AG's belligerent manner produced some electric and colourful exchanges from a bunch of gutsy and aggressive accused who were not cowed by his bullying tactics. There were some very amusing moments but most of the time it was dead boring, as seemingly irrelevant *minutiae* were dissected and all Afrikaans evidence had to be translated for the benefit of those accused who were not bilingual. Mike's wife Phyllis Hoare set up a field kitchen each morning outside the court building and, with some help from other wives and girlfriends, served outstanding tea and snacks for the duration of the marathon case.

"At one stage the late Johan Fritz's parents spent a few days listening to evidence. Their grief was evident but this didn't stop Mr. Fritz from chatting with many of us at some length and even making provisional job offers to some of the lads. He was CEO of the gold and platinum division of General Mining at the time. A stout effort I thought.

"Out of court, life was a blast. The nearby university was packed with

Zimbabweans, many of whom we knew from school or the forces. There was also an abundance of lively and pretty young ladies with whom we endeavoured, with mixed success, to become acquainted. Japie, Simon, Bob and I scrounged digs in a big colonial house rented by five ex-Rhodesian Army officers. Many festivities were partaken of, particularly the fundraising braais where we also sold T-shirts with a 'Wild Goose' design of Simon Willar's. All proceeds to go to the lawyers.

"Unbeknown to most of the guys and the press, I was relatively okay financially because I was still getting a salary from the SADF so, unlike most of the others, I was financially stable," remembers Stannard. "The big challenge was to keep the money coming in so we could pay our lawyers and this is where I got very busy with fund-raising. We were up for anything that would entertain and this included doing strip-shows which the ladies loved and they really became very involved in helping us. Nick Wilson was our star attraction – the girls loved him and he loved them. Some of the ladies who helped in fund-raising went beyond 'the call of duty' in some instances and I ended up engaging in all sorts of extra-marital shenanigans that were certainly not going to please my wife if and when she found out.

"While the trial was ongoing Pete Rauhein, one of the 'Congo crew', and Vic De Beer, one of the South Africans, were successfully robbing banks and other places when not sitting respectfully before the 'beak'. They asked Blue Kelly to join them and Blue approached me. I gave him a flat 'no' as an answer. Later I found out they broke into the municipal offices in Pietermaritzburg and stole the mayoral chain which they flogged. The cops got onto Vic, arrested him, told him to turn state evidence and nailed Rauhein who copped a long prison sentence.

"Coming out of court one day I was met by a British journalist who asked me about a medal and I was lost for answers. He then told me that I had been awarded the Honoris Crux Silver, for gallantry, for my actions on the Matola Raid. This came as a complete surprise to me and I was told I was the first Rhodesian to be awarded it. Then my mother got in touch to tell me that she and my father had been invited by the head of the army to be present at the medal presentation. But up to that point the Army had not told me anything. The journalist then pointed out that I was obviously still part of the South African Army which I denied. His point was that this was proof that the South African government was in fact involved in the

CHAPTER FOURTEEN

whole attempted coup. Meanwhile the powers that be had decided against giving me the medal because they didn't want anything to do with me. I had become a pariah."

"The court decided that hearing evidence from the Air India crew was essential. The Indians would not come to South Africa but agreed on Mahe as a compromise," says Standish. "A commission to the island was organised; we were granted bail and scattered for some three weeks. On our return in June our counsel, Mike Hannon, had to recuse himself due to a conflict of interests between Hoare and 'the rest'. We had to brief new counsel. Over the weeks lies were told, poor advice was given, evidence was suppressed and generally we had a bad time of it, but the end result was never really in doubt.

"Initially Hoare told us he would provide for our defence but that did not work out so a lot of us broke away and hired our own lawyers. We told the judge we really believed this was an official operation and I think he began to empathise with us a little. He could see we were not really 'bad guys' but soldiers who liked to fight, who followed orders, and who had made a big mistake.

"The South African prosecutors submitted that the aircraft had been cleared for landing by our own men in highly dangerous conditions when it should have been diverted to its emergency plan alternative. Our lawyers argued that by the time the plane could have been instructed to turn away it had already committed to landing and thus would not have had enough fuel to get back up to cruising height and reach its alternative destination. Other intelligence procured by the defence but unfortunately not provable due to the impossibility of obtaining documents, was that a scam with fuel at Harare airport resulted in the Boeing not having enough fuel to divert but that piece of information was of no help either.

"This was the nail in the coffin for us in court. It doesn't matter if a genuine 'agreement' had been reached or not; the threat, even if it was implicit rather than real, was enough to convict us all of common cause in commandeering an aircraft against the crew's will.

"On 27th July, after a record four-and-a-half-month trial, judgment on us (13 000 words of it) was handed down. Charlie Dukes was acquitted since the defence had played skilfully on his inability to make rational decisions with a bullet hole in his arm. The following day was sentencing. There was a strangely cheery mood and many of us had our toothbrushes in our top pockets. The rank and file received the minimum possible sentence of five years with four and a half suspended. Seven others, including Chas Goatley, received longer terms with Mike Hoare getting an effective ten years.

"We were duly bundled off to Diepkloof prison south of Joburg. Those with longer sentences, including Mike Hoare, went to 'real jail' in Pretoria Central where they were introduced to such customs as clanging the bars of their cells early in the morning when people were getting hanged.

"One point Judge James brought to our attention, was the massive costs that had been generated by our misadventure. The human cost of two dead men, losses to Air Swazi, Mahe airport, tourists marooned on the island, and the cost to tourism generally. Also, Air India and her passengers who hadn't got to Bombay, the cost of deploying the task force and flying us to Pretoria, the longest trial in South African history including a commission to the island to gather testimony and, last but never least, the insurers couldn't get out of settling claims on 'act of war' clauses.

"We were probably in a better position than the members who remained on the island, all of whom were tortured and given life sentences. Roger England, who chose to stay, ended up swimming around the peninsular and making his way back to his hotel where he waited for the inevitable knock on the door. I wonder if he had a few stiff ones out the mini bar before the Gendarmes arrived. Our other comrade, Aubrey Brooks lay wounded outside the army barracks until he was subsequently captured and beaten on a daily basis. He was given a death sentence which was later commuted and he was released some two and a half years later."

Prison

"The bright sunlight bounced off the metal roof of our new home - Diepkloof Prison, a new facility constructed just outside Johannesburg," remembers Stannard. "Subdued, with a feeling of foreboding, we all filed quietly through the prison gate and handed over our clothes and personal items. The prison garb was dark olive green with black shoes; it was like being back in the army but much worse.

"The Prison Commandant, an angry looking Afrikaner addressed us.

'Afrikaans or English – never mind I will speak to you in both languages,' he barked.

CHAPTER FOURTEEN

'Listen to me carefully people - I did not ask for you to come here? You are an embarrassment to me and the South African government. I have a prison to run, I'm not here to babysit you lot. If you step out of line, I will crush you!' It was that simple! Then he lowered his voice.

'How many bibles do you people want?'

There was a silence. The Commandant looked in vain for a 'God botherer'. Not one of us put up a hand. Being God-fearing, the non-response really pissed him off big time. There was a brief silence then a bellow that made the walls shake.

'You all a bunch of bloody Philistines,' he roared. And with that he stormed off in furious disgust leaving us trying to look sorry for ourselves. The watching warders were sniggering and trying to hide their amusement.

"We were then 'whipped' into lines and assigned dormitory-type prison cells, which could accommodate up to twenty prisoners. It was rather like being back in Crawford House hostel at Umtali Boys High school. A young warder took it upon himself to get to know me better.

'Are you an SAS officer,' he asked. I could detect the sarcasm and had to grin and bear it.

'Yes, officer,' I replied respectfully.

'Well SAS officer, go and carry that table from there and put it there.'

'Yes officer,' I replied and off I went like a good chap.

'Now get down on your knees and clean the corridor so it shines.'

I did his bidding exactly as instructed, and when he realised I wasn't going to be any 'fun', he started to leave me alone.

"In addition to us, there were about four hundred black inmates in a separate wing of the prison. This was apartheid and there was no mixing even in prison. I have to admit I was relieved – there were some real brutes in amongst them and I was pleased not to have to deal with them up close and personal. Most were covered in tattoos, much of which was to do with their lives in the gangs they belonged to. One particularly nasty looking dude had a question mark right in the middle of his forehead. Clearly, they resented our presence, insisting we were given special privileges. This was not so as we were given the same food and had the same visitation rights as they did.

"One early morning it was my turn to collect the morning porridge for breakfast for the rest of the blokes. Stirring the porridge in a huge steel pot with a thick wooden pole was a mean looking black prisoner who stared at me in a way I knew he desperately wanted to hurt or kill me. I tried to ignore him but then a challenge.

'Hey, white man. I'm going to put you in this pot one day and eat you!' He then shrieked with laughter, and this brought the house down with the other black inmates joining in and pointing at me while he told them loudly in isiZulu how he planned to kill me when he got his hands on me. Blue Kelly looked at me blankly.

'I think he means it mate,' he said quietly.

'But I'm not organic,' I said. Then a look of genuine alarm as the noise increased and the rattling of bars unnerved us.

'Fuck that, let's get out of here,' Blue said, and we were happy to do just that.

"The daily regimen became familiar. Prison cells had to be cleaned and swept by 7am and all prisoners had to be dressed and ready for roll-call, usually conducted by an unattractive, pimply faced guard, then it was single file down to the mess hall for boring bloody porridge and Rooibos tea. That never changed. The food was lousy. Lots of porridge, beans and soya pork was the main protein.

"We were allowed five visitors a month. The girls I had become 'friendly' with in the months before trial were keen to see more of me and they booked my slots out so Sylvia and my parents couldn't get to see me. This pissed her and them off terribly.

"To combat the mind-numbing boredom, Nick Wilson and I used to run around the small exercise yard, lap after lap like two hyped up hamsters. Then somehow we managed to 'liberate' a set of dumb-bells which we put to good use in a little improvised gym in one of the empty cells. There we did endless push-ups and other exercises but with a lean diet all this burning of calories meant a rapid loss of weight. I'm not a big guy and I lost a total of 15 kgs by the time I was released.

"After four months, desperate to get out, I requested a dentist to sort out a nagging toothache, hoping that just maybe I would be taken into town. I got my wish and I was escorted to a dentist in Johannesburg with an armed guard standing over as the dentist drilled away. Not the sort of outing that would normally be enjoyed, but just such a pleasure to lie in his chair and look at some different walls and colours.

CHAPTER FOURTEEN

"Later I thought I'd have another crack and went to the doctor and told him I needed an operation.

'What do you need done?' he asked quietly.

'I want my foreskin chopped off please doctor.' This did not impress him.

'Fuck off,' he shouted.

"Our boredom was broken by the arrival on the scene of the Prison psychologist who came to assess our sanity, or lack thereof, and try and help us to prepare for life upon release. This commenced with an address to all of us where we were asked if we felt any 'shame or guilt'.

'Shame my arse,' came a loud voice from the back, 'we are political prisoners, not criminals!'

This retort was closely followed by loud laughter and this did not impress the 'shrink' at all. 'Don't talk 'kak' to me', he shouted, before storming out the room ranting about 'fucking Philistines'!

"That having failed, they then sent in an Anglican priest to try and help us find our souls and seek solace in the Scriptures. This poor guy started slowly but then got carried away and ranted on about the prodigal son and the urgent need for us to seek redemption. It didn't take long for him to get heckled and he too was sent packing with his box of Bibles in a rage.

"Word was then out that we 'Philistines' were beyond help in the spiritual world. The fact is we were not seeking forgiveness or redemption, but just wanted to get back to where we could get on with our lives.

"Towards the end of my sentence Darrell Watt came to see me to bring me up to date with what was going on at *Barnacle,* and with other operations then underway. It was good to see my old mate again and I was struck by the lovely smell of deodorant and toothpaste.

"Then the conversation moved on to our mutual friends. Our old mate Hennie Pretorius, he told me, was living in his car in his garage, having been booted out the house by his wife. He had thrown a microwave oven through a kitchen window and she had banished him from home indefinitely.

"I had fond memories of Hennie. Grandson of the famous Major Philip Jacobus (PJ) Pretorius CMG DSO and Bar, who became known as 'Jungle Man', and inspired Wilbur Smith to write 'Shout At The Devil,' one of his early best-sellers. P J was the scout who found where the German Cruiser *Koningsberg* was hiding in the Rufiji River Delta during WWI and organised its sinking. He worked with Frederick Courteney Selous DSO during the East African campaign and was nearby when Selous was killed. Hennie was, in many ways, cut from the same cloth. Tough, brave and a superb bushman I was with him in the SAS when he saved our four-man callsign from certain death when he outsmarted a company-strength Frelimo detachment in hot pursuit of us.

"Darrell and I were planning to visit him on his farm on the Limpopo River as soon as I was released to shoot a few kudu and make some biltong. I was salivating at the thought when he told me he had good news and also some bad news. He confirmed that I had been awarded the Honoris Crux (Silver) for the action on the Matola raid, and that this made me the only Rhodesian to have been awarded the medal in South Africa. I was delighted. But the bad news was they were not going to give it to me because of the embarrassment I had caused the army.

'You kidding me, Darrell,' I shouted.

'Hey ... don't panic, Kafupi,' he said calmly, 'the good news is Danie Steyn and I have traced it to the Commandant's safe. We know exactly where it is, and we are working on the combination for the safe, and then we will 'liberate it for you'. And with that he gave me a big slap on the back.

'Never fear Kafupi, 'Buff' is on tracks,' he said, 'we'll get it for you, old friend.'

Then the duty warder shouted – 'Time up!' – and our conversation came to an abrupt end. Darrell came to his feet, turned, smiled, and gave me a thumbs-up as he went out through the metal grill."

Standish-White remembers: "In a way we had a much easier ride in this prison since we were, initially, the only inmates in a vast new complex and the major in charge, behind all the threatening bluster, basically made a deal with us that if we behaved he would allow us privileges. After a while our cells were open to the courtyard all day instead of only the normal two half-hour sessions. Many of us got exercise routines going and set up a basic gym but the food was both unappetising and insufficient for our exercise levels. This shortage was to some extent relieved by visits and food parcels from the 'outside'. Those of us who were 'orphans' snivelled in with a bunch of RLI guys for whom Noel Smee and his mum Shirley organised an enormous weekly resupply of fresh rations and newspapers. We got to know others from the RLI Commando officer corps well and the humour

CHAPTER FOURTEEN

generated at these sessions was copious and most un-prisonlike.

"We even got hold of a projector and had movies most nights. After some weeks we had chatted the guards up sufficiently for them to smuggle in a couple of bottles of brandy. Our radically altered digestive systems did not take kindly to the hard liquor however and this exercise was not repeated!

"We received a couple of visits from military personnel in connection with work on our release, but the sad news of Dave Berry's death on operations in southern Zimbabwe seemed to knock that project on the head. The post-sentencing, optimistic expectation of release within weeks was unfounded and, after the standard one third off for good behaviour and a non-alcoholic braai with the warders, we were released at dawn in early December after serving four months.

"A monster English breakfast at the Sandton Sun hotel lined our stomachs for an epic onslaught of ethanol with those who had so kindly done the weekly purchasing. Then we shook ourselves up and tackled the task of getting back to some sort of normality."

"I was euphoric at the news we were to be released the next day," recalls Stannard. "We were going to be chucked out at 4am in the morning to avoid the press which pleased us. But freedom did not come without shocks. I was collected by my father-in-law who immediately set about reminding me what a cunt I was before telling me his daughter had had enough and was divorcing me. I was also fired from my job as a Benoni furniture salesman.

"Back in an empty home, I was still reeling from the news when the phone rang and it was our *Barnacle* IO.

'Report to work immediately,' he said, 'you're on the next operation and it's a big one.'

'But I've just come out of prison,' I pleaded.

'Fuck you, you've just taken a six-month holiday you cunt, now get to the office.'"

Chapter Fifteen

A brotherly band of hard, dangerous, young men
Who held the fire in our hands
And the storm in our souls.

♦

Back to war

Maseru Raid

"I drove out to our secret location near Lanseria Airport. It was out in the country and I never quite figured out what was going on there. The locals thought it was a chicken farm and big men with big beards were seen going in and out at all times of the day and night.

Occasionally gunfire was reported and on more than one occasion the police raided the place suspecting some sort of secret militia – little did they know how close to the truth they were.

"I parked my car and walked to the briefing room where all the team was present, looking very serious, pouring over maps, documents and aerial photos. When I walked in, they all looked up with wry smiles. Gray Branfield approached me, clapped me on the back and roared with laughter.

'Stannard, you big *poes*! We knew you were thick but not dumb enough to go on that caper! You were blown, right from the start,' he exclaimed.

Gray, stood there stroking his blonde beard, looking me up and down, deep in thought. I returned the stare and was not really sharing the humour when my boss Neil Kriel spoke.

"'Well Kafupi, since you didn't have the good manners to tell us you were fucking off to the Seychelles, I'm posting you to 5 Recce where you will be under Captain Corrie Meerholz and you'll be working with his commandos.

'No sweat,' I said, not wanting them to think they were getting the better of me, 'I look forward to it!'

I saw Darrell looking at me with a smile on his face and gave him a wink.

CHAPTER FIFTEEN

'Jeez Kafupi,' he said, 'you can thank the prison service for all the weight you've lost. You're looking fit and trim.'

"Two days later I collected my AK and picked up two drum magazines holding 75 rounds each – it looked like a Thompson machine-gun and it was a weapon I felt very comfortable with. I drew the rest of my kit and then went home to say goodbye to poor Sylvia who had kindly taken me back into her life but was still sulking owing to the fact I had used her Edgars account to purchase all my fancy holiday clothes for my island holiday, and hadn't even bothered to bring them back. I had arrived back in Durban in a pair of rugby shorts but did manage to salvage my favourite *Hang Ten* baseball cap. I blew a kiss at her but she was still growling when I walked away.

"I didn't have to ask for leave from the 'Down-Town Furnishers' because they were getting on fine without me. I heard Tony Factor nearly had a fit when he heard about where I had been and done and told the regional managers they better stop employing mercenaries to sell their bedroom suites. I thought about all the marketing seminars I had been on as I became the best Sealy Posturepedic mattress salesman in Benoni! But that career was now definitely behind me. It was back to being a gunfighter.

"I made my way to Phalaborwa where 5 Recce were based and there Corrie briefed me on the upcoming operation. He impressed me, a highly-respected officer, well liked and decorated. I was to be his deputy. After the recent debacle it was good to be back in the company of a professionals doing things properly. I looked over the intelligence reports and photos and got a better understanding of the lie of the land and what challenges lay ahead.

"Over the years the ANC had built up a strong presence in the Lesotho capital, Maseru. The key man in the leadership element was ANC stalwart and militant, Chris Hani, who led the armed wing Umkhonto We Sizwe. Unbeknown to me at the time, Gray had become big chums with Hani while working undercover in Lesotho. In all we were tasked to attack five ANC facilities in the city including the planning and administration hub; Moscow House. The No 1 man on our hit-list was Chris Hani and I was tasked to get him.

"The various assault teams had been practising house-clearing drills using live ammunition for weeks and were pumped and ready to go. I was also excited. After preparing our kit and equipment and packing our explosives charges and grenades, we were ready to roll.

"Our departure point was a farm on the South African side of the border where we went through our drills one last time. From there, on the night of 8th December 1982 we quietly crossed the Caledon River into Lesotho, just down from the main Maseru Bridge, in our rubber inflatables. Above us the night sky was filled with stars, and I could hear the soft swish of the oars through water and dogs barking. In the distance, the lights of Maseru flickered. It all looked so peaceful and I thought to myself it would not be long before we would kill and possibly be killed.

"I had on an old trench coat, my face was blackened up, and I wore an old slouch hat similar to the ones worn by the Basotho miners. My weapon was slung off my right shoulder.

There were about forty of us and we all made it across without incident. Once off the boats, we made our way in silence to our respective targets. From the river, our heavily armed group headed to the main road and walked as nonchalantly as we could towards the city. There was no hiding under the streetlights, and I reminded myself we were just a bunch of miners walking home from a night out. Many of the assault group were black ex Selous Scouts so they blended in better than I did. Some of them were dolled up in pretty dresses. I thought of the poor people who were going to get shot by assassins in pink dresses wearing wigs; it was a funny thought in a macabre sort of way.

"Our group under Captain Corrie broke off and we quickly made our way to our main target which consisted of a block of apartments. In my section I was the only white with four former black Selous Scouts. The apartment I had been directed to was where our intelligence people said we would find Hani.

"We were making good progress up the fire escape when the night exploded with the sound of machineguns and I looked up to see a blaze of bright green tracer that streaked across the sky. I raced up the stairs as I heard the other assault groups opening up on their targets and blew a door down with a 'knock-knock' charge then went through with my AK on auto and just shot the shit out of the place. Then I stopped to look for anyone like Hani but he was nowhere to be seen. I searched hurriedly in cupboards and under beds but in vain. Frustrated, I then heard Corrie on the radio calling

CHAPTER FIFTEEN

for help – they were meeting serious resistance and were in trouble.

"As I moved to get to Corrie, I heard a shout to my left, a small window opened and out came a grenade. This was one of ours which an ANC fighter had managed to grab swiftly and chuck back at us. I dodged and it bounced off the balcony and detonated on the cars below. This one ANC guy was putting up a magnificent fight and giving Corrie's guys a tough time so they had tried to flush him with a grenade. He then came out the window, grabbed another machinegun and carried on fighting until he was finally killed.

I saw one of the ANC guys leaping off a balcony. He hit the ground, broke his ankle, but kept firing and then went for one of the black guys and tried to wrestle his RPD off him but failed. He was killed, but a brave man who fought to the end. The air was thick with the smell of explosives and cordite. Then I heard someone shout, 'He is out!'

"Some poor English chap with a Cockney accent, I think he was an academic working with the ANC, stuck his head up.

'What the bloody hell is going on here?' he asked.

'Get your fucking head down and behind that wall,' I shouted, 'otherwise it's going to get taken off.'

He ducked away and I never saw him again.

"With Corrie's guys still inside with guns blazing I kept my chaps outside to deal with any reinforcements. In the heat of battle, I still had to laugh at the crazy sight of the men in their dresses blasting away at anything that moved. A car then pulled up full of armed ANC but I shot them all before they could get out the car.

"Then the fire from the apartments adjacent to us intensified and I decided to take my guys there and deal with them. I'd always wanted to destroy a block of flats and I thought now was my chance. I poured fire into the place and the return fire subsided. There was a lull and I told Corrie I thought we had been in the area long enough and it was time to get going but he disagreed, explaining he wanted time to look for documents.

I was getting very twitchy when Corrie eventually reappeared, carrying lots of papers, looking annoyingly relaxed.

'Hey Rich,' he said, 'are you getting worried?'

'Fucking right, Corrie,' I said, 'let's get the hell out of here!'

"As it turned out I was right and the Lesotho Army was, at that time, getting ready for us on our escape route past the Victoria Hotel. As we headed down there soldiers were leaning out the hotel windows firing at us forcing us to back up against the walls. We were making progress when ahead of us a roadblock appeared which very quickly received my attention as they let us have it. Fire was coming at us from everywhere and I don't know how nobody was hit. Just when I thought we were cornered there was a loud 'boom boom' – Corrie had let rip at these guys with his 40 mm grenade launcher.

"As the grenades exploded there was a lull in the firing and this gave me and two of my guys a chance to get over the road. One of them was wearing a pink dress. If I had not been so terrified I think I'd have died laughing. But the grenades saved the night; they got a hell of a fright – they must have thought we had heavier weapons than we actually did. They lost interest in taking us on and we ran through the golf course with mortars raining down on us. My coat was slowing me down so I ditched that just as I saw one of the greens on the course demolished by a mortar bomb. Breathless but relieved, my group was the last to arrive at the river and we wasted no time in jumping into the waiting Zodiacs and racing for the South African side.

"The raid was deemed a success. We had eliminated over 30 ANC leaders, gathered intelligence and had taken no casualties. But the man we really wanted, Chris Hani, was nowhere to be seen. The international media condemned us for an attack on innocent civilians but that was to be expected. The ANC had taken a big blow.

"Not long after my return I discovered Neil Kriel had been replaced as our boss by Charl Naude. Neil was furious. He blamed us for some reason, but the truth is we had no idea what was going on at the higher level; we were just the grunts getting the jobs done. I was not happy to see Neil go, he was a tough and difficult guy, but we had worked together for a long time and I liked and respected him. Charl was also a good guy but just why the change was made, I did not know.

"Then a bit of good news when I was informed that I had been promoted to the rank of Captain. From then on I was happy to be known as 'Captain Kafupi'.

Life in Benoni

"While I was buggering around killing people, Sylvia was loving life

CHAPTER FIFTEEN

in Benoni. She was pregnant with our daughter Amanda and had been very busy decorating our small home in the suburbs in all the pastels which were the rage in the 1980s. Benoni was a very Afrikaans area and quite a rough neighbourhood. Some of the bars were only sensible if you were looking for a fight. And not only fistfights, but also gunfights. I had a gun pulled on me in a pub in nearby Springs. Although I was Rhodesian, because I wasn't Afrikaans speaking, I was seen as an 'Engelsman' (Englishman) or more often as a 'fokken Engelsman' or 'Soutie'. A 'Soutie' was short for 'Soutpiel' (salty dick because the Afrikaners said that English-speaking South Africans had one leg in South Africa, the other in England and their dicks hanging in the sea.) There were some real desperados in these mining towns. I was almost mugged by a gang outside a bank but fortunately I had my trusty .45 quickly to hand. They could see I knew how to use it and ran like hell.

"I was a little lost for friends there, but Sylvia's family, which went on forever, kept us very busy, especially on weekends when they would arrive *en masse* from the Delmas farming area. Sylvia's Afrikaner grandparents lived down the road from us in a ramshackle old house which was shrouded in a big, beautiful bougainvillea bush which sent its wonderful purple flowers cascading down from the roof on to the porch where old '*Oupa*' Koos and I would sit and waffle while drinking strong coffee and eating soggy rusks. Old Koos was troubled by me. I was from a different world and he was not sure what to make of me.

"Dressed in his normal attire, which was rugby shorts, shirt and tatty old fedora hat, he would draw heavily on his battered pipe, blowing smoke-rings in the air and give me a jaundiced look with his rheumy eyes.

'Tell me '*Engelsman*', how is it you always drive fancy BMWs; you live well and yet you never seem to work? What the fuck do you actually do for a living? I know you had a good job selling mattresses at the furniture store but then you went to jail. Since you've been out of prison you have been doing *fok* all! My granddaughter deserves better....I think you're a bloody '*skelm*' myself'. And with that he would walk off shaking his head in a huff, trailed by his faithful fox terrier who also glared at me; it always amazed me how his fedora stayed on his head, cocked at its rakish angle over his right eye.

"But Old Koos was not the problem; it was the mayhem on the weekends when the whole clan would abandon their farms and the mealie-fields and come racing into town in their dented Datsun 'bakkies' with their fat wives in their flowery dresses squeezed into the front, and kids chucked on the back. Then they would commence an eating and feeding frenzy at our house. Flip-flops or 'thongs' were regulation footwear for the parents and kids were barefoot and normally filthy. Out would come the cold boxes stuffed with booze and boerewors. Then the shouting and loud music. 'Light the *fokken* fire, *fokken Engelsman*!'

"This was a regular occurrence every weekend. Most of the time I couldn't understand what they were saying so I just got blind drunk and went to sleep. It was after one of these sessions that I passed out in my bed and left my visitors to continue gorging themselves. It was about 2 am in the morning when I was awoken by the high-pitched screams of cats mating. My head was so sore it felt like someone was scraping the inside of my cranium. We had a cat called Felix. I had no idea Felix was a female, but her suitor had arrived to have some fun and the noise just jarred my jangled brain. I grabbed my .45 from under my pillow, almost without thinking and raced through to the kitchen. As I ran in, out the corner of my eye, I heard the hiss and caught the movement of a big Tomcat about to leap out the window. Instinctively, I swung round and fired a shot which killed the cat instantly. I chucked the dead Tom in the garbage can and went back to a wide-eyed Sylvia wanting to know what the hell was happening. Only then did I feel a little remorseful, but it had all happened so fast and I suppose years of living on the edge, with all the intensive training I had done, had something to do with it. I told her not to worry and eventually she went back to sleep.

Into Botswana

"Early 1983 reports started coming through to us about massacres taking place in western Zimbabwe and some of them were horrifying. Mugabe had sent in the North Korean-trained 5th Brigade to terrorise the Matabele people and snuff out any opposition to his plans to instal a one-party-state. The commander was a nasty piece of work named Perence Shiri who had been responsible for a number of atrocities during our war and was doing again what he did best. When I was called in to see Gray Branfield I was hoping for a task back in Zimbabwe to have another crack at those bastards

CHAPTER FIFTEEN

but it was not to be. He handed me a leather brown briefcase.

'Kafupi, take this to Captain Dawie, he is the SB officer in Zeerust. He is a close contact of mine and only give him the briefcase. Understand, it's got classified material on the next operation which you and Tom are going to execute...got it? You're the demolition man.

'Oh, and you will be going up with Alan Trowsdale,' he said. Alan was another guy I got on with very well with. He had done many years in the Rhodesian BSAP Special Branch in Bulawayo and was a real character.

"Alan and I jumped in my car and raced off to Zeerust. We were thirsty on arrival and had no problem finding the main pub in town for a few cold beers. Clutching the briefcase tightly we both sauntered into the bar. One of those sparsely furnished, old-fashioned country bars that reeked of cigarettes and booze with shiny wooden floors and a heavy wooden bar-top. It was quiet when we walked in, the only sound came from a fox terrier which lay under a table licking its balls. I whistled a friendly greeting and got a growl for my trouble.

'Shut-up 'Bakkie',' shouted the barman in Afrikaans.

The dog continued to look at me as we moved closer to the bar, feeling increasingly unwanted, when I looked at a bull of a Boer in khaki shorts and shirt, with a big black beard, big belly, small black eyes glazed from drink, and rippling muscles stretching his clothes. His fingers, the size of sausages, were gnarled and cracked. This was one rough, tough brute with an attitude, and I knew our chances of a having a quiet, cold beer were fading fast. Then the barman bellowed in Afrikaans.

"*'Kan ek julle koffie-moffies help,*' (can I help you coffee-queers).

'*Twee Castle beers asseblief,*' (two Castle beers please) I replied politely, in my best Afrikaans hoping that would please him a little but it was not to be.

'*Fokken Rooineks!*' (fucking rednecks) he exclaimed and slammed two beers down on the counter, the beers spilling in the process.

'*Dankie,*' (thank you) I replied. It crossed my mind to tell these two bruisers that we were actually here fighting for South Africa against a common enemy but realised that was unlikely to help our cause. These guys hated us from the moment when we walked through the door and they realised we were not Afrikaners. I turned to Alan and mumbled.

'This ox has a hair up his arse so we better be careful.'

"We moved away to chat and mind our own business. I looked at the other drunks at the bar and they looked rough. Cattle smugglers, I thought, but definitely desperados of some sort. Then suddenly the brute with black beard stormed over to me and started shouting in my face sending spittle flying into my eye. I had no idea what he was saying and asked Alan to interpret.

'He has challenged you to arm wrestle. He says if you beat him, he won't fuck you up.'

Oh shit! I thought, here goes my shoulder. And that's precisely what happened. This bastard wrenched the right shoulder almost out the socket sending a wave of excruciating pain shooting down my arm to the tips of my fingers leaving a terrible numbness. I was left breathless and enraged.

'Jou Ma se poes,' (your mother's pussy) I shouted, and one punch flattened his nose against his face before I grabbed the briefcase and we ran for the door. We heard a scream and a thump and were pleased to see 'Blackbeard' had slipped on the step coming out and crashed into the pavement giving us valuable seconds to get away. We managed to jump in and slam the car doors shut as this madman got back on his feet and charged at us screaming about killing us with blood and snot pouring out his face. While I fumbled with one hand for the keys his huge face reared up against the passenger window splashing it with blood. The car shook as he wrenched at the door. With that, Alan pulled his 9 mm pistol, and the madman ducked away only to reappear at the rear. In the rear-view mirror I watched him trying to pull the engine cover off but I managed to fire the engine, slammed it into gear and the accelerator hit the floorboards as we screeched away. When I had enough speed, I did a violent 'U-turn' and roared up the main street with this bastard running after us pumping his fists and screaming. 'Fuck me, but that Boer has a serious problem,' said Alan in the understatement of the year.

"In silence we headed down the dusty dirt road to the old farmhouse nestled in an orchard of lovely lemon and orange trees. There was no meal cooked so we opened a can of baked beans and had a beer.

'Oh, so you met up with Tommy,' said Dawie. 'He's on bail for robbing the local abattoir. That's why he's probably a little pissed off with life.'

I did wonder to myself then if my life was at greater risk here in South Africa having to deal with Boers who hated us non-Afrikaners, or across the border in 'Injun country'.

CHAPTER FIFTEEN

"The next morning, with throbbing pain in my arm, we got to work with Dawie and his secretary, poring over maps and aerial photos. The mission was quite simple; hit a house where a bunch of ANC assassins were living and kill the lot. Later in the day Gray arrived in good cheer in a VW Kombi, armed with bottles of 'Klipdrift' brandy.

'Hey Kafupi,' he said, 'go take a look in the Kombi and tell me what you see,' he said. I wandered over and all I could see was a tractor tyre. A little puzzled, I went back to him.

'A tractor tyre you *poes*?' I said.

'Actually Kafupi, it's a bloody big bomb and you are placing it tomorrow night in Gaborone.' With that he burst out laughing and headed inside the house. It turned out the dirty tricks department at Speskop wanted me to test its destructive capacity. It was a combination of incendiary and liquid which I thought was a total overkill for this particular target but there was nothing I could do.

"Looking on at the time were a few black former Selous Scouts who also had a good laugh. I didn't even bother replying. Instead I wandered over and pulled down a piece of kudu biltong that was hanging on a wire on the veranda. Probably poached, I cut a piece off and was chewing on it when Tom screeched to a halt in a cloud of dust in front of me.

"He climbed out slowly and casually, his pipe firmly clenched between his teeth, his bushy beard looked like a Sparrow's nest. My mind raced ahead to what we were going to do. I could imagine the Botswana papers: 'WANTED: Six foot beard wandering around Gaborone with tractor-tyre.' It was thanks to people like him that the Selous Scouts were known as the 'Walking Armpits.'

"The next night Tom, I, and two black former Scouts breached the border half a mile from the Tlokweng border post. The moon was on the wane, there was a cool breeze and we soon found an old smuggler's track leading to the main road. I was smartly dressed in slacks, open shirt and blue blazer. I had my AK slung with trusty drum magazine complete with 75 rounds of armour-piercing and tracer if anyone gave us trouble. The going slowed when we walked into Acacia thorn-trees that snagged us and made a bit of mess of my attire.

Then the radio crackled into life... a whisper from Gray '...will be at your loc in five minutes.' We were on schedule. A short wait and then the

MEN OF WAR

kombi drew up. A smiling face peered out the window; 'Taxi anyone?'

"We all leapt in laughing and sat on the tractor tyre bomb. The trip into the city was uneventful and Gray stopped the car a block away from the target. We quickly disembarked and wrestled the damn tyre out and on to the road. With the help of one of the ex-Scouts I got it upright and proceeded to wheel it down the road. Tom walked ahead and a fourth operator brought up the rear. I was unsettled by the barking of dogs on both sides of us and the smell of wood smoke hung heavy in the night air. In the distance an angry woman was screaming at someone in seTswana. My black mate chuckled.

'The husband is drunk again,' he whispered, 'she is going to beat him now.'

Women never change, I thought.

As we neared the house we were going to blow I heard another dog barking frantically next door. I quickly lobbed some meat laced with lethal poison over the wall and the barking stopped instantly. I watched expectantly as it gobbled down the juicy sausage bought in the Zeerust butchery. Then to my dismay the damn dog started barking again and I stared at it in some distress. Then it just fell over dead but, unfortunately, the owner of the dog appeared to investigate and he started shouting something about 'thieves'.

"With him yelling I rolled the tyre gently down a shallow storm drain which ran along the road when suddenly there was lights on us and a car approached then stopped.

'I know what you are doing,' a loud voice proclaimed, 'you are thieves, and I am calling the police!'

"With that he sped away, and I saw alarmed ANC people hurrying out the front gate. I quickly rolled the tyre up the small incline and placed it alongside the bedroom window and lit the short fuse. Then we all ran like greased lightning and jumped into a culvert before burying ourselves and adopting a foetal position.

"The explosion shook the whole city, while the incendiaries sent flames streaking high in the night sky. A cloud of dust enveloped us, and screams filled the night. Our South African Police pick-up team heard the blast back in South Africa. There was total pandemonium. We picked ourselves up and ran into the night. Escaping the city lights, we were pleased to find the bush again but the thorns were terrible and ripped us to pieces as we tore through the trees. When we heard approaching vehicles, we knew we were moving too slow as we had to keep tearing our way through thorn bushes to pick up

CHAPTER FIFTEEN

the pace. Lacerated to hell we made it to the pick-up point and broke for the border. Dawie was there with a smile.

"'*Fok*, you all look like you've been in a cat-fight,' he said, 'let's go'. And with that, we were driven back to our safe-house for a quick debrief, coffee and rusks. We were all exhausted but confident we had achieved our aim.

"It later transpired that the explosion was so powerful that it blew the roofs off dozens of houses including the local school. The ANC operators were hit by flying corrugated roof debris as they ran for their lives. They only sustained minor injuries and were released from hospital shortly afterwards. But we knew the bomb worked!"

Operation Plexis

"Apart from the odd mugging and cat-kill, I was getting a little restless. It was after yet another weekend of debauchery that I awoke on a Monday morning and had a glimpse at the world through bloodshot eyes. It was a sparkling, sunny day outside, the air was cool and the sky was deep blue. It was about 10am when the phone rang and I was summoned to report for duty. I was told to get to the 'safe-house' soon as possible for a briefing. I moved fast to get myself cleaned and dressed, kissed Sylvia goodbye, and sped out the gate.

"When I arrived there, Gray and a couple of other intelligence guys were slumped in easy-chairs, wry smiles on their faces, drinking coffee and sucking on their fags.

Gray took a deep puff when the room went quiet and looked up at me.

'Kafupi, we have an interesting new job for you.' Just from the look on his face, I knew trouble was coming.

'On no,' I replied, 'what's it this time?'

'Relax, we're not asking you to blow anything up just yet.'

'You've just been hired to join your old Selous Scout mate Roy[54] in selling industrial chemicals in Botswana and Zambia. When not selling your wares, we have a list of ANC safe houses in Gaborone we want to know more about. We want you to work with Rudi, the (SO) Security Officer handling Botswana. I will give you a detailed briefing tomorrow but be prepared to leave for about a month while we figure out what's going on up there.'

"With that he left and I made my way to the kitchen to watch Blue.

---
[54] A pseudonym.

He was a master with a blade and I was mesmerised by his speed and skill as I pondered what lay ahead.

'Heard you're off to Botswana to carry on surveillance, Kafupi?' he said with a frown. I nodded.

'Just be bloody careful,' he said, 'they're onto us after that fucking Seychelles saga.' This had crossed my mind. After that my face had been splashed across every newspaper in Africa. I was pretty famous or notorious, so spying was not going to get any easier for me.

"Blue made me even more concerned. He told me he had been sent into Botswana as an Australian tourist after release from prison to check on ANC houses. He had been arrested and imprisoned in Gaborone and had a tough time. He was interrogated for days but Blue was a crafty bastard and knew how to deal with them. He had been through a torrid time with Scotland Yard after being arrested at Heathrow on his way home to Australia from Lebanon where he had been fighting with the Christian Phalangists. He recalled that they were very professional, smooth and extremely well informed. He had also fallen foul of the Americans when he trashed a bar in Saigon during the Vietnam War era.

"Under interrogation in Gaborone he managed to scare the hell out of them by convincing them that he was barking mad – which was not that far from the truth. Eventually, after a week of intense questioning, they gave up on him and deported him. Blue's biggest worry was the chance of having caught tuberculosis in the jail where he was packed in with all sorts of sick people coughing their lungs out. I had the added problem of being a wanted man in Zimbabwe. The artist's impression they had drawn was an excellent likeness and that had been sent around the world. If they picked me up there was a damn good chance they were going to figure out who I was and send me to Zimbabwe to stand trial and a very long spell in Chikurubi prison.

"Despite my concerns the wheels started turning and I was introduced to Rudi who I would be working with. He was based in Zeerust, a small farming town near the Botswana border. From there, in conjunction with MI (Military Intelligence) he ran a very extensive network of informers and operators throughout Botswana. I was just one more cog in the intelligence wheel corroborating and collecting information on the ANC and 'Umkonto we Sizwe' operations in the country. I was told how ANC cadres were receiving crash courses on communist weapons, explosives and grenades

CHAPTER FIFTEEN

but more information was required on where this was all actually happening. I was also given a shortlist of potential targets I would be expected to look at more closely.

"There had been a grenade attack which killed two government officials in Cape Town and another attack on a political target was expected in Pretoria. This was the reason there was a measure of urgency in the need to find out who was planning these attacks and from where. At the time there had been over 30 terrorist attacks committed in South Africa which originated in Botswana.

"My first foray into the country was with Roy and we cleared the border at Tlokweng without any problems using my forged passport. But we were driving a Land Rover with tinted windows which displeased the authorities. We explained the chemicals we were carrying reacted badly to direct sunlight and they let us go on our way. The real reason was to allow Roy to take photographs without being seen doing it. I was the driver and he was the photographer.

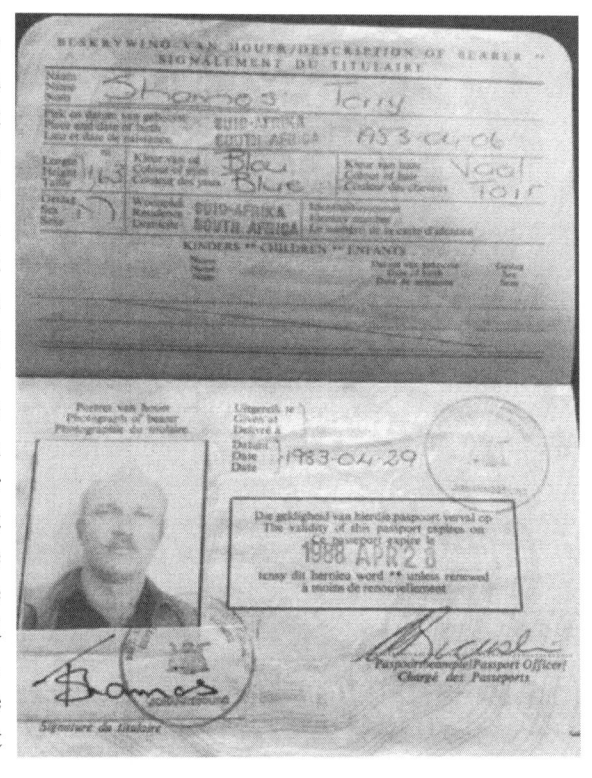

"One of our primary areas of interest was a small informal settlement near the border, also called Tlokweng. It was a shantytown filled with itinerant migrants and it was in some of these tin shacks that the ANC was training their 'bombers' for future attacks in the Transvaal and Western Cape. It was a clever location because not many whites would have any reason to go in there so our presence would easily arouse suspicion. On several occasions we were stopped by alert bystanders and asked what we were doing. We showed them our pamphlets and invoices and allayed their fears and they let us on our way, but these were always tense moments. I knew we could get caught up in a mob there and we'd have been burned alive if they tumbled to what we were actually doing. From there we made it without problem to Gaborone and snooped around for a few days, looking, listening and photographing. Then we went back to Zeerust.

"Roy and I were living comfortably in an old farmhouse on the outskirts of the town where we bided our time awaiting orders. Most nights we either did a braai or 'Potjiekos'. On this particular night I was doing the pot and was just about to put the peas into the stew when Rudi summoned me inside.

"There he was looking intently at a whole lot of maps on the kitchen table while sipping on cold coffee in a cracked enamel mug. Then he looked up and went straight into giving us our next assignment. Looking back, he must have been aware of the impending operations that had just been approved and up-to-date information was urgently required. As it turned out, the big ANC elective conference was about to take place and the young militants wanted to launch a series of attacks to send a signal to the hierarchy that they were active and effective.

"Rudi explained that he wanted detailed information on all people coming and going from three ANC safe houses in Broadhurst, a Gaborone suburb. One of these provided accommodation, another was a logistical base used to move people from Zambia and down to South Africa., and the other was a training facility where the 'bombers' were being prepared for future attacks. It was from here that the people who had bombed the Carlton Centre had come.

"The next day Roy and I loaded our vehicles with a few boxes of chemicals and left for the border. I was not too happy. Blue's warning was much on my mind, our cover was quite thin and I didn't think it would hold up for long before we were hauled in for questioning, but I thought this might be our last task in the country so I was anxious to get on and do it.

"We checked into a motel and the next morning jumped into our Land Rover and set off to Broadhurst, me in front driving, and Roy behind with camera ready. Soon we were in the target area and I had a little fun putting my foot down on corners sending Roy sprawling among our boxes of chemicals. Being an ex-Scout with an attitude, I liked making him cross. Not a big bloke, but with his huge beard and big hands, he was like an

CHAPTER FIFTEEN

enraged garden gnome being flung around in the back of the car. I knew there was not much he could do to retaliate when sneaking undercover around the ANC in Gaborone.

'Drive slower for fuck's sake!' he would growl from the back before I heard him crash into boxes and thrash around among barrels of industrial cleaning chemicals.

'I'm going to fucking kill you, I swear!'

"The first day we got good photos but did not see many people. The next day it was hot and tense. We drove and looked but again, there was little movement of people. I felt we had overstayed our welcome and it was time to head home. We had cased the targets, and MI must surely know enough about who was living there I thought. Roy wanted to stay on and gather more information.

'Let's get the fuck out of Dodge,' I hissed. We were parked on the side of the road and I was feeling uncomfortable. We had been trolling around for too long.

'I need one more pass to make sure I have the best photos,' he insisted.

'For Fuck's sake,' I shouted in frustration and I was very angry, but I felt I had to do his bidding.

"Just as I feared, when we made our next pass two men rushed out to the gate, watched us and then I saw one writing down our registration number. Unsurprisingly, someone had noticed two white dudes driving slowly up and down in a blacked-out Land Rover and decided something was not right. I'd had enough. I drove back to the city and then straight to the border without giving Roy a chance to argue. Luckily it was quiet, and we were through quickly and without incident. The drive from the border to the safe house was testy. Roy was pissed off with me but I knew we were pushing our luck there in Gaborone. He was a perfectionist and wanted to go the extra mile to get everything absolutely right but there is a fine line to be drawn between risky and being stupid, and we were stupid to stay there any longer. Looking back, I do think my nerves were fraying.

"I was pleased to see Darrell at the safe house when we arrived home and he agreed I had done the right thing by getting out when we did. Then Gray arrived in high spirits. As always, he was puffing hard on a cigarette when he addressed me with a big smile on his face.

'Some good news for you, Kafupi. The Recce Boys are going through their FIBUA (Fighting In Built-Up Areas) drills and house clearing exercises. We're going to smack those houses now. And I'm delighted to tell you, you will be leading some of them in!'

"This was not exactly what I wanted to hear, but what could I do or say. I looked at this huge man with the big beard and approached him. Towering above me he bent down knowing I had something to tell him and his hearing was poor from gunfire. 'You know something Gray?' I said quietly.

'What,' he snapped and gave me a slightly angry look.

'Smoking will kill you my mate,' I said.

Darrell and I both laughed as he hurried off with his ever-present crocodile-skin briefcase clutched firmly in his right hand. He had been mocked mercilessly for losing the last one which he left on the roof of his car in Gaborone before driving off in a hurry. He was there to pay informers so it was stuffed with cash and must have made whoever picked it up a very happy person.

"The operation was called *Operation Plexis* and it all started to happen quickly from the beginning of June 1985. There was much discussion between the intelligence people and the military about which targets to hit and how big an operation it should be. The Recce officers wanted to hit as many targets as possible, but the intelligence guys wanted to be more selective. Eventually they decided on 17 different facilities that were going to be attacked. The group that I would lead in was tasked to destroy the three houses Roy and I had watched and photographed in Broadhurst.

"We were briefed on the capabilities of the Botswana Defence Force and left in no doubt that if they were mobilised we would meet some stiff resistance. In the city were at least two infantry battalions, and they had an armoured capability and air assets. Part of our plan involved the use of loud hailers which would be used to broadcast a loud message to the civilian population informing them that this was an attack on the ANC and nobody else and to ask them to stay indoors and for the army not to get involved.

"It was a big operation involving almost a hundred soldiers. About 20 of the officers and NCOs were to be infiltrated ahead of the main body posing as tourists and people looking for business possibilities. Gray, myself and some of the intelligence guys would go in with this group. Once we were established and had checked out all the different targets the main assault group with weapons and equipment would follow hidden in a large

CHAPTER FIFTEEN

furniture removal truck. On arrival in the city we checked in at the hotel and waited. We had radios with which to communicate with our forward Tactical Headquarters.

"On 13th June the main group crossed the border at Tlokweng without any incident. The only problem for them was it was extremely hot and stuffy inside, so it was with much relief that they reached the rendezvous point. They were very pleased to be out of there and breathing some fresh air.

"Everyone then got into their pre-arranged groups and prepared for action. It was all very well planned and executed. I quickly hooked up with my three teams and we were soon on the move. All the troops were dressed in civvie clothes. Most of the guys carried R5 rifles with trigger-activated lamps attached, as well as grenades, explosives and we had a few RPG 7s to deal with any hostile vehicle activity. All the guys were issued with bulletproof vests. We started moving just after midnight. Once all the teams were in position Tac HQ was advised and then we all waited for the signal to attack. It was reassuring to know that if we got into serious trouble there were fighter aircraft, armoured assault units and helicopters standing by just across the border. One group would not get involved in any of the attacks but would be strategically placed to keep our escape route open.

"Once we received the order to attack, we closed in on our targets while using the megaphones to advise citizens and security forces in the vicinity to stay out of our way and no harm would come to them. With me leading the way we encountered no problems and once I had identified the house to be attacked, I left them to carry on. At the third house a young NCO looked at me nervously.

'Aren't you going to lead us in sir?' he asked.

'No Boet,' I said, 'this is your show. Get stuck in and give them hell.' And in they went with first a bunker bomb followed by grenades and gunfire.

"Once I dropped the last group, I started making my way back to the first group who were finishing up. I collected them and then the other two groups and it appeared everyone was safe having accomplished their respective tasks. I then led them to the pre-arranged assembly area where everyone gathered prior to heading for the border.

"The operation had been a success, targets had been eliminated and a huge amount of documentation was secured which led to the arrests of ANC personnel already deployed in South Africa. Unsurprisingly, the international reaction was an angry one. South Africa was widely condemned at the UN and elsewhere, and Britain announced they would start giving military assistance to Botswana to assist them in defending themselves against attacks of this nature.

"I know it is only a matter of opinion, but when I look back on this operation, I like to believe that what we did that night almost certainly saved the lives of innocent civilians in South Africa who would have died in bomb attacks had we not done that operation.

Time to go.
"A few days later I was relaxing at the safe house when our IO arrived in a cloud of smoke. I looked up.

'Good morning, General,' I said.

'Morning Kafupi', he replied. 'The good news is we have a new job for you to do.'

I took a deep breath.

'For fuck's sake General, can't you find someone else to do it? My wife is going to divorce me if I don't change my ways.' He pulled on his fag and laughed.

'They're really starting to use their imagination these guys. Wait till you hear what their latest idea is.'

'Nothing would surprise me, General,' I replied.

'Well, try this one.' He paused, and his suntanned face broke into laughter.

'You are going into the prisons and there we have a serious psychopath for you to get to know.'

'Are you crazy,' I said. 'I've spent enough time in prison for one lifetime: I'm not going into anymore of those places. And I'm a damn soldier, not a policeman. This is a job for you guys not me.'

'This is not my idea, Kafupi, I hold them it was ludicrous, but these are the orders.'

With that, Charl, hearing the discussion, approached us and looked at me.

'If you can't take a joke Kafupi, you should never have joined,' and with that he walked away leaving me to mull my next task.

"Before I knew it, I was inside the solid walls of Pretoria Central Prison. Just the smell of stale sweat and carbolic soap that wafted over me made me feel nauseous as the steel doors clanged closed behind me. That familiar

CHAPTER FIFTEEN

smell of fear, like rats in a cage, made me feel like I might easily vomit.

"Then there he was before me; one of the most disgusting looking human beings I had ever laid eyes on and I was in his face, locked in his cell with him. The sight of him and the smell of him almost floored me. Coal black, thick lips barely covered jagged yellow teeth, his skin was pock-marked and scars raked across his face. He grinned and it was full of menace; I knew this guy could kill quickly and cold-bloodedly. He was a huge motherfucker and my sudden appearance had brought an alertness to his eyes like when a leopard suddenly spots its prey. There was silence, his eyes cut through me and he started to sweat. He was a Zulu, and God alone knows how many people he had killed but I knew his kinfolk; they were expert knife-men, most carried cheap but dangerous Okapis, known as 'Saturday Night Specials'. While trying to figure this monster out, I heard sniggering and looked behind me to see guards chuckling; they liked seeing a white man looking bloody terrified. I had seen his rap-sheet and it was not for the faint of heart; there was hardly a violent crime he had not committed and why they had not strung him up, puzzled me.

"It immediately concerned me that the intelligence people had chosen this guy; he was a killer alright but then what? I knew beyond any doubt that if they expected me to work with him and control him, it was simply not going to happen. This guy would answer to nobody.

"I reported back to my bosses but they had decided they wanted to give this a try, so I was sent back to the dungeons to brief him. I told him he was to be released, infiltrated into Botswana with a false passport, introduced to contacts there and given names and photos of ANC operatives designated for elimination.

"I called him 'Bongo'. On the appointed day, he was slipped out of prison and I collected him. It was now my responsibility to look after him and prepare him for his infiltration into Botswana. This involved quite a big shopping spree getting him all the clothes and other stuff that he needed. He couldn't believe his luck but at the end of it there he was in his shiny black shoes, slick suit and cheap black sunglasses looking just like the Soweto gangster he was. By this time, he had warmed to me and promised me he would never let me down. I didn't believe a word of it.

"Once he had been fully briefed on who he was to meet up with and how the plan was to unfold I was tasked to take him to the border and let him

MEN OF WAR

go. We drove to the border post at Kopfontein and only when we arrived there did I give him the suitcase full of cash which he was to use to pay his contacts. This guy thought he had died and gone to heaven. After promising me for the umpteenth time that he would never let me down, he took off into the building and waved me goodbye.

"With that done I returned to the safe house in Zeerust and joined Rudi who was having a braai that night. It was an enjoyable, relaxing evening and as always, we gorged ourselves on some good beef, but Rudi was hitting his brandy hard. Most of the time he was a pretty quiet reserved guy but as the booze flowed into his veins, he became more vocal.

'How's your friend Bongo?' he said and roared with laughter. I laughed too but not as loudly. Bongo was not that much of a joke as far as I was concerned. I was pretty sure we had seen the last of that guy.

He then went quiet, then looked me in the eyes as I was stuffing a boerewors role into my mouth.

'Kafupi, how long were you in the Rhodesian army?' he asked quietly.

'Almost ten years Rudi. Why?' I asked.

'Well you must understand something Kafupi. You guys fought hard to the bitter end and never gave up. But that's not going to happen here.'

This got my attention. Coming from a dedicated operator and a real Afrikaner patriot, this was quite alarming.

'What are you saying Rudi?' I asked.

'You must understand we are going to give this country away. Our politicians do not have the stomach for a long fight. We don't fight like you Rhodesians; we fight among each other. We don't trust one another. Just now someone is going to turn on you and you are going to end up either dead or in jail on some trumped up charge, but I suggest you get the hell out of here.'

"This was a view I had not heard from him before, but it was a troubling thought which had crossed my mind. I cast my mind back to the Seychelles caper and the mulling over the possible elimination of Blue Kelly in the course of the operation. This could be me, I reminded myself. He took another big gulp of Brandy and the next words jarred.

'Kafupi, my friend, get out of this now! Time is not on your side, you're already compromised and they know it within the organisation. It's only a matter of time and you are going to be caught. And I promise, when it

CHAPTER FIFTEEN

happens, they'll walk away and disown you. You are destined for disaster and you now have a family to think about. Get out now, I tell you!'

"His warning let loose a swarm of bees in my head and they did not stop buzzing until I finally made my way to see General Kat Liebenberg, then OC Special Forces at Speskop. I did not waste his or my time and came straight to the point.

'Sir, I have come to tell you, I have decided to tender my resignation.'

He did not look pleased.

'Well tell me Captain, why do you want to leave us?'

I told him I was concerned about my family and my time had come. I did not mention the fact that I was also starting to think I was losing my nerve.

'Well, this is not the right procedure to follow Captain. You should follow the correct channels and report to your CO first,' he advised.

'I don't trust him, or them, Sir,' was my blunt reply.

"There was indeed a mandatory procedure to follow, but I was in a rush. I had told Sylvia my mind was made up and we were leaving as soon as possible. I was worried for the safety of my family and we made immediate plans to leave South Africa and go to the UK.

"One of the few people I saw after my meeting was my old SAS pal, Mike Smith, who was also with Special Forces. We met and I told him I had decided to resign. I explained to him I had lost confidence and also told him what Rudi had said to me. Mike listened but he had decided to stay. I did try to persuade him, but maybe I didn't try hard enough.

"Sure enough, he, Kevin Woods and Philip Conjwayo were later arrested in Zimbabwe going after ANC targets there. Mike and Kevin got the death sentence and spent four miserable years on Death Row in Harare before their sentences were commuted. They were finally released after 19 years in prison. Later I was accused of having gone AWOL but that was not the case. I did, however, lose all my pension benefits. It certainly was not a happy ending to my military career.

"I have made many bum decisions in my life but this time I got it right. Thank God for brandy and coke and Rudi! Between him and the booze; that's probably why I survived.

And Bongo?

Well, he was never seen again."

Addendum on Viscounts.

The question of who was responsible for the destruction of the two Viscounts; *Hunyani* on the 3rd September 1978, and *Umniati* on 12th February 1979, remains unresolved but a recent book, *'The Uncomfortable Truth'*, by Geoffrey Alp who spent five years doing highly detailed technical and circumstantial research into the two tragedies, is enlightening and disturbing. He makes a very compelling case, in support of the contention that neither aircraft was downed by Soviet-supplied Strela missiles.

This is notwithstanding the fact that Zipra and Zanla personnel were trained, armed and operationally deployed with portable anti-aircraft rockets and launchers and Rhodesian aircraft were fired upon by people using these weapons at various stages of the conflict. There is also no doubt that survivors of the Viscount *Hunyani* were murdered by terrorists some of whom may have been eliminated subsequently but this remains a point of contention.

Some of the more pertinent points Mr. Alp makes in the course of this very thorough analyses include the following.

1. The weapon and ancillary devices were very unwieldy and difficult to porter on foot over long distances. For this reason, it was essentially designed as a defensive, more than offensive, weapon.
2. The battery that armed, aimed and discharged the missile in the tube, had to be initiated and then only lasted for 30 – 40 seconds. This made it imperative for the shooter to be well positioned on a known flight-line, well before the arrival of the target.
3. From his calculations, he is certain that both aircraft were well outside the limited range of the launchers. (Another expert insists that the Dart engine on the Viscounts does not exhaust gasses at a temperature which is visible to the Strela.)
4. On studying replica aircraft, he believes it is impossible for the missiles to have entered the exhaust pipes as averred in the forensic reports.
5. He found, "The actual forensic reports are shocking with inaccuracies and false information." And noted; "It was interesting that the only attributable parts that were claimed to have come from a Strela only surfaced after three weeks or so of the event." Despite

this, an announcement was made within days of the first downing, stating categorically, that the plane was shot down. This smacks of, at best as rush to judgement, at worst, a deliberate attempt to obfuscate.
6. He is far from convinced that any certifiable parts of a Strela missile were ever discovered.
7. Alp discovered that both aircraft flew almost exactly the same distance and time form take-off before exploding. He believes it well nigh impossible, that two separate teams, operating at different times in rugged country, managed to shoot down two planes in different places at exactly the same time and distance from the airport.
8. The author asks why the shooters did not avail themselves of the opportunity to position themselves on the landing path rather. This was more predictable than the flight-line followed on departure.
9. He questions the wisdom of shooting down an aircraft that the enemy knew was a civilian airliner, incapable of attacking them.
10. Following all his investigations, Alp is convinced that both aircraft were sabotaged on the ground by the placement of timed, explosive devices, inside the wheel-well, close to the air-intake.

"I have done further research into the shrapnel patterns from military explosives. Physics simulations suggest it was a frag grenade with a 15 or 20 minute timer, placed in the wheel well. The target being the main spar and fuel tanks. As the wheel nacelle is lower than the wing the grenade being static and not moving exploded and failed to take out the main spar, however it did spray shrapnel into the fuel tanks which ignited. It also ruptured the main fuel lines and hydraulic lines which lost control to the starboard wings. Had it been a Strela which is moving, the damage would have been greater with a spay pattern into the wing. This is not in evidence when one looks at the wing parts."

Easily done by anyone with access to the planes, the charges would have ignited the fuel tanks and brought the aircraft down.

Political background to the tragedies.

March 1978 Ian Smith, tired of Britain moving the goal-posts, formed a coalition government which included Bishop Abel Muzorewa;s UANC and several other black-led political parties. By July 1978 moves were afoot for Ian Smith to meet and find some possible accommodation with Joshua Nkomo who was increasingly being seen as the lesser of two evils compared to Robert Mugabe. Ken Flower would have been fully informed and involved in these moves. At the time the British government was desperate to settle the Rhodesian problem which was bedevilling British business interests in Africa.

In the same month, on the 11th of July, the Kariba to Salisbury convoy consisting of 50 vehicles was attacked by a terrorist gang in the Vuti Purchase Area, 15 kilometres before Makuti on a section of the road that wound through a hilly area. Samuel Gondo, the driver of the Express Motorways bus, was fatally wounded in the attack but managed to get his vehicle into a gully before succumbing to his wounds. Also killed in the bus were Debra de Bres (17 years old), Margaret Turk (in her early 20s), and 5-year-old Sally Muggleton. All three were from Salisbury. At least sixteen others were injured in the ambush. It was the worst attack of the war on a civilian convoy. All the tourists targeted were white.

While Nkomo's Zipra were blamed for the attack, no evidence was ever produced to confirm this. The question then is, was this attack designed to derail the political alignment being pursued by Smith and Nkomo. If so the gambit failed and on the 14th August 1978, Ian Smith, Jack Gaylard and Derrick Robinson flew secretly to Lusaka in a Lonrho supplied aircraft to meet President Kaunda, Joshua Nkomo and Nigerian Foreign Minister Brigadier Joe Garba. With Tiny Rowland watching in the wings, the talks were very positive, and a general agreement was reached and fundamentals for a compromise that would see Nkomo accommodated within the new political structures being installed and stop fighting. Garba promised to fly to Mozambique immediately to brief Mugabe and bring him on board. Alp points out that, only the day before the *Hunyani* crashed, Ian Smith made it publicly known that he and Nkomo had met and expressed optimism an agreement was imminent.

It is now known, that then British Foreign Secretary David Owen, and the Foreign Office were solidly behind Mugabe as the man to lead an independent Zimbabwe, so this news was certain to have displeased them, calling for urgent action. The blowing up of the Hunyani, unsurprisingly, outraged Rhodesians and when it appeared Nkomo's operatives were responsible, Smith's attempt at a rapprochement with Nkomo, was doomed. Following the downing of the second plane in February the following year, all gloves came off and the Rhodesians attacked Nkomo's house in Lusaka and then followed this up with several punishing air and ground attacks on Zipra bases and Zambian infrastructure.

Questions remaining.

All the above must be understood in the light of the fact that a very senior SB officer attached to the Selous Scouts, insists, he remembers going through diaries recovered from a gang in some way connected to the Viscounts. Whether in the shooting down or the murder of survivors, is not known. He also saw weapons and equipment recovered. These items may have been connected to the controversial contact initiated by Darrell Watt on the 24th November 1978, acting on information from Keith Nell, then serving with the SFA's (Security Force Auxiliaries). What remains a mystery about this contact is why it was never reported to Combined Operations by SAS HQ or by Special Branch, but if one assumes the British were involved in the atrocities, then it is perfectly likely their agents would have been involved in the suppression of sensitive information relating to the incidents.

If the British were behind it their aims would have been three-fold:
1. To discredit Nkomo and alienate him politically from Ian Smith.
2. To provoke a Rhodesian military response aimed at Nkomo's forces in Zambia.
3. To demoralise the Rhodesian populace and pressure them into a political dispensation that would be foisted upon them by the British government.

If so, then they succeeded in achieving all three goals. In this third objective, the *Hunyani* tragedy was extremely effective. News of a successful engagement, eliminating some of the culprits involved would have triggered jubilation in the country and raised morale immeasurably. This is not what the Foreign Office would have wanted and maybe this is why the contact-report was suppressed.

Dick Oldridge, has investigated these events closely. "In the 'Black Operation' launched by Zanu PF in the aftermath of the EDM (Early Day Motion) 1029 tabled in the British Parliament on the 5th February 2013, they (the Mugabe government) expressed regret about the Viscounts but went on to say that the *Hunyani* was downed by the Rhodesian CIO who were adamant that they were out to prevent the implementation of the Smith/Nkomo military and political alliance. My personal view of the downings, is that they were not ordered by Nkomo who had too much to lose. Yes, he took ownership of the tragedies on behalf of ZIPRA, but they were most probably caused by a renegade faction of ZIPRA operating outside of his control. I have listened to the David Frost interview a hundred times and am convinced that the laughter is nervous laughter generated by a leader whose plans were going awry. Nkomo was relatively pro-white, an ardent capitalist and loathed Mugabe whom he regarded as an upstart. Nkomo was cut from the same cloth as the Robben Island Class of Nationalist and had met with and maintained close ties with Mandela whilst Mugabe was a school-boy. There has never been a scintilla of evidence to link Nkomo to any order to down civilian aircraft to my knowledge."

Author and former broadcaster Jill Baker, a close friend from childhood of the late Zipra Commander, Dumiso Dabengwa, broached the subject with him while they were working together on a book in Botswana, not long before his death.

"We had been together on this project for a while and I had an enormous amount of respect for the man. I knew it was a sensitive subject, but I asked him if they had shot the planes down. He looked me in the eyes, very sternly and said.

"Jill, I promise you, we had nothing to do with the shooting down of the Viscounts." I absolutely believe him.

Sources Consulted.

Keith Samler.
Ken Bird.
Pat Armstrong.
Bert Sachse.
Rich Stannard.
Tim Callow.
Darrell Watt.
Andrew Standish White.
Mike West.
John Jordan.
Barry Jolliffe
Frans Botha.
Rob Riddell.
Allan Hider.
Steve Lunderstedt.

Books.

Iron Fist from the Sea. Arne Soderlund and Douw Steyn. Delta Books. 2018.
Under The Skin. David Caute. Penguin Books. 1983.
The Elite. Barbara Cole. Three Knights. 1982.
The Rhodesian War. Paul Moorcroft and Peter McLaughlin. Jonathan Ball. 2008.
Three Sips of Gin. Tim Bax. Helion. 2013.
Selous Scouts; The Men Speak. Jonathan Pittaway. Dandy Agencies. 2015.
Echoes of an African War. Chas Lotter. Covos-Day. 1999.
A Pride of Eagles. Beryl Salt. Covos Day. 2001.
Anatomy of a Rebel. Peter Joyce. Graham Publishing 1974.
Special Air Service; The Men Speak. Jonathan Pittaway. Dandy Agencies. 2009.
The Valiant Years. Beryl Salt. Galaxie Press. 1978.
Serving Secretly. Ken Flower. John Murray Publishers. 2008.
The Saints. Alexandra Binda. Thirty Degrees South. 2007.

About the author

Born in 1956 in what was then Salisbury in Southern Rhodesia (now Harare, Zimbabwe) Hannes Wessels grew up in Umtali on the Mozambique border. As a young boy school holidays were spent with Rangers in the Rhodesia Game department but time in his early teens on safari in Mozambique with the late Wally Johnson were a big influence. During this time Wessels met Robert Ruark whose love of Africa, its people, politics and the written word left a lasting impression.

After leaving school he saw action in the bush-war before acquiring a law degree which he chose not to use. He hunted big game professionally in Zimbabwe, Zambia and Tanzania in a twenty-year career. In 1994 he was severely gored by a wounded buffalo which almost cost him his life.

He has published **'Strange Tales from Africa'** in America which is a collection of stories about people and places encountered by him in the course of his hunting days. His biography of PK van der Byl (former Rhodesian Defense Minister), **'P.K. van der Byl; African Statesman'**, includes a revised history of the Rhodesian political imbroglio. **'A Handful of Hard Men'** was his first book about the Rhodesian war focusing on the exploits of Captain Darrell Watt during his service in the SAS. His second book on the SAS, **'We Dared to Win'**, was written with Andre Scheepers and has been well received in South Africa and abroad. He has recently published **'Guns, Golf and Glory'** about the great golfers that came out of Rhodesia and later Zimbabwe, which he co-wrote with former world number one golfer, Nick Price.

He is married to Mandy and has two daughters; Hope and Jana and lives in Darling in the Cape Province of South Africa. While no longer directly involved, he remains keenly interested in all matters relating to African wildlife and conservation.

Other books by Hannes Wessels

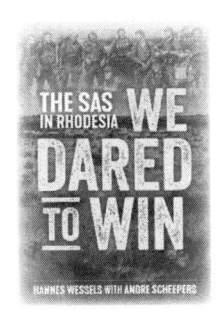

Printed in Great Britain
by Amazon